IN THEIR OWN WORDS

Criminals on Crime

Second Edition

Edited by

Paul Cromwell

Wichita State University

Roxbury Publishing Company

Los Angeles, California

Library of Congress Cataloging-in-Publication Data

Cromwell, Paul
  In their own owrds: criminals on crime / edited by Paul Cromwell.—2nd ed.
    p. cm.
  Includes bibliographical references.
  ISBN 0-935732-95-0
  1. Criminology—Field work. 2. Crime—Research.
  3. Criminals—Research. I. Cromwell, Paul F.
HV6030.I488 1999
364—dc21   98-45336
                                                           CIP

Publisher and Editor: Claude Teweles
Supervising Editor: Sacha A. Howells
Assistant Editors: Joyce Rappaport, Dawn VanDercreek, and Renee Burkhammer
Production Editors: Remy Goldsmith and Cathy Yoo
Cover Design: Marnie Deacon
Typography: Rebecca Evans & Associates

Printed on acid-free paper in the United States of America. This paper meets the standards for recycling of the Environmental Protection Agency.

ISBN 0-935732-95-0

Roxbury Publishing Company
P.O. Box 491044
Los Angeles, California 90049-9044
(310) 473-3312 Fax: (310) 473-4490
E-mail: roxbury@crl.com

Dedication

*For my wife, Jimmie; my children, Christopher Cromwell,
Rebecca Pettis, and Karen VanDerKroon; and my grandchildren,
Katheryn Elizabeth and Paul Anderson VanDerKroon,
and Erin Nicole and Victoria Anne Pettis.
They are truly my greatest treasures.*

Acknowledgements

Like the First Edition, this volume owes its existence first to the researchers and authors whose work is presented here. My task was simply to select the best exemplars of contemporary ethnographic research and to attempt to tie them together in an integrated and effective way. I gratefully acknowledge the scholarly efforts of the authors of the studies presented in this anthology. It is truly their book.

In the process of preparing the second edition I had the benefit of numerous reviewers who commented on the selections, organization, and integration of materials, and the general worth of the project. Their advice was invaluable. In most cases I accepted it gratefully. In every case, I benefitted from it. To the extent that this book has value for advancing scholarly understanding of crime and criminals and especially as a teaching tool, the credit should be given to them. To the extent that it fails in its purpose, I am to blame. Special appreciation is extended to:

Robert S. Agnew, Emory University; Mitchell B. Chamblin, University of Cincinnati; Dean J. Champion, Minot State University; Scott H. Decker, University of Missouri-St. Louis; Chris Ekridge, University of Nebraska-Omaha; Gary F. Jensen, Vanderbilt University; Stephen F. Messner, SUNY-Albany; Frank R. Scarpitti, University of Delaware; Samuel Walker, University of Nebraska-Omaha; and Richard A. Wright, University of Scranton.

Frederic L. Faust of Florida State University and Quint Thurman of Wichita State University also reviewed and commented on various aspects of the project. Richard T. Wright at the University of Missouri-St. Louis and Neal Shover at the University of Tennessee also offered valuable insights and advice.

Sacha Howells and Dawn VanDercreek at Roxbury Publishing Company provided their expertise in all stages of the manuscript preparation. I am particularly appreciative of the efforts and persistence of Claude Teweles, Publisher and President at Roxbury Publishing Company. He kept me on track and on schedule.

My wife Jimmie is owed the greatest debt. Her editing skills, attention to detail, and emotional support have always undergirded my efforts. Once again, I express my gratitude to her.

—Paul Cromwell
Wichita, Kansas

Contents

Introduction to Ethnographic Research in Criminal Justice and Criminology

   *Richard T. Wright, Scott H. Decker, Allison K. Redfern,
   and Dietrich L. Smith*

   Wright and his associates explain the process and problems associated with designing and conducting a field
   study of active burglars.

SECTION I: Criminal Lifestyles and Decision Making

   Neal Shover and David Honaker

   Shover and Honaker argue that improved understanding
   of the decision-making processes of property offenders is
   gained through exploring how their decisions are shaped
   by their lifestyles.

   Malin Åkerström

   Åkerström compares attitudes and perspectives of thieves
   and drug addicts to a population of noncriminals about
   work, leisure, the law, finances, lifestyle, and the future.

   Deborah R. Baskin and Ira Sommers

   Baskin and Sommers describes how the respondents in
   their research make a living and their progression from
   early involvement in the legal economy to their ultimate
   embeddedness in the illicit economy.

SECTION II: Property Crime

SECTION III: Occupational Crime

SECTION IV: Violent Crime

SECTION V: Gangs and Crime

SECTION VI: Drugs and Crime

Preface

This anthology provides the reader an opportunity to view the world from the perspective of criminal offenders. *In Their Own Words, Second Edition* is a collection of field studies of crime and criminals derived from a long tradition of field research in criminology (Sutherland, 1937; Cressey, 1953; Irwin, 1970; Shover, 1971; Letkemann, 1973; Klockars, 1974; Inciardi, 1977; Campbell, 1984). *In Their Own Words* is a collection of ethnographic or "field" accounts of crime and criminals. The studies presented are derived from a long tradition of field research in sociology and criminology. In the Second Edition, students will encounter gang members, burglars, shoplifters, robbers, fences, addicts, rapists, drug smugglers, and white-collar offenders—all of whom discuss their motives, perceptions, strategies, and rationalizations of crime. This new edition contains seven new studies, adding more accounts of crimes committed by women, studies of decision making by residential burglars, factors that motivate shoplifters, the use of force and threats by armed robbers, youthful car thieves, a study of crack sales in a declining market, and research that analyzes crime as work. These new research findings increase the range of criminal behaviors analyzed and offer the reader fresh insights into the criminal experience.

Methods of Field Research

Field research is not a single research methodology. Field research, also called *ethnography*, provides a way of looking at the complex contexts in which any research problem exists. Good field research results in what Glassner and Carpenter (1985) call *thick description*—access to the often conflicting and detailed views of the social world held by the subjects being studied.

According to Maxfield and Babbie (1995), field research "encompasses two different methods of obtaining data, direct observation, and asking questions."

Asking questions involves in-depth interviews (also called ethnographic interviews) with research subjects. Field study interviews are much less structured than survey research interviews. At one level, field interviews may be likened to a conversation (Maxfield and Babbie, 1995). At a more structured level, researchers ask open-ended questions in which a specific response is elicited, but the respondent is allowed and encouraged to explain more completely and to clarify responses. The question is simply a guide, structuring but not limiting the interviewee's responses. Zachary Fleming's "The Thrill of it All: Youthful Offenders and Auto Theft," Floyd Feeney's "Robbers as Decision Makers," Paul Cromwell, Lee Parker, and Shawna Mobley's "The Five-Finger Discount," and Neal Shover and David Honaker's "The Socially Bounded Decision Making of Persistent Property Offenders" in this volume are examples of the "asking questions" technique of field research.

Observation takes several forms in field research. These techniques may be categorized on a continuum according to the role played by the researcher (Gold, 1969; Maxfield and Babbie, 1995). At one degree of involvement, the researcher observes an activity or individuals without their knowledge. A researcher watching shoplifters through a one-way mirror in a department store is an example of this technique. Gold (1969) labels this method *the complete observer.*

At a more involved level of interaction, the researcher is identified as a researcher and interacts with the participants in the course of their activities, but does not actually become a participant (Maxfield and Babbie, 1995). Gold (1969) identified this technique as *observer-as-participant*. In "The Social Organization of Crack Sales," Bruce Jacobs employed the observor-as-participant technique. Paul Cromwell, James N. Olson, and D'Aunn W. Avary ("Decision Strategies of Residential Burglars") also used the technique when observing burglars in their natural habitat ("in the wild") and going with them to houses they had previously burglarized, reconstructing their crimes.

The *participant-as-observer* (Gold, 1969) technique involves participating with the group under study while making clear the purpose of conducting research. Patricia Adler ("Dealing Careers" in this anthology) makes use of this research technique. Adler writes: "I became a member of the drug dealers' and smugglers' social world and participated in their daily activities on that basis."

The most complete involvement of researcher with subjects is the *complete participant*. Gold (1969: 33) describes this role as:

> The true identity and purpose of the complete participant in field research are not known to those he observes. He interacts with them as naturally as possible in whatever areas of their living interest him and are acceptable to him in situations in which he can play or learn to play requisite day-to-day roles successfully.

There are a number of ethical, legal, and personal risk considerations involved in the *complete participant* role and the researcher must tread carefully to avoid pitfalls. Because of these problems, complete participation is seldom possible in criminological research. However, some of the material in Patricia Adler's "Dealing Careers" was obtained using this methodology. Adler reports that although most of their subjects (high-level drug dealers) knew that she and her husband were researchers, others did not. They were accepted by these individuals through their friendship and were vouched for by those same subjects. Thus, her study made use of both *complete participant* and *participant-as-observer* techniques.

Use of Field Research in Criminal Justice and Criminology

Field studies are particularly well-suited to investigating several important issues in criminology and criminal justice. Only through field research may we observe the everyday activities of offenders: how they interact with others, how they perceive the objects and events in their everyday lives, and how they perceive the sanction threat of the criminal justice system. By understanding the offenders' perspective, decision making, and motivation, field research may inform

crime prevention and control strategies. Wright and Decker (1994) point out that criminal justice policymaking is predicated on assumptions about the perceptions of criminals:

> The traditional policy of deterrence rests squarely on the notion that offenders are utilitarian persons who carefully weigh the potential costs and rewards of their illegal actions. . . .

However, the studies in this collection offer strong arguments for other, perhaps as compelling motivations for many crimes, including so-called economic crimes. Even robbery and burglary, crimes which are assumed to be driven almost entirely by instrumental (economic) motivations, may have expressive roots as well (See Zachary Taylor's "The Thrill of it All" in this volume). Burglars report that excitement, thrills, and a "rush" often accompany the criminal act. Some burglars report having occasionally committed a burglary out of revenge or anger against the victim (see Cromwell, Olson, and Avary; Wright and Decker; and Shover and Honaker, all in this volume). On the other hand, gang membership, which traditionally has been thought to be turf oriented and centered around conflict, is shown to be increasingly about money—drugs and drug sales. Thus, effective crime control strategies must take into account the factors which drive crime. Field research which allows offenders to "speak for themselves" is ideally suited to these issues.

Field studies such as those in this book also have great value in educating students in criminal justice and criminology. The field has sometimes suffered from the "distance" between student and subject of the study. Would anyone argue that it is possible to train a physician without contact with sick people? The essence of medical training is of course the gaining of experience diagnosing and treating the sick. Yet, in 15 years as a criminal justice practitioner and administrator, and 15 years more as a criminal justice and criminology educator, I have been troubled by the realization that most graduates never encounter an actual criminal during the course of their education. Some universities provide internships or practicums or arrange field trips to prisons or other correctional facilities. Despite these efforts, however, few students ever experience a "real criminal" during their education. By viewing the criminal event from the perspective of the participants, these studies can make the decision by an individual to engage in crime "up close and personal" and supplement the statistical data from other research.

In Their Own Words enriches the reader's understanding of criminal typologies, criminal decision making, criminological theories, and criminal subcultures and lifestyles. The studies contained in this book vary in terms of the settings, crimes being studied, and the researcher's involvement and role in the environment. In every case, however, the story is told from the perspective of and in the words of the offender. In each case, the researcher places the offender's words in a theoretical context and provides analyses and conclusions.

References

Campbell, A. 1984. *Girls in the Gang.* Oxford, UK: Basil Blackwell.

Cressey, D.R. 1953. *Other People's Money.* Glencoe, IL: Free Press.

Glassner, B. and C. Carpenter. 1985. *The Feasibility of an Ethnographic Study of Property Offenders: A Report Prepared for the National Institute of Justice.* Washington D.C.: NIJ Mimeo.

Gold, R. 1969. "Roles in Sociological Field Observation." In George J. McCall and J. L. Simmons (Eds.) *Issues in Participant Observation.* Reading, MA: Addison-Wesley.

Inciardi, J. 1977. "In Search of Class Cannon: A Field Study of Professional Pickpockets." In Robert S. Weppner (Ed.), *Street Ethnography: Selected Studies of Crime and Drug Use in Natural Settings.* Beverly Hills: Sage.

Irwin, J. 1970. *The Felon.* Englewood Cliffs, NJ: Prentice-Hall.

Klockars, C. 1974. *The Professional Fence.* New York: Macmillan.

Letkemann, P. 1973. *Crime as Work.* Englewood Cliffs, NJ: Prentice-Hall.

Maxfield, M. G. and E. Babbie. 1995. *Research Methods for Criminal Justice and Criminology.* Belmont, CA: Wadsworth.

Shover, N. 1971. "Burglary As an Occupation." Ph.D. dissertation, University of Illinois.

Sutherland, E.H. 1937. *The Professional Thief.* Chicago: University of Chicago Press.

Wright, R. T. and S. H. Decker (1994). *Burglars on the Job: Streetlife and Residential Break-ins.* Boston: Northeastern University Press. ✦

About the Contributors

Patricia A. Adler is a professor of sociology at the University of Colorado-Boulder.

Malin Åkerström is a professor of sociology at the University of Lund-Sweden.

D'Aunn W. Avary (deceased) was Director of Quality Management at Texas Tech University, Regional Health Sciences Center.

Deborah H. Baskin is a professor and chairperson in the Department of Criminal Justice at California State University-Los Angeles.

Michael L. Benson is an associate professor of sociology at the University of Tennessee-Knoxville.

Paul Cromwell is a professor of criminal justice and director of the Hugo Wall School of Urban and Public Affairs at Wichita State University.

Scott H. Decker is a professor of criminology and criminal justice at the University of Missouri-St. Louis.

Jeffery Fagan is a professor and director of the Center for Violence Research and Prevention in the School of Public Health at Columbia University.

Charles E. Faupel is a professor of sociology at Auburn University.

Floyd Feeney is a professor in the School of Law at the University of California-Davis.

Zachary Fleming is a policy analyst with the Road Safety Strategic Initiative Group of the Insurance Corporation of British Columbia, Canada.

Gilbert Geis is Professor Emeritus in the School of Social Ecology at the University of California-Irvine.

John M. Hagedorn is an assistant professor of criminal justice at the University of Illinois at Chicago.

David Honaker is a research associate in the Social Work Office of Research and Public Service at the University of Tennessee-Knoxville.

Geoffrey Hunt is a senior research associate at the Institute for Scientific Analysis in Alameda, California.

Bruce Jacobs is an associate professor of criminology and criminal justice at the University of Missouri-St. Louis.

Paul Jesilow is an associate professor of criminology, law, and society in the School of Social Ecology at the University of California-Irvine.

Joseph Marolla is an associate professor and chair of sociology and anthropology at Virginia Commonwealth University.

Tom Mieczkowski is a professor of criminal justice at the University of South Florida.

Shawna Mobley is Director of Correctional Counseling of Kansas in Wichita, Kansas.

Tomas Morales is a research associate at the Institute for Scientific Analysis in Alameda, California.

James N. Olson is a professor of psychology and Dean of the College of Arts and Sciences at the University of Texas-Permian Basin.

Lee Parker is assistant professor of criminal justice and public administration at Wichita State University.

Felix M. Padilla is a professor of sociology and anthropology at Northeastern University.

Henry M. Pontell is a professor and chair of the Department of Criminology, Law, and Society in the School of Social Ecology at the University of California-Irvine.

Allison K. Redfern (now Allison Rooney) is a probation officer for the state of Missouri.

Stephanie Riegel is a research associate at the Institute for Scientific Analysis in Alameda, California.

Diana Scully is a professor of sociology at Virginia Commonwealth University.

Neal Shover is a professor of sociology at the University of Tennessee-Knoxville.

Dietrich L. Smith is a senior research analyst at the University of Missouri-St. Louis.

Ira Sommers is an associate professor of criminal justice at California State University-Los Angeles.

Dan Waldorf (deceased) was a senior research associate at the Institute for Scientific Analysis in Alameda, California.

Richard T. Wright is a professor and chair of the Department of Criminology and Criminal Justice at the University of Missouri-St. Louis. ✦

1

A Snowball's Chance in Hell: Doing Fieldwork With Active Residential Burglars

Richard T. Wright
Scott H. Decker
Allison K. Redfern
Dietrich L. Smith

Criminologists long have recognized the importance of field studies of active offenders. More than 2 decades ago, for example, Polsky (1969, p. 116) observed that "we can no longer afford the convenient fiction that in studying criminals in their natural habitat, we would discover nothing really important that could not be discovered from criminals behind bars." Similarly, Sutherland and Cressey (1970) noted that:

> Those who have had intimate contacts with criminals "in the open" know that criminals are not "natural" in police stations, courts, and prisons, and that they must be studied in their everyday life outside of institutions if they are to be understood. By this is meant that the investigator must associate with them as one of them, seeing their lives and conditions as the criminals themselves see them. In this way, he can make observations which can hardly be made in any other way. Also, his observations are of unapprehended crimi-

nals, not the criminals selected by the processes of arrest and imprisonment. (p. 68)

And McCall (1978, p. 27) also cautioned that studies of incarcerated offenders are vulnerable to the charge that they are based on "unsuccessful criminals, on the supposition that successful criminals are not apprehended or at least are able to avoid incarceration." This charge, he asserts, is "the most central bogeyman in the criminologist's demonology" (also see Cromwell, Olson, and Avary 1991; Hagedorn 1990; Watters and Biernacki 1989).

Although generally granting the validity of such critiques, most criminologists have shied away from studying criminals, so to speak, in the wild. Although their reluctance to do so undoubtedly is attributable to a variety of factors (e.g., Wright and Bennett 1990), probably the most important of these is a belief that this type of research is impractical. In particular, how is one to locate active criminals and obtain their cooperation?

The entrenched notion that field-based studies of active offenders are unworkable has been challenged by Chambliss (1975) who asserts that:

> The data on organized crime and professional theft as well as other presumably difficult-to-study events are much more available than we usually think. All we really have to do is to get out of our offices and onto the street. The data are there; the problem is that too often [researchers] are not. (p. 39)

Those who have carried out field research with active criminals would no doubt regard this assertion as overly simplistic, but they probably would concur with Chambliss that it is easier to find and gain the confidence of such offenders than commonly is imagined. As Hagedorn (1990, p. 251) has stated: "Any good field researcher . . . willing to spend the long hours necessary to develop good informants can solve the problem of access."

We recently completed the fieldwork for a study of residential burglars, exploring, specifically, the factors they take into account when contemplating the commission of an offense. The study is being done on the streets of St. Louis, Missouri, a declining "rust belt" city. As part of this study, we located and interviewed 105 active offenders. We also took 70 of these offenders to the site of a recent burglary and asked them to reconstruct the crime in considerable detail. In the following pages, we will discuss how we found these offenders and obtained their cooperation. Further, we will consider the difficulties involved in maintaining an on-going field relationship with these offenders, many of whom lead chaotic lives. Lastly, we will outline the characteristics of our sample, suggesting ways in which it differs from one collected through criminal justice channels.

Locating the Subjects

In order to locate the active offenders for our study, we employed a "snowball" or "chain referral" sampling strategy. As described in the literature (e.g., Sudman 1976; Watters and Biernacki 1989), such a strategy begins with the recruitment of an initial subject who then is asked to recommend further participants. This process continues until a suitable sample has been "built."

The most difficult aspect of using a snowball sampling technique is locating an initial contact or two. Various ways of doing so have been suggested. McCall (1978), for instance, recommends using a "chain of referrals":

> If a researcher wants to make contact with, say, a bootlegger, he thinks of the person he knows who is closest in the social structure to bootlegging. Perhaps this person will be a police officer, a judge, a liquor store owner, a crime reporter, or a recently arrived Southern migrant. If he doesn't personally know a judge or a crime reporter, he surely knows someone (his own lawyer or a circulation clerk) who does and who would be willing to introduce him. By means of a very short chain of such referrals, the researcher can obtain an introduction to virtually any type of criminal. (p. 31)

This strategy can be effective and efficient, but can also have pitfalls. In attempting to find active offenders for our study, we avoided seeking referrals from criminal justice officials for both practical and methodological reasons. From a practical standpoint, we elected not to use contacts provided by police or probation officers, fearing that this would arouse the suspicions of offenders that the research was the cover for a "sting" operation. One of the offenders we interviewed, for example, explained that he had not agreed to participate earlier because he was worried about being set up for an arrest: "I thought about it at first because I've seen on T.V. telling how [the police] have sent letters out to people telling 'em they've won new sneakers and then arrested 'em." We also did not use referrals from law enforcement or corrections personnel to locate our subjects owing to a methodological concern that a sample obtained in this way may be highly unrepresentative of the total population of active offenders. It is likely, for instance, that such a sample would include a disproportionate number of unsuccessful criminals, that is, those who have been caught in the past (e.g., Hagedorn 1990). Further, this sample might exclude a number of successful offenders who avoid associating with colleagues known to the police. Rengert and Wasilchick (1989, p. 6) used a probationer to contact active burglars, observing that the offenders so located "were often very much like the individual who led us to them."

A commonly suggested means of making initial contact with active offenders other than through criminal justice sources involves frequenting locales favored by criminals (see Chambliss 1975; Polsky 1969; West 1980). This strategy, however, requires an extraordinary investment of time as the researcher establishes a street reputation as an "all right square" (Irwin 1972, p. 123) who can be trusted. Fortunately, we were able to short-cut that process by hiring an ex-offender (who, despite committing hundreds of serious crimes, had few arrests and no felony convictions) with high status among several groups of black street criminals in St. Louis. This person retired from crime after being shot and paralyzed in a gangland-style execution attempt. He then attended a university and earned a bachelor's degree, but continued to live in his old neighborhood, remaining friendly, albeit superficially, with local criminals. We initially met him when he attended a colloquium in our department and disputed the speaker's characterization of street criminals.

Working through an ex-offender with continuing ties to the underworld as a means of locating active criminals has been used successfully by other criminologists (see e.g., Taylor 1985). This approach offers the advantage that such a person already has contacts and trust in the criminal subculture and can vouch for the legitimacy of the research. In order to exploit this advantage fully, however, the ex-offender selected must be someone with a solid street reputation for integrity and must have a strong commitment to accomplishing the goals of the study.

The ex-offender hired to locate subjects for our project began by approaching former criminal associates. Some of these contacts were still "hustling," that is, actively involved in various types of crimes, whereas others either had retired or remained involved only peripherally through, for example, occasional buying and selling of stolen goods. Shortly thereafter, the ex-offender contacted several street-wise law-abiding friends, including a youth worker. He explained the research to the contacts, stressing that it was confidential and that the police were not involved. He also informed them that those who took part would be paid a small sum (typically $25.00). He then asked the contacts to put him in touch with active residential burglars.

Figure 1 outlines the chain of referrals through which the offenders were located. Perhaps the best way to clarify this process involves selecting a subject, say 064, and identifying the referrals that led us to this person. In this case, the ex-offender working on our project contacted a street-wise, non-criminal acquaintance who put him in touch with the first active burglar in the chain, offender 015. Offender 015 referred 7 colleagues, one of whom—033—put us in touch with 3 more subjects, including 035, who in turn introduced us to 038, who referred 8 more participants. Among these participants was offender 043, a well-connected burglar

Figure 1
'Snowball' Referral Chart

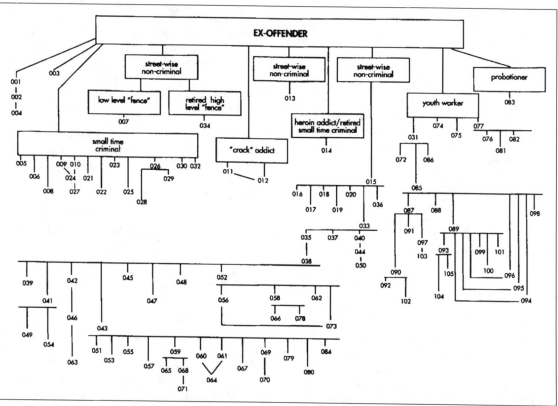

who provided 12 further contacts, 2 of whom—060 and 061—convinced 064 to participate in the research. This procedure is similar to that described by Watters and Biernacki (1989, p. 426) in that "the majority of respondents were not referred directly by research staff." As a consequence, our sample was strengthened considerably. After all, we almost certainly would not have been able to find many of these individuals on our own, let alone convince them to cooperate.

Throughout the process of locating subjects, we encountered numerous difficulties and challenges. Contacts that initially appeared to be promising, for example, sometimes proved to be unproductive and had to be dropped. And, of course, even productive contact chains had a tendency to "dry up" eventually. One of the most challenging tasks we confronted involved what Biernacki and Waldorf (1981, p. 150) have termed the "verification of eligibility," that is, determining whether potential subjects actually met the criteria for inclusion in our research. In order to take part, offenders had to be both "residential burglars" and "currently active." In practice, this meant that they had to have committed a residential burglary within the past 2 weeks. This seems straightforward, but it often was difficult to apply the criteria in the field because offenders were evasive about their activities. In such cases, we frequently had to rely on other members of the sample to verify the eligibility of potential subjects.

We did not pay the contacts for helping us to find subjects and, initially, motivating them to do so proved difficult. Small favors, things like giving them a ride or buying them a pack of cigarettes, produced some cooperation, but yielded only a few introductions. Moreover, the active burglars that we did manage to find often were lackadaisical about referring associates because no financial incentive was offered. Eventually, one of the informants hit on the idea of "pimping" colleagues, that is, arranging an introduction on their behalf in exchange for a cut of the participation fee (also see Cromwell et al. 1991). This idea was adopted rapidly by other informants and the number of referrals rose accordingly. In effect, these informants became "locators" (Biernacki and Waldorf 1981), helping us to expand referral chains as well as vouching for the legitimacy of the research, and validating potential participants as active residential burglars.

The practice of pimping is consistent with the low level, underworld economy of street culture, where people are always looking for a way to get in on someone else's deal. One of our contacts put it this way: "If there's money to make out of something, I gotta figure out a way to get me some of it." Over the course of the research, numerous disputes arose between offenders and informants over the payment of referral fees. We resisted becoming involved in these disputes, reckoning that such involvement could only result in the alienation of one or both parties (e.g., Miller 1952). Instead, we made it clear that our funds were intended as interview payments and thus would be given only to interviewees.

Field Relations

The success of our research, of course, hinged on an ability to convince potential subjects to participate. Given that many of the active burglars, especially those located early in the project, were deeply suspicious of our motives, it is reasonable to ask why the offenders were willing to take part in the research. Certainly the fact that we paid them a small sum for their time was an enticement for many, but this is not an adequate explanation. After all, criminal opportunities abound and even the inept "nickel and dime" offenders in the sample could have earned more had they spent the time engaged in illegal activity. Moreover, some of the subjects clearly were not short of cash when they agreed to participate; at the close of one interview, an offender pulled out his wallet to show us that it was stuffed with thousand dollar bills, saying:

> I just wanted to prove that I didn't do this for the money. I don't need the money. I did it to help out [the ex-offender employed on our project]. We know some of the same people and he said you were cool.

Without doubt, many in our sample agreed to participate only because the ex-offender assured them that we were trustworthy. But other factors were at work as well. Letkemann (1973, p. 44), among others, has observed that the secrecy inherent in criminal work means that offenders have few opportunities to discuss their activities with anyone besides associates—which many of them find frustrating. As one of his informants put it: "What's the point of scoring if nobody knows about it?" Under the right conditions, therefore, some offenders may enjoy talking about their work with researchers.

We adopted several additional strategies to maximize the cooperation of the offenders. First, following the recommendations of experienced field researchers (e.g., Irwin 1972; McCall 1978; Walker and Lidz 1977; Wright and Bennett 1990), we made an effort to "fit in" by learning the distinctive terminology and phrasing used by the offenders. Here again, the assistance of the ex-offender proved invaluable. Prior to entering the field, he suggested ways in which questions might be asked so that the subjects would better understand them, and provided us with a working knowledge of popular street terms (e.g, "boy" for heroin, "girl" for cocaine) and pronunciations (e.g., "hair ron" for heroin). What is more, he sat in on the early interviews and critiqued them afterwards, noting areas of difficulty or contention and offering possible solutions.

A second strategy to gain the cooperation of the offenders required us to give as well as take. We expected the subjects to answer our questions frankly and, therefore, often had to reciprocate. Almost all of them had questions about how the information would be used, who would have access to it, and so on. We answered these questions honestly, lest the offenders conclude that we were being evasive. Further, we honored requests from a number of subjects for various forms of assistance. Provided that the help requested was legal and fell within the general set "of norms governing the exchange of money and other kinds of favors" (Berk and Adams 1970, p. 112) on the street, we offered it. For example, we took subjects to job interviews or work, helped some to enroll in school, and gave others advice on legal matters. We even assisted a juvenile offender who was injured while running away from the police, to arrange for emergency surgery when his parents, fearing that they would be charged for the operation, refused to give their consent.

One other way we sought to obtain and keep the offenders' confidence involved demonstrating our trustworthiness by "remaining close-mouthed in regard to potentially harmful information" (Irwin 1972, p. 125). A number of the offenders tested us by asking what a criminal associate said about a particular matter. We declined to discuss such issues, explaining that the promise of confidentiality extended to all those participating in our research.

Much has been written about the necessity for researchers to be able to withstand official coercion (see Irwin 1972; McCall 1978; Polsky 1969) and we recognized from the start the threat that intrusions from criminal justice officials could pose to our research. The threat of being confronted by police patrols seemed especially great given that we planned to visit the sites of recent successful burglaries with offenders. Therefore, prior to beginning our fieldwork, we negotiated an agreement with police authorities not to interfere in the conduct of the research, and we were not subjected to official coercion.

Although the strategies described above helped to mitigate the dangers inherent in working with active criminals (see e.g., Dunlap et al. 1990), we encountered many potentially dangerous situations over the course of the research. For example, offenders turned up for interviews carrying firearms including, on one occasion, a machine gun; we were challenged on the street by subjects who feared that they were being set up for arrest; we were caught in the middle of a fight over the payment of a $1 debt. Probably the most dangerous situation, however, arose while driving with an offender to the site of his most recent burglary. As we passed a pedestrian, the offender became agitated and demanded that we stop the car: "You want to see me kill someone? Stop the car! I'm gonna kill that motherfucker. Stop the fuckin' car!" We refused to stop and actually sped up to prevent him jumping out of the vehicle; this clearly displeased him, although he eventually calmed down. The development of such situations was largely unpredictable and thus avoiding them was difficult. Often we deferred to the ex-offender's judgment about the safety of a given set of circumstances. The most notable precaution that we took involved money; we made sure that the offenders knew that we carried little more than was necessary to pay them.

Characteristics of the Sample

Unless a sample of active offenders differs significantly from one obtained through criminal justice channels, the difficulties and risks associated with the street-based recruitment of research subjects could not easily be justified. Accordingly, it seems important that we establish whether such a difference exists. In doing so, we will begin by outlining the demographic characteristics of our sample. In terms of race, it nearly parallels the distribution of burglary arrests for the City of St. Louis in 1988, the most recent year for which data [were] available. The St. Louis Metropolitan Police Department's Annual Report (1989) reveals that 64% of burglary arrestees in that year were Black, and 36% were White. Our sample was 69% Black and 31% White. There is divergence for the gender variable, however; only 7% of all arrestees in the city were female, while 17% of our sample fell into this category. This is not surprising. The characteristics of a sample of active criminals, after all, would not be expected to mirror those of one obtained in a criminal justice setting.

Given that our research involved only currently active offenders, it is interesting to note that 21 of the subjects were on probation, parole, or serving a suspended sentence, and that a substantial number of juveniles—27 or 26% of the total—were located for the study. The inclusion of such offenders strengthens the research considerably because approximately one third of arrested burglars are under 18 years of age (Sessions 1989). Juveniles, therefore, need to be taken into account in any comprehensive study of burglars. These offenders, however, seldom are included in studies of burglars located through criminal justice channels because access to them is legally restricted and they often are processed differently than adult criminals and detained in separate facilities.

Prior contact with the criminal justice system is a crucial variable for this research. . . . Of primary interest . . . is the extent to which our snowball sampling technique uncovered a sample of residential burglars unlikely to be encountered in a criminal justice setting, the site of most research on offenders.

More than one-quarter of the offenders (28%) claimed never to have been arrested. (We excluded arrests for traffic offenses, "failure to appear" and similar minor transgressions, because such offenses do not adequately distinguish serious criminals from others.) Obviously, these offenders would have been excluded had we based our study on a jail or prison population. Perhaps a more relevant measure in the context of our study, however, is the experience of the offenders with the criminal justice system for the offense of burglary, because most previous studies of burglars not only have been based on incarcerated offenders, but also have used the charge of burglary as a screen to select subjects (e.g., Bennett and Wright 1984; Rengert and Wasilchick 1985). Of the 105 individuals in our sample, 44 (42%) had no arrests for burglary, and another 35 (33%) had one or more arrests, but no convictions for the offense. Thus 75% of our sample would not be included in a study of incarcerated burglars. . . .

Conclusion

By its nature, research involving active criminals is always demanding, often difficult, and occasionally dangerous. However, it is possible and, as the quantitative information reported above suggests, some of the offenders included in such research may differ substantially from those found through criminal justice channels. It is interesting, for example, that those in our sample who had never been arrested for anything, on average, offended more frequently and had committed more lifetime burglaries than their arrested counterparts. These "successful" offenders, obviously, would not have shown up in a study of arrestees, prisoners, or probationers—a fact that calls into question the extent to which a sample obtained through official sources is representative of the total population of criminals.

Beyond this, researching active offenders is important because it provides an opportunity to observe and talk with them outside the institutional context. As Cromwell et al. (1991) have noted, it is difficult to assess the validity of accounts offered by institutionalized criminals. Simply put, a full understanding of criminal behavior requires that criminologists incorporate field studies of active offenders into their research agendas. Without such studies, both the representativeness and the validity of research based on offenders located through criminal justice channels will remain problematic.

References

Bennett, Trevor and Richard Wright. (1984). *Burglars on Burglary: Prevention and the Offender.* Aldershot, England: Gower.

Berk, Richard and Joseph Adams. (1970). Establishing rapport with deviant groups. *Social Problems* 18:102-17.

Biernacki, Patrick and Dan Waldorf. (1981). Snowball sampling: Problems and techniques of chain referral sampling. *Sociological Methods & Research* 10:141-63.

Blumstein, Alfred and Jacqueline Cohen. (1979). Estimation of individual crime rates from arrest records. *Journal of Criminal Law and Criminology* 70:561-85.

Chambliss, William. (1975). On the paucity of research on organized crime: A reply to Galliher and Cain. *American Sociologist* 10:36-39.

Cromwell, Paul, James Olson, and D'Aunn Avary. (1991). *Breaking and Entering: An Ethnographic Analysis of Burglary.* Newbury Park, CA: Sage.

Dunlap, Eloise, Bruce Johnson, Harry Sanabria, Elbert Holliday, Vicki Lipsey, Maurice Barnett, William Hopkins, Ira Sobel, Doris Randolph, and Ko-Lin Chin. (1990). Studying crack users and their criminal careers: The scientific and artistic aspects of locating hard-to-reach subjects and interviewing them about sensitive topics. *Contemporary Drug Problems* 17:121-44.

Greenwood, Peter. (1982). *Selective Incapacitation.* Santa Monica, CA: RAND.

Hagedorn, John. (1990). Back in the field again: Gang research in the nineties. Pp. 240-59 in *Gangs in America*, edited by C. Ronald Huff. Newbury Park, CA: Sage.

Irwin, John. (1972). Participant observation of criminals. Pp.117-37 in *Research on Deviance*, edited by Jack Douglas. New York: Random House.

Letkemann, Peter. (1973). *Crime as Work.* Englewood Cliffs, NJ: Prentice-Hall.

McCall, George. (1978). *Observing the Law.* New York: Free Press.

Miller, S. M. (1952). The participant observer and over-rapport, *American Sociological Review* 17:97-99.

Petersilia, Joan, Peter Greenwood, and Marvin Lavin. (1977). *Criminal Careers of Habitual Felons.* Santa Monica, CA: RAND.

Polsky, Ned. (1969). *Hustlers, Beats, and Others.* Garden City, NJ: Anchor.

Rengert, George and John Wasilchick. (1985). *Suburban Burglary: A Time and a Place for Everything.* Springfield, IL: Charles C. Thomas.

———. (1989). *Space, Time and Crime: Ethnographic Insights into Residential Burglary.* Final report submitted to the National Institute of Justice, Office of Justice Programs, U.S. Department of Justice.

Sessions, William. (1989). *Crime in the United States—1988.* Washington, DC: U.S. Government Printing Office.

St. Louis Metropolitan Police Department. (1989). *Annual Report, 1988–1989.* St. Louis, MO: St. Louis Metropolitan Police Department.

Sudman, Seymour. (1976). *Applied Sampling.* New York: Academic Press.

Sutherland, Edwin and Donald Cressey. (1970). *Criminology—8th Edition.* Philadelphia, PA: Lippincott.

Taylor, Laurie. (1985). *In the Underworld.* London: Unwin.

Walker, Andrew and Charles Lidz. (1977). Methodological notes on the employment of indigenous observers. Pp. 103-23 in *Street Ethnography*, edited by Robert Weppner. Beverly Hills, CA: Sage.

Watters, John and Patrick Biernacki. (1989). Targeted sampling: Options for the study of hidden populations, *Social Problems* 36:416-30.

West, W. Gordon. (1980). Access to adolescent deviants and deviance. Pp. 31-44 in *Fieldwork Experience: Qualitative Approaches to Social Research*, edited by William Shaffir, Robert Stebbins, and Allan Turowitz. New York: St. Martin's.

Wright, Richard and Trevor Bennett. (1990). Exploring the offender's perspective: Observing and interviewing criminals. Pp. 138-51 in *Measurement Issues in Criminology*, edited by Kimberly Kempf. New York: Springer-Verlag.

Richard T. Wright, Scott H. Decker, Allison K. Redfern, and Dietrich L. Smith, "A Snowball's Chance in Hell: Doing Field Research With Residential Burglars." In *Journal of Research in Crime and Delinquency* 29 (2), pp. 148–157, 159–161. Copyright © 1992 by Sage Publications. Reprinted with permission. ✦

Section I

Criminal Lifestyles and Decision Making

This section explores the lifestyles and the decision-making strategies of criminals. We are concerned here with offenders' views and attitudes about both criminal and conventional activities and their perceptions of the risks and benefits associated with a criminal lifestyle. How those perceptions are formed and how they change over time are also examined. Because the nature of the criminal lifestyle is covert, hidden from public view and open only to the initiated, criminologists know little about these important issues. The research studies in this book are a step toward understanding the dynamics of criminal lifestyles and criminal decision making in that context.

In the first selection, Neal Shover and David Honaker ("The Socially Bounded Decision Making of Persistent Property Offenders") argue that an adequate understanding of the decision-making processes of property offenders can only be gained through exploring how their decisions are influenced by their lifestyles. They argue that offenders' risk assessments can best be understood by exploring the personal and social contexts in which decisions are made. They examine how lifestyles of persistent property offenders affect their assessment of the risks and benefits of crime. The research focuses on the decision to commit a crime, emphasizing how

closely that decision fits the rational choice model, in which decisions are based on an "assessment of potential returns from alternative courses of action and the risk of legal sanctions" (in this anthology, p. 11).

The article by Malin Åkerström ("Looking at the Squares") compares a sample of thieves and addicts to non-criminals on the basis of attitudes about work, leisure, law, finances, lifestyles, and the future. "Most of the time," she states, "the criminal life won." Criminals see their lives as more rewarding in terms of personal freedom, excitement, variety of experience, challenges, and thrills. Far from offering a deterministic view of criminal life, Åkerström contends that in the absence of acceptable alternatives, criminals clearly choose crime over the life of the "square john."

Finally, Deborah R. Baskin and Ira Sommers ("Women, Work, and Crime") analyze how female offenders make a living. They describe their progression from early involvement in the legitimate, formal economy to their ultimate embeddedness in the illegal, informal economy. Through a description of their experiences, the women provide us with an understanding of the basis for and types of decisions they make when choosing their "professions." ✦

2

The Socially Bounded Decision Making of Persistent Property Offenders

Neal Shover
David Honaker

The past decade has witnessed a renewal of interest in understanding crime based on the degree of rationality attributed to criminals as they contemplate offending. The rational-choice model recognizes that individuals choose crime from other possible alternative courses of action. The argument holds that prospective criminals weigh the possible consequences of their actions—potential risks and possible gains—and take advantage of a criminal opportunity only when it is in their self-interest to do so. This model stresses the offender's perceptions of the costs and benefits and the anticipated net utilities of crime, arguing that an objective appraisal of the costs and benefits of any course of action cannot be completely known or acted upon.

In the following selection, Neal Shover and David Honaker argue that the risk assessments of offenders are best understood by exploring the personal and social contexts in which decisions are made. They examine the lifestyles of persistent property offenders as influences on how they assess the risks and benefits of crime. The focus of the research is on the decision to commit a crime with emphasis on how

closely that decision fits the rational choice model.

The study population includes a sample of 60 recidivist property offenders incarcerated in Tennessee state prisons but who were nearing their release date. Subjects ranged in age from 23 to 70 years of age, with an average age of 34.1 years. Each member of the sample was interviewed approximately one month before his release from prison. Seven to ten months after release, the authors traced, contacted and interviewed 46 of the original sample of 60 men. The data used in this study was collected in the post-release interviews. Semi-structured ethnographic interviews were the principal data collection technique.

The interviews produced detailed descriptions of the most recent, easiest recalled crime that each subject had committed prior to the interview. Some of these crimes were committed before their incarceration and some after release. The objective was to gain, through the eyes of the offender, an understanding of the decision to commit a specific criminal act. The subjects were asked to focus their recollection on how the decision was made and to provide a detailed account of the risks and rewards they assessed while doing so.

The 1970s were marked by the eclipse of labeling theory as the dominant individual-level criminological theory and by the reappearance of interest in approaches originally advanced by classical theorists. Economists and cognitive psychologists along with many in the criminological mainstream advanced an interpretation of crime as *choice*, offering models of criminal decision making grounded in the assumption that the decision to commit a criminal act springs from the offender's assessment of its anticipated net utilities (e.g., Becker 1968; Heinke 1978; Carroll 1978; Reynolds 1985). This movement in favor of rational-choice approaches to crime spurred empirical investigation of problems that heretofore were limited primarily to studies of the death penalty and its impact on the homicide rate.

Early investigations of a rational choice interpretation of crime reported a weak but persistent relationship between the certainty of punishment and rates of serious property crimes (Blumstein, Cohen, and Nagin 1978). It was recognized, however, that an understanding of criminal decision making also requires knowledge about individual perceptions and beliefs about legal threats and other constraints on decision making (e.g., Manski 1978). Investigators moved on two main fronts to meet this need. Some used survey methods to explore differential involvement in minor forms of deviance in samples of restricted age ranges, typically high school and college students (e.g., Waldo and Chiricos 1972). Alternatively they examined the link between risk assessments and criminal participation in samples more representative of the general population (e.g., Tittle 1980). Serious shortcomings of these studies are that most either ignore the potential rewards of crime entirely or they fail to examine its emotional and interpersonal utilities. Still other investigators turned attention to serious criminal offenders and began expanding the narrow existing knowledge base (e.g., Claster 1967), chiefly through the use of cross sectional research designs and survey methods.

For more than a decade now, investigators have studied offenders' attitudes toward legitimate and criminal pursuits, their perceptions of and beliefs about the risks of criminal behavior, and their estimates of the payoffs from conventional and criminal pursuits (e.g., Petersilia et al. 1978; Peterson and Braiker 1980). These studies raise serious questions about the fit between offenders' calculus and a priori assumptions about their utilities and criminal decision making. One investigation of 589 incarcerated property offenders concluded, for example, that the subjects apparently do not utilize "a sensible cost-benefit analysis" when weighing the utilities of crime (Figgie 1988, p. 25). They substantially underestimate the risk of arrest for most crimes, routinely overestimate the monetary benefit they expect, and seem to have "grossly inaccurate perceptions of the costs and benefits associated with property crime" (Figgie 1988, p. 81). Unfortunately, both design and conceptual problems undermine confidence in the findings of this and similar studies. Cross sectional survey methods, for example, are poorly suited for examining dynamic decision-making *processes*.

Most such studies also fail to examine offenders' estimates of the likely payoffs from noncriminal alternatives or their non-monetary utilities, such as emotional satisfaction (Katz 1988).

As newer, empirically-based models of criminal decision making have been developed (e.g., Clarke and Cornish 1985; Cornish and Clarke 1986), a growing number of investigators are using ethnographic methods to examine the offender's criminal calculus, often in real or simulated natural settings (e.g., Carroll 1982; Carroll and Weaver 1986). The research reported here continues this line of ethnographic inquiry by using retrospective interviews to examine criminal decision making by serious and persistent property offenders. The focus of our attention is the decision to commit a crime rather than the target-selection decision that has received substantial attention elsewhere (e.g., Scarr 1973; Repetto 1974; Maguire 1982; Bennett and Wright 1984a; Rengert and Wasilchick 1985; Cromwell, Olson, and Avary 1991). The first objective is to examine how closely the decision to commit crime conforms to a classical rational choice model in which decisions assumedly are based largely on an assessment of potential returns from alternative courses of action and the risk of legal sanctions. A second objective is to examine the influence of the lifestyle pursued by many persistent property offenders on the salience of their utilities and the risks they assess in criminal decision making. . . .

Findings

Analysis reveals the most striking aspect of the subjects' decision making for the crimes they described is that a majority gave little or no thought to the possibility of arrest and confinement. Of 34 subjects who were asked specifically whether they considered the risk of arrest or who spontaneously indicated whether they did so, 21 (62 percent) said they did not. The comments of two subjects are typical:

Q: Did you think about . . . getting caught?

A: No.

Q: [H]ow did you manage to put that out of your mind?

A: [It] never did come into it.

Q: Never did come into it?

A: Never did, you know. It didn't bother me.

Q: Were you thinking about bad things that might happen to you?

A: None whatsoever.

Q: No?

A: I wasn't worried about getting caught or anything, you know. I was a positive thinker through everything, you know. I didn't have no negative thoughts about it whatsoever.

The 13 remaining subjects (38%) acknowledged they gave some thought to the possibility of arrest but most said they managed to dismiss it easily and to carry through with their plans:

Q: Did you worry much about getting caught? On a scale of one to ten, how would you rank your degree of worry that day?

A: [T]he worry was probably a one. You know what I mean? The worry was probably one. I didn't think about the consequences, you know. I know it's stupidity, but it didn't—that I might go to jail, I mean—it crossed my mind but it didn't make much difference.

Q: As you thought about doing that [armed robbery], were there things that you were worried about?

A: Well, the only thing that I was worried about was . . . getting arrested didn't even cross my mind—just worrying about getting killed is the only thing, you know, getting shot. That's the only thing. . . . But, you know, you'd have to be really be crazy not to think about that . . . you could possibly get in trouble. It crossed my mind, but I didn't worry about it all that much.

Some members of our sample said they managed deliberately and consciously to put out of mind all thoughts of possible arrest:

When I went out to steal, I didn't think about the negative things. 'Cause if you think negative, negative things are going to happen. And that's the way I looked at it . . . I done it just like it was a job or something. Go out and do it, don't think about getting caught, 'cause that would make you jumpy, edgy, nervous. If you looked like you were doing something wrong, then something wrong is 'gonna happen to you. . . . You just, you just put [the thought of arrest] out of your mind, you know.

Q: Did you think about [the possibility of getting caught] very much that night?

A: I didn't think about it that much, you know. . . . [I]t comes but, you know, you can wipe it away.

Q: How do you wipe it away?

A: You just blank it out. You blank it out.

Another subject said simply that "I try to put that [thought of arrest] the farthest thing from my mind that I can."

Many subjects attribute their ability to ignore or to dismiss all thought of possible arrest to a state of intoxication or drug altered consciousness:

Q: You didn't think about going to prison?

A: Never did. I guess it was all that alcohol and stuff, and drugs. . . . The day I pulled that robbery?—no. I was so high I didn't think about nothing.

Another subject told us that he had been drinking the entire day that he committed the crime and, by the time it occurred, he was in "nightlight city."

While it is clear that the formal risks of crime were not considered carefully by most members of the sample, equally striking is the finding that very few thought about or assessed legitimate alternatives before opting to commit a criminal act. Of 22 subjects who were asked specifically whether they had done so, 16 indicated they gave no thought whatsoever to legitimate alternatives. The six subjects who did either ignored or quickly dismissed them as inapplicable, given their immediate circumstances.

We recognize the methodological shortcomings of the descriptions of criminal decision making and behavior used as data for this study. Since the subjects were questioned in detail only about specific offenses they could remember well, the sample of descriptions may not be representative of the range of crimes they committed. By definition, they are memorable ones. Moreover, the recall period for these crimes ranged from one to 15 years, raising the possibility of errors caused by selective recall. Whether or not this could have produced systematic bias in the data is unknown. We cannot rule out the possibility that past crimes are remembered as being less rational than they actually were at the time of commission. Such a tendency could account in part for our interpretation of the data and our description of their style of decision making. The fact that we limited the sample to recidivists means also that we cannot determine how much their behavior may reflect either innate differences (Gottfredson and Hirschi 1990) or experiential effects, i.e., the effects of past success in committing crime and avoiding arrest (Nagin and Paternoster 1991). It could be argued that the behavior of our subjects, precisely because they had demonstrated a willingness to commit property crimes and had done so in the past, limits the external validity of their reports. Given sample selection criteria and these potential data problems, generalizations beyond the study population must be made with caution.

This said, we believe that the remarkable similarity between our findings and the picture of criminal decision making reported by others who have studied serious property offenders strengthens their credibility significantly. A study of 83 imprisoned burglars revealed that 49 percent did not think about the chances of getting caught for any particular offense during their last period of offending. While 37 percent of them did think about it, most thought there was little or no chance it would happen (Bennett and Wright 1984a, Table A14). Interviews with 113 men convicted of robbery or an offense related to robbery revealed that "over 60 percent . . . said they had not even thought about getting caught." Another 17 percent said that they had thought about the possibility but "did not believe it to be a problem" (Feeney 1986, pp. 59-60). Analysis of prison interviews with 77 robbers and 45 burglars likewise revealed

their "general obliviousness toward the consequences [of their crimes] and no thought of being caught" (Walsh 1986, p. 157). In sum, our findings along with the findings from other studies suggest strongly that many serious property offenders seem to be remarkably casual in weighing the formal risks of criminal participation. As one of our subjects put it, "you think about going to prison about like you think about dying, you know." The impact of alcohol and drug use in diminishing concern with possible penalties also has been reported by many others (e.g., Bennett and Wright 1984b; Cromwell, Olson, and Avary 1991).

If the potential legal consequences of crime do not figure prominently in crime commission decision making by persistent thieves, what do they think about when choosing to commit crime? Walsh (1980; 1986) shows that typically they focus their thoughts on the money that committing a crime may yield and the good times they expect to have with it when the crime is behind them. Carroll's data (1982) likewise indicate that the amount of gain offenders expect to receive is "the most important dimension" in their decision making while the certainty of punishment is the least important of the four dimensions on which his subjects assessed crime opportunities. Our findings are consistent with these reports; our subjects said that they focused on the expected gains from their crimes:

> I didn't think about nothing but what I was going to do when I got that money, how I was going to spend it, what I was going to do with it, you know.

> See, you're not thinking about those things [possibility of being arrested]. You're thinking about that big pay check at the end of thirty to forty-five minutes worth of work.

> [A]t the time [that you commit crime], you throw all your instincts out the window. . . . Because you're just thinking about money, and money only. That's all that's on your mind, because you want that money. And you throw, you block everything off until you get the money.

Although confidence in our findings is bolstered by the number of points on which they are similar to reports by others who have explored crime commission decision making, they do paint a picture of decision making that is different from what is known about the way at least some of them make target selection decisions. Investigators (e.g., Cromwell, Olson, and Avary 1991) have shown that target decisions approximate simple common-sense conceptions of rational behavior (Shover 1991). A resolution of the problem presented by these contradictory findings is suggested by others (Cromwell, Olson, and Avary 1991) and also apparent in our data: Criminal participation often results from a *sequence* of experientially and analytically discrete decisions, all of potentially varying degrees of intentional rationality. Thus, once a *motivational* crime commission decision has been made, offenders may move quickly to selecting, or to exploiting an apparently suitable target. At this stage of the criminal participation process, offenders are preoccupied with the *technical* challenge of avoiding failure at what now is seen as a *practical* task. As one subject put it, "you don't think about getting caught, you think about how in hell you're going to do it *not* to get caught, you know." His comments were echoed by another man: "The only thing you're thinking about is looking and acting and trying *not* to get caught." Last, consider the comments of a third subject: "I wasn't afraid of getting caught, but I was cautious, you know. Like I said, I was thinking only in the way to prevent me from getting caught." Just as bricklayers do not visualize graphically or deliberate over the bodily carnage that could follow from a collapsed scaffold once there is a job to be done, many thieves apparently do not dwell at length on the likelihood of arrest or on the pains of imprisonment when proceeding to search out or exploit suitable criminal opportunities.

The accumulated evidence on crime commission decision making by persistent offenders is substantial and persuasive: the rationality they employ is limited or bounded severely (e.g., Carroll 1982; Cromwell, Olson, and Avary 1991). While unsuccessful persistent offenders may calculate potential benefits and costs before committing criminal acts, they apparently do so differently or weigh utilities differently than as sketched in a priori decision making models. As Walsh (1980, p. 141) suggests, offenders' "definitions of costs and rewards seem to be at variance with society's estimates of them." This does not mean their decision making is *irrational* but it does point to the difficulties of understanding it and then refining theoretical models of the process. Our objective in the remainder of this paper is an improved understanding of criminal decision making based on analysis of the socially anchored purposes, utilities, and risks of the acts that offenders commit. Put differently, we explore the contextual origins of their bounded rationality.

Lifestyle, Utilities, and Risk

It is instructive to examine the decision making of persistent property offenders in context of the lifestyle that is characteristic of many in their ranks: *life as party*. The hallmark of life as party is the enjoyment of "good times" with minimal concern for obligations and commitments that are external to the person's immediate social setting. It is a lifestyle distinguished in many cases by two repetitively cyclical phases and correspondingly distinctive approaches to crime. When offenders' efforts to maintain the lifestyle (i.e., their party pursuits) are largely successful, crimes are committed in order to sustain circumstances or a pattern of activities they experience as pleasurable. As Walsh (1986, p. 15) puts it, crimes committed under these circumstances are "part of a continuing satisfactory way of life." By contrast, when offenders are less successful at party pursuits, their crimes are committed in order to forestall or avoid circumstances experienced as threatening, unpleasant or precarious. Corresponding to each of these two phases of party pursuits is a distinctive set of utilities and stance toward legal risk.

Life as Party

Survey and ethnographic studies alike show that persistent property offenders spend much of their criminal gains on alcohol and other drugs (Petersilia et al. 1978; Maguire 1982; Gibbs and Shelley 1982; Figgie 1988; Cromwell, Olson, and Avary 1991). The proceeds of their crimes, as Walsh has noted (1986, p. 72), "typically [are] used for personal, non-essential consumption (e.g., 'nights out'), rather than, for example, to be given to family or used for basic needs." Thieves spend much of their leisure hours enjoying good times. Our subjects were no different in this regard. For example,

> I smoked an ounce of pot in a day, a day and a half. Every other day I had to go buy a bag of pot, at the least. And sometimes I've went two or three days in a row. . . . And there was never a day went by that I didn't [drink] a case, case and a half of beer. And [I] did a 'script of pills every two days.

While much of their money is consumed by the high cost of drugs, a portion may be used for ostentatious enjoyment and display of luxury items and activities that probably would be unattainable on the returns from blue-collar employment:

> [I]t was all just, it was all just a big money thing to me at the time, you know. Really, what it was was impressing everybody, you know. "Here Floyd is, and he's never had nothing in his life, and now look at him: he's driving new cars, and wearing jewelry," you know.

Life as party is enjoyed in the company of others. Typically it includes shared consumption of alcohol or other drugs in bars and lounges, on street corners, or while cruising in automobiles. In these venues, party pursuers celebrate and affirm values of spontaneity, autonomy, independence, and resourcefulness. Spontaneity means that rationality and long range planning are eschewed in favor of enjoying the moment and permitting the day's activities and pleasures to develop in an unconstrained fashion. This may mean, for example, getting up late, usually after a night of partying, and then setting out to contact and enjoy the company of friends and associates who are known to be predisposed to partying:

> I got up around about eight-thirty that morning. . . .

Q: Eight-thirty? Was that the usual time that you got up?

A: Yeah, if I didn't have a hangover from the night before. . . .

Q: What kind of drugs were you doing then?

A: I was doing . . . Percadans, Dilauds, taking Valiums, drinking. . . . [A]nyway, I got up that morning about eight-thirty, took me a bath, put on some clothes and . . . decided to walk [over to his mother's home]. [T]his particular day, . . . my nephew was over [there]. . . . We was just sitting in the yard and talking and drinking beer, you know. . . . It was me, him and my sister. We was sitting out there in the yard talking. And this guy that we know, he came up, he pulled up. So my nephew got in the car with him and they left. So, you know, I was sitting there talking to my sister. . . . And then, in the meantime, while we was talking, they come back, about thirty minutes later with a case of beer, some marijuana and everything, and there was another one of my nephews in the car with them. So me, two of my sisters, and two of my nephews, we got in the car with this guy here and we just went riding. So we went to Hadley Park and . . . we stayed out there. There were so many people out there, they were parked on the grass and things, and the vice squad come and run everybody away. So when they done that, we left. . . . So we went back out [toward his mother's home] but instead of going over to my mother's house we went to this little joint [tavern]. Now we're steady drinking and smoking weed all during this day. So when we get there, we park and get out and see a few friends. We [were] talking and getting high, you know, blowing each other a shotgun [sharing marijuana].

Enjoyment of party pursuits in group context is enhanced through the collective emphasis on personal autonomy. Because it is understood by all that participants are free to leave if they no longer enjoy or do not support group activities, the continuing presence of each participant affirms for the remainder the pleasures of the lifestyle. Uncoerced participation thus reinforces the shared assumption that group activities are appropriate and enjoyable. The behavioral result of the emphasis on autonomy is acceptance of or acquiescence in group decisions and activities.

Party pursuits also appeal to offenders because they permit conspicuous display of independence (Persson 1981). This generally means avoidance of the world of routine work and freedom from being "under someone's thumb." It also may include being free to avoid or to escape from restrictive routines:

> I just wanted to be doing something. Instead of being at home, or something like that. I wanted to be running, I wanted to be going to clubs, and picking up women and shooting pool. And I liked to go to [a nearby resort community] and just drive around over there. A lot of things like that. . . . I was drinking two pints or more a day. . . . I was doing Valiums and I was doing Demerol. . . . I didn't want to work.

The proper pursuit and enjoyment of life as party is expensive, due largely to the costs of drugs. As one of our subjects remarked: "We was doing a lot of cocaine, so cash didn't last long, you know. If we made $3,000, two thousand of it almost instantly went for cocaine." Some party pursuers must meet other expenses as well if the lifestyle is to be maintained:

> Believe it or not, I was spending [$700] a day.
>
> Q: On what?
>
> A: Pot, alcohol, women, gas, motel rooms, food.
>
> Q: You were living in hotels, motels?
>
> A: Yeah, a lot of times, I was. I'd take a woman to a motel. I bought a lot of clothes. I used to like to dress pretty nicely, I'd buy suits.

Party pursuits require continuous infusions of money and no single method of generating funds allows enjoyment of it for more than a few days. Consequently, the emphasis on spontaneity, autonomy, and independence is matched by the importance attached to financial resourcefulness. This is evidenced by the ability to sustain the lifestyle over a period of time. Doing so earns for offenders a measure of respect from peers for their demonstrated ability to "get over." It translates

into "self-esteem . . . as a folk hero beating the bureaucratic system of routinized dependence" (Walsh 1986, p. 16). The value of and respect for those who demonstrate resourcefulness means that criminal acts, as a means of sustaining life as party, generally are not condemned by the offender's peers.

The risks of employing criminal solutions to the need for funds are approached blithely but confidently in the same spontaneous and playful manner as are the rewards of life as party. In fact, avoidance of careful and detailed planning is a way of demonstrating possession of valued personal qualities and commitment to the lifestyle. Combined with the twin assumptions that peers have chosen freely and that one should not interfere with their autonomy, avoidance of rational planning finds expression in a reluctance to suggest that peers should weigh carefully the possible consequences of whatever they choose to do. Thus, the interaction that precedes criminal incidents is distinguished by circumspection and the use of linguistic devices that relegate risk and fear to the background of attention. The act of stealing, for example, is referred to obliquely but knowingly as "doing something" or as "making money":

> [After a day of partying,] I [got] to talking about making some money, because I didn't have no money. This guy that we were riding with, he had all the money. . . . So me and him and my nephew, we get together, talking about making some money. This guy tells me, he said, "man, I know where there's a good place at."
>
> Q: Okay, so you suggested you all go somewhere and rob?
>
> A: Yeah, "make some"—well, we called it "making money."
>
> Q: Okay. So, then you and this fellow met up in the bar. . . . Tell me about the conversation?
>
> A: Well, there wasn't much of a conversation to it, really. . . . I asked him if he was ready to go, if he wanted to go do something, you know. And he knew what I meant. He wanted to go make some money somehow, any way it took.

To the external observer, inattention to risk at the moment when it would seem most appropriate may seem to border on irrationality. For the offender engaged in party pursuits, however, it is but one aspect of behaviors that are rational in other respects. It opens up opportunities to enjoy life as party and to demonstrate commitment to values shared by peers. Resourcefulness and disdain for conventional rationality affirm individual character and style, both of which are important in the world of party pursuits (Goffman 1967).

Party Pursuits and Eroding Resources

Paradoxically, the pursuit of life as party can be appreciated and enjoyed to the fullest extent only if participants moderate their involvement in it while maintaining identities and routines in the straight world. Doing so maintains its "escape value" but it also requires an uncommon measure of discipline and forbearance. The fact is that extended and enthusiastic enjoyment of life as party threatens constantly to deplete irrevocably the resources needed to sustain enjoyment of its pleasures. Three aspects of the life-as-party lifestyle can contribute to this end.

First, some offenders become ensnared increasingly by the chemical substances and drug using routines that are common there. In doing so, the meaning of drug consumption changes:

See, I was doing drugs every day. It just wasn't every other day, it was to the point that, after the first few months doing drugs, I would have to do "X amount" of drugs, say, just for instance, just to feel like I do now. Which is normal.

Once the party pursuer's physical or psychological tolerance increases significantly, drugs are consumed not for the high they once produced but instead to maintain a sense of normality by avoiding sickness or withdrawal.

Second, party pursuits erode legitimate fiscal and social capital. They can not be sustained by legitimate employment and they may in fact undermine both one's ability and inclination to hold a job. Even if offenders are willing to work at the kinds of employment available to them, and evidence suggests that many are not (Cromwell, Olson, and Avary 1991), the time schedules of work and party pursuits conflict. The best times of the day for committing many property crimes are also the times the offender would be at work and it is nearly impossible to do both consistently and well. For those who pursue life as a party, legitimate employment often is foregone or sacrificed (Rengert and Wasilchick 1985). The absence of income from noncriminal sources thus reinforces the need to find other sources of money.

Determined pursuit of life as party also may affect participants' relationships with legitimate significant others. Many offenders manage to enjoy the lifestyle successfully only by exploiting the concern and largesse of family and friends. This may take the form of repeated requests for and receipt of personal loans that go unreturned, occasional thefts, or other forms of exploitation:

I lived well for awhile. I lived well . . . until I started shooting cocaine real bad, intravenously. . . . [A]nd then everything, you know, went up in smoke, you know. Up my arm. The watches, the rings . . . the car, you know. I used to have a girl, man, and her daddy had two horses. I put them in my arm. You know what I mean? I made her sell them horses. My clothes and all that stuff, a lot of it, they went up in smoke when I started messing with that cocaine.

Eventually, friends and even family members may come to believe that they have been exploited or that continued assistance will only prolong a process that must be terminated. As one subject told us, "Oh, I tried to borrow money, and borrow money and, you know, nobody would loan it to me. Because they knew what I was doing." After first refusing further assistance, acquaintances, friends, and even family members may avoid social contacts with the party pursuer or sever ties altogether. This dialogue occurred between the interviewer and one of our subjects:

Q: [B]esides doing something wrong, did you think of anything else that you could do to get money? . . . Borrow it?

A: No, I'd done run that in the ground. See, you burn that up. That's burned up, right there, borrowing, you know. . . . Once I borrow, you know, I might get $10 from you today and, see, I'll be expecting to be getting $10 tomorrow, if I could. And then, when I see you [and] you see me coming, you say, "no, I don't have none." [A]s the guys in the penitentiary say, "you absorb all of your remedies," you see. And that's what I did: I burned my remedies up, you know.

Last, when party pursuits are not going well, feelings of shame and self-disgust are not uncommon (Frazier and Meisenhelder 1985). Unsuccessful party pursuers as a result may take steps to reduce these feelings by distancing themselves voluntarily from conventional others:

Q: You were married to your wife at that time?

A: Yeah, I was married . . . .

Q: Where was she living then?

A: I finally forced her to go home, you know. . . . I made her go home, you know. And it caused an argument, for her to go home to her mother's. I felt like that was the best thing I did for her, you know. She hated me . . . for it at the time, didn't understand none of it. But, really, I intentionally made her go. I really spared her the misery that we were going to have. And it came. It came in bundles.

When party pursuers sustain severe losses of legitimate income and social resources, regardless of how it occurs, they grow increasingly isolated from conventional significant others. The obvious consequence is that this reduces interpersonal constraints on their behavior.

As their pursuit of life as party increasingly assumes qualities of difficulty and struggle, offenders' utilities and risk perceptions also change. Increasingly, crimes are committed not to enhance or sustain the lifestyle so much as to forestall unpleasant circumstances. Those addicted to alcohol or other drugs, for example, must devote increasing time and energy to the quest for monies to purchase their chemicals of choice. Both their drug consumption and the frequency of

their criminal acts increase (Ball et al. 1983; Johnson et al. 1985). For them, as for others, inability to draw on legitimate or low risk resources eventually may precipitate a crisis. One of our respondents retold how, facing a court appearance on a burglary charge, he needed funds to hire an attorney:

I needed some money bad or if I didn't, if I went to court the following day, I was going to be locked up. The judge was going to lock me up. Because I didn't have no lawyer. And I had went and talked to several lawyers and they told me . . . they wanted a thousand dollars, that if I couldn't come up with no thousand dollars, they couldn't come to court with me. . . . [S]o I went to my sister. I asked my sister, I said, "look here, what about letting me have seven or eight hundred dollars"— which I knowed she had the money because she . . . had been in a wreck and she had gotten some money out of a suit. And she said, "well, if I give you the money you won't do the right thing with it." And I was telling her, "no, no, I need a lawyer." But I couldn't convince her to let me have the money. So I left. . . . I said, shit, I'm fixin' to go back to jail. . . . [S]o as I left her house and was walking—I was going to catch the bus—the [convenience store] and bus stop was right there by each other. So, I said I'm going to buy me some gum. . . . [A]nd in the process of me buying the chewing gum, I seen two ladies, they was counting money. So I figured sooner or later one of them was going to come out with the money. . . . I waited on them until . . . one came out with the money, and I got it.

Confronted by crisis and preoccupied increasingly with relieving immediate distress, the offender eventually may experience and define himself as propelled by forces beyond his control. Behavioral options become dichotomized into those that hold out some possibility of relief, however risky, and those that promise little but continued pain. Legitimate options are few and are seen as unlikely solutions. A criminal act may offer some hope of relief, however temporary. The offender may imbue the criminal option with almost magical prospects for ending or reversing the state of discomfort:

I said, "well, look at it like this"; if I don't do it, then tomorrow morning I've got the same [problems] that I've got right now. I could be hungry. I'm going to want food more. I'm going to want cigarettes more. I'm going to want everything more. But, if I do it, and if I make it, then I've got all I want.

Acts that once were the result of blithe unconcern with risk can over time come to be based on a personal determination to master or reverse what is experienced as desperately unpleasant circumstances. As a result, inattention to risk in the offender's decision making may give way to the perception that he has *nothing to lose:*

It . . . gets to the point that you get into such a desperation. You're not working, you can't work. You're drunk as hell, been that way two or three weeks. You're no good to yourself, and you're no good to anybody else. Self-esteem is gone [and you are] spiritually, mentally, physically, financially bankrupt. You ain't got nothing to lose.

Desperate to maintain or reestablish a sense of normality, the offender pursues emotional relief with a decision to act decisively, albeit in the face of legal odds recognized as narrowing. By acting boldly and resolutely to make the best of a grim situation, one gains a measure of respect, if not from others, then at least from oneself.

I think, when you're doing drugs like I was doing, I don't think you tend to rationalize much at all. I think it's just a decision you make. You don't weigh the consequences, the pros and the cons. You just do it.

You know, all kinds of things started running through my mind. If I get caught, then there, there I am with another charge. Then I said, well if I don't do something, I'm going to be in jail. And I just said, "I'm going to do it."

The fact that sustained party pursuits often cause offenders to increase the number of offenses they commit and to exploit criminal opportunities that formerly were seen as risky should not be interpreted as meaning they believe they can continue committing crime with impunity. The opposite is true.

Many offenders engaged in crimes intended to halt or reverse eroding fortunes are aware that eventually they will be arrested if they continue doing so:

Q: How did you manage not to think about, you know, that you could go to prison?

A: Well, you think about it afterwards. You think, "wow, boy, I got away with it again." But you know, sooner or later, the law of averages is "gonna catch up with you. You just can't do it [commit crime] forever and ever and ever. And don't think you're not gonna get caught," cause you will.

Bennett and Wright (1984a) likewise show that a majority of persistent offenders endorse the statement that they will be caught "eventually." The cyclical transformations of party pursuits from pleasant and enjoyable to desperate and tenuous is one reason they are able to commit crimes despite awareness of inevitable and potentially severe legal penalties.

The threat posed by possible arrest and imprisonment, however, may not seem severe to some desperate offenders. As compared to their marginal and precarious existence, it may be seen as offering a form of relief:

[When he was straight], I'd think about [getting caught]: I could get this, and that [penalties]. . . . [A]nd then I would think, well, I know this is going to end one day, you know. But, you know, you get so far out there, and get so far off into it that it really don't matter, you know. But you think about that. . . . I knew, eventually, I would get caught, you know. . . . I was off into drugs and I just didn't care if I got caught or not.

When I [got] caught—and they caught me right at the house—it's kind of like, you feel good, because you're glad it's over, you know. I mean, a weight being lifted off your head. And you say, well, I don't have to worry about this shit no more, because they've caught me. And it's over, you know.

In sum, due to offenders' eroding access to legitimately secured funds, their diminishing contact with and support from conventional significant others, and their efforts to maintain drug consumption habits, crimes that once were committed for recreational purposes increasingly become desperate attempts to forestall or reverse uncomfortable or frustrating situations. Pursuing the short term goal of maximizing enjoyment of life, legal threats can appear to the offender either as remote and improbable contingencies when party pursuits fulfill their recreational purposes or as an acceptable risk in the face of continued isolation, penury, and desperation.

We analyzed the descriptions of crime provided by our subjects, and their activities on the day the crime occurred. We focused specifically on: (1) the primary purpose of their crimes, i.e., whether they planned to use the proceeds of crime for pleasure or to cope with unpleasant contingencies, and (2) the extent and subjective meaning of their drug use at the time they decided to commit the crime in question. Based on the analysis, we classified the crimes of 15 subjects as behaviors committed in the enjoyment of life as a party and 13 as behaviors committed in order to enhance or restore enjoyment of this lifestyle. The 12 remaining offenders could not be classified because of insufficient information in the crime descriptions or they are isolated criminal acts that do not represent a specific lifestyle. Two subjects, for example, described crimes that were acts of vengeance directed at the property of individuals who had treated them or their relatives improperly. One of the men related how he decided to burglarize a home for reasons of revenge:

> I was mad. . . . When I was in the penitentiary, my wife went to his house for a party and he give her a bunch of cocaine. . . . It happened, I think, about a week before I got out. . . . I just had it in my mind what I wanted to do: I wanted to hurt him like I was hurt. . . . I was pretty drunk, when I went by [his home], and I saw there wasn't no car there. So, I just pulled my car in.

The other subject told how an acquaintance had stolen drugs and other possessions from his automobile. In response the subject "staked out the places where he would be for several days before I caught him, at gun point, [and] made him take me to his home, [which] I ransacked, and found some of the narcotics that he had stolen from me." Although neither of these crimes was committed in pursuit of life as party, other crimes committed by both these subjects during their criminal careers did occur as part of that lifestyle. Other investigators have similarly reported that revenge is the dominant motive in a minority of property offenses (e.g., Cromwell, Olson, and Avary 1991, p. 22).

Implications

We have suggested that daily routines characteristic of the partying lifestyle of persistent and unsuccessful offenders may modify both the salience of their various decision utilities and their perceptions of legal risk in the process of their crime commission decisions. This is not to say that these decisions are irrational, only that they do not conform to decision making as sketched by rational choice theories. Our objective was not to falsify the rational choice approach to criminal decision making, for we know of no way this could be accomplished. Whatever it is, moreover, rationality is not a dichotomous variable. Indeed, offenders' target selection decision making appears more rational in the conventional sense than do crime commission decisions.

The lesson here for theories of criminal decision making is that while utilities and risk assessment may be properties of individuals, they also are shaped by the social and personal contexts in which decisions are made. Whether their pursuit of life as party is interpreted theoretically as the product of structural strain, choice, or even happenstance is of limited importance to an understanding of persistent offenders' discrete criminal forays. What is important is that their lifestyle places them in situations that may facilitate important transformations in the utilities of prospective actions. If nothing else, this means that some situations more than others make it possible to discount or ignore risk. We are not the first to call attention to this phenomenon:

> [The] situational nature of sanction properties has escaped the scales and indicators employed in official record and self-report survey research. In this body of

research an arrest and a year in prison are generally assumed to have the same meaning for all persons and across all situations. The situational grounding of sanction properties suggests [however] that we look beyond official definitions of sanctions and the attitudinal structure of individuals to the properties of situations. (Ekland-Olson et al. 1984, p. 174)

Along the same line, a longitudinal survey of adult offenders concludes that decision making "may be conditioned by elements within the immediate situation confronting the individual . . . [such that] perceptions of the opportunity, returns, and support for crime within a given situation may influence . . . perceptions of risks and the extent to which those risks are discounted" (Piliavin et al. 1986, p. 115). The same interpretation has been suggested by Shover and Thompson (1992) for their failure to find an expected positive relationship between risk estimates and crime desistance among former prison inmates.

In light of the sample and data limitations of this study we cannot and have not argued that the lifestyle we described *generates* or produces the characteristic decision making behaviors of persistent property offenders. The evidence does not permit such interpretive liberties. It does seem reasonable to suggest, however, that the focal concerns and shared perspectives of those who pursue life as party may function to *sustain* offenders' free-wheeling, but purposeful, decision making style. Without question there is a close *correspondence* between the two. Our ability to explain and predict decision making requires that we gain a better understanding of how utilities and risk perceptions are constrained by the properties of situations encountered typically by persons in their daily rounds. In other words, we must learn more about the daily worlds that comprise the immediate contexts of criminal decision making behavior.

Bibliography

Ball, J. C., Shaffer, J. W., and Nurco, D. N. (1983) The day-to-day criminality of heroin addicts in Baltimore: A study in the continuity of offense rates, *Drug and Alcohol Dependence*, 12, 119-142.

Becker, G. (1968) Crime and punishment: An economic approach, *Journal of Political Economy*, 76, 169-217.

Bennett, T. and Wright, R. (1984a) *Burglars on Burglary*, Hampshire, U. K.: Gower.

——. (1984b) The relationship between alcohol use and burglary, *British Journal of Addiction*, 79, 431-437.

Blumstein, A., Cohen, J. and Nagin, D. (Eds.) (1978) *Deterrence and Incapacitation: Estimating the Effects of Criminal Sanctions on Crime Rates*, Washington, D.C.: National Academy of Sciences.

Carroll, J. S. (1978) A psychological approach to deterrence: The evaluation of crime opportunities, *Journal of Personality and Social Psychology*, 36, 1512-1520.

——. (1982) Committing a crime: The offender's decision, in: J. Konecni and E. B. Ebbesen (Eds.), *The Criminal Justice System: A Social-Psychological Analysis*, San Francisco: W.H. Freeman.

Carroll, J. S. and Weaver, F. (1986) Shoplifters' perceptions of crime opportunities: A process-tracing study, in: D. B. Cornish and R. V. Clarke (Eds.), *The Reasoning Criminal: Rational Choice Perspectives on Offending*, New York: Springer-Verlag.

Clarke, R. V. and Cornish, D. B. (1985) Modeling offenders' decisions: A framework for research and policy, in: M. Tonry and N. Morris (Eds.), *Crime and Justice: A Review of Research*, Vol. 4, Chicago: University of Chicago Press.

Claster, D. S. (1967) Comparison of risk perception between delinquents and nondelinquents, *Journal of Criminal Law, Criminology and Police Science*, 58, 80-86.

Cornish, D. B. and Clarke, R. V. (Eds.) (1986) *The Reasoning Criminal: Rational Choice Perspectives on Offending*, New York: Springer-Verlag.

Cromwell, P. F., Olson, J. N. and Avary, D. W. (1991) *Breaking and Entering: An Ethnographic Analysis of Burglary*, Newbury Park, Ca: Sage.

Ekland-Olson, S., Lieb, J. and Zurcher, L. (1984) The paradoxical impact of criminal sanctions: Some microstructural findings, *Law & Society Review*, 18, 159-178.

Feeney, F. (1986) Robbers as decision-makers, in: D. B. Cornish and R. V. Clarke (Eds.), *The Reasoning Criminal: Rational Choice Perspectives on Offending*, New York: Springer-Verlag.

Figgie International (1988) *The Figgie Report Part VI—The Business of Crime: The Criminal

Perspective, Richmond, Va: Figgie International Inc.

Frazier, C. E. and Meisenhelder, T. (1985) Criminality and emotional ambivalence: Exploratory notes on an overlooked dimension, *Qualitative Sociology*, 8, 266-284.

Gibbs, J. J. and Shelley, P. L. (1982) Life in the fast lane: A retrospective view by commercial thieves, *Journal of Research in Crime and Delinquency*, 19, 299-330.

Goffman, E. (1967) *Interaction Ritual*, Garden City, N.Y.: Anchor.

Gottfredson, M. R. and Hirschi, T. (1990) *A General Theory of Crime*, Stanford, Ca: Stanford University Press.

Heineke, J. M. (Ed.) (1978) *Economic Models of Criminal Behavior*, Amsterdam: North-Holland.

Johnson, B. D., Goldstein, P. J., Preble, E., Schmeidler, J. Lipton, D. D., Spunt, B. and Miller, T. (1985) *Taking Care of Business: The Economics of Crime by Heroin Addicts*, Lexington, Mass.: D.C. Heath.

Katz, J. (1998) *Seductions of Crime*, New York: Basic Books.

Maguire, M. in collaboration with T. Bennett (1982) *Burglary in a Dwelling*, London: Heinemann.

Manski, C. F. (1978) Prospects for inference on deterrence through empirical analysis of individual criminal behavior, in: A. Blumstein, J. Cohen and D. Nagin (Eds.), *Deterrence and Incapacitation: Estimating the Effects of Criminal Sanctions on Crime Rates*, Washington, D.C.: National Academy of Sciences.

Nagin, D. S. and Paternoster, R. (1991) On the relationship of past to future participation in delinquency, *Criminology*, 29, 163-189.

Persson, M. (1981) Time-perspectives amongst criminals, *Acta Sociologica*, 24, 149-165.

Petersilia, J. (1980) Criminal career research: A review of recent evidence, in: N. Morris and M. Tonry (Eds.), *Crime and Justice: An Annual Review of Research*, Vol. 2, Chicago: University of Chicago Press.

———, Greenwood, P. W. and Lavin, M. (1978) *Criminal Careers of Habitual Felons*, Washington, D.C.: U.S. Department of Justice, National Institute of Law Enforcement and Criminal Justice.

Peterson, M. A. and Braiker, H. B. (1980) *Doing Crime: A Survey of California Prison Inmates*, Santa Monica, Ca: Rand Corporation.

Piliavin, I., Gartner, R. and Matsueda, R. (1986) Crime, deterrence, and rational choice, *American Sociological Review*, 51, 101-119.

Rengert, G. F. and Wasilchick, J. (1985) *Suburban Burglary*, Springfield, Ill.: Charles C. Thomas.

Repetto, T. A. (1974) *Residential Crime*, Cambridge, Mass.: Ballinger.

Reynolds, M. O. (1985) *Crime by Choice: An Economic Analysis*, Dallas: Fisher Institute.

Scarr, H. A. (1973) *Patterns of Burglary* (second edition), Washington, D.C.: U. S. Department of Justice, National Institute of Law Enforcement and Criminal Justice.

Seidel, J. V., Kjolseth, R. and Seymour, E. (1988) *The Ethnograph: A User's Guide*, (Version 3.0), Littleton, Co: Qualis Research Associates.

Shover, N. (1991) Burglary, in: M. Tonry (Ed.), *Crime and Justice: An Annual Review of Research*, Vol. 14, Chicago: University of Chicago Press.

Shover, N. and Thompson, C. Y. (1992) Age, differential expectations, and crime desistance, *Criminology*, 30, 89-104.

Waldo, G. P. and Chiricos, T. G. (1972) Perceived penal sanction and self-reported criminality: A neglected approach to deterrence research, *Social Problems*, 19, 522-540.

Walsh, D. (1980) *Break-Ins: Burglary from Private Houses*, London: Constable.

———. (1986) *Heavy Business*, London: Routledge & Kegan Paul.

3

Looking at the Squares: Comparisons With the Square Johns

Malin Åkerström

I*n the previous chapter, Neal Shover dem-*
onstrated that persistent property offenders
lead a unique lifestyle which he characterized
as "life as party," and how their decision-making
processes were affected by this social context.
In the following selection, Swedish criminolo-
gist Malin Åkerström compares the lifestyles of
criminals with those of non-criminals—
"square johns." Åkerström writes that crimi-
nals are often portrayed as wanting to be like
ordinary people or having deep-seated hostility
toward them. Neither is true. In fact, she as-
serts, criminals hold a slightly condescending
attitude toward "square johns." They see their
own lives as exciting and special and the lives
of non-criminals as dull, boring, and insipid.
Moreover, many of the offenders she inter-
viewed believed that non-criminals secretly
wished "to do what they, the criminals, had
done, if only they dared." The criminal life is
thus seen as filled with thrill and adventure
and the square life as "more terrifying than do-
ing time."

For this study, the author compared the re-
sponses of 150 Swedish male prison inmates
with those of 198 non-criminal respondents re-
garding attitudes toward drugs, different types
of legal occupations, illegal ways of support-
ing oneself, opinions of the "square-johns,"
and about crime as a way of life. She con-
ducted extensive interviews over several years,

combining the data from three separate studies
into these findings.

. . . in the interviews comparisons between
the criminal life and that of the squares were
a constantly reoccurring theme. Most of the
time the criminal life won. This does not
mean that the inmates saw the criminal life
as the perfect life, but as Irwin (1980) has
pointed out, a criminal life can be seen as
more rewarding in the absence of other acceptable alternatives. The alternative as they
see it is the negatively stereotyped lifestyle of
the square-johns: their activities are dull, leisure means looking at TV, their outlook on life
is narrow, they have experienced so little, etc.
It is thought provoking that half of the inmates said "no" to the question "If you could
choose now, would you prefer to live a square
type of life?"

Shover points out that really committed
and successful burglars even derive a psychological reward from the comparison with the
squares:

> Many *good burglars* derive feelings of sat-
> isfaction from a weighing of how their life
> compares with the lives they believe are
> experienced by many *square johns*. When
> they take into account their incomplete
> education and lack of job skills, the only
> alternative legitimate role which they can
> imagine as being open to them is one
> which they evaluate with extreme negativ-
> ism. They know it as the *working stiff*, a
> name which, by itself, tells worlds.
> (1971:122)

This negative outlook is well known in the
criminological literature. Here, however, I
wish to examine this attitude a bit more extensively than is usually done.

In a question from a study of mine in 1978,
the inmates were asked if they thought that
the life of the squares contained anything
positive. Of the 88 respondents, more than a
third categorically stated "no," while the rest
mentioned some aspects as being attractive,
such as having a family, a job, or a more secure life. There is thus not a total negativism
against the lifestyle of the squares. The result
of another question in a later study about who
gets the most appreciation and most respect
in the criminal world agrees with this. A

fourth of those interviewed felt that the one who could earn his money illegally but at the same time live like the average man had the most respect. That is, he had really been able to beat the system, arrange a front and avoid having too many of the insecurities of the criminal life. For example, a young addict and thief wanted to straighten up in the following, unexpected way:

> I used to say this life is worth it even if I'm only out three months a year. I live those months much more than the working stiffs. But I've changed and now I don't think it's true.

> Are you going to live like the working stiffs now?

> No, I don't think I can take a nine-to-five job. My body hasn't got that in its computer. . . . No, I have to straighten out and put things into some kind of order. I've been inside here too long. I can start dealing drugs but you can't organize that if you're an addict yourself, it's just not possible. . . . And if that doesn't work out, I can start studying and get a job.

Why the Squares Are Looked Down On

Boring Life

Table 1

What Would Be the Disadvantages if You Were to Live a Square Lifestyle?

	% of Inmates
Difficulties in establishing contact with the squares	20
Problems with finances	35
Miss my friends	14
Miss drugs	5
Miss partying	10
Boring life, no excitement	72
N	(117)

What do the inmates feel is negative about living like the squares? First of all, as seen above, the main criticism is that they find the squares' life boring: no thrills or adventures. The spectre of the regularity of this type of life is more terrifying than the thought of doing time, as is seen in the biography of a thief:

> The alternative—the prospect of vegetating the rest of my life in a steady job, catching the 8.13 to work in the morning, and the 5.50 back again at night, all for ten or fifteen quid a week—now that really terrify [*sic*] me, far more than the thought of a few years in the nick. (Parker and Allerton, 1962:88)

Part of the negative attitude towards the [squares] comes from their being seen as prisoners in their way of life—that they cannot imagine anything outside their own lifestyle. Criminals want more in terms of experiences than what an ordinary life seems to offer:

> "Do you enjoy having done things like that, that are a bit odd, unusual, compared to most people's experiences?"

> "Yeah, they have fun in their way, I guess. Maybe they think back on old family stories, I don't know, but. . . . Maybe I want a bit more, and I do get more, living as I do."

Due to the Joneses' taken-for-granted, routine-like lives, they lack "hope" for finding anything better:

> I've got something that most guys, especially the Joe Squares, don't have. I've got hope! I've got the streets, and I'm going out there again. I've got something to look forward to. Joe Square has the rut, the routine, and there's no hope for him. When I get out there again I can make up for everything that is happening to me now. I'll be free, free to live the way I want and to do what I want. I can shoot dope, steal, rob, pimp whores. I can live as fast and as good as I want. (Manocchio and Dunn, 1970:33)

Naive and 'Imprisoned'

Another criticism is that the ordinary man is sometimes "naive." This, however, can also be advantageous when doing business: they will not cheat you. Some of the respondents said in a slightly condescending tone that they are nice, but not smart, and they are grateful:

> They're good, the workers, good to do business with, never any problems. They'll pay and that's it . . . they're grateful, you

know, and it's nice somehow when people are grateful.

Coupled with this is the theme that the squares are also a type of prisoner, of conventional and formal rules. Being a prisoner of conventionalism is expressed in statements such as "They care so much about what others think of them." The other major theme is that they are trapped in "the system."

> "I just can't see why ordinary people don't see through the system. They'll work their ass off and they'll die before retiring. . . ."

> "You think that they adjust. . . ?"

> "They are driven into a trap and then they can't get away from it. They get stuck with a family, having kids and a job, and after that, you know. . . ."

They are also seen as conforming, without resistance, even to clearly unfair treatment:

> Of course we need laws and I'm prepared to follow them, but in that case I want something in exchange. Because I don't think the laws are proportioned to the individual's right to live. Look at the squares, like if he wants to get drunk on Saturday night, he can get thrown in a cell, beaten by the police, and he takes it. What kind of life is that? Then you might as well be in prison. At least there are clear boundaries here, because they'll lock you up. And then you can have your Christmas when you get out. . . .

Bad Finances

Thirty-five percent of the inmates' answers about negative features in the squares' lifestyle concerned bad finances. Through low pay, bad living arrangements, mortgages, etc. they are considered to be financially harassed. This view often derives from the interviewees' own experiences of problems at times when they tried to go straight. Just the thought of being forced to plan a household budget is repellant:

> "Of course you can get yourself a woman and kids and move out to Rosengard [a suburban housing area] and get yourself a job and get stuck in one of those cells. It's a cell-system just like the prison, but you see, I'm not interested in that kind of thing. That's not happiness to me. I tried

it for a while but it was only worries and bills and problems. And to have to plan your . . . what in hell are you planning for? Well, it ended up planning to make ends meet."

> "You planned your household finances?"

> "Yeah, and that's nothing I want to keep doing, it's crazy. . . . I don't think that anyone should have more time left over if you're going to work and have a family. You should be better off. . . . If that's the way it's going to be, I think it's better just drifting around. . . ."

Envy

Due to their restricted economy, the squares are said to be envious of each other. The criminals' picture of the ordinary man is thus in line with the general view of him as being much concerned with "keeping up with the Joneses":

> "Most workers are envious of each other. If one of them has something, the other one wants the same."

> "Aren't you?"

> "No, you know we have the same opportunities.

Envy is even said to be the "real" reason for why the police won't "leave you alone":

> I was really determined to quit, on a larger scale anyway, just having small "jobs" earning some money. But the police won't leave you alone there's such envy: "How can you afford to go out to restaurants?" etc. . . .

Lack of Nerve

Quite a few of the inmates believed that many squares really wished to do what they, the criminals, had done, if only they dared. Thus, Polsky (1969) warns students dealing with deviants to be aware of their assumption that the students want to be like them, and the only thing holding them back is their lack of nerve. A young thief even generously offered to exchange jobs with an ordinary man one week at a time. The respondents decided, however, that the project would flop due to the latter's being too scared:

> I don't dislike them, but I feel sorry for them. They live all their lives toiling and wearing themselves out, complaining

about their jobs and their bosses and they never get any money, can only take a month of vacation a year. . . . Of course someone has to do that. Maybe one could take turns, you know, he'd be at the factory a week, and I, one week. Nice thought but unfortunately unrealistic, maybe. . . . But they might not have the nerve anyway, they get nervous just getting twelve scores [out of thirteen] in the soccer betting it could have been thirteen [laughter].

Just dreaming about the things one wants to do is looked down upon in general:

And their talk . . . the man, if you can get down to it, he always "fancies" the woman next door, but of course he never gets around to actually doing her. It's frightening, it's chronic. At least criminals have something interesting to talk about, their talk is deeper and more real, the life they lead goes at a much faster tempo and has got more excitement in it. (Parker and Allerton, 1962:109)

A Condescending View

Criminals are often portrayed as either wanting deep down to be like ordinary people, or regarding them with hostility and bitterness.

McKorkle and Korn (1954) write about "a rejection of the rejectors," and Sykes and Matza (1957) have described one of the neutralizing techniques used by juvenile delinquents as "condemnation of the condemners." The authors use words like bitterness, and describe the psychological function of reversing a negative attitude: " . . . by attacking others, the wrongfulness of his own behavior is more easily repressed or lost to view." Cohen (1955) makes a similar conclusion in his work about the subculture of juvenile delinquents. Since they "really" want a middle class type of life, due to influences from school and the rest of society, they react with frustration and hostility to their own lower class living conditions.

I have however not found that such attitudes of bitterness and hostility are common. An attitude of superiority or condescension seems to be more accurate. Gibbons' description of thieves' attitudes towards straight people is illustrative:

Thieves tend not to demonstrate hostility toward any of these individuals; instead they simply regard themselves as different from, and superior to, these others. (1968:247)

The quotes given earlier in this chapter confirm this attitude; the relative frequency of the answers to the question in Table 2 illustrates it further.

The most common answer is "I like him, he is okay, I guess." Many, however, after answering this added things like "It's admirable that they don't give up," "Society can't exist without them," "They've got a nice attitude—go to work and be pleased with what they've got." These statements demonstrate a condescending attitude rather than bitterness or expressions of frustration, as some criminologists have claimed as typical.

Table 2	
What Is Your Opinion About the Ordinary Working Guy?	
	% of Inmates
He does not dare to live, he is boring	27
He is so suspicious about everything	16
He knows so little about our life	41
He does not like people like us	25
I like him, he is okay, I guess	44
N	(122)

Stereotype Derived From Society

A Negative View From Society

The negative view of squares' lifestyle is in some ways taken from other parts of society. Firstly, I think it is equalled in much of what is published in newspapers, books, etc., by "professional debaters" and authors, discussion shows on television, and so on. Also, as the criminologist Laurie Taylor (1971) has pointed out, some sociologists . . . described "the lower class" existence in the industrial world as monotonous, and claimed that these people are reduced to mere objects.

The second source of experiencing their lives as exciting and special lies in the attention that criminals get. The thieves talked, for example, about "reading the reviews" after committing a crime. Addicts today might get even more publicity and are seen as an even more deviant and special group than the thieves. Waldorf gives this attention from society as one reason why addicts feel they belong to such an interesting group:

> Society's heavy and abiding concern and the flurry of police activity are often interpreted by the addict as evidence of heroin's importance and power. The reasoning is often thus: "If heroin is *not* such an important and powerful drug, why is society so concerned about it? They enact all these laws and put us in jail because they themselves are afraid of it." Being illegal, makes the drug attractive in the eyes of many, and the cat-and-mouse game with the police, makes drug-seeking by the addict an exciting and dramatic activity. . . . This is, I am sure, the basis for the addict's belief that he is leading a far more different and exciting life than the square. (1973:16)

Criminals also sense that people have a somewhat romantic attitude towards those who lead such an unusual life; this enhances their way of seeing themselves as leading a less boring life than the rest of us. The practice of selling things by telling people that goods are stolen, i.e. pretending a false gold chain is real, stolen gold, can be viewed in this light. That this method is successful is probably not only due to people believing they are making a smart deal. By buying something illegal, people can get a feeling of being part of something that is a bit fascinating due to its secretness.

Experiencing 'More' as a Criminal

In everyday life the concept of "experience" often has the connotation of something odd or new. A man or a woman is said to be experienced in the field of love if he or she has had many relationships, as opposed to one long one, learning, maybe, different and more subtle things.

Criminals often picture themselves as adventurers, as is shown later on in this work, and as such they derive a feeling of being closer to real life and experiencing "more." Simmel has pointed out that the adventurer:

> . . . makes a system of life out of his life's lack of system, when out of his inner necessity he seeks the naked, external accidents and builds them into that necessity. (1971:191)

The interviewed criminals often talked about themselves as "really having lived," and having experiences, as opposed to ordinary people. I guess that the basis for this is what was said above, experiences that are a bit odd or unusual compared to those that most of us acquire.

> If I'd been a working stiff, I don't think I would have *lived*, not like I have. And had the chance to take drugs and drink and have lots of buddies. Got to know lots of unusual, interesting guys, ya know. I've seen a lot, done a lot. . . .

The way criminals regard "real life" as opposed to most people's everyday life with all its conventions has a societal background and is shared with other groups. Shils, in his book *Tradition*, makes the following comment:

> Traditions of respectability and hypocrisy repressed "true individuality" and stood in way for life. . . . The "cry for life" was just not a slogan of a socialistic propagandist; it was deeper. It was a cry for an unknown object called "life" because life was held to be antithetical to custom and convention. Many less intellectuals and many less cultivated persons, too, were bored by what they received. Society seemed too cut and dried, too much the same thing. . . . (1981:235)

Unusual, often "heavy" experiences are also seen as giving a specially valid knowledge of life, not the ordinary practical everyday type but one that transcends the commonplace.

I once met a manager of a very sleazy hotel occupied by addicts and prostitutes. Earlier, he had had a middle-class job, but quit this after a divorce. The way he looked at his present situation was in terms of wanting to get out of it, but at the same time appreciating the experiences it had given him. "I haven't learned as much during my whole life as during these two years when I've been down here in this skid-row." It is an interesting attitude, since the knowledge he gets under his present circumstances is something that may be difficult to translate if he returns to middle-class life.

An ex-criminal views his former life in a similar light:

> One thing that's good with such a life, if it doesn't break you, is that you learn how to take care of yourself. Nobody picks you up if you fall. . . . If you fall you'll hurt yourself real bad. The experience that I now have of life and of people, that's the most precious thing I own. 'Cause it hasn't all been bad, I've learnt a lot about how it *really* is.

This is of course knowledge that they feel the squares lack. A young man's description of his view of the squares as being untroubled and seeking perfection:

> "First of all, he doesn't know anything."

> "About what?"

> "About the world. He kind of lives inside a shell with white inner-walls, and he scrubs and polishes them to make 'em even whiter, even more bright and shining."

Different Experiences

Table 3

Do You Find it Difficult at Times to Talk to Ordinary People?

	% of Inmates
Yes, sometimes	60
No, seldom	40
N	(138)

Table 3a

If You Do Find it Difficult to Talk to Squares, Why?

	% of Inmates
Difficult to find things to talk about	46
We do not share the same experiences	46
I cannot tell them about my life	31
Ordinary people do not like people like me	38
I do not like them	6
N	(72)

Experiencing different things does not only imply a sort of superior attitude from the inmates in that they felt that they experienced "more" but also led to difficulties in communication with the average guy. As can be seen in the table above, they emphasize that the difficulties in talking with squares lie in not sharing the same experiences.

The quote below is illustrative of the subtleties in everyday life that can be difficult if one has different outlooks on the world:

> I've worked as a cab-driver, but I don't like it. They're a pain in the ass. A lot of drunks. Drunks talk, I can't take it . . . the boss at the job, and the old lady at home, I don't see that as particularly interesting. It's none of my business. I'm not interested in 'em, and why should I be?

This man saw himself as having been through a lot and the events of his customers, quarrelling with the boss and the wife, being drunk, etc., somehow seemed petty and definitely alien to his own concerns. Not only the problems of the squares but also their definition of risk seems petty for criminals. The cab-driver above also told about events that his customers thought were daring and exciting, such as being drunk on ordinary working days or flirting with unknown women, things which he would not deign to call "risks." Since criminals are accustomed to taking risks this often leads to a lack of understanding towards the concerns of ordinary people.

As Goffman has noted, "different individuals and groups have somewhat different personal base-lines from which to measure risk and opportunity; a way of life involving much risk may cause the individual to give little weight to a risk that someone else might find forbidding" (1967:157-158).

Not sharing the same experiences and problems also gives rise to practical considerations in making conversation with the squares since the groups do not speak "the same language ":

> "I find it hard to communicate with the square-johns, it's like we don't have the same interests . . . we haven't experienced the same things . . . if I start at a new job, I can't tell 'em 'bout my break-ins, about who I've been seeing and. . . ."

> "So what do they speak about?"

". . . Their work and their family . . . my kid's got two teeth now, and stuff like that. . . . And the vacation last year, you know. What damn vacation?" (laugh)

The difficulties are, of course, not only practical, these different experiences and interests also cause lacks of intimacy, relaxation and spontaneity, since small talk becomes problematic:

> Just take you and I together here, for instance, you get acquainted with me someplace and like me, so we go out to dinner or something together and I have to keep avoiding you. See, just little tiny normal questions that you would ask another guy without any thought and he would answer without any thought. But I have to cover up so I have to continuously stay on my toes and I can't enjoy a square-john's company. (Chambliss and King, 1972:76)

A similar example is given by Martin, who has written about the thief Gene. The author recalls how he invited Gene to his suburban home during weekends, and how he reacted with unease when the author's friends dropped in:

> I noticed that he was not entirely at ease around them. He had been so long away from the company of non-criminal people. . . . You would think him rather dull because he wouldn't be very talkative. Most of his interests involve crime and he cannot talk crime to laymen; and as for small talk, it is a little hard to make small talk if everything reminds one of crime, as it does to him. The other day during a lull in conversation he pointed to my typewriter and said "I know a fellow makes a living stealing them." (1952:5)

On the other hand, differing experiences can of course be rewarding. Some of the interviewees expressed a wish to see people in their free time who were not criminals, since they had enough shop talk in prison. Others stated that they wanted to talk about more general things such as politics, society-related questions, etc., that their criminal friends did not know too much about.

Going Straight and Yet Not Straight—The Third Alternative

So far we have mainly examined the negative features of the squares' lifestyle as seen by the interviewees. In order to see whether this alternative held any attraction, I posed the following question:

Table 4	
What Are the Advantages in the Lifestyle of the Ordinary Man?	
	% of Inmates
You meet other kinds of people	24
Better finances	18
The family appreciates it	24
Get away from drugs	13
Get away from liquor	15
More interesting life	18
Don't have to spend time in prison	72
N	(118)

It is interesting that the only statement about the squares' lives that really got any response was "Don't have to spend time in prison." If one considers this rather negative view, it is natural that those who want to quit look for a third alternative—something in between the criminal world and the squares' world. The results of the question below show the wish for the third alternative.

Table 5	
If You Are Not Planning to Live as a Criminal in the Future, What Type of Life Can You Consider Living?	
	% of Inmates
That of an ordinary square-john	21
Support myself legally, but not live like the square john	72
There is no style of life outside the criminal world that would suit me	7
N	(138)

What this third alternative meant, however, seemed hard to define. There was space left in the questionnaire, where they could add what they meant by "Support myself legally, but not live like the square-johns." Very few did, however, which I think mirrors the difficulty many have in envisioning something apart from the two worlds which they knew about—the criminal and the square. This is especially interesting, I think, since we are living in a time where many alternative ways of living are made possible.

Some, however, described alternatives in the taped interviews. A young inmate spoke, for example, about a friend who worked as a delivery man whose hours were fairly free: he could take time off, smoke some pot in a park before continuing, and have free afternoons—not working nine-to-five. This was something the interviewee saw as a possible alternative.

The main reason for quitting crime seems to be due to a "burning-out" effect, or that criminal life in itself can become boring. Shover (1971) noted that precisely that which was considered an advantage in the criminal world can become boring: too much leisure, too many late nights, too much gambling and entertainment, and for some, too much drugs. This, as I see it, can become just as much routine as any other experience in any other type of life and can thus create a wish for new life alternatives. A few quotes to illustrate:

"You said you wanted to quit because this life has become boring?"

"Yeah. I've been doing this for ten or twelve years now and then you wanna try something new. Because I've done this thing and it gets to be the same experience time after time. The same things happen, so it starts to get boring."

Another:

"Is this life exciting?"

"Yeah, it has been fun a lot of times, trying, but fun at many times. Fun episodes."

"Is that a factor that makes you keep on?"

"No, no. I don't know why. It gets to be a sort of routine. . . ."

It is thus important to note that it is often not because of moral reasons that one wants to quit:

"You said you want to change your life-style?"

"Crime doesn't turn me off, it's far from that. But then you have to weigh pros and cons, what's most important. I'm just as criminal as I've always been, it's just that I've found more important things in life."

"What?"

"Well, you mature. You get to be interested in new things. This is really a narrow world. It's as petty as the squares'. It's the same damned talk, and the same way of being all the time. In ninety-nine cases out of a hundred, it's the same type of people. There ain't no personal exchange."

A new life then, requires other and different activities than the ones they have experienced but at the same time not be defined as "square" and boring. Finally, a quote that illustrates both the importance of a third alternative and the difficulties in quitting if one does not know what to do outside criminal life:

What's the damn meaning in sitting in a place and tilting a chair? Going to the employment office, looking for jobs you hardly ever get? At best you get hold of a TV, and sit there and brood in front of it with a beer. . . . You need some kind of stimulation.

This guy had tried at times to get some friends [criminals] to go with him to sport events, but they just laughed at him, because this was "square" stuff. Since he did not have any other friends, this effort of doing "something else" had thus not succeeded—an illustration of tiny things having a symbolic value and importance but which are still obviously so difficult.

References

Chambliss, B. and King, H. 1972. *Box-Man*. Harper and Row: San Francisco.

Cohen, A. 1955. *Delinquent Boys*. The Free Press: Glencoe.

Gibbons, D. 1968. *Society, Crime and Criminal Careers*. Prentice-Hall: Englewood Cliffs, N.J.

Goffman, E. 1967. *Interaction Ritual*. Doubleday & Co.: New York.

Irwin, J. 1980. *Prisons in Turmoil*. Little, Brown and Co.: Boston and Toronto.

McCorkle, L. and Korn, R. 1954. "Prison in Transformation: Resocialization Within Walls." *Annals of American Academy of Political and Social Science*, vol. 293: 88-98.

Martin. J. 1952. *My Life In Crime*. Harper and Brothers: New York.

Parker, T. and Allerton, R. 1962. *The Courage of His Convictions*. Hutchinson: London.

Polsky, N. 1969. *Hustlers, Beats and Others*. Anchor Books: New York.

Shils, E. 1981. *Tradition*. Faber and Faber: Boston.

Shover, N. 1971. *Burglary as an Occupation*, Ph.D. Dissertation. Department of Sociology, University of Illinois. Urbana, Ill.

Simmel, G. 1971. *On Individuality and Social Forms*. Ed. Levine, D. University of Chicago Press: Chicago.

Sorokin, P. 1943. *Sociocultural Causality, Space and Time*. Duke University Press: Durham.

Sykes, G. and Matza, D. 1957. "Techniques of Neutralization." *American Sociological Review*, vol. 22: 667-670.

Taylor, L. 1971. *Deviance and Society*. Michael Joseph: London.

Waldorf, D. 1973. *Careers in Dope*. Prentice-Hall: Englewood Cliffs, N.J.

4

Women, Work, and Crime

Deborah R. Baskin
Ira Sommers

The purpose of this study was to explore the impact of women's life experiences on their involvement in legal and illegal work. The authors consider issues such as how job opportunities, skills, and aspirations affect the work-crime relationship, and how illegal activities attract women away from jobs in the licit economy, and from involvement in gender stereotypical crimes such as prostitution. The authors describe how a sample of women involved in violent street crime make a living and follows their involvement in the legal and illegal economies.

The research is based on in-depth life-history interviews with 170 women who committed non-domestic violent felony crimes (robbery, assault, homicide) in New York City. The women were recruited from various social settings including: (1) those arrested and arraigned for violent crimes (N=49); (2) those in state prison for violent crimes (N=48); and (3) women actively involved in violent criminal offending (N=73).

Interviews were open-ended, in-depth, and, when possible, audiotaped. The open-ended technique created a context in which respondents were able to speak freely and in their own words. Furthermore, it facilitated the pursuit of issues that were raised by the women during the interview but were not recognized beforehand by the researchers. The in-depth interview approach enabled the authors to pursue information about specific events, as well as provide an opportunity for respondents to reflect on those events. As a result, they were able to gain insight into the women's attitudes, feelings, and other subjective orientations to their experiences.

A typical member of the sample was a black woman, 27 years old, a high-school dropout with two children, possessing limited legal work experience. The youngest was 16 years old and the oldest 43. The median age of the respondents was 30 years. Seventy-five percent of the subjects were high-school dropouts, typically leaving school by 11th grade. Although most of the women had worked in a legitimate job (80%), the median number of months employed was only 16 and the average was 35.9 months. Most of the women worked in unskilled and semi-skilled working-class occupations (e.g., clerical and factory jobs).

The relationship between crime and work has become the focus of much criminological research (Bourgois, 1995; Crutchfield, 1997; Fagan, 1996; Fagan and Freeman, 1994; Grogger, 1994; Reuter, 1990; Sommers, et al., 1996; Sullivan, 1989; Wilson, 1996). This is due, in part, to major shifts over the past two decades in inner-city legal and illegal labor markets as well as to important changes in the social, cultural, and political dynamics within urban communities. Thus far, research in this area has concentrated almost exclusively on males with only passing reference to and/or conjecture regarding women.

Nonetheless, the macro transformations in urban communities that have been identified as affecting male's decisions concerning criminal involvement have also had an impact on women's choices as they relate to work and crime. Therefore, the purpose of the present research is to explore key issues concerning the interaction between legal and illegal work in terms of the impact that the study women's life experiences had on that relationship. Here, we will explore how such human capital issues as job opportunities, skills and aspirations mediated the work-crime relationship; how illegal work, especially drug distribution and robbery, drew women away from their positions in the licit economy, as well as from their involvement in gender stereotypical crimes such as prostitution; and how an increasing and eventual full-time commitment to street life and drug abuse ended their relationship to careers in both the legal and illegal labor markets altogether.

The Literature on Crime and Work

The sharp rise in violent crime and drug trafficking that characterized many inner cities during the 1980s and early 1990s has often been associated with a precipitous decline in formal employment opportunities. This "disappearance of work" (Wilson, 1996) has been seen as altering the basic calculus used by young people to influence their choice of economic activities. By and large, the outcome of such decision-making, in the context of dwindling wages and satisfactory job opportunities in the legal world of work, has been increased participation in illegal income-generating activities (Fagan, 1992; Freeman, 1983; Hagedorn, 1994; Witte and Tauchen, 1994).

In recent years, research based on this model of decision-making has flourished. Elements of the economic calculus have been dissected and results supporting the choice of crime *over* legal work have been reported. Increasing unemployment and underemployment have been identified as significantly related to crime participation (Chiricos, 1987; Blackburn, Boom, and Freeman, 1990; Corcoran and Parrott, 1992; Fagan and Freeman, 1994); income from crime, especially from drug dealing, has been found to be higher than income from other, legal sources (Vicusi, 1986; Reuter, MacCoun, and Murphy, 1990; Fagan 1992, 1994a; Freeman, 1992); and the social and psychic payoffs from illegal work seem to outweigh the concern over, if not the risks of legal sanctions (Fagan, 1996). Thus, the choice of illegal work is understandable, at least, intellectually.

Once the decision to enter the world of illegal enterprise has been made, another body of research has sought to explain the persistence of illicit income-generation activities. Here, ethnographic studies have documented a renouncement of the secondary labor market by inner-city males. Young males who have turned to the illegal economy now rely on street networks for status (Anderson, 1990, 1994; Fagan, 1994a, 1994b; Hagedorn, 1994; Hagedorn and Macron, 1988; Padilla, 1992, 1993; Taylor, 1990; Moore; 1991, 1992). And, they use the discourse of work, like "get-ting paid," or "going to work" (Sullivan, 1989) to describe their criminal careers. Thus, for these young males, money from crime and reputation from criminal success form the bases for commodity consumption and status that would be unavailable to them from the legal workaday world.

The persistence of criminal careers from adolescence to adulthood is also understood in terms of the structural changes in legal employment patterns in urban centers. Where once manufacturing jobs and other semiskilled labor market positions provided egresses from criminal careers as young males moved from adolescence to adulthood, the disappearance of such opportunities has resulted in cross-generational joblessness with attendant cultural, social, and legal disadvantages (Wilson, 1996; Tienda, 1989; Sullivan, 1989). Thus, young males in the transition to adulthood who suffer from social capital deficits (Bourgois, 1995), the stigma of legal sanctions (Anderson, 1990; Sullivan, 1989), and exaggerated tastes and preferences (Anderson, 1990; Bourgois, 1995) further narrow their options for economic and social success in the world of licit work (Hagan and Pallioni, 1990; Bourgois, 1995; Anderson, 1990; Sampson and Laub, 1993).

Over time, the perception that entry into the world of legal work is possible dwindles. At this stage of criminal career development, research points to the rise of a rigid bifurcation between licit and illicit economic activities (Anderson, 1990, 1994; Hagedorn, 1994; Hagedorn and Macron, 1988; Taylor, 1990; Moore, 1992). Thus, young males eventually choose to *either* abandon their involvement in illegal work and accept the economic and social parameters of the conventional workaday world, or they commit themselves to illegal work and its concomitant social and legal implication. However, once the decision to commit to the illicit economy is made, the option to return to the licit world is narrowed, if not eliminated altogether (Hagan, 1993). This bifurcation has become, if not an empirical reality, one that at least characterizes much thinking in this area.

Recent research, however, suggests that participation in the *worlds* of work may not be exclusive. In fact, several studies show a much more dynamic and flexible interaction between legal and illegal work. Some qualitative studies have documented regular career "shifts" from illegal to legal sources of income and even simultaneous participation in both economies over the course of an individual's work history (Shover, 1985; Biernacki, 1986; Sullivan, 1989; Padilla, 1992; Adler, 1992; Baskin and Sommers, 1998).

Despite the talk of "young people," "individuals," and "inner-city residents," much of what we know about the interaction between legal and illegal work is based on information obtained from male respondents. This is unfortunate. Recent research on female offenders has documented dramatic changes in women's participation in income-generating criminal activities. From robbery to drug dealing, women in inner cities have increased their involvement as well as other aspects of their participation in crime, such as roles and statuses. Thus, we find more women acting as principals in criminal events, as crew bosses and owners of drug distribution enterprises, and as recruiters of other women into the illicit world of work (Baskin and Sommers, 1998; Fagan, 1994b; Inciardi et al., 1993; Mieczkowski, 1994; Miller, 1998; Taylor, 1993). Further, we find more women entering crime apart from domestic partnerships, more within single-sex peer groups, and more ready to employ violence as part of doing business (Baskin and Sommers, 1998; Curry, Ball, and Fox, 1994). And, we find that for some women, their involvement in other forms of street crime, such as robbery, burglary, and drug dealing, has led to a decrease in their participation in prostitution (Sommers, Baskin, and Fagan, 1996).

Nonetheless, these changes do not *erase* the fact that gender does indeed make a difference in daily life experiences and in decision-making patterns (Brown and Gilligan, 1992; Pipher, 1994), albeit in different ways for different groups of women. Therefore, research needs to focus on women within specific contexts if we are to understood on how the dynamics of gender impact on particular criminal career decisions.

The research reported within is a step in that direction. Here, we describe how a sample of women involved in violent street crime tried to make a living. We explore their progression from early involvement in the legal and formal economy, their joint involvement in these two spheres and their ultimate embeddedness in the informal and illicit economy. Through a description of their experiences in these various "work" sectors, the women provide us with an understanding of the bases for and types of decisions they made when choosing their "vocations."

It is clear from their accounts that even from the outset, a tension always existed between their involvement in legal and illegal work and between the asocial world of formal labor and the seemingly social atmosphere promised by criminal involvement. Further, we find that the "economic" calculus so often reported in the literature is only partially the basis for their decision making; and that their maintenance in these criminal activities comes to resemble less the workaday world described in relation to male criminal careers and more the world of drug addicts that the traditional literature on females and crime suggests (Bourgois and Dunlap, 1993; Maher and Daly, 1996; Hunt, 1990). . . .

Participation in the Secondary Labor Market

For the women we interviewed, legal employment was viewed as important, at least initially. By the time they were sixteen, the majority had left school. Therefore, securing a job took on great significance. And, at least at first, they were successful. Unlike their male counterparts, most of whom experienced high rates of joblessness from the start (Wilson, 1996), 80% of the women we interviewed were able to secure employment in the formal economy. These jobs were exclusively in the secondary labor market.

Research on the effects of labor distribution on criminal involvement has suggested that relegation to the secondary labor market, that is, working at jobs that are low-paying, have few, if any benefits, and offer little in terms of advancement, will result in greater participation in violent crime (Crutchfield,

1989).[1] Further, it is hypothesized that the mechanism through which this relationship is fostered is that of social bonding. In other words, the "weaker bonds . . . associated with employment in secondary occupations, will lead to higher crime rates" (Crutchfield, 1989:6). Those who work in the secondary labor market, therefore, are less likely both to develop attachments and commitments to their jobs as well as stakes in conformity as compared to their peers in the primary labor market. Thus, the "qualities" of a job, rather than the presence or absence of employment, seem to affect criminal involvement (Rosenfeld and Messner, 1989; Sampson and Laub, 1993; Uggen, 1992), at least among males.

Of the women in our study who worked, the vast majority were employed in entry level, unskilled positions as office clerks (32%), factory laborers (28%), and salespeople (25%). Fifteen percent (15%) of the women were able to obtain "aide" positions in home health care or education. These positions were acquired either through temporary employment agencies or public programs, never through personal networks. They lasted no more than a few months and were characteristically low paying and offered little long term security and no chances for advancement.

The women in our study entered the labor force with an acute awareness that their employment, even in the future, would, in all probability, be sporadic or remain in the lowest echelons of the secondary market. For the few women who hoped for more lucrative futures in the licit job sector, training in cosmetology and having their own "station" at the local beauty salon was their loftiest goal. But, even at the outset, these women did not think that the jobs available to them would bring the "prestige, pride, and self-respect" (Liebow, 1967:60) found in white-collar occupations. Thus, like the men Liebow described in *Tally's Corner* (1967), these women ascribed "no lower value on the job than does the larger society (p. 57)." In other words, these women were keenly aware of the social value of the types of jobs available to them.

The work descriptions offered by the women we interviewed confirmed this perspective. Furthermore, like the men Liebow

described and those studied by Bourgois (1995), the women eventually came to view these jobs with an active disinterest. They were routinely fired due to excessive absenteeism or were absent frequently as a way of quitting. They would often show up for work high on drugs, or coming down from a night of heavy drinking and partying. Often, especially towards the end of their involvement in the formal economy, they used their work environments as settings for their increasingly prevalent criminal activities.

Descriptions of Initial Experiences in the Legal Economy

Herminia told us about her first job:

I worked for like minimum wage at Duane Read Pharmacy. I enjoyed it cause, you know, I felt, like independent. I was bringing a little money home. But, fast I stopped liking it. I never liked a job that would be just standing like in one place, you know, like doing the same thing over and over. I got tired of it—the monotony, the routine everyday, so I stopped showing up. I lasted there about four months. Then, I worked in MacDonald's for maybe four weeks. I hated MacDonald's. It was boring. I was there for about four weeks. So, I went through a few other jobs. These were the only ones I could get. I had to lie about my age just to get these. I was only 15 and 16 and who was going to hire me?

Herminia's description was typical of the women in this study. For that matter and without exception, regardless of the actual position, and like the men who Liebow spoke with in *Tally's Corner*, the women did not display an "overt interest in job specifics . . . in a large part perhaps because the specifics are not especially relevant" (Liebow, 1967:57). This was due to the fact that the secondary job market was comprised of "a narrow range of nondescript chores calling for nondescript, undifferentiated, unskilled labor" (Liebow, 1967:57).

Janelle, too, described her dissatisfaction with the types of jobs available to her. Furthermore, given her early involvement in violent street crime and drug use, it was especially difficult for her to accept the drudgery and routine of employment in the secondary market. Clearly, these types of jobs did not compete with the excitement she had and enjoyment she received from hanging out and partying with her friends.

> I used to work at—this was when I was 16—I used to work at Wendy's. Yeah, at Roy Rogers too. I worked like, for six months at the first job and two months for the second. I quit because I couldn't function every day, gettin' up and goin' to work and then partyin' the night before. I didn't feel too great about these jobs. Wearing a stupid uniform and flipping burgers. That's lame.

> Yeah, I was trying to do something for myself by working these jobs. But it wasn't working. I rather go home and get high and hang out with my people. So, it wasn't workin' and neither was I.

Interestingly, even among those who worked in the human service sector, principally as home attendants, work was viewed similarly as demeaning, boring, and no different from clerical or sales work:

> I started out as a home health aide. It was O.K. for a little while. But then I got sick of it. You know what I'm saying—they like, they were driving me crazy. I felt like a housekeeper. It was nothing special, no different than working burgers or cleaning tables. There's not much else to say about it. (Denise)

Thus, the women in our study came to view their involvement in the licit job world with the same emptiness as the countless ghetto, barrio, and streetcorner males studied by other researchers. The difference for the women in our study, though, was that they were at least initially drawn to the legal economy and remained there for almost three years.

The Intermingling of Licit and Illicit Work

At the beginning of their employment careers, the women attempted to make a living, primarily through legitimate employment. Over time, however, they decided that the low economic and cultural returns from their marginal employment were not satisfactory. They then turned to crime and illegal hustles for supplementation. For many women, the workplace itself came to serve as a setting for these activities. And, it was these activities that provided them with important sources of income, identity, and excitement.

Here Denise, a former home attendant, describes how she combined licit and illicit work to augment her desires for more money, more excitement, and the respect of her peers on the street:

> Yeah, so I hated doing things for these rich people, so after a while me and my friends developed a gimmick. I would go into the house, and I would case it out and get all the necessary information. When they would be out, my friends would come in and like vandalize it. Then we'd all go out and party and celebrate our success. I was really a key connection for them. And, funny thing is, I would go back to work the next day like nothing ever happened and act shocked.

> I did that for about six months. But I really couldn't stand cleaning up after these rich people and so I went to work at _____ Hospital in their dietary department. Then I got the key to the supplies and I had my girlfriends come up with a truck and unload the block. This was fun and made us lots of money too. But, I got arrested and had to give them my paycheck. I worked there for about six months too.

Monica, too, used her place of employment for her illegal enterprises. In this case, she dealt drugs from her office.

> I started as a summer youth worker for a City agency. But then they kept me permanently as a floater, which means like I worked diversified duties. I made, like, $9,000 a year. At this point I was already indulging in cocaine and I started selling drugs. So, uh, I started going to work and showing people my material—people that I knew that got high. And they started buying from me. So then they started buying weight which would mean that I would have to get more material—and give it to them. And, uh, it's like I used the messenger companies from the office. I used to call the messenger companies, and they used to pick everything up. And they

would come pick it up at the agency and drop it off at someone else not knowing what was really inside. I made like $4000 to $5200 a week. But then I just started using all the money for getting high and I stopped going to the office.

"Doubling up" in crime and work (Fagan, 1994a), as these women had done, is not unusual among active offenders, regardless of gender, especially among those involved in drug distribution. Research has indicated that between 25% and 57% of active offenders report participating in income producing crime, thereby optimizing extant opportunities (Grogger, 1994; Hagedorn, 1994; Fagan, 1992; Reuter et al., 1990). Nonetheless, research in this area, again using predominately male respondents, has explained such behavior solely in economic terms. It has been argued that young males will "double up" for the purpose of optimizing income generation opportunities, plain and simple.What was different for the women in our study was the fact that "doubling up" provided these women with opportunities for optimizing *both* the economic *and* the social facets of their lives; one no less important than the other. Thus, "doubling up" permitted the intermingling of fun, excitement, and adventure with occasions for both legal and illegal income generation—all within the same work setting.

Crime on the Side

For some of the women with whom we spoke, "doubling up" took a different form. These women recounted for us incredible work schedules in which, for the majority of the time that they were employed in the legal sector, they would also hold down "second jobs" during their *off* hours. Many, but not all, of these women had an overarching addiction to drugs that pushed them to secure money by any means possible—legal and otherwise. April was one such woman:

I was makin' like $7 an hour at this Sears job. That was actually pretty good money, but I was gettin' high. I was stealin', robbin'. I used to forge checks to get more money. I worked there for maybe six months. I guess I was into fast money, a

fast life. I needed money to support my habit. So I went out, and, uh, the person that I was buying from, I asked him, you know, how can I get into it.

So, after I was done with my day at Sears, I was selling on the street. I turned out to be one of the carriers—the person that, uh, pick up the drugs and distribute it to people on the street to sell. I bring in about $2000 to $3000 a week. Sometimes I, I would be up two or three days in a row because the money would be coming so fast that I'd be, I wouldn't want to go to sleep because I knew if I would go to sleep, I would miss money—the Sears money and the other—I wanted both.

For the drug addicted women, losing sleep, being absent from legal work, partying, and hustling formed their day to day experiences.

For other women, crime on the side was a continuation of their long-term involvement in offending. Initially, it counterbalanced the asocial and boring nature of their jobs in the legal sector. It provided these women with the excitement, adventure, and camaraderie absent from jobs in the secondary labor market. Further, and not unimportantly, crime on the side supplemented the meager incomes they received from their marginal jobs.

As L.G. recounts:

When I was like 15—when I dropped out of school after, you know, a lot of places weren't taking people that didn't have a high school diploma and stuff like that—I went to a temporary agency, you know, which allowed me to work for different companies. I did clerical work for the Department of Probation. I did clerical work for AT&T and Citibank. I worked six or seven months in each of these places. Usually the job itself had ended and I'd go back to the agency and they place me again. But they were all boring—no one to talk to, to hang out with, but I kept going. But even though I was workin' and still doin', you know, the right thing, I always was drawed to doin' the wrong thing somewhere down the line.

When I'd get home from work, I'd go hang out with my friends. We got hooked up with some people who were, uh, transportin' drugs from New York to New Jersey to Washington, and I started doin' that for a while after work, on weekends, or between jobs. I would get paid large sums of money and I, you know, I clung to that for a while. But I was really into for the fun and for things to do with my friends. I did like the real money, though.

I did other stuff during this time, like stealin' in stores and rippin' people off. Me and friends would go to parks and 34th and 42nd streets and stick people up. We got money, real money for clothes, jewelry, and fun. But really soon getting the real money became the important thing.

L.G. was socialized initially into illegal behavior and violence for principally non-pecuniary reasons. The money she received at the early stages of her criminal career was secondary to the excitement and adventure she received from her participation. However, as L.G. and her counterparts entered their late teens and experienced a desire for a more sustained source of income, they applied the criminal "skills" learned earlier to economically motivated activities. But, even within this context, noneconomic motives were still important. For these women, committing crime with friends and enjoying the fruits together were still meaningful.

We should say that at this point in their lives, and unlike their male counterparts, these women were relatively successful in avoiding serious legal sanctions for their already lengthy involvement in criminal activity. On the average, first arrests occurred when these women were in their early (for robberies) to mid-twenties (assault and drugs), later than for males (Fagan, 1996; Fagan and Freeman, 1994; Grogger, 1994; Sampson and Laub, 1993; Good et al., 1986). Therefore, commitment to the illegal economy was viewed by these women as a relatively low-risk endeavor and the length of time that they were able to "double up" far exceeded that of their male counterparts.

Furthermore, the deterrent influences of social sanctions, such as family, peer, and community disapproval, also did not seem to affect the decisions of these women in the same way as for men (Fagan, 1989). For that matter, by the time these women were in their very early twenties, they were emotionally, if not physically, estranged from their foster or families of origin. By and large, as the women's commitment to their criminal careers increased, they became increasingly estranged from their families. This estrangement followed several patterns: the women would initially maintain legal residence with their families but come to spend more of their time in and out of apartments with friends, lovers, or other strangers; or these women eventually would be kicked out of their families' households or their own project apartments due to their increasing involvement in criminal and drug careers, most often permanently leaving their children behind with family or friends, or in the custody of child welfare; or, when they experienced a downturn in their criminal careers they would wander the streets, living in abandoned buildings, welfare hotels, or shelters, avoiding contact with their significant others, including children.

There were a few women with children who left their "always nagging and interfering" families when welfare found them and their children an apartment in the projects. And, for those fortunate and very few who were lucky enough to have a steady income from drug dealing, they moved into public housing or low-income apartments. However, the continued involvement of the majority of these women in drug dealing and other street crimes led eventually to eviction and often pushed them into the street.

One thing was clear though, when speaking about families, especially their children, these women considered all such relationships as fetters—fetters, initially on their criminal careers and social lives and later on, in their missions to obtain drugs and stay high. Accounts of children getting in the way abounded. As Wanda told us:

Yeah, I have a son. I have been away from him for five years while I've been runnin' the streets. I was never with my son. He lives with his grandmother. BCW took him away from me. My mother called them because I was neglectin' him. I was always out leaving him alone in the house. Never thought anything about how my mom and him felt.

Another woman recounted:

Oh yeah, my kids. I have three of them. But they never stayed with me. They always lived with my mom or my sister. I started dropping them off when I would be out doing stuff. But then I finally stopped bringin' them back to my place. They were always gettin' in the way. What with my hours, I couldn't be there and then, all that cryin'. It used to bother my friends when we'd come back to the apartment to party.

The estrangement of these women from their families reduced the salience of both formal and informal social networks and therefore did not influence their "calculus" on the risks and benefits of participation in the illegal economy. As Danelle explained:

Who's going to care? My ma gets money from me and doesn't ask where it's from. She just takes care of my kid for me and doesn't complain. Sometimes she tells me to be careful. I got my friends to run with me and we're doin' just fine. No one bothers us, not even the cops. Yeah, my brother's in prison, but he just got stupid. He'll be out and back into it. It's the way things are here. So, I don't get the question. Why should I think about the problems of doing business? They're not my problems. Who cares, anyway?

Here, Danelle expresses a very common theme in the narratives offered by most of the women. Not only did the women not perceive arrest or incarceration as a risk, but when commenting on others' criminal justice involvements, they dismissed them as endurable, temporary, and not the least bit unusual. Furthermore, most perceived their families and communities as highly tolerant or just plain indifferent to their behavior, whether the behavior was "decent" or "street" (Anderson, 1994). For some of the women, the fact that their families were receiving "benefits," i.e. money [or] commodities, as a result of their involvement in criminal enterprises, seemed to reduce, further, any perception of familial rejection. Thus, for these women, commitment to the illegal economy did not produce any particularly strong strains between them and their families and communities.

Commitment to the Illegal Economy

Patterns of illegal work varied among the women. As we have heard, some abandoned work after periods of licit employment, others drifted in and out of legal work while firmly committed to the illegal economy. Herminia's account was typical of this latter group of women:

I had lots of little jobs, but selling cocaine was always how I really made my living. My last job was, I was 18, I was a receptionist at a showroom. I was there maybe one year. It was okay. But I was already into selling cocaine. I started that much earlier when my father went to jail. I felt that as my duty as taking care of my family I started selling coke. My father didn't know anything about it at first. But there came a time when we were doin' it together. We were selling together.

Now, I'd be selling for about seven years. I went up and down. I could make $500. I could make $3000 a week. I never stood on the corner and sold bags or anything like that. It would always be quantity. I had a few customers, four or five customers. I was selling ounces with some Colombians. They became like my suppliers and stuff. I started like with myself, when my father came out I started like working with him. Then I stopped working in offices altogether.

Alicia, too, considered her criminal activities as more important and more regular than her sporadic experiences within the legal economy:

I had two jobs. I used to do factory work. I didn't like . . . it was too much labor, you know. You had to everything. I did home attendant for a little while. It was okay. But, my main commitment was to doing robberies. After awhile doing both things, the home attendant thing and the robbery thing, I tried to slow down a bit. So, I had to devote myself to one thing. I went full time to robbing people.

Other women from the outset considered the illegal economy as their primary job commitment. They chose *exclusive* "careers" in crime and never participated in the secondary labor market. For these women, given the alternatives of low-wage payoffs from legal work and the expectation of relatively high returns from income-generating criminal activities, they viewed illegal work as a rational choice not unlike choices made among legitimate occupational pursuits and not unlike their male counterparts (Fagan, 1994a).

Jocorn and Rose both had a rich history of pre- and early adolescent involvement in violence and crime. For them, by the time they reached their mid-teens, hustling was a way of life. As Rose recalls:

> Like I said, I use to live in a neighborhood full of hustlers. And um, they use to watch me go to school, giving me $5 or $10 buy clothes off the street for all the kids in the neighborhood. And then just, we started hanging down there by them. Then we started holding drugs for them. And paying us, $100 a day, and we would hold a 100 quarters, now if I would have gotten caught with that, lord knows how much time, but I was too naive and young to know what was going on. The money was good to me. I thought I was rich, you know what I am saying. And I liked to buy. So, by the time I left school, I was already into my job on the streets. I knew how to do the job and I had no problem protecting myself while I was doing it.

Jocorn, too, was deeply entrenched in her "career" by the time she left school. And, she stayed in this one "job," advancing through the ranks until she had her own organization.

> I was about 11 or 12 when I started selling drugs. It was fast money. I guess that's what attracted me to it, the fast money and the fun. I was makin' about $500 a week. Much later on, when I was about 17, I started like putting people to work for me. I was pulling in $10,000 a day.

> I sold it all. Crack too. I've been dealing for 19 years. The more I had, you know, the more money I wanted. I had people in Brooklyn, Manhattan, the Bronx, Boston, in upstate. All I was basically doing was gettin' the drugs and receiving the money.

The "career" trajectories of the women in the above accounts reflect the influences of structure and context in shaping their choices and options. With limited access to

satisfying legal work, and in segregated neighborhoods with high concentrations of joblessness, alienated views of legal work and diminished expectations for conventional employment became normative. For some of the women, the criminal involvement of family, friends, and neighbors were more likely to integrate them into the criminal world than into referral networks for legal and stable employment. For others, immersion in crime during childhood and early adolescence marginalized them early on from interest in or access to job contacts in the licit workaday world.

But, for those women who had some experience in the secondary labor market, commitment to criminal careers eventually ended their involvement in legal work. Denise, who earlier described her job experiences, told us about her break with marginal labor:

> Well, I still went from job to job pulling new scams. Worked for some lawyers and ran a prostitution thing out of their office. I quit working for the lawyers and with my two babies of my own and I got on welfare. Once I had that system figured out, I took the bus over to another town, and, uh, I got on welfare out there. I used a wig and glasses, somebody else's baby, and I had a birth certificate printed up with my name, and I go on welfare out there too. I tried this from town to town. I was collecting numerous checks. It was good money.

> But there was more money to be made. About when I was 20, I started to sell drugs with my father and uncle. I made about $1500 a day! I dealt heroin for about two years. Then I went into business for myself. I sold heroin and coke. I was clearing $4500 to $5500 a week.

For other women, drug use exerted a strong influence on their ultimate commitment to the illegal economy over employment in the secondary labor market. Even at the outset, commitment to licit work was weak. But, with the onset of cocaine smoking, such investments diminished and quickly disappeared. Further, once addicted to harder drugs, i.e., crack cocaine, most of the women in this study experienced the ultimate rupture in ties to the licit workaday world and a decline in the importance of excitement, adventure, and peer participation in criminal activities. Thus, drug addiction and not peers came to organize most of daily life's activities.

Barbara's involvement in legitimate work ended with her abuse of crack:

I worked for the Board of Education as a teacher's aide from like '84 to '86. When I was working I didn't need to be involved in crime at that time because I had my own income. But I was smoking crack. I was fired from the Board of Ed because of my lateness and absenteeism.

I got so involved in getting high that I was kind of glad that I didn't have to get up in the morning anymore. I didn't care about that job or those people on that job, or even the kids like I was supposed to. That's when I started gettin' into crime.

For some, cocaine smoking intensified the illicit activities in which they already were active. Evelyn recalls:

What happen was I didn't have any money, I didn't have any way of getting a job, I was already addicted into crack. Like I said, my parents threw me out of the house, there was no way means of getting any money from them or anything like that, I had bumped into people who were selling, and I got connected with them Two Spots selling drugs with their bosses. I said can help you out, be your look out or whatever, and from there I started working and I met the bosses and I started working like that.

From Some Involvement in the Legal Economy to Immersion in the Cocaine Economy and Ultimate Withdrawal from Crime as Work

While the women's stories show that illicit behaviors were continuous over time, their intensification suggests some important transitions. These transitions were structured by economic changes and social opportunities as well as key developments within drug markets. For instance, the development of the cocaine economy created opportunities for drug selling that did not exist in prior, especially heroin, markets. The changing economic structure of inner-city neighborhoods also created the possibility of changes in gender roles that in the past determined options for status and income within street drug networks.

At one time, women were excluded from selling by rigid gender roles and male hegemony in deviant street networks. The expanding cocaine economy and the increasing presence of women in the public domain may have neutralized the social processes that in the past consigned them to secondary roles in street networks. As a result, the women were able to form new organizations for drug selling, or pursue independent careers in drug selling.

For Gayle, making money through drug selling was her career ambition:

I sold all kinds of drugs. I knew from the start that I wanted to be big in this. From weed I went to selling heroin and to coke. I started dealing weed at 15. I used to steal weed from my father and deal it. Somebody approached me to deal crank [speed]. I was making $200 a week. I sold in this parking lot where kids hung out. I made $800 to $900 a week from speed.

Then I sold heroin. I already had the knowledge of dealing. I went straight to somebody who sold heroin. The idea was strictly to make money. At first I sold it myself. Then I would cut ounces and bag it and let my female friends sell it for me off the street. I was making $2500 a week. I dealt heroin for years and I started dealing coke. At this point I really learned how to make lots of money selling drugs.

Viewing women's involvement in drug markets in economic and career terms suggests an active role in decision-making. Earlier deterministic conceptions of women and drugs described a passive drift into the secondary roles of hustling and prostitution in a street world dominated by men. However, the accounts provided by the women in this paper indicate that within contemporary drug markets, women often made decisions to enter based on a logical evaluation of career options. Here, the women considered both economic (wages) and non-pecuniary (status) returns from work in the secondary labor market. Furthermore, they realistically assessed their chances of obtaining economic and social support from domestic arrangements. Recognizing their constrained options, these women opted for illicit work which to them seemed to represent a rational choice.

Stephanie's account reflects this weighing of options:

> Well, I've been working off and on in different cashiers and stuff like since I'm 15 years old. I always knew that a woman couldn't depend on a man to take care of her. I grew up on Public Assistance. I saw how it affected my mom when we on PA. People always coming to check up on your home.

> So, I knew I would have to get a career or something. But work was just menial jobs to me, and they really didn't matter.

> But then I saw that dealing drugs was a way to make real money. I started freelancing. I purchased coke from a guy that I used to cop for myself. So I began to bring people to him. But since I still had a job, in the hair business there's a lot of drugs flowing. So I used to just buy in large quantities and sell to people at work. I sold to people I knew, who I knew were into drugs. When I got off from work, I usually went to a friend's house that I know got high. I sat and got high with them, and I usually sold to whoever was in their home.

For Stephanie and many of the other women, criminal career choices provided them with higher incomes than were reachable by their peers in conventional careers. Furthermore, their involvement and success in these career trajectories placed them in contexts offering status (Williams 1989; Padilla 1992), excitement (Adler 1985; Anderson 1990), and commodities.

Dealing also helped many women avoid or exit from the types of street hustling, including prostitution, that characterized women's illicit income-generating strategies (Goldstein et al., 1992; Ouellet et al., 1993; Ratner, 1993). Stephanie's preference for dealing was typical among the women we studied:

> You see, as a prostitute or hooker, you know, I don't know. For me it's like, uh, you would rather sell drugs or even rob somebody than to perform a service. The last thing I wanted to do is lay down for somebody. I'd rather deal or rip people off.

Further, dealing provided new ways to expand their traditionally limited roles, statuses and incomes within the street economy.

For many of the women in our study, however, their involvement in the workaday world of criminal enterprise was shortlived. The same drug—crack—that opened new career opportunities for a lot of them, also brought many of them down. Crack *abuse* resulted in their immersion in a social world where options became narrower and exploitation more likely (Rosenbaum, 1981). The narrowing options reflected both the social contexts where crack was used and the effects of the drug itself.

Similar to heroin use in past eras, heavy crack use closed off social exits from drug use or hustling (Fagan, 1994b; Rosenbaum, 1981). One woman said that the intense pleasure from smoking crack, and the reinforcement when it was repeated, made it impossible "to make any space between [herself] and the world where [she] smoked it."

Reinarman et al. (1989) described the isolation that accompanies obsessive crack use, the suspicions toward friends and family members, the withdrawal from social interactions, the rejection of activities that do not lead to refilling the pipe, and the cashing in of limited economic and social assets in pursuit of an elusive but mythically powerful high. Thus, it is not surprising that with an increase in crack use, prostitution returned as an important income source for the women who used crack.

Prolonged crack use eventually led to deeper immersion in the social scenes and behaviors that limited their participation in both the licit and illicit work and social worlds. Although some walked away from crack after experimentation or maintained limits on their use of crack, others immersed themselves in crack use and reconstructed their social and economic lives to accommodate their frequent crack use.

The point of immersion into the world of crack was an important turning point for the women in our study. Their *economic* lives, for instance, became increasingly intertwined with their *social* worlds. They organized their lives around drugs and immersed themselves in those activities and with those people with whom they shared economic and social behaviors. Their roles and identities, as well as their primary sources of status and income, became defined, exclusively, within these street networks. Their options for transition to legal work, marriage, or educational settings were limited. And, their engulfment in street networks reinforced their pathway into an abyss. Any notion of a "calculus" disappeared as "chasing the pipe" became the one and only goal of daily life.

For the majority of women, then, the problem of maintaining an addiction came to take precedence over other interests and participation in both the legal and illegal work worlds. The women also came to define themselves in relationship to their drug problems. They were "junkies," "crackheads," or "coke-bitches." Few women came to see themselves as criminals, workers, or in any way other than as addicts. Whatever deviant behaviors they engaged in came to be justified by their "drug compulsion."

The increased salience or primacy of their drug habits led to their "role engulfment." Schur pointed out that one major consequence of the processes through which deviant identity is ascribed is the tendency "of the deviator to become 'caught up in' a deviant role . . . that his behavior is increasingly organized 'around' the role . . . and that cultural expectations attached to the role come to have precedence in the organization of his general way of life" (Schur, 1971:69). As a result, the women progressively became totally immersed in the networks of the drug markets. They became committed to the drug world's norms, values, and lifestyle, and they limited their involvement with nondeviant individuals and groups.

As the circumstances of the women's lives changed, and they became more engulfed in the drug world, it became less and less likely that they actively considered working, even at crime. Thus, for the majority of the women in our study, the short period between adolescence and adulthood took them through various positions vis-à-vis the workaday worlds. For many there was, indeed, an early engage-

ment in the legal economy; all went on to embrace the social and pecuniary benefits of criminal participation; and most disengaged totally from both economies, immersed instead in an all-consuming search for the next hit of crack.

Conclusion

There remains little doubt that women's experiences within the worlds of licit and illicit work remain gendered. This is the case, especially, as one reaches through the upper echelons of both the primary and illegal labor markets. In the primary market, women's gains during the 1970s and 80s were tempered by their placement in lower status specialties, less desirable work settings, lower paying industries and professions, and part-time rather than full-time work (Baca Zinn and Eitzen, 1998; Jacobs, 1989; Reskin and Roos, 1990; Herz and Wootton, 1996).

In terms of the upper levels of criminal networks, women continued to confront sex discrimination. In part, the ethnic and family segmentation of drug labor markets made it difficult for women to achieve higher ranks. The retail drug trades, particularly in immigrant communities, reproduced traditional perceptions of women's limited capabilities. Thus, women involved in the drug trade in Hispanic communities were often refused access to upper level roles that required the routine use of violence or involved the handling of large sums of money or drugs (Williams 1992; Waterston 1993).

However, such a pattern seems somewhat moderated in both the legal secondary labor and the lower levels of illicit, street markets. In both these venues, the 1980s opened doors for inner-city women. In terms of the secondary labor market, transformations in the economy resulted in poor women having greater success than their male counterparts in claiming service sector and clerical jobs (Baca Zinn and Eitzen, 1998; Wilson, 1987). At the same time, inner-city women were faced with new opportunities that were brought about by demographic, social, and particularly, drug market changes. These opportunities resulted in increased participation in street crime (Sommers and Baskin,

1992) as well as greater diversification in roles and statuses and types of crimes. For instance, most of the women crack dealers were involved in direct sales either in curbside or indoor locations, a relatively rare role in earlier drug markets (Baskin and Sommers, 1998; Johnson et al., 1985).

Nonetheless, the "success" of women in street crimes such as robbery and drug distribution was temporary. And, it is perhaps the transitory nature of their fortuity that is most the result of gendered life experiences. Despite evidence that that women enter into street crime for many of the same reasons as their male counterparts (Baskin and Sommers, 1998; Miller, 1998) and are more successful at avoiding legal sanctions, they are less successful than men at avoiding the pitfalls of addiction. Furthermore, despite the doors opened to these women as a result of changes associated with crack cocaine, it was also this drug that made their downfall so dramatic and their return to gendered crimes, such as prostitution, almost unavoidable.

Again, the role that crack-cocaine played in the lives of inner-city women during the 1980s cannot be minimized. It was far reaching and profound. Unlike the underrepresentation of females in street heroin scenes (Rosenbaum, 1981), several studies have documented that women accounted for almost 50% of crack customers (Bourgois and Dunlap, 1993; Deschenes, 1988; Greenleaf, 1989). Furthermore, whereas males who worked in crack distribution during this time period were less likely to use crack (Ratner, 1993), this was not the case for women. In addition, the effects of crack use on females was far more serious than for males (Ouellet et al., 1993) resulting in greater depravation, devastation, and re/turn to prostitution (Bourgois and Dunlap, 1993).

In conclusion, the women we interviewed were members of distinct communities that mediated between them and the larger society. It was within these local communities that the women interacted and made decisions regarding school, family, and work. Additionally, it was within these local communities that they devised ways of handling the exigencies that were imposed by the larger economic and political structures. Commu-

nity levels of family dysfunction, economic and social dislocation, and changing demographics as well as the presence of illegitimate opportunities all contributed to a landscape in which decisions were made concerning key aspects of everyday life, including work.

These landscapes, though, exist within specific time frames. As such, they are dynamic. Therefore, changes both in legal and illegal labor markets as well as in gender socialization should be considered in future research. In this way, we will be able to understand better the complex processes that influence local criminal and drug career decisions. Certainly, it will be interesting to see whether the decline in crack cocaine markets in inner-city neighborhoods have had any impact on women's roles on the street.

Note

1. Similar to the primary labor sector, in the secondary sector there is a white-collar upper level (which includes sales and clerical workers), where working conditions, pay, and benefits are better than in the blue-collar lower level (private household, laborer, and most service jobs). Turnover is high in both levels of this sector because these workers have relatively few marketable skills and are easily replaced (Kelly, 1991).

References

Adler, Patricia. 1992. "The Post Phase of Deviant Careers: Reintegrating Drug Traffickers." *Deviant Behavior* 13:103-26.

——. 1985. *Wheeling and Dealing: An Ethnography of an Upper-Level Dealing and Smuggling Community*. New York: Columbia University Press.

American Correctional Association. 1990. *The Female Offender: What Does the Future Hold?* Arlington, VA: Kirby Lithographic Company.

Anderson, Elijah. 1994. "The Code of the Streets." *The Atlantic Monthly* May:81-94.

——. 1990. *Streetwise*. Chicago: University of Chicago Press.

Baca Zinn, Maxine and Stanley D. Eitzen. 1998. "Economic restructuring and systems of inequality." In Margaret L. Andersen and Patricia Hill Collins (eds.) *Race, Class and Gender: An Anthology*. Belmont, CA: Wadsworth Publishing Co.

Baskin, Deborah and Ira Sommers. 1998. *Casualties of Community Disorder: Women's Careers in Violent Crime.* Boulder, CO: Westview Press.

Baunach, Phyllis Jo. 1992. "Critical Problems of Women in Prison." In I. L. Moyer (ed.) *The Changing Roles of Women in the Criminal Justice System.* Prospect Heights, IL: Waveland Press.

——. 1982. "You Can't Be a Mother and in Prison . . . Can You? Impact of the Mother-Child Separation." In Barbara Raffel Price and Natalie J. Sokoloff (eds.) *The Criminal Justice System and Women: Women Offenders/Victims/Workers.* New York: Clark, Boardman Company, Ltd.

Bertram, J. 1982. "My Real Prison Is Being Separated From My Children." *Prison MATCH.* San Francisco: CA: National Council on Crime and Delinquency.

Biernacki, P. 1986. *Pathways from Heroin Addiction: Recovery Without Treatment.* Philadelphia: Temple University Press.

Blackburn, M., D. Bloom and R. Freeman. 1990. "The Declining Economic Position of Less Skilled American Men." In Gary Burtless (ed.) *A Future of Lousy Jobs? The Changing Structure of U.S. Wages.* Washington, DC: The Brookings Institution.

Bourgois, Phillipe. 1995. *In Search of Respect: Selling Crack in El Barrio.* New York: Cambridge University Press.

——. 1989. "In Search of Horatio Alger: Culture and Ideology in the Crack Economy." *Contemporary Drug Problems* 16:619-649.

Bourgois, Phillipe and Eloise Dunlap. 1993. "Exorcising Sex for Crack: An Ethnographic Perspective From Harlem." In Mitchell S. Ratner (ed.) *Crack Pipe as Pimp: An Ethnographic Investigation of Sex-for-Crack Exchanges.* New York: Lexington Books.

Brown, Lyn Mikel and Carol Gilligan. 1992. *Meeting at the Crossroads: Women's Psychology and Girls' Development.* New York: Ballantine Books.

Campbell, Anne. 1991. *The Girls in the Gang.* Cambridge, MA: Basil Blackwell.

Carlen, Pat. 1988. *Women, Crime and Poverty.* Milton Keynes: Open University Press.

Chesney-Lind, Meda, Marilyn Brown, and Dae-Gyung Kwack. 1996. "Gender, Gangs and Violence in a Multiethnic Community." Presented at the annual meeting of the American Society of Criminology, November 21, Chicago, IL.

Chiricos, Ted. 1987. "Rates of Crime and Unemployment: An Analysis of Aggregate Research." *Social Problems* 334:187-212.

Church, George. 1990. "The View From Behind Bars." *Time Magazine* (Fall) 135:20-22.

Corcoran, Mary and Susan Parrott. 1992. "Black Women's Economic Progress." Paper presented at the Research Conference on the Urban Underclass: Perspectives from the Social Sciences. Ann Arbor, Michigan: June.

Crutchfield, Robert. 1997. "Labor Markets, Employment, and Crime." *National Institute of Justice Research Preview.* Washington, DC: U.S. Department of Justice.

——. 1989. "Labor Stratification and Violent Crime." *Social Forces* 68 (2):513-530.

Curry, David, Richard Ball, and Robert J. Fox. 1994. "Gang Crime and Law Enforcement Record Keeping." *Research in Brief.* Washington, DC: National Institute of Justice.

Daly, Kathleen and Meda Chesney-Lind. 1988. "Feminism and Criminology." *Justice Quarterly* 5:497-538.

Datesman, Susan and G. Cales. 1983. "I'm Still the Same Mommy." *The Prison Journal* 63(2) 142-154.

Deschenes, Elizabeth, Fran Bernat, Finn Esbensen, and D. Wayne Osgood. 1996. "Gangs and School Violence: Gender Differences in Perceptions and Experiences." Presented at the annual meeting of the American Society of Criminology, November 20, Chicago, IL.

Deschenes, Elizabeth. 1988. "Cocaine Use and Pregnancy." Drug Abuse Series Paper of the Drug Abuse Information and Monitoring Project, California Department of Alcohol and Drug Programs, Health and Welfare Agency.

Fagan, Jeffrey. 1996. "Legal and Illegal Work: Crime, Work and Unemployment." In Burton Weisbrod and James Worthy (eds.) *Dealing with Urban Crisis: Linking Research to Action.* Evanston, IL: Northwestern University Press.

——. 1994a. "Legal and Illegal Work: Crime, Work and Unemployment." Paper presented at Metropolitan Assembly on Urban Problems: Linking Research to Action. Northwestern University, Center for Urban Affairs and Policy Research.

——. 1994b. "Women and Drugs Revisited: Female Participation in the Cocaine Economy." *Journal of Drug Issues* 24:179-226.

——. 1992. "Drug Selling and Licit Income in Distressed Neighborhoods: The Economic Lives of Drug Users and Drug Sellers." In Adele Harrell and George Peterson (eds.) *Drugs, Crime and Social Isolation: Barriers to Urban Opportunity.* Washington DC: The Urban Institute Press.

——. 1989. "Cessation of Family Violence: Deterrence and Dissuasion." In Lloyd Ohlin and Michael Tonry (eds.) *Family Violence*, Volume 11 of *Crime and Justice: An Annual Review of Research*. Chicago: University of Chicago Press.

Fagan, Jeffrey and Richard Freeman. 1994. "Crime and Work." Unpublished. Newark, NJ: Rutgers University, School of Criminal Justice.

Freeman, Richard. 1992. "Crime and the Employment of Disadvantaged Youths." In George Peterson and Wayne Vroman (eds.) *Urban Labor-Markets and Job Opportunities*. Washington, DC: Urban Institute Press.

——. 1983. "Crime and Unemployment." In James Q. Wilson (ed.) *Crime and Public Policy*. San Francisco: Institute for Contemporary Studies Press.

Goldstein, Paul. 1979. *Prostitution and Drugs*. Lexington, MA: Lexington Books.

Goldstein, Paul, Laurence Ouellet, and Michael Fendrich. 1992. "From Bag Brides to Skeezers: An Historical Perspective on Sex-for-Drugs Behavior." *Journal of Psychoactive Drugs* 24:349-361.

Good, David H., Maureen Pirog-Good, and Robin Sickles. 1986. "An Analysis of Youth Crime and Employment Patterns." *Journal of Quantitative Criminology* 2:219-236.

Greenleaf, V.D. 1989. *Women and Cocaine: Personal Stories of Addiction and Recovery*. Los Angeles: Lowell House.

Grogger, Jeffrey. 1994. "Criminal Opportunities, Youth Crime, and Young Men's Labor Supply." Unpublished. Department of Economics, University of California, Santa Barbara.

Hagan, John. 1993. "The Social Embeddedness of Crime and Unemployment." *Criminology* 31:465-492.

Hagan, John and Alberto Pallioni. 1990. "The Social Reproduction of a Criminal Class in Working Class London, Circa 1950–1980." *American Journal of Sociology* 96:265-299.

Hagedorn, John. 1994. "Neighborhoods, Markets and Gang Drug Organization." *Journal of Research in Crime and Delinquency* 31:264-294.

Hagedorn, John and Parry Macron. 1988. *People and Folks: Gangs, Crime and the Underclass in a Rustbelt City*. Chicago: Lake View Press.

Herz, Diane and Barbara Wooten. 1996. "Women in the Workforce: An Overview." In Cynthia Costello and Barbara Kivimae Krimgold (eds.) *The American Woman, 1996–1997*. NY: W.W. Norton.

Hossfield, Karen J. 1997. " 'Their Logic Against Them': Contradictions in Sex, Race, and Class in Silicon Valley." In Maxine Baca Zinn, Pierette Hondagneu-Sotelo, and Michael A. Messner (eds.) *Through the Prism of Difference*. Boston, MA: Allyn and Bacon.

Hunt, Dana. 1990. "Drugs and Consensual Crimes: Drug Dealing and Prostitution." In

Michael Tonry and James Q. Wilson (eds.) *Drugs and Crime. Crime and Justice, Volume 13*. Chicago: University of Chicago Press.

Inciardi, James A., Dorothy Lockwood, and Anne Pottieger. 1993. *Women and Crack Cocaine*. New York: MacMillan.

Jacobs, Jerry. 1989. "Long Term Trends in Occupational Sex Segregation." *American Journal of Sociology* 95:160-173.

Joe, Karen and Meda Chesney-Lind. 1995. "Just Every Mother's Angel: An Analysis of Gender and Ethnic Variations in Youth Gang Membership." *Gender and Society* 9:408-430.

Johnson, Bruce, Paul Goldstein, Edward Preble, James Schmeidler, Douglas Lipton, Barry Spunt, and Thomas Miller. 1985. *Taking Care of Business: The Economics of Crime by Heroin Abusers*. Lexington, MA: Lexington Books.

Kelly, Rita Mae. 1991. *The Gendered Economy: Work Careers, and Success*. Newbury Park, CA: Sage Publications.

Koban, Linda A. 1983. "Parent in Prison: A Comparative Analysis of the Effects of Incarceration on the Families of Men and Women." *Research in Law, Deviance and Social Control* 5:171-183.

Laub, John and R. Sampson. 1993. "Turning Points in the Life Course: Why Change Matters to the Study of Crime." *Criminology* 31:301-326.

Liebow, Elliot. 1967. *Tally's Corner: A Study of Negro Streetcorner Men*. Boston, MA: Little, Brown and Company.

Maher, Lisa and Ric Curtis. 1992. "Women on the Edge of Crime: Crack Cocaine and the Changing Contexts of Street-Level Sex Work in New York City." *Crime, Law, and Social Change* 18-221-258.

Maher, Lisa and Kathleen Daly. 1996. "Women in the Street-Level Drug Economy: Continuity or Change?" *Criminology* 34:465-492.

Mieczkowski, Thomas. 1994. "The Experiences of Women Who Sell Crack: Some Descriptive Data from the Detroit Crack Ethnography Project." *Journal of Drug Issues* 24:227-248.

Miller, Eleanor. 1986. *Street Woman*. Philadelphia: Temple University Press.

Miller, Jody. 1998. "Up It Up: Gender and the Accomplishment of Street Robbery." *Criminology* 36:37-66.

Moore, Joan. 1991. *Going Down to the Barrio: Homeboys and Homegirls in Change*. Philadelphia: Temple University Press.

——. 1992. "Institutionalized Youth Gangs: Why White Fence and El Hoyo Maravilla Change so Slowly." In J. Fagan (ed.) *The Ecology of Crime and Drug Use in Inner Cities*. New York: Social Science Research Council.

——. 1990. "Mexican-American Women Addicts: The Influence of Family Background." In Ronald Glick and Joan Moore (eds.) *Drugs in Hispanic Communities*. New Brunswick, NJ: Rutgers University Press.

National Advisory Commission on Criminal Justice Standards and Goals. 1973. *Task Force on Corrections*. Washington, DC: U.S. Government Printing Office.

Ouellet, Lawrence, W. Wayne Weibel, A.D. Jimenez, and W.A. Johnson. 1993. "Crack Cocaine and the Transformation of Prostitution in Three Chicago Neighborhoods." In Mitchell Ratner (ed.) *Crack Pipe as Pimp An Ethnographic Investigation in Sex-for-Crack Exchanges*. New York: Lexington Books.

Padilla, Felix. 1992. *The Gang as an American Enterprise*. Boston, MA: Northeastern University Press.

Pettiway, Leon. 1987. "Participation in Crime Partnerships by Female Drug Users: The Effects of Domestic Arrangements, Drug Use, and Criminal Involvement." *Criminology* 25:741-766.

Pipher, Mary. 1994. *Reviving Ophelia: Saving the Selves of Adolescent Girls*. New York: Ballantine Books.

Rafter, Nicole. 1985. *Partial Justice: Women in State Prisons, 1800–1935*. Boston: Northeastern University Press.

Ratner, Mitchell. 1993. "Sex, Drugs and Public Policy: Studying and Understanding the Sex-for-Crack Phenomenon." In Mitchell Ratner (ed.) *Crack Pipe as Pimp: An Ethnographic Investigation of Sex-for-Crack Exchanges*. New York: Lexington Books.

Reinarman, Craig, Dan Waldorf, and Sheila Murphy. 1989. "The Call of the Pipe: Freebasing and Crack Use as Norm-Bound Episodic Compulsion." Paper presented at the Annual Meeting of the American Society of Criminology, Reno, Nevada, November.

Reskin, Barbara and Patricia Roos. 1990. *Job Queues, Gender Cues: Explaining Women's Inroads into Male Occupations*. Philadelphia, PA: Temple University Press.

Reuter, Peter, Robert MacCoun, and Patrick Murphy. 1990. *Money from Crime*. Report R-3894. Santa Monica, CA: The Rand Corporation.

Rosenbaum, Marsha. 1981. *Women and Heroin*. New Brunswick, NJ: Rutgers University Press.

Rosenfeld, Richard, and Steven Messner. 1989. *Crime and the American Dream*. Albany, NY: SUNY Press.

Sampson, Robert J., and Laub, John H. 1993. *Crime in the Making*. Cambridge, MA: Harvard University Press.

Sarri, Rosemary. 1987. "Unequal Protection Under the Law." In J. Figuera-McDonough and R. Sarri (eds.) *The Trapped Woman*. Newbury Park, CA: Sage.

Schur, E. 1971. *Labeling Deviant Behavior: Its Sociological Implications*. New York: Harper and Row.

Shover, Neil. 1985. *Aging Criminals*. Newbury Park, CA: Sage.

Sommers, I., D. Baskin and J. Fagan. 1996. "The Structural Relationship Between Drug Use, Drug Dealing and Other Income Support Activities Among Women Drug Dealers." *Journal of Drug Issues* 26:975-1006.

Sullivan, Mercer. 1989. *Getting Paid*. Ithaca, NY: Cornell University Press.

Taylor, Avril. 1993. *Women Drug User: An Ethnography of a Female Injecting Community*. Oxford: Clarendon Press.

Taylor, Carl. 1993. *Girls, Gangs, Women and Drugs*. East Lansing: Michigan State University Press.

——. 1990. "Gang Imperialism." In R. Huff (ed.) *Gangs in America*. Newbury Park, CA: Sage Publications.

Tienda, Marta. 1989. "Neighborhood Effects and the Formation of the Underclass." Paper presented at the Annual Meeting of the American Sociological Association, San Francisco, August.

Uggen, Christopher, Irving Piliavin, and Ross Matsueda. 1992. *Job Programs and Criminal Desistance*. Washington, DC: The Urban Institute.

Vicusi, W. Kip. 1986. "The Risks and Rewards of Criminal Activity: A Comprehensive Test of Criminal Deterrence." *Journal of Labor Economics* 4:317-340.

Waterston, Alisse. 1993. *Street Addicts in the Political Economy*. Philadelphia: Temple University Press.

Williams, Terry. 1989. *The Cocaine Kids*. New York: Addison-Wesley.

Wilson, William J. 1996. *When Work Disappears: The World of the New Urban Poor*. New York: Alfred Knopf.

——. 1987. *The Truly Disadvantaged*. Chicago: University of Chicago Press.

Witte, Ann and Helen Tauchen. 1994. "Work and Crime: An Exploration Using Panel Data." Unpublished paper.

Wolf, Naomi. 1997. *Promiscuities: The Secret Struggle for Womanhood*. New York: Random House.

Section II

Property Crime

Most crime is nonviolent, solely intended to bring financial benefit to the offender. Property crime is usually differentiated from violent crime by the lack of the use of force or serious injury to the victim.

Property crimes make up more than 90 percent of all victimizations. In addition to being more frequent than violent crimes, property crimes usually occur without interaction between the victim and the criminal. In contrast, violent offenders and their victims interact with each other and are often known to each other, although stranger-to-stranger violence is becoming more common.

This section includes studies of nonviolent property offenders: burglars, thieves, and buyers and sellers of stolen property. The offenders discuss their perspectives on crime as a way of life and the strategies and decisions involved in their criminal activities.

In the first selection, Paul Cromwell, James Olson, and D'Aunn Avary ("Decision Strategies of Residential Burglars") analyze the target selection strategies of a sample of residential burglars in Texas. They delineate a decision model based on occupancy, surveillability, and accessibility of the target.

In the next selection, Paul Cromwell, Lee Parker, and Shawna Mobley ("The Five-Finger Discount") analyze the motivations which underlie shoplifting. They find, that while most shoplifters do so in order to obtain cash or desired merchandise, there were few individuals who employed a single, stable criminal calculus. In the next selection, Zachary Fleming ("The Thrill of It All") looks at young car thieves in British Columbia. He argues that most youthful auto theft is done for recreational purposes, as opposed to stealing for profit. Excitement and thrills were the motives behind most of the thefts he analyzed.

Next, Neal Shover ("Aging Criminals") examines changes in the criminal calculus—how offenders evaluate the costs and benefits of crime—over time. He illustrates the increasing importance of risk in the decision process as offenders age.

Finally, Ira Sommers, Deborah R. Baskin, and Jeffrey Fagan ("Getting Out of the Life") consider the role of life events, cognitions, and life situations in female offenders' decisions to desist from crime. Their findings were consistent with those described by Shover. They reported that women offenders desist when they begin to take the threat of incarceration seriously and attempt to reestablish links with conventional society while severing relationships in the deviant subculture.

The studies included in this section and throughout the book illustrate that criminal decision making is neither purely opportunistic nor completely rational. It is frequently directed at solving immediate problems and satisfying immediate needs. Age, lifestyle, and previous criminal experience combine to create a "limited rationality" based upon what seems reasonable to the offender. ✦

5

Decision Strategies of Residential Burglars

Paul Cromwell
James N. Olson
D'Aunn W. Avary

This selection is part of a larger study of residential burglary. The authors sought to determine how offenders go about their business and the kinds of things they do or fail to do before and during the commission of a crime, and to understand their perceptions of the risks and rewards involved in criminal activity, particularly in residential property crime. Of particular interest was their perception of the sanction threat of the criminal justice system and how those perceptions are formed, evolve, and are modified over time. One specific purpose of the research was to determine the extent to which residential burglars utilize rational processes to select burglary targets and what environmental factors are used as discriminative cues in the target selection process. This selection focuses on the target selection strategy.

Thirty active burglars in an urban Texas metropolitan area of 250,000 population were recruited as respondents using a snowball sampling procedure. The first respondent was referred by a local burglary detective who introduced the authors to one of his confidential informants. That person recruited another respondent and the sample grew through a chain of referrals. Respondents were promised complete confidentiality, anonymity, and a stipend for each interview with the authors and for each additional "active" burglar referred by them and accepted for the study. Informants who usually worked with partners (co-offenders) were encouraged to recruit their co-offenders.

The authors conducted extensive interviews and "ride alongs," during which the respondents were asked to discuss and evaluate residential sites they had previously burglarized and sites previously burglarized by other subjects in the study. Each respondent participated in as many as nine sessions with the researchers.

The authors found that while burglars tend to utilize rational processes, they were also opportunistic. They chose targets that were vulnerable at the time they became aware of them. Most of the burglaries committed by the respondents appeared to be the result of propitious juxtaposition of target, offender and situation.

One of the most critical questions for the formulation of burglary prevention strategies is: "Do burglars carefully plan their crimes and choose their targets by rational means, or do they primarily choose targets of opportunity?" Recent studies of residential burglary have focused on decisionmaking strategies in target selection (Cromwell, Olson, & Avary, 1991; Rengert & Wasilchick, 1985; Nee & Taylor, 1988; Bennett & Wright, 1984). The findings from these studies have been inconsistent with regard to the degree of planning which characterizes decisionmaking by burglars. Some early research (Reppetto, 1974) portrays burglars as planning and executing their crimes in a rational manner, weighing the potential risks versus the potential gains, and choosing a course of action that optimizes gain. Other researchers (Shover, 1971; Bennett & Wright, 1984) have recognized an opportunistic quality in the techniques of some burglars, but have generally supported a "rational planner" perspective. Still others (Rengert & Wasilchick, 1985) have portrayed the burglar as primarily opportunistic. The extent to which these studies have classified burglars as rational planners appears to be at least partially associated with the circumstances under which the data were gathered. In most cases the data were obtained through interviews conducted in prisons or with burglars contacted through criminal justice sources. The interviewers necessarily relied on self-reports concerning level of expertise, experience and "style" of burglary. We believe that this methodology may produce misleading results. Burglars interviewed in prison, or those recalling crimes from the past, might tend to reinterpret their past behavior in a manner consistent with "what should have been" rather than "what was." Few individuals will admit to being opportunistic. Rational decisionmaking is much more valued behavior and is more consistent with a positive self-image. Retrospective accounts of past crimes might therefore give the appearance of highly rational decision strategies. If, however, most burglars are less rational and more opportunistic, crime prevention tactics based on a rational decisionmaker model might prove to be ineffective or overly complex and expensive.

Our findings suggest that a burglar's decision to "hit" a target is based primarily on environmental cues which are perceived to have immediate consequences. Most burglars appear to attend only to the present; future events or consequences do not appear to weigh heavily in their risk-gain calculation. Many informants described how they would identify a target, case, probe, and undertake a hypothetical burglary. The process they described was carefully planned and completely rational. Yet, when their past burglaries were carefully reconstructed, over 75 percent of the 460 burglaries reconstructed were found to be crimes of opportunity—hastily planned—if at all.

Drug using burglars and juveniles are particularly oriented to this immediate gain and immediate risk decision process. Non-drug using, experienced burglars are probably less likely to attend only to immediate risks and gains. Our respondents, while experienced burglars, were all drug users, and tended to have a "here and now" orientation toward the rewards and costs associated with burglary.

Reconstructions of past burglaries revealed that burglars are much more spontaneous and opportunistic than previously reported. The reconstructed burglaries followed three patterns: (a) The burglar happened by the potential burglary site when the occupants were clearly absent and the target was perceived vulnerable (open garage door,

windows, etc.); (b) the site had been previously visited by the burglar for a legitimate purpose (as a guest, delivery person, maintenance worker, etc.); or, (c) the site was chosen after "cruising" neighborhoods and detecting an overt or subtle cue that signaled vulnerability.

The Decision Strategy

We found that most burglars use a simple, yet highly efficient three-component decision making strategy (See also Walsh, 1980). The decision model rests on two assumptions. The first assumption is that while offenders are not completely rational, they may usually be characterized as exercising free will in choosing among alternatives (Clarke & Cornish, 1985; Cornish & Clarke, 1986; Cook, 1980). Unlike the economic model of crime which relies on the concept of maximization of outcomes, the "limited rationality" explanation (see Simon, 1957; Becker, 1968; Cook, 1980) of burglary assumes that burglars are seeking satisfactory target choices, not optimal ones. They do not assess all the available information about a target, rather they consider only those variables which in their own experience and that of other burglars (mentors, co-offenders, acquaintances) are perceived to be reasonable predictors of success or failure in burglary. As Paul and Patricia Brantingham (1978) have noted, burglars develop a mental "template" that defines a good or a bad target. They conclude that, "Potential ... targets are compared to the template and are either accepted or rejected depending upon the congruence" (Brantingham & Brantingham, 1978:108). The content of the burglars "template" is developed and refined through experience. Likewise, Philip Cook (1980) observed that people have limited capacity to acquire and process information and tend to economize on this scarce capacity by adopting "standing decisions" or "rules of thumb" which eliminate the need to completely analyze every new decision. These opportunistic burglars did not heavily weigh long term costs, risks, or benefits. The second assumption is that burglars expect some minimal gain from each potential burglary target. Holding gain as a constant, risk cues then are assessed to answer the question: Do the immediate risks exceed the minimal expectation of gain?

Assessing Risk

Immediate risks, unlike immediate gains, are not assumed to be constant, and vary widely from target site to target site. The net effect is that when only the immediate gains and risks are weighed, and some minimal gain is assumed, the burglar has only to assess risks and then rule out sites which are perceived to pose risks which exceed that which he or she is willing to assume given the expected gain. The immediate risk cues considered by burglars in the target selection decision are of three types: surveillability, occupancy, and accessibility. Risk cues appear to be assessed sequentially, although the evidence from this study suggests that occupancy and surveillabilty may be considered almost simultaneously.

Occupancy Cues. The first category of risk cues are those which indicate occupancy. Occupancy cues appear to be considered first, or simultaneously with the determination that he or she is not likely to be observed and reported while in the act of committing the burglary. Occupancy cues include the presence of cars in drive or garage, visible residents, noise or voices emanating from the house, and other cues which indicate that someone is at home.

Prior research has consistently reported that a primary concern of the residential burglar is whether or not a target site is occupied. Twenty-eight of the 30 burglars in our study stated that they would never purposely enter an occupied residence. Many reported that their greatest fear was that they would encounter the resident upon entering or that the resident would return home while they are still there. The burglar, therefore, not only scans the physical environment for signs of occupancy, he or she also probes the proposed target site to determine if it is occupied. One experienced burglar respondent reported:

> First thing ya gotta do is make sure nobodies home. It's pretty easy. I can do it driving by most times. Like, you know, cars in the carport, front door open, kids playing, shit like that.

Another stated:

> I'm always looking to find a house all shut down. Doors shut, curtains closed. Ya gotta check though. I been fooled before.

Respondents consistently advised that it was important for burglars develop techniques to probe the potential target site to determine if anyone is at home. There are various ways, some quite ingenious, in which burglars probe the target to determine occupancy. These occupancy probes are quite similar across studies. This may be the result of simple common sense, or it may result from sharing of techniques by burglars on street corners, in bars, and in prisons and jails.

The most common probe used by our informants was to send one of the burglars, usually the most presentable (or the woman), to the door to knock or ring the doorbell. If someone answered the prober would ask directions to a nearby address or for a nonexistent person, e.g. "Is Ray home?" The prospective burglar would apologize and leave when told that he or she had the wrong address. Burglars also occasionally ring the doorbell and ask the resident to use the phone: "My car broke down across the street. May I use your phone to call a garage?" This is a good strategy. If the resident refuses, the prober can leave without arousing suspicion. If, however, the resident agrees, the prober has the additional opportunity to assess the quality and quantity of the potential take and to learn more about the security, location of windows and doors, dogs, alarms, etc. Several who used this strategy reported that they usually raised the hood of their car or removed a tire in order to give their story legitimacy. Rengert and Wasilchick (1985) reported similar strategies:

> One of our burglars likes to pretend to have car problems. He would turn into a driveway of a likely house and raise the hood of his car. If the doorbell was answered, he asked for water for his overheated radiator. (p. 89)

One respondent reported that he usually telephoned the prospective target house to determine if anyone was at home.

> I usually go up to the door and ring the bell. If they don't come to the door, then I figure its empty. . . . It's better to call if you know who lives there. Some people won't come to the door. If theys a name on the mailbox, I check the number in the directory and call 'em. I leave it ringing and go back to the door. If I can hear the phone ringing, I know they gone.

Some burglars, particularly the more professional, will probe neighbors next door to and across the street from the target. The ideal target is one where no one is home adjacent to and in houses overlooking the target. One burglar informant chose houses next door to homes that exhibited a "For Sale" sign. She would dress and act like a potential buyer, walking around the yard of the "For Sale" home, peering in windows, etc., finally entering the back yard of the "For Sale" home and from there climbing the adjoining fence into the back yard of the target home.

Some burglars watch a target home until they see the occupants leave for work in the morning; after a quick probe for a remaining occupant, they enter the house. One informant drives around residential neighborhoods until he sees a resident leaving. He enters after a quick probe for remaining occupants.

One informant in the study dressed in jogging gear and removed a piece of mail from the potential target house mailbox. He then knocked on the door and if the resident answered, he told them he had found the piece of mail in the street and was returning it. The jogging gear gave him legitimacy in a strange neighborhood, and returning the mail made him appear to be a good citizen. Thus, he aroused no suspicions.

Another informant, a female heroin addict, carried her two-year-old child to the target residence door, asking for directions to a nearby address. She advised:

> Everybody will open the door when you got a baby. Makes you automatically honest to them. Even when they are suspicious, they usually let me come in to get a drink [of water] for my baby. That way, I

get to scope out what they got and see around the house a little.

Surveillability Cues. Surveillability refers to the extent to which a house is overlooked by and observable by neighbors or passersby. Surveillability cues include the location of the house on the block, visibility of the target site from neighbors' houses, and visibility from the street of doors and other entry points. These cues provide answers to several questions of primary importance to the burglar. Are there neighbors present? Can the neighbors observe the target house from inside their homes? Can the proposed point of entry into the target site be overlooked by passersby? Are there dogs which might bark and arouse neighbors? Are there shrubs, blind doorways, corners, or fences which will hide the burglar as he enters? Is there traffic near the house which might see and report the burglar? Are there people in the neighborhood who "watch the street and know who is and who is not at home?" Debbie, a 23 year old heroin addict, who had been a burglar for seven years observed:

> These people [elderly retirees in one neighborhood] are nosy. The watch for strangers and they call the police. I stay away from neighborhoods where old people live.

The location and type of windows at both the target site and at neighbors houses was considered critical by almost all informants. One respondent stated:

> Notice how that picture window looks out onto the street. The curtains stay open all the time and both the houses across the street can see straight into the living room. I wouldn't do [burglarize] this place.

Another said:

> I'm looking at that upstairs window next door. You can see almost everything that goes on at this house from there. I'm worried about that window.

While the "average" burglar fears being seen, many professional burglars do not. Rather, they fear being seen *and reported*. The more experienced burglars reported that it was important to fit into a neighborhood or situation. They attempted to make their presence in a neighborhood seem normal and natural.

The most experienced of the burglars in our study, Robert, always drove a car that fit the neighborhood socioeconomic level or a van disguised as a delivery vehicle. He dressed befitting the circumstances: as a plumber, deliveryman, or businessman. He would walk to the door of a potential target residence, open the screen door, and unobtrusively hold it open with his foot while he pantomimed a conversation with a nonexistent person inside. He would then enter the house if the door was unlocked. (He reported that many of his target houses were unlocked). If the door was locked, he pantomimed a conversation which appeared to instruct him to go around to the back yard. He would then walk around the house, sometimes stopping to gaze at some feature of the house or landscape, and take notes on a clipboard. When he got to the backyard, he entered the house from that point. To possible onlookers, he had knocked on the door, talked with the owner, and, following instructions, had gone to the rear of the house on some legitimate errand. Other times he would stop his car near a proposed target residence, open the hood, tinker around under the hood, appear to be angry, kick a tire, and angrily walk over to the potential target house. A neighbor or anyone else who might be watching saw only an angry man with a broken car, walking to a house to ask for assistance. Robert stated:

> Trick is to make 'em think I'm legit. Hell, I've even been helped by neighbors who see me trying to get in a house. . . . Acting like you belong is better than sneaking around. . . . You'd be surprised how much credibility you have when you're carrying a clipboard.

Surveillability cues also include the extent of natural cover such as trees, shrubbery, and other landscaping. Houses with dense shrubbery near windows and doors were considered very vulnerable by the informants. Among the most important forms of cover was the "privacy" fence, a six to eight foot high board or masonry fence enclosing a back yard. These fences were common in the area studied, and most respondents considered them important to the target selection process. Some stated that they would not consider burglarizing a house which did not have a privacy fence. Although burglars were at risk while climbing the fence or entering through an unlocked gate, once inside, they were effectively protected from prying eyes by the fence. As one burglar stated:

> Once I'm inside this fence, I can slow down and take my time. The place is mine.

Accessibility Cues. The third level of cues used in the decision strategy are those which indicate how easily the residence may be entered and how well the site is protected. These accessibility cues include location and type of doors and windows, as well as the extent of "target hardening" such as locks, burglar alarms, fences, walls, burglar bars, and dogs.

Our respondents expressed a preference for easily entered houses. While many of them initially told us that they possessed skills which enabled them to disable alarms and overcome deadbolt locks, we found that when reenacting their previous crimes and when they evaluated potential targets, they chose to burglarize the least protected sites. As one said:

> I might could beat that deadbolt. I could. But it takes time and makes noise. Why mess with that shit when the house next door probably got nothing [no security devices].

Almost every respondent considered the presence or absence of dogs when evaluating accessibility. While there was some individual variation among burglars, the general rule was to bypass a house with a dog—any dog. Large dogs represent a physical threat to the burglar and small ones are often noisy, attracting attention to his or her activities. We found that while many burglars have developed contingency plans to deal with dogs (petting them, feeding them, or even killing them), most burglars prefer to avoid them. When asked what were considered absolute "no go" factors, most burglars responded that dogs were second only to occupancy. The sight or sound of a dog at a potential target site almost invariably resulted in a "no go" decision. As one respondent said:

I don't mess with no dogs. If they got dogs I go someplace else.

Debbie, a professional burglar, told us that she was concerned primarily with small dogs:

> Big dogs don't bark much. I talk to them through the fence or door and get them excited. Then I open the gate or the door and when they charge out, I go in and shut the door behind me. They are outside and I'm in. Little dogs "yap" too much. They [neighbors] look to see what they are so excited about. I don't like little yapping dogs.

The ability to "beat" a security system or to enter a protected house was one of the skills that separated the novice from the more experienced and professional burglars. The greater the experience and skill of the burglar, the less important are the accessibility cues in the decisionmaking process.

Using Risk Cues in the Decision Strategy

As stated earlier, the components of the decision process appear to be addressed sequentially. Most burglars in our study assessed cues relating to occupancy first, cues relating to surveillability second, and cues relating to accessibility last. A study by Carol DeFrances and Richard Titus (1993) appears to support the sequential nature of the target selection decision. They found that occupancy and surveillability are assessed first as they can be estimated from a distance (at least as far away as the street). Accessibility cues usually require the burglar to move closer to the proposed target before such factors as deadbolt locks, alarm systems, and the existence of a dog in the house can be determined. Clearly, however, the order in which burglars address each component may vary between burglars. The order may even vary from context to context. Furthermore, the assumptions of occupancy, surveillability and accessibility may be assessed simultaneously. The critical point is that all three components must be addressed before a decision to burglarize is made. Such a three-component decision process maximizes the burglar's outcomes by minimizing the risks. However, the decision *not* to enter is made whenever information consistent with an immediate risk is found. Thus, such a decision making strategy is biased toward personal safety since the decision to enter is always reached through a more complex and time-consuming process than the decision to abort.

Summary and Implications for Crime Prevention

We found that burglars use three categories of environmental cues to assess these "risk" factors: (1) cues which indicate the surveillability of the proposed target site, (2) cues which indicate whether the target site is occupied, and (3) cues which indicate the degree of difficulty which might be expected in actually breaking into the site. The specific content of these cues has varied widely across prior studies.

The study revealed that burglars are opportunistic and are easily deterred or displaced from one target site to another. Situational factors such as the presence of a dog, alarm system, security hardware, and alert neighbors may be the most effective deterrents. When one or more of these risk cues are discerned by the burglar, the target is usually considered too risky and the burglary is aborted or displaced. This is especially true for the opportunistic burglar and less so for the non-drug using "professional." These findings have particular relevance for burglary prevention, for they suggest that burglary is more easily prevented by situational measures than previously thought.

The opportunistic burglar chooses targets based upon their perceived vulnerability to burglary at a given time. Given a large number of potential targets, the burglar tends to select the most vulnerable of the target pool. The rational planning burglar chooses his targets on the basis of other factors than situational vulnerability alone and conceives ways in which he or she can overcome impediments to the burglary. Programs designed to prevent burglary must be based upon valid assumptions about burglars and burglary. Measures designed to combat the relatively small population of high incidence "professional" burglars tend to overemphasize the skill and determination of most burglars. They are expensive, complex, and require long term commitment at many levels. The typical burglar is not a calculating professional against whom complex prevention tactics must be employed. In fact, most burglars are young, unskilled, and opportunistic. This suggests that emphasis should be directed at modifying situational cues relating to surveillability, occupancy, and accessibility. Dogs, good locks, and alarm systems deter most burglars. Methods which give a residence the "illusion of occupancy" deters almost all burglars and are maintained with little effort or cost. Increasing the surveillability of a dwelling is often only a matter of trimming trees and shrubs. Our study suggests that these simple steps may be the most cost efficient and effective means by which residents may insulate themselves from victimization by burglars.

References

Bennett, Trevor (1986). A decision-making approach to opioid addiction. In Cornish, Derek & Clarke, R.V. (Eds.) *The Reasoning Criminal*. New York: Springer-Verlag.

Bennett, T. & Wright, R. (1984). *Burglars on Burglary: Prevention and the Offender*. Aldershot: Gower.

Brantingham, P.J. & Brantingham, P.L. (1978). A theoretical model of crime site selection. In Marvin D. Krohn & Ronald L. Akers (Eds.), *Crime, Law and Sanctions*. Beverly Hills: Sage.

Clarke, R.V. & Cornish, Derek (1985). Modeling offenders' decisions: A framework for policy and research. In Michael Tonry and Norval Morris (Eds.) *Crime and Justice: An Annual Review of Research*, 4th Ed. Chicago: University of Chicago Press.

Cook, Philip J. (1980). Research in criminal deterrence: laying the groundwork for the second decade. In Norval Morris & Michael Tonry (Eds.), *Crime and Justice: An Annual Review of Research*, vol. 2, Chicago: University of Chicago Press.

Cornish, Derek B. & Clarke, Ronald V. (1986). Situational prevention, displacement of crime and rational choice theory. In K. Heal & G. Laycock (Eds.), *Situational Crime Prevention: From Theory into Practice*. London: H.M.S.O.

Cromwell, Paul, James N. Olson and D'Aunn Wester Avary (1991). *Breaking and Entering: An Ethnographic Analysis of Burglary*. Beverly Hills, CA: Sage.

DeFrances, Carol and Richard M. Titus (1993). Urban Planning and Residential Burglary Outcomes. *Landscape and Urban Planning*, vol. 26.

Nee, C. & Taylor, M. (1988). Residential burglary in the republic of Ireland: A situational perspective. *The Howard Journal*, 27, (2).

Rengert, G. & Wasilchick, J. (1985). *Suburban Burglary: A Time and a Place for Everything*. Springfield: Charles C. Thomas.

Reppetto, T. G. (1974). *Residential Crime*, Cambridge, MA.: Ballinger.

Shover, Neal (1971). *Burglary as an Occupation*, Ph.D. Dissertation. The University of Illinois. Ann Arbor, Michigan: University Microfilms, 1975.

Simon, Herbert A. (Ed.) (1982). *Behavioral Economics and Business Organization*, vol.2. Cambridge, MA.: M.I.T. University Press.

Walsh, Dermot P. (1980). *Break-Ins: Burglary From Private Houses*. London: Constable.

6

The Five-Finger Discount: An Analysis of Motivations for Shoplifting

Paul Cromwell
Lee Parker
Shawna Mobley

The purpose of this study was to analyze the various motives that underlie shoplifting behavior and to suggest prevention strategies based on the types of shoplifters identified and the motives that drive their behavior. The study is based on data obtained over a nine-year period in three states. The initial data were gathered during the course of a field study of burglary in 1988–89 in Texas (Cromwell, Olson, and Avary, 1991). Many of the 30 active burglars interviewed for that study were also shoplifters. The data were obtained through extensive interviews with 20 burglars who also shoplifted regularly.

The second wave of shoplifter interviews occurred in Miami, Florida, between 1991 and 1994. The first group of respondents was located with the assistance of a graduate student who was employed part-time in a methadone maintenance clinic in the city. She introduced the first author to a pair of heroin addicts receiving methadone at the clinic. After some initial hesitancy (and assurances from the employee they trusted), they discussed their shoplifting experiences. They related that they supported their considerable heroin habits exclusively through shoplifting. Using a snowball referral technique, 19 additional shoplifter subjects were obtained over the next 12 months. These 22 subjects were extensively interviewed from one to five times each during 1990–91. All were current or former substance abusers, and all were active shoplifters at the time of the study.

During 1992–94, anonymous surveys were conducted with undergraduate students in sociology classes at a university in Miami. Two hundred and twenty-eight (n=228) completed surveys were obtained. Of these, 141 (62%) admitted to one or more instances of shoplifting and completed an additional survey questionnaire regarding their shoplifting experiences. Thirty-nine (n=39) agreed to participate in a more extensive interview concerning their shoplifting experiences. These interviews lasted from one to three hours. Several student respondents were interviewed on more than one occasion.

Finally, in 1997, in Wichita, Kansas, the authors obtained access to a court-ordered diversion program for adult "first offenders" charged with theft. Of these, the majority were charged with misdemeanor shoplifting. These individuals were required to attend an eight-hour therapeutic/education program as a condition of having their records expunged. The authors participated in the sessions as observers, recording their stories and experiences and occasionally asking questions. The participants were told that the authors were studying shoplifting and were asked to participate in a more extensive interview after the sessions were concluded. Data were obtained regarding shoplifting experiences from 137 subjects during the eight-hour sessions and the authors subsequently conducted more extensive interviews with 34 of these informants. Although the diversion program was designed for first offenders, many of the participants had lengthy histories of shoplifting and a smaller percentage had been arrested and convicted of shoplifting in the past.

In summary, shoplifting data were gathered from 320 persons who admitted to one or more shoplifting incidents and more extensive interviews were conducted with 115 of those respondents. The respondents ranged from youthful first offenders to professionals who made the bulk of their living from shoplifting.

One hundred and fifteen (115) subjects were interviewed more extensively. Although they provided clarification, detail, and a richer description of their shoplifting, they did not appear to differ significantly in their motivation, extensiveness of shoplifting behavior, or attitude toward shoplifting from those in the group who completed the survey instrument only.

The study found that shoplifting is not simple behavior with a simple causal dynamic. While shoplifters appeared to make conscious decisions to shoplift and did usually attend to considerations of risk and gain in their decision calculus, many reported that they stole for different reasons at different times. There were few individuals who employed a single, stable criminal calculus. While most stole for economic reasons, they also occasionally chose to steal to satisfy some emotional need, and an otherwise rational offender might on occasion steal some item for which he or she had no need or purpose. The findings, while supporting a rational choice model of offending, noted some cases of shoplifting with apparent nonrational motives.

Shoplifting may be the one crime that most people have committed at one time or another in their lives, and yet it is a relatively unstudied crime. There have been few large-scale studies yielding systematically collected data. Prior research on this subject tends to focus on small convenience or student populations (Katz, 1988; Turner and Cashdan, 1988; Moore, 1983), data gathered from criminal justice or store security records (Cameron, 1964; Moore, 1984; Robin, 1963), special populations, such as the elderly (Feinberg, 1984), juveniles (Klemke, 1982; Hindelang et al., 1981; Osgood et al., 1989), or psychiatric patients (Arboleda-Florez et al., 1977), or involve a few questions about shoplifting as part of a larger more general survey (*Monitoring the Future*, 1984–1995). And, while there have been some large-scale studies (e.g. Griffin, 1970, 1971; Fear, 1974; Won and Yamamoto, 1968), most of these have been conducted with apprehended shoplifters and have concentrated primarily on collecting demographic data on the subjects.

There are several apparent reasons for the lack of interest on the part of scholars and the public. First, most shoplifting is a minor, nonviolent offense. It does not engender public outrage or fear. It is seldom the focus of legislative or media investigations. In fact, most studies place shoplifting near the bottom of the seriousness scale, along with such offenses as painting graffiti and trespassing (Warr, 1989). In her classic study, Mary Cameron (1964) wrote:

> Most people have been tempted to steal from stores, and many have been guilty (at least as children) of "snitching" an item or two from counter tops. With merchandise so attractively displayed in department stores and supermarkets, and much of it apparently there for the taking, one may ask why everyone isn't a thief. (p. xi)

Lloyd Klemke (1992) explains that shoplifting does not result in "eye-catching 'body counts' or astronomical dollar losses generated by individual shoplifters" (p. 5). He argues:

> Without sensational evidence of cataclysmic harm to foster and fuel public concern, most people consider shoplifting to be an interesting but not a very serious type of crime. (p. 6)

Second, shoplifters do not conform to most people's perception of what a criminal is like. Instead, shoplifters tend to be demographically similar to the "average person." In a large-scale study of nondelinquents, Klemke (1982) reported that as many of 63 percent had shoplifted at some point in their lives. Students, housewives, business and professional persons, as well as professional thieves constitute the population of shoplifters. Loss prevention experts routinely counsel retail merchants that there is no "profile" of a potential shoplifter. Klemke (1992) contends, ". . . adult middle-class female shoplifters continue to be a significant segment of the contemporary shoplifting population" (p. 24). Turner and Cashdan (1988) conclude, "While clearly a criminal activity, shoplifting borders on what might be considered a 'folk crime.' "

Another reason for the relative lack of interest in shoplifting is the public's attitude toward the "victim." While most people understand that the costs of shoplifting are passed on to the consumer through higher prices, few people view a large, impersonal department store or other commercial establishment with much sympathy. Shoplifters themselves frequently characterize their crimes as "victimless," or, the victim as deserving it.

So, Why Study Shoplifting?

It is for many of these same reasons that shoplifting should be more widely and systematically examined. It is perhaps the most commonly committed crime. It is widely distributed in the population and appears to cross racial, ethnic, gender, and class lines. Studies have shown that one in every 10–15 shoppers shoplifts (Lo, 1994; Russell, 1973; Turner and Cashdan, 1988). The Federal Bureau of Investigation estimates that shoplifting accounts for approximately 15 percent of all larcenies (Freeh, 1995). According to the *Monitoring the Future* data, shoplifting is the most prevalent and most frequent crime among high-school seniors over time, with over 30 percent of respondents reporting having taken something from a store without paying on one or more occasions (Johnston, Bachman and O'Malley, 1984–1995). And, a study by Ellen Nimick (1990) identified shoplifting as the most common offense for which youth under the age of 15 are referred to juvenile court. Estimates of losses attributable to shoplifting range from 12 to 30 billion dollars annually (Klemke, 1992; Nimick, 1990; Griffin, 1988).

While shoplifting is considered by most to be a relatively minor offense, it is a violation of the law, and when the stolen items exceed a certain value, it is a felony. Petty offenses, while not as dramatic as more serious ones, raise the same questions of explanation and policy as do more serious offenses.

The very fact that shoplifting is considered to be a "folk crime" enables us to see some things about the origin and motivation for crime that more serious offenses such as burglary and robbery may not. And explaining why people shoplift may help explain why most of us at some time or another engage in deviant behavior and why some persist and some do not.

If shoplifting is as prevalent as studies have shown and the losses attributed to shoplifting as great as estimates indicate, this criminal activity has major economic and social consequences and should be more widely and systematically studied.

Purpose of This Study

The purpose of this study is to analyze the various motives that underlie shoplifting behavior and to suggest prevention policy strategies based on the types of shoplifters identified and the motives which drive their behavior.

Conceptual Framework

Rational Choice Theory

This research focuses on the factors that motivate an offender to commit a crime—in this case, to shoplift. While some studies have attributed shoplifting to psychological maladjustments, to compulsion, or to other forces beyond the conscious control of the offender (Arboleda-Florez et al., 1977; Beck and McEntyre, 1977; Solomon and Ray, 1984), most research has noted that shoplifters often employ decision strategies involving calculation of the risks and gains associated with committing the offense. This rational choice perspective is predicated on the assumption that individuals choose to commit crimes. It predicts that individuals will evaluate alternative courses of action, weigh the possible rewards against the costs and risks, and choose the action that maximizes their gain. The benefits of a criminal action are the net rewards of crime and include not only the material gains but also intangible benefits such as emotional satisfaction. The individual may receive immense satisfaction from the excitement of crime, from the independent lifestyle afforded by crime, or from outwitting the authorities. The risks or costs of crime are those associated with the formal punishment should the individual be discovered, apprehended, and convicted, as well as psychological or social costs, such as pangs of conscience, social disapproval, marital and family discord, or loss of self esteem (Vold and Bernard, 1986).

Rational choice theory is a theory of crime, not a theory of criminality. It assumes a general "readiness" for crime, that is, someone who has sufficient criminal motivation to act upon a criminal opportunity or to seek out an opportunity to commit a crime (Brantingham and Brantingham, 1991, 1984). Criminal "readiness" is not constant in any individual. It varies over time and space according to an individual's background, circumstances, and opportunity structure. On one occasion, shoplifting might be a product of the individual's mood and perceptions brought on on by drugs or alcohol, and by the need for money on another (Brantingham and Brantingham, 1993).

The degree of rationality that can be attributed to offenders in planning and executing their crimes and how rationality is related to crime prevention measures has been a central issue of debate (Clarke and Cornish, 1986; Cook, 1989). In the classical version of rational choice, the individual gathers information relevant to risk and gain and combines this information in making a reasoned decision. There is little reason to believe that this "strict" form of rationality is correct. Offenders seldom have all the information regarding risk and gain and have little or no accurate knowledge of the probabilities of reward or punishment associated with the act. However, in order for an act to be rational, it is not necessary that it be carefully preconceived and planned. Behavioral decision making theorists (March, 1994; Newell and Simon, 1972; Slovic et al., 1977; Kahneman et al., 1982) have shown that individuals do not behave consistently with normative rationality; rather, they take shortcuts or make simplifications that are reasonable but may not produce maximized outcomes (Carroll and Weaver, 1986). This view of rationality does not require deliberate weighing of carefully considered alternatives and consequences. It is sufficient that decision makers choose between alternatives based upon their immediate perception of the risks and gains involved. The decision does not have to be the best possible under the circumstances, nor does it have to be based upon an accurate

assessment of the situation. And, as Wilson and Herrnstein (1985) conclude, the value of any reward or punishment associated with a criminal action is always uncertain. It is enough that decisions are perceived to be optimal.

The concept of "limited rationality" recognizes the limited capacity and willingness of most persons to acquire and process information from more than one input or source simultaneously. Clarke and Cornish (1986) concluded that people usually pay attention to only some of the facts or sources at their disposal, employing short cuts or rules of thumb to speed the decision process. These rules of thumb are analogous to Cook's (1989) concept of "standing decisions" which negate the need to carefully weigh all the alternatives and consequences before making a decision in many cases. A standing decision may simply be a decision made beforehand to take advantage of certain types of criminal opportunities or to avoid others. None of this, however, implies irrationality. Rational choice theories need only presume that some minimal degree of planning and foresight occurs (Hirschi, 1986).

Many prior studies have noted a rational element in the motivations of shoplifters. Cameron (1964) classified shoplifters into two classes: *boosters*, who "steal merchandise as one way of making a living," and *snitches*, described as "deliberate thieves who manifest intent to steal by preparation beforehand and who carry out their crimes with system and method." (pp. 58–59). She noted that they are "not impulsive, erratic individuals who are suddenly 'taken' with an uncontrollable urge for a pretty bauble" (p. 59). She concluded that there may be individuals who act impulsively; however, their numbers are few and their impact on the justice system or on business institutions is minimal.

Moore (1983) also found little evidence that pathology or maladjustment were significant contributing factors in shoplifting. He found no meaningful differences in the MMPI between shoplifters and nonshoplifters. Instead, he found that college students experience psychological satisfaction from acquiring personally attractive goods and saving money for other purposes. Kraut

(1976) also argued that the motive for most shoplifting was the acquisition of goods at minimum cost. He claimed that the decision to shoplift is "an inverse function of the perceived risks associated with stealing" (Kraut, 1976:365).

Turner and Cashdan (1988) asked college students to provide information about the reasons their classmates and friends shoplifted. It was assumed that their responses would function as a projective self-report, in effect, revealing information about the respondents' real or potential motives for shoplifting. They found that poverty, "self-indulgence," and some variant of "thrill," "risk," "fun," or "challenge" were the most prevalent motives reported. Those who reported poverty (mentioned by 64% of the subjects) as a motive shoplifted to obtain items they needed but could not afford to buy. Self-indulgence (mentioned by 40% of the respondents) was defined as stealing items that were desired, but not necessarily needed. Sixty-six percent of the respondents listed "excitement," "thrill," "challenge," or "fun" as a primary motive for their illegal behavior.

Katz (1988), in research with a college student population, concluded that "various property crimes share an appeal to young people, independent of the material gain or esteem from peers" (Katz, 1988:52). He found that such offenses as vandalism, joyriding, and shoplifting are "all sneaky crimes that frequently thrill their practioneers" (p. 53).

Each of these studies—whether attributing shoplifting to the desire to obtain material goods at minimal cost or to attain some psychosocial reward (thrill, excitement, fun, self-indulgence, etc.)—involves a choice by the offender based upon (at least minimally) his or her perceptions of the risks and gains associated with the act.

Results

The subjects were asked to explain the primary motivation for their shoplifting. They were asked, "Why do you shoplift?" They were allowed to list as many reasons as they believed applied to them, but were asked to be specific about the "main reason you shop-

lift." Many subjects reported more than one motive for their behavior. Table 1 illustrates the range of responses reported by the study subjects:

Table 1

Reported Motivations for Shoplifting
N = 320

Primary Motivation	N	Percent
1. Wanted item but did not want to pay for it.	82	25.6
2. Peer pressure.	49	15.3
3. Steal for a living.	46	14.4
4. Wanted the item but could not afford it.	41	12.8
5. I don't know why? It was an impulse thing.	37	11.6
6. I was under the influence of drugs or alcohol.	17	5.3
7. I enjoy the thrill/rush/the danger involved.	15	4.7
8. I was under a lot of stress.	13	4.1
9. I can't help myself. It's compulsive.	10	3.1
10. Other.	10	3.1
Total	**320**	**100**

It was difficult to determine the *primary* motivation driving the shoplifting activity for most of the informants, as they shoplifted for different reasons at different times. Many reported multiple reasons for single shoplifting events. For example, one Wichita subject stated, "I wanted it. It's kinda of a rush to take things, and I was mad at my mother at the time." When a subject expressed difficulty listing a primary motivation, the first motivation mentioned was considered primary. In the example above, the primary motive was recorded as "I wanted it." The subject was then asked if he had the money to pay for the item. If he or she said "yes," the motive was classified as "I wanted the item but did not want to pay for it." If he or she said "no," the motive was classified as "I wanted the item but could not afford to pay for it."

A Miami student reported, "My girlfriend dared me to do it. It was real exciting—I was pumped." In this case, the motive was recorded as "peer pressure."

This finding of within-individual variation in motivation may be important, as most of the literature in criminal decision making suggests a single, stable criminal calculus. However, it appears that many of the subjects in this study shoplifted for economic gain on some occasions and to satisfy some psychosocial need on others. Occasionally, the two motives were intertwined in a single offense.

In the following section each of the identified motives for shoplifting and representative statements by study subjects are presented.

'I Wanted the Items(s) but Didn't Want to Pay for It'

Eighty-two subjects listed this motive as primary. These shoplifters admitted to having the money to pay for the items they stole, but preferred to steal them anyway. Over 60 percent (64.6%) of males and only 47.5 percent of females reported this motivation as their primary reason for shoplifting. Many of these subjects also reported stealing for the thrill or rush, by impulse, or for some other "noneconomic" reason on occasion. White respondents (42.6%) were more likely than black respondents (24.4%) or Hispanics (32.9%) to report this motivation. Some examples of their responses include:

> I did it because I didn't want to pay for anything. I've got better things to do with my money. (Wichita: 18-year-old white male)

> I have a long shoplifting history. There are a lot of expensive things and I want them. (Miami student: 22-year-old white female)

> I got two kids I gotta raise and I don't get no help from that shit of an ex-husband of mine. They like nice things and it makes me feel good seeing them dressed nice to go to school. It ain't hard to take stuff. I just take what I want, anytime I want it. I've got three televisions and three VCRs in my house. I took 'em all from Wal Mart. . . . I once went a whole year without washing clothes. Just threw them in the basement when they was dirty and "went shopping" for some more. (Wichita: 29-year-old black female)

> I've got better things to spend my money on. Some things you can't lift—movie tickets, a Big Mac, gas, stuff like that—everything that I can lift, I do. (Miami student: 23-year-old black male)

'It Was Peer Pressure'

Forty-nine (49) subjects reported peer pressure as the primary motivation for their

shoplifting. Peer pressure—the second most cited motive in the present study—may be a highly rational motive for behavior as perceived by the offender. Approval from peers is one of the most powerful motivators of youthful behavior. Robert Agnew writes, "This pressure might be direct, with respondents reporting that their friends explicitly encouraged them to commit the delinquent act. This pressure might also be indirect, with respondents stating that they were trying to impress their friends or simply act in conformity with them" (Agnew, 1990: 279).

Two-thirds of all the subjects reported shoplifting because of peer influences at one time or another in their life. However, only those subjects who were in the early stages of a shoplifting career or those who had shoplifted only a few times reported peer influence as the primary motivation for their current behavior. White respondents were three to four times more likely to report peer pressure as their main motive. Males were somewhat more likely than females to report peer pressure as a motive for their behavior. Many of the professional thieves reported shoplifting due to peer influence, but they seemed to be referring to their early experiences. Twenty-two Miami students (15 male and 7 female) and 27 Wichita informants (20 male and 7 female) listed peer influence as the primary motivation of their behavior.

> My mom is a shoplifter. Both my sisters do it. I got it from them. My oldest sister said, "Don't be stupid. Take what you want." (Wichita: 20-year-old black female)

> I started out learning from my cousins. They always stole candy from the [neighborhood store]. They let me go with them but at first I just was the lookout—watching if the manager was looking. If he looked at them, I dropped a can or a box on the floor and he looked at me and they knew he was watching. (Wichita: 38-year-old Hispanic male)

> My mother taught me. Ever since I was a baby she used me to hide stuff. She'd push me in my stroller and put things under my blanket. After I got older she would give me stuff to walk out of the store with. Nobody paid any attention to a little kid. (Wichita: 25-year-old white female)

I never stole anything in my life until I changed schools in the seventh grade. These girls had a sorority and to get in you had to shoplift something. They would tell you what to take. . . . I had to get a pair of earrings from a Woolworth store. Red ones. It was too easy. I still do it sometimes. (Miami student: 22-year-old white female)

In some cases, need or greed supplied the primary motive, but peer pressure facilitated the actual offense. One Wichita subject stated:

I had been wanting this CD and my friend started egging me on to steal it. I was afraid I'd get caught and stuff, but he just kept bugging me about it and finally I went in the store and put in down my pants and just walked out. It set off the alarm by the door and I just ran out. Now I can't ever go back in there 'cause they know what I look like. (Wichita: 19-year-old female)

'I Steal for a Living'

These subjects shoplifted for resale and much of their income was derived from shoplifting. Most, but not all, were or had been drug addicts with daily habits which ranged from $50 to $500. They engaged in a range of legal and illegal activities to support their habits. Most preferred shoplifting to other criminal activity because of the ease of committing the crime and the minimal sanctions associated with apprehension and conviction. Twenty of the Texas subjects (18 males and 2 females), 22 of the Miami drug clinic informants (21 males and 1 female), and four of the Wichita subjects (1 male and 3 females) were so categorized. In every case, these subjects looked on their shoplifting as "work." One subject in Wichita told the interviewer, "I'm a self-employed thief." Typical responses included:

I changed from doing houses [burglary] to boosting cause it was getting too hot for me in Odessa. I couldn't go out of the house without being dragged down for some burglary I didn't commit. I've been down to TDC [Texas Department of Corrections] two times already and I could get the "bitch" next time [life imprisonment as a habitual criminal] so I went to boosting. It's a misdemeanor. Oughta have changed

years ago. Boosting is easy and safer. [Y]ou steal a TV from a house and maybe you get $50 for it. I got a 19-inch Magnavox at Walmart last week and sold it for half the sticker price. (Texas: 47-year-old Hispanic male)

I make more than you do [referring to the writer] just stealing from stores. Yesterday I rolled up six silk dresses inside my shirt and walked out of Dillards [an upscale department store in Ft. Lauderdale]. They was worth over $1000 and I sold 'em for $300. That was 30 minutes' work. (Miami drug clinic: 39-year-old white female)

I'm the Prince of Thieves. Everybody in my family are crooks. My father is a shoplifter. My mother is a shoplifter. My sister is a shoplifter. I'm sure my son will probably be a shoplifter, too. I can't imagine making a living any other way. I'm proud of what I do and I'm proud that I've only been caught once—after over 20 years. (Wichita: 40-year-old white male)

I don't boost every day. Sometimes not even every week. My girlfriend and I go out whenever we need some money and spend the whole day. We fill up big garbage bags full of stuff—clothes mostly. We make enough to live good for a week, two weeks. (Wichita: 28-year-old black female)

I gotta have $200 every day—day in and day out. I gotta boost a $1000, $1500 worth to get it. I just do what I gotta do. . . . Do I feel bad about what I do? Not really. If I wasn't boosting, I'd be robbing people and maybe somebody would get hurt or killed. (Miami drug addict: 28-year-old white male)

Taking stuff from stores is a lot easier than robbing people or burglary. Nobody ever shoots boosters. Even if I get caught, nothing much gonna happen. Probation—a few days in county. It's like it's my job. (Texas drug addict: 35-year-old black female)

'I Wanted the Item(s) and Could Not Afford It'

Another common response to the motivation question was "I wanted [the item] and didn't have enough money, so I lifted it." This motivation was reported much more often by women (80%) than by men. Some of the women who reported this motivation were single parents with few financial resources. However, the majority simply coveted some item they could not then afford to buy and took it. In many cases this was one of the motivations for their first shoplifting experience. Five Miami student respondents (0 males and 5 females) and 36 Wichita subjects (8 males and 28 females) listed this as their primary motive for shoplifting. Typical responses included:

> I want nice things for my family but I can't afford to buy them. My husband and kids have the best wardrobe in town. My husband doesn't know, but I don't know how he doesn't. Where does he think all this stuff comes from? He never asks. Course, he doesn't know how much anything costs. (Wichita: 39-year-old white female)

> My mom wouldn't buy me a pair of $30 jeans . . . so I took 'em. (Wichita: 18-year-old black female)

> I stole a wallet from Sears for my boyfriend. I didn't have the money so I took it. After that I became quite the klepto. If I saw something I wanted, I took it. . . . it's hard to raise three children without help and my ex hasn't paid a cent of child support. . . . I was willing to steal to give them things they needed. It's hard to see something you want and can't have it. (Wichita: 33-year-old white female)

> The first time I ever lifted anything, there was this CD I wanted real bad. I didn't have any money and me and my friend decided to steal it. We were scared to death, but it was easy. I've probably stolen $10,000 worth of stuff since. (Miami student: 22-year-old white female)

'I Don't Know Why. It Was Just an Impulse'

A few subjects expressed the belief that their acts were impulsive and done without thought or planning. Nine Miami college students (4 males and 5 females) and 28 Wichita subjects (10 males and 18 females) reported impulse as the primary motive for their shoplifting. Over one-half of all the subjects reported impulse as one of the motives for their first shoplifting experiences. Typical responses included:

> I want to say "spur of the moment." It was a watch and I just wanted that watch then. The amazing thing was that I had the money in my pocket to pay for it. . . . I wish I could say that I had been drinking, but I can't. (Wichita: 33-year-old black male)

> It was sort of an impulse. I didn't plan to do it. I'm really embarrassed by all this. (Wichita: 22-year-old white female)

> I didn't really plan on it. It just kinda happened. I've never stolen anything before. (Wichita student: 19-year-old white male)

> I've been doing it since I was in elementary school. [I] see something in a store and even if I don't need it, I just take it. I don't know why. I'm a klepto. (Miami student: 18-year-old Hispanic female)

> I've done this since I was eight. To me it comes natural. I don't know why I do it. I've done it so many times that I don't think about it. (Wichita: 18-year-old white male)

> I took a shirt at K-Mart. I don't understand why I did it. I have friends who take things, but I never did. I liked this shirt and on the spur of the moment I stuffed it in my purse. (Wichita: 19-year-old white female)

'I Was Under the Influence of Drugs or Alcohol'

Eleven of the subjects in the Wichita diversion sample (7 males and 4 females) and six in the Miami student sample (3 males and 3 females) reported shoplifting only when intoxicated or under the influence of drugs. Many stated that they never stole when sober and blamed the disinhibition of alcohol or drug use for their crimes. In fact, in most cases, they reported taking minor items such as beer, cigarettes, or candy. Subjects reported:

> I picked up a pack of cigarettes and put them into my pocket. I forgot I had them there. I'd been drinking most of the afternoon. (Wichita: 30-year-old white male)

> Drinking causes it. I should stop altogether. Makes me impulsive. That's when I take things. Usually I'm too drunk to be a good thief. (Wichita: 40-year-old black male)

Sometimes when everybody is drinking or smoking, we go down to the [shopping area] and pick up stuff. It doesn't seem bad then but sometimes I do feel guilty about it the next day. (Miami: 21-year-old white female)

When I'm drunk or stoned, it's like I'm invisible. No, it's like I'm Superman. I ain't scared of nothing. Nobody can touch me. It seems like that's what always gets me in trouble. I'll just walk in and take something and walk out. (Wichita: 37-year-old white male)

We were sitting around drinking. My roommate bet me I couldn't go across the street and steal a pack of cigarettes. (Miami: 20-year-old white male)

'I Enjoy the Thrill/Excitement/Rush/Danger'

Many informants viewed shoplifting as a challenge and a thrill. They enjoyed the risk taking and many discussed the "rush" they received from the act. Many of the subjects reported "excitement" or "rush" as one of the motivations for their illegal behavior, however, only 15 informants, six Miami students (6 males and 0 females) and nine Wichita subjects (7 males and 2 females), considered this motivation as primary.

I do it for the rush. Adrenaline rush, you know. You get all excited and you feel kinda crazy inside. I can't explain it. It's adrenaline. (Wichita: 25-year-old white male)

It's like an addiction. I like the feeling I get when I might get caught. Once you get in the car and you got away with it, it's like, wow, I did it. It's a buzz. An adrenaline buzz. I love that feeling—while I'm still in the store, my hear is pumping real loud and fast. It's so loud I know people can hear it. I'm really scared, but once I get away, I'm exhilarated. (Miami student: 21-year-old white female)

It is really fun. It got to be quite a lark doing it. It was an art and I was good at it. (Wichita: 44-year-old white male)

It's not hard. Actually, it's fun. It's fun when you get away with it. It's scary in the store. Heart pumping—adrenaline pumping. It's exciting. Addicting. (Wichita: 30-year-old white female)

It's a thrill—the excitement, danger. Fear. Dude, my heart pounded like a drum. Like it was gonna come out of my chest. It made me feel alive. (Miami: 20-year-old white male)

'I Can't Help Myself. It's Compulsive'

A small number of informants reported that their behavior was beyond their control. This category is differentiated from the "Impulse" category by the subjects' assertions that they could not seem to stop. Many argued that they were addicted to shoplifting. There was significant crossover between those who reported compulsive behavior and those who reported shoplifting for thrill and excitement. Seven Miami students (0 males and 7 females) and six Wichita subjects (2 males and 4 females) reported that they could not easily control their shoplifting behavior. Typical responses include:

I don't plan on stealing. I tell myself I'm not going to do it again and then I see something I want and I lift it. I already have it in my purse before I think about it. It's like, you know, automatic pilot. I'm addicted—that's all I know. (Miami student: 19-year-old white female)

I'm a kleptomanic. I steal anything I can get in my purse. The other day I stole a key chain—can you believe it? Took a chance on going to jail with a stupid key chain. (Wichita: 35-year-old white female)

Shoplifting is an addiction for me. It built up over time. I tried seeing a counselor but it didn't help. Didn't stop me. (Wichita: 44-year-old black male)

'I Was Under a Lot of Stress'

A small number of subjects reported shoplifting as a response to stressful life situations. Five Wichita (2 male and 3 females) and five Miami students (0 males and 5 females) listed stress as the primary factor in their shoplifting behavior. Typical responses included:

I was worried about my ex-wife back in New York. She was being evicted from her apartment. I also didn't get a promotion I thought I was going to get. (Wichita: 46-year-old black male)

I was working long hours and not getting along with my wife and we had a lot of bills and some sickness. I don't know what happened to me. Next thing I know I'm stealing things. Books from Barnes and Nobles, cigarettes, meat from [grocery store]. (Wichita: 40-year-old white male)

I used to shoplift before I got married. Then I stopped. . . . The divorce started me up again. It gave me something to think about, I guess. I think maybe I wanted to get caught, but I didn't for a long time. (Wichita: 35-year-old white female)

I get depressed. Things start to pile up and I start shoplifting. Sometimes it's at finals [final exams] or when I have a fight with my boyfriend. One time when I thought I was pregnant. Who knows why. It's like I take out my feelings on them [the stores]. (Miami student: 24-year-old white female)

Other Responses

Other responses not mentioned often enough to rate a separate category included: "It was so easy" (n=1), "I had a fight with my husband and I wanted to embarrass him" (n=1), "I hate my boss. When he gives me shit about something, I give myself a little reward" (n=1), "I needed some condoms and was too embarrassed to take them to the check-out" (n=2), and "the check-out line was too long and I didn't want to wait" (n=5). Six Wichita respondents (3 males and 3 females) and four Miami students (2 males and 2 females) listed these motives.

Conclusions and Discussion

It is obvious, now, that to speak of shoplifting as having a simple causal dynamic is to misunderstand the diversity and complexity of the behavior. When asked "Why do you shoplift?" the 320 shoplifters in this study revealed motivations that ranged from purely economic to apparent manifestations of emotional maladjustment. Most of the subjects reported that they shoplifted for some economic benefit. These subjects chose to steal as a means of satisfying their material needs and desires. Others satisfied some emotional need by their shoplifting activity. Still others sought to avoid some unpleasant or painful encounter or activity. These behaviors—satisfying economic or emotional needs—may be seen as highly utilitarian and rational. Moti-

vations in these categories included (1) wanting the item but not being able to afford it, (2) wanting the item but not wanting to pay for it, (3) pressure from peers, (4) stealing for a living, and (5) feelings of thrill, rush, or danger. A small number of subjects reported that they stole to avoid embarrassment of paying for condoms, to avoid long lines at the check-out station, to embarrass a spouse or parent, or to exact revenge on an employer or store where they perceived they had been mistreated.

Of critical importance, however, was the finding that people who shoplift steal for different reasons at different times. In the 115 cases more extensively interviewed, there were few individuals who reported a single, stable criminal calculus. An otherwise "rational" shoplifter might occasionally act impulsively, stealing some item for which he or she had no need or purpose. The informants often expressed bewilderment over their motives in such cases. Of course, it is recognized that subjects may not have good insight into their own behavior or motives. Subjects may have reported their motive as "impulse" or "compulsive" because they could not articulate the dynamics of their behavior. Others may have reported stealing because of the disinhibition brought on by drugs or alcohol as a rationalization for behavior which they could not otherwise justify.

This points out the situational nature of offending. The motivation to shoplift is closely tied to the offenders' current circumstances. In most instances offenders perceive the act as a means of satisfying some need. The "need" may be for cash, for some item(s) they wish to obtain for their personal use, or to satisfy some psychosocial need, such as revenge, self-esteem, peer approval, or for thrill and excitement. However, the same individuals might also commit offenses without a clear motive. Several informants reported that they simply went along with friends who decided to shoplift during an otherwise legitimate shopping excursion. They joined in for no reason other than, as one informant said, "It seemed like a good idea at the time." Crozier and Friedberg (1977) argued that people seldom have clear objectives. They do not know exactly where they are going or what they want. Maurice Cusson (1983) notes that to imagine that people carry out only projects that are conceived in advance and act in terms that are clearly foreseen is "sheer idealism" (p. 19). A shoplifter may drift into crime on one day, following the lead of a friend or acquaintance, while on another occasion he or she may utilize a more thoughtful planning strategy before committing a crime. Wright and Decker (1994) argued that this type of offending is not the result of a thoughtful decision strategy, but rather "emerges out of the natural flow of events, seemingly coming out of nowhere" (p. 40). They conclude:

> [i]t is not so much that these actors consciously choose to commit crime, as they elect to get involved in situations that drive them toward lawbreaking. (p. 40)

Some "otherwise rational" shoplifters reported that they occasionally took an item, not out of need or because they wanted it, but because they could do so without being observed. In these cases, the relative lack of risk appeared to be the major factor in the offenders' calculus. They were individuals with a "readiness" to commit offenses if the circumstances were favorable, and they did so even when they had no specific need for the items taken. Like the proverbial mountain that was climbed "because it was there," these shoplifters stole because they could.

Approximately 20 percent (n=60) informants reported occasionally committing offenses for what appeared to be nonrational motives. These included shoplifting as a response to stress, as a result of compulsion, or impulse. Women were more than twice as likely to report a nonrational motive than men. Of the 60 individuals who reported a nonrational motive for their shoplifting, 42 were women. Such shoplifters often asserted that they did not know why they committed their acts or that they did not understand their own behavior. The behavior was seldom obviously goal-oriented and it frequently did not have a significant acquisitive element. Many of these shoplifters took small, inexpensive items such as candy, cigarettes, and nonsensical items like keychains or small toys for which they had no use. However, upon closer examination, we found that all of these individuals recognized that they had a tendency to "compulsively" or "impulsively" shoplift, and yet they consciously entered places of business for that very purpose. Others appeared to attribute their shoplifting to forces over which they had no control as a means of maintaining their sense of self-worth or to impress the interviewer with their "basic goodness." One informant summed it up stating, "I'm basically a good person. Sometimes I lift things and when it's over, I can't even tell you why. It's not like me at all."

These findings are important because they call attention to a wider range of behaviors and motives associated with shoplifting than have previous studies, which depended upon limited samples or on data developed through criminal justice sources. They also suggest the need for further systematic research with both apprehended and nonapprehended shoplifter populations.

Implications for Prevention Strategies

The study suggests that shoplifting is not simple behavior with simple motives. Shoplifting is more complex than previously thought and the motives of shoplifters, while not stable, are more rational than those noted in some previous research. These findings, if borne out by further research, have policy implications both for law enforcement and for businesses.

If a substantial proportion of shoplifters are compulsive and nonrational, policies based on deterrence have little impact. They do not calculate the risks and gains, but rather steal without "reason." However, if shoplifting is perceived as rational behavior, then deterrence-based policies may be effective. The existence of a strong deterrent effect does not require that the individual be fully informed or fully rational in their decisions. The deterrence argument holds that an increase in the probability or severity of punishment for a particular crime will reduce the rate at which that crime is committed, other things being equal (Cook, 1989: 51). This suggests that arrest and prosecution for shoplifting might reduce its incidence. However, during the course of this study we discussed store policy regarding shoplifting with store mangers and loss-control personnel. A substantial number of these individuals reported that they prosecuted few shoplifters because of fear of lawsuits by those arrested or belief that penalties for the offense were so minor compared to the time and effort required for the store to carry out the prosecution as to render prosecution not worthwhile. Others reported that their loss-control technology or manpower was too limited to provide the evidence needed to prosecute suspected shoplifters. In many of these stores, suspected shoplifters were detained briefly, the stolen items recovered, and the thieves warned not to return to the store under threat of prosecution.

Interviews revealed that shoplifters are easily deterred if the threat of apprehension is obvious. Their perceptions of the risks involved at a particular store were gained from their own experiences and those of friends and acquaintances. They said that when a store had a reputation for arresting and prosecuting shoplifters, they tended to give it a wide berth. They also reported that once in a store, if they were being overtly watched by clerks or loss-prevention staff, they left the store immediately. These findings have several implications for loss control.

First, effective shoplifting control requires visible and obvious threat communication. Stores should post signs stating their policies regarding shoplifting. Clarke (1992) has shown that "rule setting" has a significant effect on behavior. Where the rules are clearly and openly established and stated, people tend to adhere to them. Where the rules are ambiguous or unclear, there is less adherence.

Second, shoplifting can be effectively reduced by strategic siting of store clerks' work stations, proper layout of display counters, check-out areas and dressing rooms. Stores which pile merchandise high, crowd aisles, and do not maintain adequate sight line between aisles and check-out stations may expect higher rates of shoplifting. Unattended dressing rooms and inattentive clerks also facilitate theft. Some small but expensive items, such as cigarettes, batteries, and razor blades should be placed in locked display cabinets or immediately under the watchful eyes of clerks. Clerks should be trained in shoplifting prevention and incentives should be established to encourage attentiveness. Closed-circuit television, strategically placed mirrors, and merchandise tagging, bar-coding, and "electronic point of sales" systems also play a major role in theft reduction.

Third, if store personnel openly and overtly observed suspected shoplifters, following them about the store, most of them would leave without committing an offense. However, there is little glory or credit given to employees who "scare off" potential thieves. Most store security personnel prefer to apprehend suspected shoplifters and will thus observe them covertly, waiting for a theft to occur before revealing themselves. This course of action results in lost time spent processing the shoplifter in the store, taking statements, calling the police, if warranted by the evidence and store policy, and subsequently testifying in court if necessary.

Fourth, if store policy demands that the shoplifter be apprehended, then the store should be committed to carrying out the prosecution to the end. If word gets out in the shoplifter population (and it will) that a store releases apprehended shoplifters with a warning, or does not follow up with charges and court appearances by its staff, shoplifters will not weigh risk too heavily in their risk-gain calculus. That store will become a favorite for shoplifters.

Finally, police, prosecutors, and courts must agree to aggressively prosecute shoplifting. If shoplifters find that they are rarely arrested, unlikely to be convicted if arrested, and unlikely to receive a substantial punishment if convicted, then they may justifiably begin to believe that they are free to commit their offenses at will.

Policies, once established and communicated to the public, should be carried out faithfully. If the policy is to prosecute "to the fullest extent of the law," as the anti-shoplifting signs often threaten, then stores should follow through on the promise. These actions reverberate throughout the shoplifter population and should quickly pay dividends in reduced levels of theft.

These conclusions suggest that most shoplifters can be deterred. Their behavior, while not rational in the Benthamite sense, has a rational component in most cases.

References

Abelson, Elaine S. (1989) The Invention of Kleptomania. *Journal of Women in Culture and Society* 15 (1).

Agnew, Robert (1990) The Origins of Delinquent Events: An Examination of Offender Accounts. *Journal of Research in Crime and Delinquency* 27(3) 267-294.

Akers, Ronald L. (1985) *Deviant Behavior: A Social Learning Approach* (Belmont, CA: Wadsworth).

Arboleda-Florez, J., Helen Durie, and John Costello (1977) Shoplifting—An Ordinary Crime. *Journal of Offender Therapy and Comparative Criminology* 21(3) 201-207.

Beck, E .A. and S.C. McEntyre (1977) MMPI Patterns of Shoplifters within a College Population. *Psychological Reports* 41, 1035-1040.

Brantingham, Paul J. and Patricia L. Brantingham (1991) *Environmental Criminology* (Prospect Heights, IL: Waveland Press).

Brantingham, Patricia L. and Paul J. Brantingham (1993) Environment, Routine, and Situation: Toward a Pattern Theory of Crime. In Ronald V. Clarke and Marcus Felson (Eds.) *Routine Activity and Rational Choice* (New Brunswick, NJ: Transaction Publishers).

Cameron, Mary (1964) *The Booster and the Snitch* (New York: The Free Press).

Carroll, John and Frances Weaver (1986) Shoplifters' Perceptions of Crime Opportunities: A Process Tracing Study. In Derek B. Cornish and Ronald V. Clarke (Eds.) *The Reasoning Criminal: Rational Choice Perspectives on Offending* (New York: Springer-Verlag).

Clarke, Ronald V. (Ed.) (1992) *Situational Crime Prevention: Successful Case Studies* (New York: Harrow and Heston).

Clarke, Ronald V. and Derek Cornish (1986) *The Reasoning Criminal: Rational Choice Perspectives on Offending* (New York: Springer-Verlag).

Cook, Philip J. (1989) in M.L.Friedland (Ed.) *Sanctions and Rewards in the Legal System: A Multidisciplinary Approach* (Toronto: University of Toronto Press).

Cressy, Donald R. (1954) The Differential Association Theory and Compulsive Crimes. *Journal of Criminal Law, Criminology and Police Science* 45: 29-40.

Cromwell, Paul, James N. Olson, and D. W. Avary (1991) *Breaking and Entering: An Ethnographic Analysis of Burglary.* (Beverly Hills: Sage).

Crozier, M. and E. Friedberg (1977) *L'Acteur et le systeme* (Paris: Le Seuil). Cited in Cusson (1983).

Cusson, Maurice (1983) *Why Delinquency?* (Toronto: University of Toronto Press).

Fear, R.W.G. (1974) An Analysis of Shoplifting. *Security Gazette* (July): 262-263.

Feinburg, Gary (1984) Profile of the Elderly Offender. In Evelyn Newman, Donald J. Newman and Mindy Gerwitz (Eds.) *Elderly Criminals* (Cambridge, MA: Oelgeshlager, Gunn and Hain).

Freeh, Louis (1996) *Crime in the United States—1995* (Washington, DC: U.S. Department of Justice).

Griffin, R.K. (1970) Shoplifting: A Statistical Survey. *Security World* 7, Part 10: 21-25.

—— (1971) Behavioral Patterns in Shoplifting. *Security World* 10, Part 2: 21-25.

Griffin, Roger (1988) *Annual Report: Shoplifting in Supermarkets* (Van Nuys, CA; Commercial Service Systems).

Hindelang, Michael, Travis Hirschi, and Joseph Weis (1981) *Measuring Delinquency* (Beverly Hills: Sage).

Hirschi, Travis (1986) On the Compatibility of Rational Choice and Social Control Theories. In Derek R. Cornish and Ronald V. Clarke (Eds.) *The Reasoning Criminal: Rational Choice Perspectives on Offending* (New York: Springer-Verlag).

Johnston, Lloyd D., Jerald G. O'Malley, and Patrick M. O'Malley (1984–1995) *Monitoring the Future* (Ann Arbor, MI: Institute for Social Research, University of Michigan). Data adapted by and cite from Bureau of Justice Statistics (1997). *Sourcebook of Criminal Justice Statistics—1996* (Washington, D.C.: United States Department of Justice).

Kahneman, D., P. Slovic and A. Tversky (Eds.) *Judgement Under Uncertainty: Heuristics and Biases* (New York: Cambridge University Press).

Karpman, Benjamin (1949) Criminality, Insanity and the Law. *Journal of Criminal Law and Criminology* 39: 584-605.

Katz, Jack (1988) *The Seductions of Crime* (New York: Basic Books).

Klemke, Lloyd W. (1992) *The Sociology of Shoplifting: Boosters and Snitches Today* (Westport, CT: Praeger).

—— (1982) Exploring Juvenile Shoplifting. *Sociology and Social Research* 67: 59-75.

Kraut, Robert (1976) Deterrent and Definitional Influences on Shoplifting. *Social Problems* 25 (February) 358-68.

Lo, Lucia (1994) Exploring Teenage Shoplifting Behavior. *Environment and Behavior* 26(5): 613-639.

March, James G. (1994) *A Primer on Decision Making: How Decisions Happen* (New York: Free Press).

Moore, Richard (1983) College Shoplifters: Rebuttal of Beck and McIntyre. *Psychological Reports* 53, 1111-1116.

—— (1984) Shoplifting in Middle America: Patterns and Motivational Correlates. *International Journal of Offender Therapy and Comparative Criminology* 28(1): 53-64.

Newell, A. and H.A. Simon (1972) *Human Problem Solving* (Englewood Cliff, NJ: Prentice-Hall).

Nimick, Ellen (November, 1990) Juvenile Court Property Cases. *OJJDP Update on Statistics*. (Washington, D.C.: United States Department of Justice) 1-5.

O'Brien, Patricia (1983) Bourgeois Women and Theft. *Journal of Social History* 17 (Fall) 65-77.

Ordway, J. (1962) "Successful" Court Treatment of Shoplifters. *Journal of Criminal Law, Criminology and Police Science* 8 27-29.

Osgood, Wayne D., Patrick M. O'Malley, Gerald G. Bachman, and Lloyd D. Johnston (1989) Time Trends and Age Trends in Arrests and Self-Reported Behavior. *Criminology* 27(3): 389-415.

Robin, Gerald D. (1963). Patterns of Department Store Shoplifting. *Crime and Delinquency* 9 (April): 163-72.

Russell, D.H. (1973) Emotional Aspects of Shoplifting. *Psychiatric Annals* 3: 77-79.

Schlueter, Gregory R., Francis C. O'Neal, JoAnn Hickey, and Gloria Seiler (1989) Rational and Nonrational Shoplifter Types. *International Journal of Offender Therapy and Comparative Criminology* 33 (3): 227-238.

Solomon, G. S. and J. B. Ray (1984) Irrational Beliefs of Shoplifters. *Journal of Clinical Psychology*, 40 (4).

Turner, C. T. and S. Cashdan (1988) Perceptions of College Students Motivations for Shoplifting. *Psychological Reports* 62: 855-862.

Vold, George and Thomas Bernard (1986) *Theoretical Criminology* (New York: Oxford University Press).

Warr, Mark (1989) What is the Perceived Seriousness of Crimes? *Criminology* 27(4): 801.

Wilson, James Q. and Richard J. Herrnstein (1985) *Crime and Human Nature* (New York: Simon and Schuster).

Won, G. and G. Yamamoto (1968) Social Structure and Deviant Behavior: A Study of Shoplifting. *Sociology and Social Research* 53, Part 1: 45-55.

7

The Thrill of It All: Youthful Offenders and Auto Theft

Zachary Fleming

For *this study, originally prepared for the Insurance Corporation of British Columbia, Canada, Zach Fleming interviewed 31 incarcerated youthful offenders, each of whom had a history of auto theft. Most of the subjects could be described as multiple-offense, persistent, frequent offenders. Using a semi-structured format, the author interviewed each youth for about one and one-half hours. The subjects were queried about their family characteristics, employment history, school involvement, recreational activities, friends, involvement in auto theft, knowledge of the techniques of auto theft, and perceptions of the deterrent effect of the criminal justice system. Fleming found that in contrast to professional criminals who stole for economic gain, the young offenders in his sample stole automobiles primarily for recreational purposes and occasionally for transportation. His subjects expressed disdain for the square lifestyle, preferring instead a "fast lane" approach to life (Also see Shover and Honaker, and Malin Åkerström in this volume). These youngsters appeared to have a good understanding of the workings of the criminal justice system and recognized that as juveniles they could expect few serious consequences from their criminal behavior. Similar to the findings of other studies concerning the lifestyles of persistent property offenders (Cromwell et al., 1991; Shover and Honaker, 1996), many in this sample described patterns of offending as extensions of social activities with drinking and drug use at* the core. Fleming's findings suggest that thrill and excitement may be as rational a goal as economic gain, especially for youth.

In contrast to decade-long national trends in both the US and Canada which have seen auto theft levels rise and fall with other property crimes, the incidence of auto theft in the Canadian province of British Columbia increased over 200% during the past decade, outpacing the passenger vehicle fleet growth by a factor of 20, and greatly outdistancing the growth rates of other property crimes. Much of this increase came in two pronounced spurts. The first saw annual theft counts double between 1987 and 1991 before leveling off. Then in early 1995, monthly auto theft counts began a meteoric rise ending with an unprecedented 74% increase within a 12-month period before again leveling off.

In response to the first rapid increase in auto theft, authorities undertook a province-wide study intended to triangulate information about offenders, victims, and vehicle characteristics, the auto theft event, and the justice system's response to the problem. These areas of interest were explored using multiple methods and data sources, including an examination of auto theft claims reported to one of the study's participants, the Insurance Corporation of British Columbia, which provides comprehensive automobile insurance coverage to three-quarters of the two million passenger vehicles licensed in the province. The availability of a very large sample of auto theft insurance claims information proved invaluable in the efforts to profile the nature of the auto theft problem.

Auto Theft Motivations

Because the kinds of policies one would pursue to reduce the incidence of organized professional car theft differ significantly from those undertaken to thwart thrill-seeking youth, useful policy hinges on accurately profiling the nature of the auto theft problem in a given jurisdiction. Challinger's (1987) tripartite division of auto theft motivation adequately describes the sources of motivation uncovered in British Columbia:

I. *Profit motives*—including thefts for re-sale, chopping, stripping, and/or fraud;

II. *Transportation motives*—temporary appropriation for short-term or extended use, including use in the commission of other crimes; and

III. *Recreation motives*—temporary appropriation of automobiles for thrill and status-seeking by young persons (e.g., "joyriding).

It is commonly believed that profit motives drive more or less organized, adult, "professional" offenders; recreation motives characterize disorganized juvenile offenders; and transportation motives underlie both juveniles and adults. Stolen automobiles not recovered or those recovered minus a significant percentage of their parts are thought to have been stolen because of the profit motive. Stolen autos that are recovered either intact, damaged, or vandalized are usually thought to have been stolen for recreation or out of need for temporary transportation.

During the past decade, 90–95% of all passenger vehicles stolen in British Columbia have been recovered. This high recovery rate existed even during periods when annual auto theft frequency counts increased greatly. Even among the small portion going unrecovered, very few have been the kinds of vehicles associated with professional auto thieves (e.g., late-year model German imports like BMW, Mercedes Benz, or Porsche; high-end luxury models such as Jaguar, Lexus, or Infiniti; or expensive sport utility models such as Toyota Landcruiser). Other analyses of auto theft insurance claims filed in recent years found that the vast majority of part replacement costs (other than door and ignition lock assemblies) stemmed from damage to vehicle body parts as opposed to systematic part stripping associated with organized offenders. Insurance data thus tend to point the finger at youth as the source of the rapid increase in auto theft.

In the late 1980s, police in British Columbia began seeing a growing number of stolen vehicles being intentionally damaged by new forms of reckless joyriding. Teenagers began stealing cars not merely to get to "bush" parties held in remote locations, but also for the expressed purpose of "trashing" them to entertain other partygoers. Police began to recover groups of totaled automobiles stolen to use in impromptu demolition derbies. By all accounts, auto stealing in British Columbia was becoming more thrill-focused.

The purpose of this study was to determine the motives and strategies underlying theft of automobiles by youthful offenders and to discover their perceptions of the deterrent effect of the criminal justice sanction.

Findings

Rational choice perspectives argue for analytical distinctions between *criminal involvement* which entails long-term, multistaged decision making processes concerning initial involvement, continuance, and desistance in crime, and *criminal event* decisions which involve shorter processes in response to immediate circumstances and situations (Cornish and Clarke, 1986). In an effort to put their criminal event decisions in context, I begin with a look at how these young repeat offenders described their lives.

Frequent Offenders' Lives in Context

The average age of offenders in the sample was 16. About a quarter of the sample had no siblings; and one-third lived in female-headed households. Ten percent indicated that their mothers stayed at home as full-time housemothers. About half of the sample described their family's financial situation as "comfortable" or "stable"; another 10% said they were "well-off" or "wealthy"; the reminder described their family as "poor." Most of the offenders indicated that their parents are employed in blue-collar occupations, and many described varied and sporadic work histories for both their mothers and fathers. A quarter of the sample indicated that their fathers had been unemployed at least once in the last three years, a fifth had been unemployed two or more times during that period. Frequent house moves are also a common characteristic of the sample—more than 60% had moved six or more times since birth.

Slightly more than half said they got along with their parents most of the time, and indicated that they liked living at home. Most were expected to do some household chores. About half said they had curfews on both weeknights and weekends, but most did not abide by those curfews. About a third described the rules at home as "strict." Most receive some type of punishment for breaking household rules; a third said they are routinely subject to beatings with closed fists and/or being kicked or struck with belts or other hard objects. Most respondents indicated they leave the house when "grounded" by their parents.

While nearly all the respondents said they plan to finish high school, most voiced low levels of interest in school achievement and involvement in school-sponsored activities like sports and clubs (even amongst the 25% who said they plan to attend college/university). On average, respondents skipped school nine days a month. The vast majority said they disliked school and their teachers. About half thought their teachers disliked them personally; however, this did not appear to adversely affect their self-esteem: three quarters of the respondents said their peers look up to them for advice (albeit, often times for criminal advice), and almost 40% believed they were more knowledgeable than their peers about things in general.

Almost half of the sample thought they would have it "easier" or "about the same" as their parent's generation; and many planned to begin working full-time in a semi-skilled job directly after high-school. Most believed their financial prospects are good even with little or no post-secondary education. When asked how old they thought they would be when they could afford to purchase their first home, the majority thought they would do so before age 26, at an anticipated median cost of $250,000; however, few could say from where the down payments for these quarter-million-dollar homes would come, save a few "jokes" about financing via a crime spree. It is of course possible that these kids did hold more fatalistic views but chose not to share them with the interviewer.

Lifestyle and Routine Activities

Ethnographic research on offender lifestyles has identified their involvement in crime as a means to obtain money in order to fulfill largely expressive needs (Rengert and Wasilchick, 1985; Clarke and Cornish, 1985; Cromwell et al., 1991; Shover and Honaker, 1996; Shover, 1996). The desire to live "life in the fast lane" was likewise true for many in this sample. Due to their ages, most of the respondents had few job experiences. More than half of the sample reported having no legitimate source of income, yet the reported average figure for reported monthly spending was roughly $1,750 (arrived at through itemizing weekly spending habits). Several offenders described spending sprees in the wake of obtaining money from crime in order to impress friends and show them a good time. Describing a three-day road trip where he put a group of friends up at an expensive hotel and took them all to an amusement park, a 17-year-old remarked:

> I probably spent about $5000, but it was worth it . . . easy come easy go. We partied hardy. That's the kind of stuff memories are made of.

Many expressed their disdain for the opposite of the fast life, the dullness of ordinary, unskilled work, what one subject referred to as being a "ham and egger :

> I worked as a busboy for a week once. It was like being a pig in everyone else's slop. Why should I put up with that shit? . . . Doing crime [referring to a smash and grab where he ran a truck through the front window of a Safeway store in order steal cigarettes] is a lot more fun and pays a lot better. (17-year-old)

Similar to the findings of other studies concerning the lifestyles of persistent property offenders (Cromwell et al., 1991; Shover and Honaker, 1996) many in this sample described patterns of offending as extensions to social activities with drinking and psychoactive drug use at the core. The most prevalent "recreational" activity reported by offenders was "hanging-out" with friends, and using drugs and alcohol. Fifty-five percent of the respondents said they used hallucinogens at least once a month; 23% said they did so between 12 and 20 times a month. Fifty-eight percent said they drank to intoxication at least twice a week; 20% did so five times a week. This latter 20% may well be on their way to severe adult drinking problems. On average, respondents used cocaine five times a month and marijuana almost daily. The majority of respondents indicated that they were motivated to steal cars when they were high on drugs and alcohol.

Most of those interviewed said they spend a considerable amount of time hanging around shopping malls. A few were cognizant of the effect frequent exposure to consumer goods played in motivating them to commit crime. Said one 14-year-old:

> I go to the mall almost every day and see stuff I want to buy. I do crime in order to buy nice stuff.

Auto Theft Involvement

It is likely true of most jurisdictions that the bulk of auto stealing can be attributed to transportation and recreation motives. Some portion of transportation motives involve the use of stolen vehicles for the anonymity they provide when doing other crime; however, this would probably account for a lesser proportion than the perceived need to steal a car simply to get somewhere. For the most part, auto theft appears by and large to be a crime against the property rights of others in the sense of unauthorized use.

Where youth are involved, motives for auto stealing are largely affective, and the heightened sense of risk-taking among today's youth has served to enlarge thrill- and status-seeking motives. The past decade has witnessed the cultivation of a daredevil ethic now rooted in popular culture and much of youth-focused product advertising. This growing desire to feel the "rush" of fear-induced adrenaline appears to have been the major driving force behind the massive increase in auto stealing in British Columbia.

Most in the sample described their auto stealing as thrill-seeking behavior from which they derive an "adrenaline rush" unmatched by legitimate thrill activities like skiing or snow boarding. "I got hooked on the thrill," said one 16-year-old reflecting on his commitment to auto theft. Seventy-one percent of the sample described themselves as thrill-seekers. The appeal of auto theft in this respect was threefold: (1) driving fast and recklessly; (2) the prospect of getting into a police pursuit; and (3) the prospect of getting caught. For many in the sample, thrill and status seeking were intertwined:

> I like to shock people, intimidate them, make them back down. We used to play tag with stolen cars and my friends couldn't believe the things I would do. (17-year-old)

> I like crime. I like to get in police chases. I do crimes for the adrenaline rush. Car theft, B&E, smash and grab, whatever. (15-year-old)

> Me and two other friends competed with two others for the number we could steal in a week. (15-year-old)

Offenders with varying involvement in auto theft were interviewed. The most prolific in the sample claimed to have stolen hundreds of cars in recent years; the least active offender said he took three in his life. For the most part, differences in the level of auto theft involvement among offenders living in different regions of the province appear to be a function of urban versus rural living. The lack of anonymity perceived by youth in small towns appears to be a significant deterrent. All of the low-involvement offenders in this sample lived in small towns in the Interior or Northern regions of the province. The auto stealing they described was very opportunistic: they took vehicles left running in driveways on cold winter mornings. These offenders were inhibited both by a limited local street network and by the perceived likelihood of being caught if they drove the stolen car through towns where residents know each others' vehicles.

Juvenile Auto Thief Typologies

Of course each interviewed offender was uniquely motivated to steal automobiles; however, many described themselves and their motivations in ways that made it possible to draw some generalizations. What follows are profiles for the three most evident auto stealing personalities encountered in the interviews with young offenders:

Acting out joyrider

- most emotionally disturbed of the offenders interviewed—likes to convince his peers he's crazy

- engages in outrageous driving stunts—dangerous to pursue
- vents anger via car—responsible for large proportion of totaled and burned cars
- most committed to crime—irrational, immature
- least likely to be deterred—doesn't care what happens

Thrill-Seeker

- heavily into drugs—doing crime is a way to finance the habit—entices others to feel the "rush" of doing crime
- engages in car stunts and willful damage to cars, but also steals them for transportation and to use in other crimes
- steals parts for sale in a loosely structured friendship network
- likely to look for the "rush" elsewhere if autos become too difficult to steal—"rush" might be legitimately substituted

Instrumental Offender

- doing auto theft for the money—most active of the offenders but the smallest proportion of the sample—connected to organized theft operations
- rational, intelligent—does crimes with least risk—gravitated to auto theft from burglary—thinks about outcomes doing crime while young offender status affords them lenient treatment—indicate that they will quit crime at age 18

Even among this sample of multiple-offense, persistent young offenders, thrill-seeking motives were identified in more than half of their auto thefts. One variant of joyriding often incorporates deliberate destruction of the vehicles—68% indicated that they had stolen vehicles for the express purpose of "trashing" them.

> It's not your car. You can do whatever you want, beat it up, go as fast as you want, bake the tires, do jumps. (16-year-old)

Many offenders expressed the belief that this kind of activity did not really hurt anyone as the vehicles they typically stole to intentionally wreck were "old beaters" whose owners "probably got insurance money to buy a better one."

Profit-motivated auto stealing in this sample was evidenced in two areas: (1) vehicle acquisition for an adult-run theft ring; (2) haphazard stripping of parts for which a ready market existed. In stark contrast to the acting-out joyrider and thrill-seeker, instrumental offenders expressed little interest in adrenaline producing behavior. They took precautions to avoid police and usually worked alone. They possessed a reflective, business-like attitude about their crime of choice and this is what probably enabled them to find work with relatively rare organized theft rings.

> The newbies [younger kids just beginning their frequent involvement in auto stealing] are real heat scores [do things that attract police attention]. They wear the black Bulls [NBA team logo] skull caps and drive like idiots. If the guys I steal for ever saw one of them around, I'd never get another call. (17-year-old)

Target Selection and Acquisition

Perhaps the simplest way to dichotomize the targets of auto theft is to think in terms of supply and demand. Instrumental motives for auto stealing are driven by the *demand* for certain models sought in whole or for their parts. Why? People who like to drive fast and take risks much of the time (e.g., young males) are drawn to vehicles engineered and marketed for this "need for speed." They buy American "muscle cars" like Mustangs, Camaros, and Corvettes; European and Japanese sports coupes such as the Porsche 911 and Honda Prelude; or, if they are looking for off-road thrills, 4X4 pick-ups and sport utility vehicles.

One would expect that risk-taking drivers would crash with greater frequency, driving the demand for replacement parts. Because they are likely at fault in the majority of their crashes, drivers of these kinds of vehicles are greatly motivated to cover needed repairs outside the legitimate economy where they can stretch their repair dollar with stolen replacement parts. Relative to their fleet proportions, the kinds of models identified above are often over-represented in organized auto theft activities uncovered by police stings and task forces in many jurisdictions. The targets of instrumental theft, then, are in response to the demand for specific models.

On the affective motivation side, we would not expect to see much in the way of target specificity aside from general performance requirements—sporty cars that go fast and impress girls, or 4X4 trucks and sport utility vehicles sought for off-road thrill potential. A *supply* orientation should dominate this realm wherein largely opportunistic offenders steal whatever is most readily available.

A victimization survey done for the larger study found that 20% of vehicles were stolen with the owners' keys, roughly half of which were left in the ignition or elsewhere in the vehicle. As might be expected, no target specificity was exhibited amongst this subset of auto thefts—any car with the keys in it will do as far as most thrill or transportation seeking offenders are concerned. We did, however, find pronounced model specificity for the remainder serving to define the "path of least resistance" amongst the fleet of passenger vehicles.

Virtually all interviewed offenders identified older Japanese models as the targets of choice for thrill and transportation motives due to the relative ease with which their door and ignition locks could be defeated with ordinary objects such as scissors or screwdrivers. Simplistic, brute force techniques are the favored *modus operandi* of juvenile delinquents everywhere, and so it is with young car thieves.

We were able to quantify the degree of this target specificity by analyzing insurance claims data relative to the fleet of licensed passenger vehicles. When theft rates by vehicle make (e.g., Chevrolet, Ford, Mazda, etc.) were rank-ordered, we found Japanese nameplates occupying eight of the 10 makes most at risk of theft. Like many places in North America, Japanese makes are popular with British Columbians. In the early 1990s, they accounted for roughly one-quarter of the fleet; however, the 10-year-old models most at risk of theft made up a much smaller proportion.

Insurance claim data analyses replicated following the sharp auto theft increase witnessed between 1995 and 1996 found that passenger vehicles manufactured by the US conglomerate Chrysler, Plymouth, Dodge, Jeep, Eagle, Mitsubishi—makes exhibiting the lowest theft rates in the early 1990s—to be most disproportionately at risk of theft. Largely ignored in the first half of the decade, auto stealers in British Columbia learned in the intervening years that many older Chrysler, Plymouth, Dodge products were likewise vulnerable to their favored brute-force techniques. In 1996, 30 passenger vehicle models making up just 12% of the fleet accounted for more that a third of all auto thefts in the province.

The most obvious implication regarding the relative rarity of favorite targets has to do with offender search patterns. Motivated offenders would waste huge amounts of time if they settled on wandering about aimlessly in the hopes of finding the relatively few vehicles on which their limited theft skill-set would likely work. This limited competence funnels them to places where they are apt to find their favorite prey—large parking lots. Conveniently, the large amounts of time young offenders spend in and around shopping malls provide a good match between their routine activities and a sufficiently large pool of easy-to-steal vehicles. Mall parking lots were noted as prime "hunting grounds." Roughly a third of the offenders thought underground parking lots the best place to steal vehicles.

Individual Theft Frequency

Two-thirds of the offenders interviewed could provide confident estimates of the number of vehicles they were stealing per week on average over the course of the year prior to being incarcerated. Excluding the three most prolific offenders and the four expressing minimal auto theft involvement, this sample of persistent young offenders claimed to have stolen almost three vehicles a week prior to their incarceration. These self-reported figures are consistent with other yearly auto stealing figures reported by high involvement offenders (e.g., Wilson and Abrahamse, 1992). If the total number of autos reported stolen by this small sample of juveniles were halved to allow for a good deal of bragging and lesser auto stealing levels for some portion of the year, it would still account for approximately 7% of the auto thefts known to police in British Columbia in 1992, or roughly $3 million in direct costs.

Offenders' Thoughts on Deterrence

Offenders' perceptions of deterrence was gauged in two areas—the prospects of target hardening (alarms, steering wheel and ignition locks, etc.) and how they viewed the criminal justice system's response to their offending. Notwithstanding the possibility of functional displacement in the form of "carjacking," or displacement to less protected vehicles, target-hardening appears, on the basis of interviews with these offenders, the best prospect for reducing auto theft.

Three-quarters of the offenders said they avoid cars equipped with alarms and flee if an alarm goes off while attempting to steal a car. Few had encountered many mechanical anti-theft devices such as the "Club;" however, two-thirds said they would avoid a car equipped with such a device. Several offenders expressed their dislike of being encumbered with special tools needed to defeat anti-theft devices:

> It's easy to get a car [equipped] with a "club" . . . you can saw through the steering wheel in 30 seconds, but it's too big of a heat score carrying around a gym bag with a hacksaw. . . . Why go through all the hassle when you can just steal another one with a pen knife? (17-year-old)

The findings offer little encouragement for the deterrent value of the Combat Auto Theft (CAT) sticker program as intended. The CAT program attempts to assist police in the identification of stolen autos by having owners who do not routinely operate their vehicles between the hours of 1:00 and 5:00 AM place a brightly colored sticker on the inside of the rear window where it is visible to patrolling police officers. Among other things, the sticker grants police blanket permission to stop and search a vehicle bearing this sticker whenever it is observed in operation during the proscribed hours.

Only three offenders correctly identifying a CAT sticker said they would avoid a car so marked. The majority of offenders believed the sticker indicated the car was equipped with an alarm, so presumably, three-quarters of these young offenders would avoid cars marked with CAT stickers in order to avoid the assumed alarms. The rest of the offenders did not recognize the CAT sticker as a police signaling device and said the presence of the sticker on a car would not influence their auto stealing decisions. Because the majority of offenders believe the CAT sticker indicative of an alarmed car that most said they would avoid, it may be advantageous for the true nature of the CAT sticker to remain obscure. If more offenders knew what the sticker signifies, they might be more inclined to promptly peel them off once they gain entry to a vehicle so marked.

Offenders' Thoughts on the Criminal Justice System

On average, offenders in this sample stole their first vehicle at age 13, and were passengers in stolen cars an average of two and a half times prior to their first theft. Nearly a quarter of the sample identified auto theft as a "starter crime" leading to their involvement in other crimes. Sixteen percent indicated that they had curtailed burglary in favor of auto theft in the last year as "judges are getting tougher on B&Es." Several articulated a perception that they stood less chance of being incarcerated for auto theft:

> I told my friends they were stupid for doing robberies. . . . I'd make $500–$2000 a pop [for a stolen car]; they got chump change. . . . If I get caught I may get a month or two, they're gonna get 18. (15-year-old)

The deterrent value of existing sanctions were zealously assailed by offenders. They were confident about prevailing at nearly every stage of the process.

On Evading the Police. Offenders were aware of the policy constraints under which police operate and expressed an eagerness to exploit them:

> [c]ops pull their guns out but I know they can't shoot at me for joyriding (14-year-old);

> We can drive anyway we want . . . up on the sidewalk, down a one-way street, cops have to obey the rules . . . police can't wreck cars so they won't follow you in the bush. (15-year-old)

The heat [police] won't chase you during the day when there's a lot of traffic cause they'll get sued if they hit someone. (17-year-old)

I never use the middle lane during rush hour because that where cops can box you in when you get stuck behind cars at a light. (17-year-old)

It's easy to get away. You just jump out and leave it in drive. The cops have to go get it while you are running the other way. They can't use dogs on you if it is only a stolen car. (15-year-old)

If they get you in the car they got you. If you get away from the scene they've got nothing. (16-year-old)

On Evading Punishment. More than half of the sample was confident of prevailing in court once charged, and almost 60% percent said they did not worry about being punished by the court. Consistent with other findings regarding persistent property offenders' perceptions that offenses resulting in probation are "free crimes" (Cromwell et al., 1991), young offenders in this sample were nearly unanimous about the uselessness of probation. Virtually all the offenders characterized it as a "joke." They didn't abide by the conditions, especially the curfew imposed, and no one ever checked up on them:

It's a joke! I'm going up for breach [probation violation] for the first time since age 12. . . . I never obeyed. (15-year-old)

Reflecting on his involvement in auto theft, another 15-year-old remarked:

I think it's pretty much worth it. I've only spent two and a half months in jail and I have gotten away with hundreds [of auto thefts].

Many respondents identified the leniency of the juvenile system as a factor in their offending, though several expressed the view that a more punitive criminal justice system would not make a difference in their offending. While several offenders displayed an obvious lack of moral development, for example indicating that they thought it was great that lawyers work to get them off even when they committed the offense charged, most possessed a sense of the unique position in which the adolescent finds himself in Western society, hinting that they were involved in crime because they could do so without much repercussion:

Q: Did you ever worry about getting caught?

A: No, I was so young . . . it's no big deal, I was let off easy. . . . I got nine days open custody for robbery. (12-year-old)

Q: Did you ever think about getting punished by the court?

A: No, it was worth the risk . . . nothing happens . . . you get community hours or probation . . . I never abide by my curfew. (17-year old)

Q: What do you think about getting probation?

A: It's a joke . . . for four car thefts, a B&E and three breaches, I got seven days in closed custody, most charges were dropped. The juvenile system doesn't scare anyone, it just bores people to death . . . coming in here means nothing to me. (17-year-old)

Q: Do you think what is happening to you is fair?

A: I lucked out. I only got nine months and I even killed someone [in a high speed chase].

Many of the young offenders in this study asserted that they did not consider the consequences of their actions, however this appears to be mostly situational. Based on our interviews, it becomes evident that many offenders do weigh the costs and benefits of their actions and conclude that crime is worth pursuing so long as their young offender status insulates them from what they themselves would see as meaningful sanctions.

The obvious conclusions to be drawn from these findings involve the use of (1) target hardening technology, including alarms, and steering wheel and ignition locks, and (2) increased likelihood and severity of punishment.

Consistent with the findings in the burglary study by Cromwell, Olson, and Avary (1991) the extra time and "hassle" required to overcome locks and alarms often discourages young, nonprofessional criminals. And, as many of the young offenders stated, the relative lack of punishment due to their status as juveniles encourages many to engage in offenses which they otherwise might not.

References

Challinger, D. (1987) Car Security Hardware—How Good is it? In *Car Theft: Putting on the Brakes, Proceedings of Seminar on Car Theft*, May 21. Sydney: National Roads and Motorists' Association and the Australian Institute of Criminology.

Clarke, R. and D. Cornish (1985) Modeling offenders' decisions: a framework for research and policy, in: M. Tonry and N. Morris (Eds.), *Crime and Justice: An Annual Review of Research*, 6. Chicago: University of Chicago Press.

Clarke, R. and P. Harris (1992) Auto Theft and Its Prevention, in M. Tonry (Ed.), *Crime and Justice: An Annual Review of Research*, 16. Chicago: University of Chicago Press.

Cornish, D. and R. Clarke (Eds.) (1986) *The Reasoning Criminal: Rational Choice Perspectives on Offending*. New York: Springer-Verlag.

Cromwell, P., J. Olson, and D. Avary (1991) *Breaking and Entering: An Ethnographic Analysis of Burglary*. Newbury Park, CA: Sage.

Fleming, Z., P. Brantingham, and P. Brantingham (1994) "Exploring Auto Theft in British Columbia," in: R. Clarke (ed.), *Crime Prevention Studies*, Vol. 3. Monsey, NY: Willow Tree Press.

Gottfredson, M and T. Hirschi (1990) *A General Theory of Crime*, Stanford, CA: Stanford University Press.

Rengert, G. and Wasilchick, J. (1989) Space, time and crime: ethnographic insights into residential burglary. A report prepared for the National Institute of Justice.

Shover, N. (1996) Aging Criminals: Change in the Criminal Calculus, in: P. Cromwell, (Ed.), *In Their Own Words: Criminals on Crime*, Los Angeles: Roxbury.

Shover, N. and D. Honaker (1996) The Socially Bounded Decision Making of Persistent Property Offenders, in: P. Cromwell, (ed.), *In Their Own Words: Criminals on Crime*, Los Angeles: Roxbury.

Norrie, A. (1986) Practical Reasoning and Criminal Responsibility: A Jurisprudential Approach in: D. Cornish and R. Clarke (Eds.), *The Reasoning Criminal: Rational Choice Perspectives on Offending*, New York: Springer-Verlag.

Wilson, J. and A. Abrahamse (1992) Does Crime Pay? *Justice Quarterly* 9(3), 357-377.

8

Aging Criminals: Changes in the Criminal Calculus

Neal Shover

In *this selection, Neal Shover compares the decision-making processes of juvenile and young adult offenders to those of older criminals to discover the changes in the criminal calculus—the perception of risk and gain associated with a criminal opportunity—as offenders age. "Clearly," he argues, "something about advancing age produces reduced participation in ordinary crime, even by those with extensive criminal records" (p. 22). Shover concludes that aging offenders undergo a number of changes, including development of new commitments and increasing fear of incarceration. This causes them to alter their calculus—to evaluate the risks and benefits of crime differently.*

Shover's research methodology involved identifying, locating, and interviewing a group of men aged 40 and over who were involved in ordinary property crime earlier in their careers. Shover and his assistants interviewed 50 subjects whose dominant criminal pattern consisted of ordinary property offenses such as grand larceny, burglary, robbery, and auto theft. All had been convicted of such offenses at least once. The research subjects were identified through the files of the U.S. Probation Offices in Baltimore and Washington, D.C. (22), and U.S. Probation Offices in other cities (5), through introduction by an ex-convict employed to work on the project (13), and by referral from an ex-convict who had been part of an earlier study (4). Six additional subjects were interviewed in federal prisons. Interviews, which were tape recorded and later tran-
scribed, lasted from 30 minutes to three hours, averaging two hours.

Calculus and Offenses of Youth

For many juveniles, involvement in delinquency contains a rich variety of motives and subjective meanings. Juveniles "slide into" their initial delinquent acts for a variety of nonrational, often situationally based reasons (Matza, 1964). Although there is little new in this, it is interesting that the interview subjects recalled their earliest crimes this way. A 45-year-old man said,

> I was, like years ago, I was a peeping Tom—when I was a kid, you know. . . . I enjoyed this, you know. . . . But, anyway, then I got married young, and I had two children. And I had bills, you know. I was a kid and I had a man's responsibility. . . . Now, what's the best way to make money? With something you know. I had been peeping in windows when I was a kid. So, I knew, you know, like where the windows would open, where the—you understand what I mean? And then [I] broadened my sense. After awhile I started mixing business with pleasure, you know. I would peep and then later come back and, you know, take this or that.

Another man told of his adolescent fascination with automobiles. As a youth, he often roamed through parking lots, admiring the steering wheels of cars. From there it was a short, tentative step to breaking into the cars and stealing their contents.

A great deal of delinquency begins simply as risk-taking behavior and it is only later, with the benefit of accumulated incidents, that it takes on the character and meaning of "crime" (Short and Strodtbeck, 1965). Braley (1976: 11-12) writes,

> I began to steal seriously as a member of a small gang of boys. We backed into it, simply enough, by collecting milk and soda bottles to turn in for the deposits, but, after we had exhausted the vacant lots, empty fields, and town dumps, we began to sneak into garages . . . and, having dared garages and survived, we next began to loot back porches, and, finally, breathlessly, we entered someone's

kitchen. . . . Clearly, this was an exercise of real power over the remote adult world and I found it exciting. I liked it. . . . [A]nd it is only now, some forty years later, that I begin to see how stealing cast me in my first successful role.

Many of the crimes committed by youth are impulsive and poorly planned:

Q: Did you do a lot of stickups [when you were young]?

A: Oh yeah, you know. . . . [We] stole and shit like that, you know. I didn't give it no thought, no plan, don't know how much money's in it. You know what I mean? Just go in there and say, "we're gonna do it, we're gonna do it." . . . That was it.

The spontaneous pursuit of fun and excitement provides the impetus for some delinquency:

[When I was a kid] I wasn't a sports enthusiast. I played sports very rarely, but it just wasn't exciting enough. . . . None of [the "normal" adolescent activities] were exciting to me. . . . It's just that we, there was a feeling of participating in something that was daring and dangerous.

To some extent, these collective definitions of misconduct based on expressive vocabularies of motive explain why participants do not always see their activities as criminal. Instead of resulting from a rational decision-making process, they simply "happen," and participants do not appreciate sufficiently the seriousness. A former gang member writes,

It's funny, but we didn't see ourselves as delinquents or young criminal types. Most of what we were into was fighting other gangs. . . . Sure, we got into other kinds of scrapes sometimes, like vandalism and petty larceny from a street vendor or a store. Most of the time we thought of that kind of stuff as "just playing around"— never as crime. [Rettig et al., 1977: 28]

For other youths, participation in delinquency results from the interactional dynamics of peer groups. Some boys experience a situational need to maintain personal status and face with their peers (Short and Strodtbeck, 1965; Jansyn, 1966). Theft or other acts of delinquency may function to buttress or solidify one's informal ranking within a small group. Youths may occasionally use them as a dramatic, incontrovertible demand for a higher as compared with a lower rank:

Everybody would look up to me, you know, when I was young. . . . And seem like every time they wanted something, they'd come to me and say, "Jack, well, come on and do this," or "help me do this," you know. Fuck it, you know. I had an image I had to live up to, you know. I'd say, "fuck it, man, come on."

Precisely because many of the criminal incidents of youth are responses to group dynamics or moods, they occasionally "break out" in situationally propitious circumstances. An interview subject related an incident of armed robbery that occurred when he was young. His account illustrates some of the foregoing observations about the impetuous nature of juvenile crime:

[One day] we were just walking up First Street and [one of my companions] said as we were approaching Rhode Island Avenue, "let's go in here and rob this drug store," because [another companion] had a gun. We said, "okay, let's go in here and rob the drug store." Went in there, the soda fountain was filled up . . . robbed everybody on the stools. Went back in the post office, stole money orders and stamps and stuff, took the cash box. And we turned our backs on everybody in the store, going out! We didn't know whether the proprietor had a gun or what, but it just so happened that he didn't. But, that's just the atmosphere in which, you know, that took place.

Overall, the interview subjects said that as juveniles and young adults they pursued crime with considerable intensity:

[W]hen you're young, or when—the people that I've known who are young, it was nothing to go out and break into two or three places a week just *looking* for money.

Similarly, a retired English thief writes that "when you're young you tend to have a go at anything" (Quick, 1967: 142).

While juvenile crime is impetuous and fun, it is also monetarily rewarding. Indeed, to juveniles from economically deprived backgrounds it may appear more rewarding than any legitimate employment available to them. The sums of money garnered from crime may seem princely indeed. Crime opens up for them new worlds of consumption and leisure activities. The 49 imprisoned armed robbers studied by Petersilia et al. reported that often their youthful crimes were motivated by a desire for and pursuit of "high times" (1978: 76).

It seems apparent that many youth become involved in property offenses without having developed an autonomous and rationalized set of criminal motives. Petersilia et al. discovered a similar pattern in their research on imprisoned armed robbers. Their subjects reported using little or no sophistication in planning the offenses they committed in their youth (1978: 60–65). At the same time, they found that the juvenile offenses committed by men in their sample included "expressive elements" far more than was true of the offenses they committed later (1978: 76). (Expressive reasons for committing offenses include such things as hostility, revenge, thrills, or peer influence.)

Juveniles and young adults often have little awareness or appreciation of the legal and personal repercussions of their criminality. This is true especially of their perceptions of time spent in institutions such as training schools and prisons:

> I've seen the time in my life, man, where it might seem foolish, 'cause it seems foolish to me now. When I was in the street, hustling, I'd say, "if I get knocked off and don't get but a nickel"—five years—I said, "hell with it," you know. The only thing would be in my mind, if I got busted could I hang around, try to have my lawyer try to get me some kind of plea or something so I wouldn't get but a nickel. 'Cause I knew I could knock five years out.

A 47-year-old man echoed these remarks, saying that when he was young,

> I don't know, man, I just didn't give a fuck, you know. I was young, simple, man. I didn't care, you know. Shit, doing time, you know, I didn't know what doing time was all about. Doing time to me was nothing, you know.

The net result of these youthful meanings and motives is that the potential repercussions of crime to some extent are blunted. Juveniles neither possess nor bring to bear a precise, consistent metric for assessing the potential consequences of delinquent episodes. They fail to "see" or to calculate seriously their potential losses if apprehended. For many youth, crime is a risk-taking activity in which the risks are only dimly appreciated or calculated.

Calculus and Offenses of Young Adults

This poorly developed youthful calculus is transformed both by the approach of adulthood and by the experience of arrest and adult felony confinement. Young adults develop the ability to see, to appreciate, and to calculate more precisely some of the potential penalties that flow from criminal involvement. Consequently, by late adolescence to their early 20s men begin to develop a keener awareness of the potential costs of criminal behavior. Gradually supplanting the nonrational motives and calculus of youthful offenders is a more clearly articulated understanding of the price they will pay if convicted of crime. In this sense, aging and its associated experiences are accompanied by an increasing rationalization of ordinary property crime.

Their growing rationalization of crime seems to be a turning point for many ordinary property offenders. As Zimring (1981: 880) has noted,

> At some point in adolescence or early adult development, most of those who have committed offenses in groups either cease to be offenders or continue to violate the law, but for different reasons and in different configurations. Either of these paths is a significant change from prior behavior.

A substantial majority of the uncommitted apparently drop out of crime at this point.

Paradoxically, others—this includes many unsuccessful and most successful offenders—respond to their developing rationalization of crime with a strengthened belief that they can continue committing crime and make it a lucrative enterprise. This is because they convert their developing rationalization of crime into an increased confidence that they can avoid arrest.

For those who continue at crime, theft increasingly springs from a more autonomous set of motives and meanings. The salience of "expressive elements" gradually declines in the process of criminal decision making. Offenders also develop an awareness of the importance of making crime a rational process. They learn the importance of assessing and committing crimes on the basis of an increasingly narrow and precise metric of potential benefits and costs. In this sense as well, their crimes became more calculating and rational. Money increasingly assumes more importance as a criminal objective. After serving a term in the National Training School, one subject and his friends began robbing gamblers and bootleggers. I asked him,

Q: Did the desire for excitement play any part in those crimes?

A: No, I think the desire for excitement had left. It was, we recognized that it was a dangerous mission then, because we knew that gamblers and bootleggers carried guns and things like that. And it was for, you know, just for the money.

Another man made the same point succinctly, saying that "whatever started me in crime is one thing. But at some point I know that I'm in crime for the money. There's no emotional reason for me being into crime." Finally, an ex-thief has written,

When I first began stealing I had but a dim realization of its wrong. I accepted it as the thing to do because it was done by the people I was with; besides, it was adventurous and thrilling. Later it became an everyday, cold-blooded business, and while I went about it methodically . . . I was fully aware of the gravity of my offenses. [Black, 1926: 254]

Interestingly, during their young adult years the 49 California armed robbers expressed a new confidence in their ability to avoid arrest for their crimes (Petersilia et al., 1978: 69-70). They reported a marked increase in the sophistication of their criminal planning (although the researchers indicate the men never achieved tactical brilliance)

(1978: 60). Pursuit of "high times" declined in importance as a motive for crime (1978: 78) and the need to meet ordinary financial exigencies became more important (1978: 76). Concern about arrest declined substantially (1978: 70).

Young men, however, tend to exaggerate their ability to rationalize their crimes and to commit them successfully:

Whenever I began to steal it was always with the rationale I wouldn't make the mistakes I had made before. . . . It didn't occur to me there were literally thousands of ways I could get caught. I was sustained by the confidence nothing truly awful could happen to me. [Braly, 1976: 65]

Often they confidently assume there are a finite, manageable number of ways that any particular criminal act can fail (Shover, 1971). Consequently, they analyze past offenses for information they believe will lead to ever more perfect criminal techniques and success. Parker's interview (Parker and Allerton, 1962: 149) with an English thief reveals this reasoning process:

Q: When you're arrested, what are your reactions at that moment?

A: I think the first thing's annoyance—with myself. How could I be so stupid as to get nicked? What's gone wrong, what have I forgotten, where have I made the mistake?

In most cases, young adult offenders' newly acquired faith in their ability to rationalize theft and thereby make it safer proves to be self-defeating. Few of them are equipped by temperament, intelligence, or social connections to follow through on their plans and dreams. Consequently, subsequent offenses usually only repeat the pattern established in their youthful criminal forays.

Calculus and Offenses of Aging Adults

As men age, fail at crime, and experience . . . [other] contingencies, their rationalization of the criminal calculus changes apace. Now they enter a third and final stage of their criminal careers. Increasingly, they realize that the expected monetary returns from criminal involvement are paltry, both in relative and in absolute terms.

Simultaneously, their estimation of the likelihood of being arrested increases, as do the objective probabilities of arrest (Petersilia et al., 1978: 36-39).

Because of the nature and length of their previous criminal record, they generally assume that they will be sentenced to prison again if convicted of another felony. There is evidence to support this assumption (Petersilia et al., 1978: 39). Also, older men assume that any prison sentence they receive, given the length of their previous criminal record, will be long. Finally, those who experience an interpersonal contingency are increasingly reluctant to risk losing their new-found social ties. For all these reasons, aging men begin to include factors that previously were absent from their calculus of potential criminal acts. A 46-year-old former addict said,

> If I go out there and commit a crime now, I got to think about this: Hey, man, I ain't *got* to get away. See what I'm saying? I have—man, it would be just my luck that I would get busted. Now I done fucked up everything I done tried to work hard for, man, you know, to get my little family together.

Perhaps it is not surprising that they increasingly begin to see that their potential losses, if imprisoned again, will be immense.

In sum, as offenders age, their expectations of the potential outcome of criminal acts changes. Their perception of the odds narrows. Now the perceived risks of criminal behavior loom larger. Note that the Rand Corporation's research on 49 armed robbers found that fear of arrest increases during this age period (Petersilia et al., 1978: 70). Little wonder then that a 56-year-old man said,

> I realized that, even though in crime, even though you might get away, let's say 99 times, the one time eliminates your future. You don't have no future. Regardless of what you have gained, you lost all of that. A rabbit can escape 99 times and it only takes one shot to kill him. So, I was a rabbit. . . . I want to enjoy life. But I know I can't do it successfully by committing crimes.

This does not mean that men cease *thinking* about crime altogether. Rather, they develop a more complex set of reasons for avoiding it in most situations. However, in more advantageous circumstances, some believe they still are capable of resorting to crime:

> Now, I'm not going to tell you that if you put $100,000 on that table and I saw an opportunity, that I felt that I could get away with it, that I wouldn't try to move it. But there's no way, even now, there's no way that I would endanger my freedom for a measley four, five, ten thousand dollars. I make that much a year now, you know. And I see the time that I wasted— well, I figure I wasted four or five years when I was younger.
>
> Q: What do you mean, you "wasted" it?
>
> A: In and out of jail.

Those men who continue to pursue a criminal career change their approach to crime. Most decide to avoid some of the crimes more characteristic of their youth. They shift to offenses that are less confrontative and, therefore, less *visible*. Armed robbery is the prototypical highly visible and highly confrontative offense. Shoplifting or selling marijuana represent the other extreme. An imprisoned man said,

> When I go out, I'm goin' for the "soft" stuff. I'm going to book the numbers, you know . . . but *hard* crime . . . I gave that up a long while ago.

Thus, there is evidence that ordinary property offenders, once their fear of arrest and confinement increases, shift to other types of criminal activities. In doing so, they believe that they simultaneously reduce the chances of arrest and, even if arrested, increase the chances of receiving less severe penalties:

> You know, it's funny but there's only a few things that a man goes to the penitentiary for: burglary or robbery or something like that. But how many ways of making money are there that you don't have to revert to robbery or burglary? Thousands. I mean [where you're] between being legit and being crooked. You're skating on thin ice and if that ice breaks it's not going to break bad. You might get your foot wet, you might get a fine or something. What

they're [police, prosecutors, courts] really concerned with are these violent cases, man, these people who are causing these headlines and stuff. . . . If I am going to be a thief I might as well be the one who is skating on that thin ice. And a person who is skating on thin ice is less likely to go to the penitentiary. . . . 'Cause if you get arrested boosting, shoplifting, it is generally a fine. If worse comes to worst, you're going to have to have to do a year in the county jail—in some places, nine months.

I caught one number—that ten years, all them robberies—and then, you know, everything I did then was more like a finesse thing. . . . I'm not gonna stick no pistol in nobody's face, man, you know. I'm not gonna strong arm nobody, you know. I'm not gonna go in nobody's house. You understand what I'm sayin'? I'm not gonna do that.

Q: You figure as long as you don't do those things you won't go to the penitentiary?

A: Hey, you better believe it. You better believe it.

Along with this reduction in the visibility of their offenses, men try to reduce the *frequency* of their crimes. One subject, who still engages occasionally in nonviolent felonies, told me how he had changed:

I done got a little *softer*, you know. I done got, hey man, to the point, you know, where, like I say, I don't steal, I don't hustle, you know. But I don't pass the opportunity if I can get some free money. I'm not gonna pass. . . . I don't hustle, you know. I don't make it a everyday thing. I don't go out *lookin'* for things, you know.

Another man said,

When you're younger, you can . . . steal to pay the rent, you know. Hell, you can go out and steal seven days a week. And sooner [or later] . . . you learn that—to me, it's exposure time, you know. You don't want to get "exposed" too much.

Petersilia et al. (1978: 27) found the same pattern. The average monthly offense rates reported by their subjects decreased from 3.28 when they were juveniles to 0.64 in their adult years. After changing their approach to crime, some men do continue to commit

crime for several years, but eventually they desist from crime. Only a handful of ordinary property offenders continue their criminal behavior into old age. . . .

Negative Cases

Three aspects of the experiences of successful offenders distinguish them from the other types of offenders. First, the former usually develop an autonomous, rationalized calculus of crime at an earlier age, albeit in the same general fashion discussed here. By their late teens, some successful offenders are engaging in carefully planned crimes primarily for the expected monetary gains. Even some successful thieves, however, never entirely slough off all nonmonetary meanings of and motivations for crime:

I know a guy who's relatively well connected, if you know what I mean, with the Outfit. [Nevertheless, he would] [g]o on any score! Now he needed money like I need a double hernia. But [he] just loved—don't care if there's any money there or not. "Let's go." [It was] [t]he thrill. I never got any thrills like that myself. . . . The only thrill I got [was] counting the money.

Second, the crimes of successful offenders generally are substantially more rewarding than the crimes committed by other types of offenders. Third, they are more successful than other types of offenders in avoiding incarceration; they spend fewer years in prison. For these reasons, failure at crime does not produce in successful offenders the same impetus to modify their criminal calculus as it does in their unsuccessful peers.

Despite these differences, however, some successful offenders also experience one or more of the contingencies described [earlier]. . . . In such circumstances, they respond in ways similar to unsuccessful offenders (Hohimer, 1975).

Unlike unsuccessful offenders, however, they sometimes make adjustments in their criminal activities without discontinuing them entirely. They can do so, in part, because their theft activities provide them late career opportunities not available to unsuccessful offenders. For example, because some of them establish extensive social contacts through their work, they can change the nature of their criminal involvement. They are able to shift to other roles in the social organization of theft. Now they eschew the role of *front-line participant* in favor of the role of *background operator* (Mack and Kerner, 1975; Shover, 1983a). Still others manage to save enough money from their working years to retire with a degree of material comfort. One man suggested these two strategies account for most late-life patterns of successful offenders like himself. As he put it, "[T]hey're either sitting in the rocking chair or out finding something soft for somebody else to pick up."

Nevertheless, a substantial percentage of successful offenders apparently continues "going to the well" despite advancing age. An English thief, who already had served several prison sentences, has written,

> I content myself with the dream—the one that all criminals have—that one day I'll get the really big tickle. . . . That's all I can do now, take my time and wait for the chance to come. I've no intention of going straight, I'm just being more careful, that's all—and I'm getting cagey, I won't take unnecessary risks. It used to be I wanted a fifty-fifty chance, now I want it better than that, somewhere like seventy-five to twenty-five. But sooner or later it'll come, the job will be there, I'll do it, get the big tickle, and then I'll retire. . . . This is it, this is the dream, the great rock candy mountain that beckons us all. (Parker and Allerton, 1962: 189)

This man subsequently was reimprisoned several times (Parker, 1981).

Among the unsuccessful offenders, there are two distinctly different categories of negative cases. Some men simply do not experience the orientational and interpersonal changes described [earlier], and so they fail to modify significantly their calculus of ordinary property crime. In assessing their past criminal behavior these men use almost identical verbalizations: "They [police and the courts] could never get even." They use this description to support their contention that they have avoided arrest and prosecution for so many crimes that, even if they were caught in the future, the ledger books still would show an advantage for them. A man who shoplifts almost daily as a means of support had this to say:

> Q: Have you ever thought that you were a good thief, or a good hustler?
>
> A: Yeah, I am. . . .
>
> Q: What makes you think you're a good hustler?
>
> A: 'Cause I *produce*.
>
> Q: Yeah, but you've done a lot of time, too, haven't you?
>
> A: Yeah, but considering, you know, in comparison, I ain't did that much. I think, if they gave me 199 years they couldn't get even. . . . They couldn't get even.

References

Braley, Malcolm (1976). *False Starts*. New York: Penguin.

Hohimer, Frank (1975). *The Home Invaders*. Chicago: Chicago Review Books.

Jansyn, Leon R. , Jr. (1966). Solidarity and Delinquency in a Street Corner Group. *American Sociological Review* 31 (October): 600-614.

Mack, John and Hans-Jurgen Kerner (1975). *The Crime Industry*. Lexington, MA: D.C. Heath.

Matza, David (1964). *Delinquency and Drift*. New York: John Wiley.

Parker, Tony (1981). Letter to the Author (July 10).

Parker, Tony and Robert Allerton (1962). *The Courage of His Conviction*. London: Hutchinson.

Petersilia, Joan, P. W. Greenwood and M. Lavin (1978). *Criminal Careers of Habitual Felons*. Washington, DC: National Institute of Justice.

Quick, Harry (1967). *Villain*. London: Jonathon Cape.

Short, James F. and Fred L. Strodtbeck (1965). *Group Processes and Gang Delinquency*. Chicago: University of Chicago Press.

Shover, Neal (1971). Burglary as an Occupation. Ph.D. dissertation, University of Illinois, Urbana.

Zimring, Franklin (1981). Kids, Groups, and Crime: Some Implications of a Well-Known Secret. *Journal of Criminal Law and Criminology* 72 (Fall): 867-885.

Adapted from Neal Shover, *Aging Criminals*, Sage Publications, pp. 105–126. Copyright © 1985 by Neal Shover. Notes deleted. Reprinted with permission. ✦

9

Getting out of the Life: Crime Desistance by Female Street Offenders

Ira Sommers
Deborah R. Baskin
Jeffrey Fagan

This selection considers the role of life events and the relationship of cognitions and life situations to the desistance process. The authors are concerned with whether the social and psychological processes and the events leading up to their desistance from crime vary by gender. In other words, do men and women differ in the processes and events which bring them to the decision to give up crime?

The authors constructed a sample of 30 women. Initially, 16 subjects were recruited through various drug and alcohol treatment programs in New York. An additional 14 women were obtained through a chain of referrals process. To be included in the sample, a woman had to have had at least one official arrest for a violent street crime and to have desisted from crime for at least two years prior to the study. Life history interviews were conducted by the first two authors. Each interview lasted approximately two hours.

The subjects had engaged in a wide range of criminal activities. Eighty-seven percent were addicted to crack, 63% had been involved in robberies, 60% had committed burglaries, 94% had sold drugs, and 47% had at some time been involved in prostitution. The mean number of prior incarcerations was 3.

The authors found that the reasons for desistance from crime were remarkably similar to those found for men. Like the male subjects in Shover's (1985 and in this volume) desistance study, the women in this study had begun to take the threat of incarceration seriously and attempted to reestablish links with conventional society while severing relationships in the deviant subculture.

Studies over the past decade have provided a great deal of information about the criminal careers of male offenders. (See Blumstein et al. 1986 and Weiner and Wolfgang 1989 for reviews.) Unfortunately, much less is known about the initiation, escalation, and termination of criminal careers by female offenders. The general tendency to exclude female offenders from research on crime and delinquency may be due, at least in part, to the lower frequency and comparatively less serious nature of offending among women. Recent trends and studies, however, suggest that the omission of women may seriously bias both research and theory on crime.

Although a growing body of work on female crime has emerged within the last few years, much of this research continues to focus on what Daly and Chesney-Lind (1988) called generalizability and gender-ratio problems. The former concerns the degree to which traditional (i.e., male) theories of deviance and crime apply to women, and the latter focuses on what explains gender differences in rates and types of criminal activity. Although this article also examines women in crime, questions of inter- and intragender variability in crime are not specifically addressed. Instead, the aim of the paper is to describe the pathways out of deviance for a sample of women who have significantly invested themselves in criminal social worlds. To what extent are the social and psychological processes of stopping criminal behavior similar for men and women? Do the behavioral antecedents of such processes vary by gender? These questions remained unexplored.

Specifically, two main issues are addressed in this paper: (1) the role of life events in triggering the cessation process, and (2) the relationship between cognitive and life situation changes in the desistance process.

First, the crime desistance literature is reviewed briefly. Second, the broader deviance literature is drawn upon to construct a social-psychological model of cessation. Then the model is evaluated using life history data from a sample of female offenders convicted of serious street crimes.

The Desistance Process

The common themes in the literature on exiting deviant careers offer useful perspectives for developing a theory of cessation. The decision to stop deviant behavior appears to be preceded by a variety of factors, most of which are negative social sanctions or consequences. Health problems, difficulties with the law or with maintaining a current lifestyle, threats of other social sanctions from family or close relations, and a general rejection of the social world in which the behaviors thrive are often antecedents of the decision to quit. For some, religious conversions or immersion into alternative sociocultural settings with powerful norms (e.g., treatment ideology) provide paths for cessation (Mulvey and LaRosa 1986; Stall and Biernacki 1986).

. . . A model for understanding desistance from crime is presented below. Three stages characterize the cessation process: building resolve or discovering motivation to stop (i.e., socially disjunctive experiences), making and publicly disclosing the decision to stop, and maintaining the new behaviors and integrating into new social networks (Stall and Biernacki 1986; Mulvey and Aber 1988). These phases . . . describe three ideal-typical phases of desistance: "turning points" where offenders begin consciously to experience negative effects (socially disjunctive experiences); "active quitting" where they take steps to exit crime (public pronouncement); and "maintaining cessation" (identity transformation):

Stage 1 Catalysts for change

Socially disjunctive experiences

- Hitting rock bottom
- Fear of death
- Tiredness
- Illness

Delayed deterrence

- Increased probability of punishment
- Increased difficulty in doing time
- Increased severity of sanctions
- Increasing fear

Assessment

- Reappraisal of life and goals
- Psychic change

Decision

- Decision to quit and/or initial attempts at desistance
- Continuing possibility of criminal participation

Stage 2 Discontinuance

- Public pronouncement of decision to end criminal participation
- Claim to a new social identity

Stage 3 Maintenance of the decision to stop

- Ability to successfully renegotiate identity
- Support of significant others
- Integration into new social networks
- Ties to conventional roles
- Stabilization of new social identity

Stage 1: Catalysts for Change

When external conditions change and reduce the rewards of deviant behavior, motivation may build to end criminal involvement. That process, and the resulting decision, seem to be associated with two related conditions: a series of negative, aversive, unpleasant experiences with criminal behavior, or corollary situations where the positive rewards, status, or gratification from crime are reduced. Shover and Thompson's (1992) research suggests that the probability of desistance from criminal participation increases as expectations for achieving rewards (e.g., friends, money, autonomy) via crime decrease and that changes in expectations are age-related. Shover (1983) contended that the daily routines of managing criminal involvement become tiring and burdensome to aging offenders. Consequently, the allure of crime diminishes as offenders get older. Aging may also increase the perceived formal risk of criminal participation. Cusson and Pinsonneault (1986, p. 76) sposited that "with age, criminals raise their estimates of the certainty of punishment." Fear of reimprisonment, fear of longer sentences, and the increasing difficulty of "doing time" have often been reported by investigators who have explored desistance.

Stage 2: Discontinuance

The second stage of the model begins with the public announcement that the offender has decided to end her criminal participation. Such an announcement forces the start of a process of renegotiation of the offender's social identity (Stall and Biernacki 1986). After this announcement, the offender must not only cope with the instrumental aspects (e.g., financial) of her life but must also begin to redefine important emotional and social relationships that are influenced by or predicated upon criminal behavior.

Leaving a deviant subculture is difficult. Biernacki (1986) noted the exclusiveness of the social involvements maintained by former addicts during initial stages of abstinence. With social embedment comes the gratification of social acceptance and identity. The decision to end a behavior that is socially determined and supported implies withdrawal of the social gratification it brings. Thus, the more deeply embedded in a criminal social context, the more dependent the offender is on that social world for her primary sources of approval and social definition.

The responses by social control agents, family members, and peer supporters to further criminal participation are critical to shaping the outcome of discontinuance. New social and emotional worlds to replace the old ones may strengthen the decision to stop. Adler (1992) found that outside associations and involvements provide a critical bridge back into society for dealers who have decided to leave the drug subculture. With discontinuance comes the difficult work of identity transformations (Biernacki 1986) and establishing new social definitions of behavior and relationships to reinforce them.

Stage 3: Maintenance

Following the initial stages of discontinuance, strategies to avoid a return to crime build on the strategies first used to break from a lengthy pattern of criminal participation: further integration into a noncriminal identity and social world and maintenance of this new identity. Maintenance depends in part on replacing deviant networks of peers and associates with supports that both censure criminal participation and approve of new nondeviant beliefs. Treatment interventions (e.g., drug treatment, social service programs) are important sources of alternative social supports to maintain a noncriminal lifestyle. In other words, maintenance depends on immersion into a social world where criminal behavior meets immediately with strong formal and informal sanctions.

Despite efforts to maintain noncriminal involvement, desistance is likely to be episodic, with occasional relapses interspersed with lengthening of lulls in criminal activity. Le Blanc and Frechette (1989) proposed the possibility that criminal activity slows down before coming to an end and that this slowing down process becomes apparent in three ways: deceleration, specialization, and reaching a ceiling. Thus, before stopping criminal activity, the offender gradually acts out less frequently, limits the variety of crimes more and more, and ceases increasing the seriousness of criminal involvement.

Age is a critical variable in desistance research, regardless of whether it is associated with maturation or similar developmental concepts. Cessation is part of a social-psychological transformation for the offender. A strategy to stabilize the transition to a noncriminal lifestyle requires active use of supports to maintain the norms that have been substituted for the forces that supported criminal behavior in the past.

Findings

Resolving to Stop

Despite its initial excitement and allure, the life of a street criminal is a hard one. A host of severe personal problems plague most street offenders and normally become progressively worse as their careers continue. In present study, the women's lives were ominated by a powerful, often incapacitating, need for drugs. Consequently, economic problems were the most frequent complaint voiced by the respondents. Savings were quickly exhausted, and the culture of addiction justified virtually any means to get money to support their habits. For the majority of the women, the problem of maintaining an addiction took precedence over other interests and participation in other social worlds.

People the respondents associated with, their primary reference group, were involved in illicit behaviors. Over time, the women in the study became further enmeshed in deviance and further alienated, both socially and psychologically, from conventional life. The women's lives became bereft of conventional involvements, obligations, and responsibilities. The excitement at the lifestyle that may have characterized their early criminal career phase gave way to a much more grave daily existence.

Thus, the women in our study could not and did not simply cease their deviant acts by "drifting" (Matza 1964) back toward conventional norms, values, and lifestyles. Unlike many of Waldorf's (1983) heroin addicts who drifted away from heroin without conscious effort, all of the women in our study made a conscious decision to stop. In short, Matza's concept of drift did not provide a useful framework for understanding our respondents' exit from crime.

The following accounts illustrate the uncertainty and vulnerability of street life for the women in our sample. Denise, a 33-year-old black woman, has participated in a wide range of street crimes including burglary, robbery, assault, and drug dealing. She began dealing drugs when she was 14 and was herself using cocaine on a regular basis by age 19.

I was in a lot of fights: So I had fights over, uh, drugs, or, you know, just manipulation. There's a lot of manipulation in that life. Everybody's tryin' to get over. Everybody will stab you in your back, you know. Nobody gives a fuck about the next person, you know. It's just when you want it, you want it. You know, when you want that drug, you know, you want that drug.

There's a lot of lyin', a lot of manipulation. It's, it's, it's crazy!

Gazella, a 38-year-old Hispanic woman, had been involved in crime for 22 years when we interviewed her.

I'm 38 years old. I ain't no young woman no more, man. Drugs have changed, lifestyles have changed. Kids are killing you now for turf. Yeah, turf, and I was destroyin' myself. I was miserable. I was . . . I was gettin' high all the time to stay up to keep the business going, and it was really nobody I could trust.

Additional illustrations of the exigencies of street life are provided by April and Stephanie. April is a 25-year-old black woman who had been involved in crime since she was 11.

I wasn't eating. Sometimes I wouldn't eat for two or three days. And I would . . . a lot of times I wouldn't have the time, or I wouldn't want to spend the money to eat— I've got to use it to get high.

Stephanie, a 27-year-old black woman, had used and sold crack for 5 years when we interviewed her.

I knew that, uh, I was gonna get killed out here. I wasn't havin' no respect for myself. No one else was respecting me. Every relationship I got into, as long as I did drugs, it was gonna be constant disrespect involved, and it come . . . to the point of me gettin' killed.

When the spiral down finally reached its lowest point, the women were overwhelmed by a sense of personal despair. In reporting the early stages of this period of despair, the respondents consistently voiced two themes: the futility of their lives and their isolation.

Barbara, a 31-year-old black woman, began using crack when she was 23. By age 25, Barbara had lost her job at the Board of Education and was involved in burglary and robbery. Her account is typical of the despair the women in our sample eventually experienced.

. . . the fact that my family didn't trust me anymore, and the way that my daughter was looking at me, and, uh, my mother wouldn't let me in her house any more, and I was sleepin' on the trains. And I was sleepin' on the beaches in the summertime. And I was really frightened. I was real scared of the fact that I had to sleep on the train. And, uh, I had to wash up in the Port Authority.

The spiral down for Gazella also resulted in her living on the streets.

I didn't have a place to live. My kids had been taken away from me. You know, constantly being harassed like 3 days out of the week by the Tactical Narcotics Team [police]. I didn't want to be bothered with people. I was gettin' tired of the lyin', schemin', you know, stayin' in abandoned buildings.

Alicia, a 29-year-old Hispanic woman, became involved in street violence at age 12. She commented on the personal isolation that was a consequence of her involvement in crime:

When I started getting involved in crime, you know, and drugs, the friends that I had, even my family, I stayed away from them, you know. You know how you look bad and you feel bad, and you just don't want those people to see you like you are. So I avoided seeing them.

For some, the emotional depth of the rock bottom crisis was felt as a sense of mortification. The women felt as if they had nowhere to turn to salvage a sense of well-being or self-worth. Suicide was considered a better alternative than remaining in such an undesirable social and psychological state. Denise is one example:

I ran into a girl who I went to school with that works on Wall Street. And I compared her life to mine and it was like miserable. And I just wanted out. I wanted a new life. I was tired, I was run down, looking bad. I got out by smashing myself through a sixth-floor window. Then I went to the psychiatric ward and I met this real nice doctor, and we talked every day. She fought to keep me in the hospital because she felt I wouldn't survive. She believed in me. And she talked me into going into a drug program.

Marginalization from family, friends, children, and work—in short, the loss of traditional life structures—left the women vulnerable to chaotic street conditions. After initially being overwhelmed by despair, the women began to question and reevaluate basic assumptions about their identities and their social construction of the world. Like Shover's (1983) male property offenders, the women also began to view the criminal justice system as "an imposing accumulation of aggravations and deprivations" (p. 212). They grew tired of the street experiences and the problems and consequences of criminal involvement.

Many of the women acknowledged that, with age, it is more difficult to do time and that the fear of incurring a long prison sentence the next time influenced their decision to stop. Cusson and Pinsonneault (1986, p. 76) made the same observation with male robbers. Gazella, April, and Denise, quoted earlier, recall:

Gazella: First of all, when I was in prison I was like, I was so humiliated. At my age [38] I was really kind of embarrassed, but I knew that was the lifestyle that I was leadin'. And people I used to talk to would tell me, well, you could do this, and you don't have to get busted. But then I started thinking why are all these people here. So it doesn't, you know, really work. So I came home, and I did go back to selling again, but you know I knew I was on probation. And I didn't want to do no more time.

April: Jail, being in jail. The environment, having my freedom taken away. I saw myself keep repeating the same pattern, and I didn't want to do that. Uh, I had missed my daughter. See, being in jail that long period of time, I was able to detox. And when I detoxed, I kind of like had a clear sense of thinking, and that's when I came to the realization that, uh, this is not working for me.

Denise: I saw the person that I was dealing with—my partner—I saw her go upstate to Bedford for 2 to 4 years. I didn't want to deal with it. I didn't want to go. Bedford is a prison, women's prison. And I couldn't see myself givin' up 2 years of my life for something that I knew I could change in another way.

As can be seen from the above, the influence of punishment on these women was due to their belief that if they continued to be olved in crime, they would be apprehended, convicted, and incarcerated.

For many of the women, it was the stresses of street life and the fear of dying on the streets that motivated their decision to quit the criminal life. Darlene, a 25-year-old black woman, recalled the stress associated with the latter stage of her career selling drugs:

The simple fact is that I really, I thought that I would die out there. I thought that someone would kill me out there and I would be killed; I had a fear of being on the front page one day and being in the newspaper dying. I wanted to live, and I didn't just want to exist.

Sonya, a 27-year-old Hispanic woman, provided an account of what daily life was like on the streets:

You get tired of bein' tired, you know. I got tired of hustlin', you know. I got tired of livin' the way I was livin', you know. Due to your body, your body, mentally, emotionally, you know. Everybody's tryin' to get over. Everybody will stab you in your back. Nobody gives a fuck about the next person. And I used to have people talkin' to me, "You know, you're not a bad lookin' girl. You know, why you don't get yourself together."

Perhaps even more important, the women felt that they had wasted time. They became acutely aware of time as a diminishing resource (Shover 1983). They reported that they saw themselves going nowhere. They had arrived at a point where crime seemed senseless, and their lives had reached a dead end. Implicit in this assessment was the belief that gaining a longer-range perspective on one's life was a first step in changing. Such deliberations develop as a result of "socially disjunctive experiences" that cause the offender to experience social stress, feelings of alienation, and dissatisfaction with her present identity (Ray 1961).

Breaking Away from the Life

Forming a commitment to change is only the first step toward the termination of a criminal career. The offender enters a period that has been characterized as a "running struggle" with problems of social identity (Ray 1961, p. 136). Successful desisters must work to clarify and strengthen their nondeviant identity and redefine their street experience in terms more compatible with a conventional lifestyle. The second stage of the desistance process begins with the public announcement or "certification" (Meisenhelder 1977, p. 329) that the offender has decided to end her deviant behavior. After this announcement, the offender must begin to redefine economic, social, and emotional relationships that were based on a deviant street subculture.

The time following the announcement was generally a period of ambivalence and crisis for the study participants, because so much of their lives revolved around street life and because they had, at best, weak associations with the conventional world. Many of the women remembered the uncertainty they felt and the social dilemmas they faced after they decided to stop their involvement in crime.

Denise: I went and looked up my friends and to see what was doing, and my girlfriend Mia was like, she was gettin' paid. And I was livin' on a $60 stipend. And I wasn't with it. Mia was good to me, she always kept money in my pocket when I came home. I would walk into her closet and change into clothes that I'm more accustomed to. She started calling me Pen again. She stopped calling me Denise. And I would ride with her knowing that she had a gun or a package in the car. But I wouldn't touch nothin'. But that was my rationale. As long as I don't fuck with nothin'. Yeah, she was like I can give you a grand and get you started. I said I know you can, but I can't. She said I can give you a grand, and she kept telling me that over and over; and I wasn't that far from taking the grand and getting started again.

Barbara: After I decided to change, I went to a party with my friend. And people was around me and they was drinkin' and stuff, and I didn't want to drink. I don't have the urge of drinking. If anything, it would be smokin' crack. And when I left the party, I felt like I was missing something—like something was missing. And it was the fact that I wasn't gettin' high. But I know the consequences of it. If I take a drink, I'm gonna smoke crack. If I, uh, sniff some blow, I'm gonna smoke crack. I might do some things like rob a store or something stupid and go to jail. So I don't want to put myself in that position.

At this stage of their transition, the women had to decide how to establish and maintain conventional relationships and what to do with themselves and their lives. Few of the women had maintained good relationships with people who were not involved in crime and drugs. Given this situation, the women had to seek alternatives to their present situation.

The large majority of study participants were aided in their social reintegration by outside help. These respondents sought formal treatment of some kind, typically residential drug treatment, to provide structure, social support, and a pathway to behavioral change. The women perceived clearly the need to remove themselves from the "scene" to meet new friends, and to begin the process of identity reformation. The following account by Alicia typifies the importance of a "geographic" cure:

> I love to get high, you know, and I love the way crack makes me feel. I knew that I needed long-term, I knew that I needed to go somewhere. All away from everything, and I just needed to away from everything. And I couldn't deal with responsibility at all. And, uh, I was just so ashamed of the way that I had, you know, became and the person that I became that I just wanted to start over again.

Social avoidance strategies were common to all attempts at stopping. When the women removed themselves from their old world and old locations, involvement in crime and drugs was more difficult.

> **April:** Yeah, I go home, but I don't, I don't socialize with the people. I don't even speak to anybody really. I go and I come. I don't go to the areas that I used to be in. I don't go there anymore. I don't walk down the same blocks I used to walk down. I always take different locations.

> **Denise:** I miss the fast money; otherwise, I don't miss my old life. I get support from my positive friends, and in the program. I talk about how I felt being around my old associates, seeing them, you know, going back to my old neighborhood. It's hard to deal with, I have to push away.

Maintaining a Conventional Life

Desisters have little chance of staying out of the life for an extended period of time if they stay in the social world of crime and addiction. They must rebuild and maintain a network of primary relations who accept and support their nondeviant identity if they are to be successful (the third stage of this model). This is no easy task, since in most cases the desisters have alienated their old nondeviant primary relations.

To a great extent, the women in this study most resemble religious converts in their attempts to establish and maintain support networks that validate their new sense of self. Treatment programs not only provide a ready-made primary group for desisters, but also a well-established pervasive identity (Travisano 1970), that of ex-con and/or ex-addict, that informs the women's view of themselves in a variety of interactions. Reminders of "spoiled identities" (Goffman 1963) such as criminal, "con," and "junkie" serve as a constant reference point for new experiences and keep salient the ideology of conventional living (Faupel 1991). Perhaps most important, these programs provide the women with an alternative basis for life structure—one that is devoid of crime, drugs, and other subcultural elements.

The successful treatment program, however, is one that ultimately facilitates dissociation from the program and promotes independent living. Dissociation from programs to participate in conventional living requires association, or reintegration, with conventional society. Friends and educational and occupational roles helped study participants reaffirm their noncriminal identities and bond themselves to conventional lifestyles. Barbara described the assistance she receives from friends and treatment groups:

> . . . a bunch of friends that always confronts me on what I'm doing' and where I'm goin', and they just want the best for me. And none of them use drugs. I go to a lot outside support groups, you know. They help me have more confidence in myself. I have new friends now. Some of them are in treatment. Some have always been straight. They know. You know, they glad, you know, when I see them.

In the course of experiencing relationships with conventional others and participating in conventional roles, the women developed a strong social-psychological commitment not to return to crime and drug use. These commitments most often revolved around renewed affiliations with their children, relationships with new friends, and the acquisition of educational and vocational skills. The social relationships, interests, and investments that develop in the course of desistance reflect the gradual emergence of new identities. Such stakes in conventional identity form the social-psychological context within which control and desistance are possible (Waldorf et al. 1991).

In short, the women in the study developed a stake in their new lives that was incompatible with street life. This new stake served as a wedge to help maintain the separation of the women from the world of the streets (Biernacki 1986). The desire to maintain one's sense of self was an important incentive for avoiding return to crime.

> **Alicia:** I like the fact that I have my respect back. I like the fact that, uh, my daughter trusts me again. And my mother don't mind leavin' me in the house, and she don't have to worry that when she come in her TV might be gone.

> **Barbara:** I have new friends. I have my children back in my life. I have my education. It keeps me straight. I can't forget where I came from because I get scared to go back. I don't want to hurt nobody. I just want to live a normal life.

Janelle, a 22-year-old black woman, started dealing drugs and carrying a .38-caliber gun when she was 15. She described the ongoing tension between staying straight and returning to her old social world:

> It's hard, it's hard stayin' on the right track. But letting myself know that I'm worth more. I don't have to go in a store today and steal anything. I don't deserve that. I don't deserve to make myself feel really bad. Then once again I would be steppin' back and feel that this is all I can do.

Overall, the success of identity transformations hinges on the women's abilities to establish and maintain commitments and involvements in conventional aspects of life. As the women began to feel accepted and trusted within some conventional social circles, their determination to exit from crime was strengthened, as were their social and personal identities as noncriminals.

Discussion

The primary purpose of this study was to describe—from the offenders' perspective—how women embedded in criminal street subcultures could end their deviance. Desistance appears to be a process as complex and lengthy as that of initial involvement. It was interesting to find that some of the key concepts in initiation of deviance—social bond, differential association, deterrence, age—were important in our analysis. We saw the aging offender take the threat of punishment seriously, reestablish links with conventional society, and sever association with subcultural street elements.

Our research supports Adler's (1992) finding that shame plays a limited role in the decision to return to conventional life for individuals who are entrenched in deviant subcultures. Rather, they exit deviance because they have evolved through the typical phases of their deviant careers.

In the present study, we found that the decision to give up crime was triggered by a shock of some sort (i.e., a socially disjunctive experience), by a delayed deterrence process, or both. The women then entered a period of crisis. Anxious and dissatisfied, they took stock of their lives and criminal activity. They arrived at a point where their way of life seemed senseless. Having made this assessment, the women then worked to clarify and strengthen their nondeviant identities. This phase began with the reevaluation of life goals and the public announcement of their decision to end involvement in crime. Once the decision to quit was made, the women turned to relationships that had not been ruined by their deviance, or they created new relationships. The final stage, maintaining cessation, involved integration into a nondeviant lifestyle. This meant restructuring the entire pattern of their lives (i.e., primary relationships, daily routines, social situations). For most women, treatment groups provided the continuing support needed to maintain a nondeviant status.

The change processes and turning points described by the women in the present research were quite similar to those reported by men in previous studies (Shover 1983, 1985; Cusson and Pinsonneault 1986). Collectively, these findings suggest that desistance is a pragmatically constructed project of action created by the individual within a given social context. Turning points occur "part of a process over time and not as a dramatic lasting change that takes place at any one time" (Pickles and Rutter 1991, P. 134). Thus, the return to conventional life occurs more because of "push" than "pull" factors (Adler 1992), because the career of involvement in crime moves offenders beyond the point at which they find it enjoyable to the point at which it is debilitating and anxiety-provoking.

Considering the narrow confines of our empirical data, it is hardly necessary to point out the limits of generalizability. Our analysis refers to the woman deeply involved in crime and immersed in a street subculture who finds the strength and resources to change her way of life. The fact that all the women in this study experienced a long period of personal deterioration and a "rock bottom" experience before they were able to exit crime does not justify a conclusion that this process occurs with all offenders. Undoubtedly, there are other scenarios (e.g., the occasional offender who drifts in and out of crime, the offender who stops when criminal involvement conflicts with commitments to conventional life, the battered woman who kills) in which the question of desistance does not arise. Hence, there is a need to conceptualize and measure the objective and subjective elements of change among various male and female offender subgroups.

Furthermore, the evidence presented here does not warrant the conclusion that none of the women ever renewed their involvement in crime. Because the study materials consist of retrospective information, with all its attendant problems, we cannot state with certainty whether desistance from crime is permanent. Still, it is also clear that these women broke their pattern of involvement in crime for substantial lengths of time and have substantially changed their lives.

References

Adler, Patricia. 1992. "The 'Post' Phase of Deviant Careers: Reintegrating Traffickers." *Deviant Behavior* 13: 103-126.

Anglin, Douglas, and George Speckhart. 1988. "Narcotics Use and Crime: Multisample, Multimethod Analysis." *Criminology* 26: 197-234.

Biernacki, Patrick A. 1986. *Pathways from Heroin Addiction: Recovery Without Treatment*. Philadelphia: Temple University Press.

Biernacki, Patrick A., and Dan Waldorf. 1981. "Snowball Sampling: Problems Techniques of Chain Referral Sampling." *Sociological Methods and Research* 10: 141-163.

Blumstein, Alfred, Jacqueline Cohen, Jeffrey A. Roth, and Christy A. Visher. 1986. *Careers and Career Criminals*. Washington, DC: National Academy Press.

Collins, J., R. Hubbard, and J. V. Rachal. 1985. "Expensive Drug Use and Income: A Test of Explanatory Hypotheses." *Criminology* 23: 743-764.

Cusson, Maurice, and Pierre Pinsonneault. 1986. "The Decision to Give Up Crime." In *The Reasoning Criminal: Rational Choice Perspectives on Offending*, edited by Derek Cornish and Ronald Clarke. New York: Springer-Verlag.

Daly, Kathy, and Meda Chesney-Lind. 1988. "Feminism and Criminology." *Justice Quarterly* 5: 101-143.

Faupel, Charles. 1991. *Shooting Dope: Career Patterns Of Hard-Core Heroin Users*. Gainesville: University of Florida Press.

Goffman, Erving. 1963. *Stigma: Notes on the Management of Spoiled Identity*. Englewood Cliffs, NJ: Prentice-Hall.

Hirschi, Travis, and H. C. Selvin. 1967. *Delinquency Research: An Appraisal of Analytic Methods*. New York: Free Press.

Le Blanc, Marc, and M. Frechette. 1989. *Male Criminal Activity from Childhood Through Youth: Multilevel and Developmental Perspective*. New York: Springer-Verlag.

Matza, David. 1964. *Delinquency and Drift*. New York: Wiley.

Meisenhelder, Thomas. 1977. "An Exploratory Study of Exiting from Criminal Careers." *Criminology* 15: 319-334.

Mulvey, Edward P., and John F. LaRosa. 1986. "Delinquency Cessation and Adolescent Development: Preliminary Data." *American Journal of Orthopsychiatry* 56: 212-224.

Petersilia, Joan, Peter Greenwood, and Marvin Lavin. 1978. *Criminal Careers of Habitual Felons*. Washington, DC: Law Enforcement Assistance Administration, U.S. Department of Justice.

Peterson, M., and H. Braiker. 1980. *Doing Crime: A Survey of California Prison Inmates*. Santa Monica, CA: Rand.

Pickles, Andrew, and Michael Rutter. 1991. "Statistical and Conceptual Models of 'Turning Points' in Developmental Processes." In *Problems and Methods in Longitudinal Research: Stability and Change*, edited by D. Magnusson, L. Bergman, G. Rudinger, and B. Torestad (pp. 110-136). New York: Cambridge University Press.

Ray, Marsh. 1961. "The Cycle of Abstinence and Relapse Among Heroin Addicts." *Social Problems* 9: 132-140.

Shover, Neil. 1983. "The Latter Stages of Ordinary Property Offenders' Careers." *Social Problems* 31: 208-218.

——. 1985. *Aging Criminals*. Newbury Park, CA: Sage.

Shover, Neil, and Carol Thompson. 1992. "Age, Differential Expectations, and Crime Desistance." *Criminology* 30: 89-104.

Stall, Ron, and Patrick Biemacki. 1986. "Spontaneous Remission from the Problematic Use of Substances: An Inductive Model Derived from a Comparative Analysis of the Alcohol, Opiate, Tobacco, and Food/Obesity Literatures." *International Journal of the Addictions* 2: 1-23.

Travisano, R. 1970. "Alteration and Conversion as Qualitatively Different Transformations." In *Social Psychology Through Symbolic Interaction*, edited by G. Stone and H. Farberman (pp. 594-605). Boston: Ginn-Blaisdell.

Waldorf, Dan. 1983. "Natural Recovery from Opiate Addiction: Some Social Psychological Processes of Untreated Recovery." *Journal of Drug Issues* 13: 237-280.

Waldorf, Dan, Craig Reinerman, and Sheila Murphy. 1991. *Cocaine Changes*. Philadelphia: Temple University Press.

Weiner, Neil, and Marvin E. Wolfgang. 1989. *Violent Crime, Violent Criminals*. Newbury Park, CA: Sage.

Weis, Joseph G. 1989. "Family Violence Research Methodology and Design." In *Family Violence*, edited by Lloyd Ohlin and Michael Tonry (pp. 117-162). Chicago: University of Chicago Press.

Ira Sommers, Deborah R. Baskin, and Jeffery Fagan, "Getting out of the Life: Desistance by Female Street Offenders." In *Deviant Behavior*, vol. 15 (2) 1994, pp. 125–149. Washington, D.C.: Taylor and Francis, Inc. Reprinted with permission. ✦

Section III

Occupational Crime

The term *occupational crime* refers to crimes committed through opportunities created in the course of a legal occupation. The use of labels such as *white-collar crime* in the past almost always connoted crimes committed by the rich and powerful. Most criminologists today have broadened the term to refer to crimes committed by persons in a wide range of situations. The focus today is on the nature of the crime and not on the person committing it, thus the term "occupational crime."

Research reported in this book (Åkerström, Shover and Honaker, Wright and Decker, and Feeney) tends to support the idea that most offenders accept responsibility for their crimes. For example, Floyd Feeney's ("Robbers as Decision Makers") subjects reported:

[I did it] just to cause some trouble.

I don't know. It sounded easy and I guess we needed the money.

I did it because I didn't care.

I was mad and I had to do something to get it out of my system.

Åkerström's respondents (thieves and addicts) also appeared to accept the responsibility for their criminal actions. One stated:

It's not society's fault that I'm here [in prison]—it's the good money you can earn through crime. That's why I'm here.

However, the consistent theme in the following articles, which deal with occupational crime, is that these offenders concoct elaborate justifications, excuses, and rationalizations to avoid accepting responsibility for their criminal behavior. Perhaps it is because their primary identity is noncriminal. They are doctors, lawyers, bankers, stockbrokers, etc. To conceive of themselves as criminals is difficult, if not impossible.

In this section Michael Benson ("Denying the Guilty Mind") explains how individuals convicted of occupational crimes attempt to avoid the stigmatization of criminality by denying criminal intent. In a similar vein, Paul Jesilow and his associates ("How Doctors Defraud Medicaid") also focus on occupational criminals' use of "techniques of neutralization" to cast their actions in a more favorable light.

These studies are somewhat unusual in that ethnographic research of crime "in the suites" is much more difficult to accomplish than studies of crime "in the streets." Potential subjects are less likely to talk with researchers and not as easily approached. Patricia Adler (personal communication, 1995) correctly noted that it is easier to "study down than to study up." Thus, the pool of field studies of so-called "white-collar" crime is small; however, the papers included here are excellent examples of what can be accomplished with a difficult population. ✦

10

Denying the Guilty Mind: Accounting for Involvement in a White-Collar Crime

Michael L. Benson

The author examines the excuses and justifications used by white-collar offenders to explain their involvement in criminal activities
and to deny their criminality.

Michael L. Benson's study is based on interviews with a sample of 30 convicted white-collar offenders. The interviews were supplemented with an examination of the files maintained by federal law enforcement authorities
(prosecutors, probation officers, judges) concerned with the prosecution of white-collar
offenses. The authors defines white-collar offenders as ". . . those convicted of economic
offenses committed through the use of indirec-
tion, fraud, or collusion" (p. 586). The offenses
represented in the sample included such offenses as securities and exchange fraud, antitrust violations, embezzlement, false claims,
and tax evasion. All of the offenders were men.

Adjudication as a criminal is, to use Garfinkel's (1956) classic term, a degradation
ceremony. The focus of this article is on how
offenders attempt to defeat the success of this
ceremony and deny their own criminality
through the use of accounts. However, in the
interest of showing in as much detail as possible all sides of the experience undergone by
these offenders, it is necessary to treat first
the guilt and inner anguish that is felt by
many white-collar offenders even though
they deny being criminals. This is best accomplished by beginning with a description of a
unique feature of the prosecution of white-
collar crimes.

In white-collar criminal cases, the issue is
likely to be *why* something was done, rather
than *who* did it (Edelhertz, 1970:47). There is
often relatively little disagreement as to what
happened. In the words of one Assistant U.S.
Attorney interviewed for the study:

> If you actually had a movie playing, nei-
> ther side would dispute that a person
> moved in this way and handled this piece
> of paper, etc. What it comes down to is, did
> they have the criminal intent?

If the prosecution is to proceed past the
investigatory stages, the prosecutor must in-
fer from the pattern of events that conscious
criminal intent was present and believe that
sufficient evidence exists to convince a jury
of this interpretation of the situation. As Katz
(1979:445-446) has noted, making this inference can be difficult because of the way in
which white-collar illegalities are integrated
into ordinary occupational routines. Thus,
prosecutors in conducting trials, grand jury
hearings, or plea negotiations spend a great
deal of effort establishing that the defendant
did indeed have the necessary criminal intent. By concentrating on the offender's motives, the prosecutor attacks the very essence
of the white-collar offender's public and personal image as an upstanding member of the
community The offender is portrayed as
someone with a guilty mind.

Not surprisingly, therefore, the most consistent and recurrent pattern in the interviews, though not present in all of them, was
denial of criminal intent, as opposed to the
outright denial of any criminal behavior
whatsoever. Most offenders acknowledged
that their behavior probably could be con-
strued as falling within the conduct proscribed by stature, but they uniformly denied
that their actions were motivated by a guilty
mind. This is not to say, however, that offenders *felt* no guilt or shame as a result of conviction. On the contrary, indictment, prosecu-

tion, and conviction provoke a variety of emotions among offenders.

The enormous reality of the offender's lived emotion (Denzin, 1984) in admitting guilt is perhaps best illustrated by one offender's description of his feelings during the hearing at which he pled guilty.

> You know (the plea's) what really hurt. I didn't even know I had feet. I felt numb. My head was just floating. There was no feeling, except a state of suspended animation. . . . For a brief moment, l almost hesitated. I almost said not guilty. If I had been alone, I would have fought, but my family. . . .

The traumatic nature of this moment lies, in part, in the offender's feeling that only one aspect of his life is being considered. From the offender's point of view his crime represents only one small part of his life. It does not typify his inner self, and to judge him solely on the basis of this one event seems an atrocious injustice to the offender.

For some the memory of the event is so painful that they want to obliterate it entirely, as the two following quotations illustrate.

> I want quiet. I want to forget. I want to cut with the past.

> I've already divorced myself from the problem. I don't even want to hear the names of certain people ever again. It brings me pain.

For others, rage rather than embarrassment seemed to be the dominant emotion.

> I never really felt any embarrassment over the whole thing. I felt rage and it wasn't false or self-serving. It was really (something) to see this thing in action and recognize what the whole legal system has come to through its development, and the abuse of the grand jury system and the abuse of the indictment system. . . .

The role of the news media in the process of punishment and stigmatization should not be overlooked. All offenders whose cases were reported on by the news media were either embarrassed or embittered or both by the public exposure.

> The only one I am bitter at is the newspapers, as many people are. They are un-

fair because you can't get even. They can say things that are untrue, and let me say this to you. They wrote an article on me that was so blasphemous, that was so horrible. They painted me as an insidious, miserable creature, wringing out the last penny. . . .

Offenders whose cases were not reported on by the news media expressed relief at having avoided that kind of embarrassment, sometimes saying that greater publicity would have been worse than any sentence they could have received.

In court, defense lawyers are fond of presenting white-collar offenders as having suffered enough by virtue of the humiliation of public adjudication as criminals. On the other hand, prosecutors present them as cavalier individuals who arrogantly ignore the law and brush off its weak efforts to stigmatize them as criminals. Neither of these stereotypes is entirely accurate. The subjective effects of conviction on white-collar offenders are varied and complex. One suspects that this is true of all offenders, not only white-collar offenders.

The emotional responses of offenders to conviction have not been the subject of extensive research. However, insofar as an individual's emotional response to adjudication may influence the deterrent or crime-reinforcing impact of punishment on him or her, further study might reveal why some offenders stop their criminal behavior while others go on to careers in crime (Casper, 1978:80).

Although the offenders displayed a variety of different emotions with respect to their experiences, they were nearly unanimous in denying basic criminality. To see how white-collar offenders justify and excuse their crimes, we turn to their accounts. The small number of cases rules out the use of any elaborate classification techniques. Nonetheless, it is useful to group offenders by offense when presenting their interpretations.

Antitrust Violators

Four of the offenders had been convicted of antitrust violations, all in the same case involving the building and contracting industry. Four major themes characterized their accounts. First, antitrust offenders focused on the everyday character and historical continuity of their offenses.

> It was a way of doing business before we even got into the business. So it was like why do you brush your teeth in the morning or something. . . . It was a part of the everyday. . . . It was a method of survival.

The offenders argued that they were merely following established and necessary industry practices. These practices were presented as being necessary for the well-being of the industry as a whole, not to mention their own companies. Further, they argued that cooperation among competitors was either allowed or actively promoted by the government in other industries and professions.

The second theme emphasized by the offenders was the characterization of their actions as blameless. They admitted talking to competitors and admitted submitting intentionally noncompetitive bids. However, they presented these practices as being done not for the purpose of rigging prices nor to make exorbitant profits. Rather, the everyday practices of the industry required them to occasionally submit bids on projects they really did not want to have. To avoid the effort and expense of preparing full-fledged bids, they would call a competitor to get a price to use. Such a situation might arise, for example, when a company already had enough work for the time being, but was asked by a valued customer to submit a bid anyway.

> All you want to do is show a bid, so that in some cases it was for as small a reason as getting your deposit back on the plans and specs. So you just simply have no interest in getting the job and just call to see if you can find someone to give you a price to use, so that you don't have to go through the expense of an entire bid preparation. Now that is looked at very unfavorably, and it is a technical violation, but it was strictly an opportunity to keep your name in front of a desired customer. Or you may find yourself in a situation where somebody is doing work for a customer, has done work for many, many years and is totally acceptable, totally fair. There is no problem. But suddenly they (the customer) get an idea that they ought to have

> a few tentative figures, and you're called in, and you are in a moral dilemma. There's really no reason for you to attempt to compete in that circumstance. And so there was it way to back out.

Managed in this way, an action that appears on the surface to be a straightforward and conscious violation of antitrust regulations becomes merely a harmless business practice that happens to be a "technical violation." The offender can then refer to his personal history to verify his claim that, despite technical violations, he is in reality a law-abiding person. In the words of one offender, "Having been in the business for 33 years, you don't just automatically become a criminal overnight."

Third, offenders were very critical of the motives and tactics of prosecutors. Prosecutors were accused of being motivated solely by the opportunity for personal advancement presented by winning a big case. Further, they were accused of employing prosecution selectively and using tactics that allowed the most culpable offenders to go free. The Department of Justice was painted as using antitrust prosecutions for political purposes.

The fourth theme emphasized by the antitrust offenders involved a comparison between their crimes and the crimes of street criminals. Antitrust offenses differ in their mechanics from street crimes in that they are not committed in one place and at one time. Rather, they are spatially and temporally diffuse and are intermingled with legitimate behavior. In addition, the victims of antitrust offenses tend not to be identifiable individuals, as is the case with most street crimes. These characteristics are used by antitrust violators to contrast their own behavior with that of common stereotypes of criminality. Real crimes are pictured as discrete events that have beginnings and ends and involve individuals who directly and purposely victimize someone else in a particular place and a particular time.

> It certainly wasn't a premeditated type of thing in our cases as far as I can see. . . . To me it's different than _____ and I sitting down and we plan, well, we're going to rob this bank tomorrow and premeditatedly go in there. . . . That wasn't the case

at all. . . . It wasn't like sitting down and planning I'm going to rob this bank type of thing. . . . It was just a common everyday way of doing business and surviving.

A consistent thread running through all of the interviews was the necessity for antitrust-like practices, given the realities of the business world. Offenders seemed to define the situation in such a manner that two sets of rules could be seen to apply. On the one hand, there are the legislatively determined rules—laws—which govern how one is to conduct one's business affairs. On the other hand, there is a higher set of rules based on the concepts of profit and survival, which are taken to define what it means to be in business in a capitalistic society. These rules do not just regulate behavior; rather, they constitute or create the behavior in question. If one is not trying to make a profit or trying to keep one's business going, then one is not really "in business." Following Searle (1969:33-41), the former type of rule can be called a regulative rule and the latter type a constitutive rule. In certain situations, one may have to violate a regulative rule in order to conform to the more basic constitutive rule of the activity in which one is engaged.

This point can best be illustrated through the use of an analogy involving competitive games. Trying to win is a constitutive rule of competitive games in the sense that if one is not trying to win, one is not really playing the game. In competitive games, situations may arise where a player deliberately breaks the rules even though he knows or expects he will be caught. In the game of basketball, for example, a player may deliberately foul an opponent to prevent him from making a sure basket. In this instance, one would understand that the fouler was trying to win by gambling that the opponent would not make the free throws. The player violates the rule against fouling in order to follow the higher rule of trying to win.

Trying to make a profit or survive in business can be thought of as a constitutive rule of capitalist economies. The laws that govern how one is allowed to make a profit are regulative rules, which can understandably be subordinated to the rules of trying to survive and profit. From the offender's point of view,

he is doing what businessmen in our society are supposed to do—that is, stay in business and make a profit. Thus, an individual who violates society's laws or regulations in certain situations may actually conceive of himself as thereby acting more in accord with the central ethos of his society than if he had been a strict observer of its law. One might suggest, following Denzin (1977), that for businessmen in the building and contracting industry, an informal structure exists below the articulated legal structure, one which frequently supersedes the legal structure. The informal structure may define as moral and "legal" certain actions that the formal legal structure defines as immoral and "illegal."

Tax Violators

Six of the offenders interviewed were convicted of income tax violations. Like antitrust violators, tax violators can rely upon the complexity of the tax laws and an historical tradition in which cheating on taxes is not really criminal. Tax offenders would claim that everybody cheats somehow on their taxes and present themselves as victims of an unlucky break, because they got caught.

> Everybody cheats on their income tax, 95% of the people. Even if it's for ten dollars it's the same principle. I didn't cheat. I just didn't know how to report it.

The widespread belief that cheating on taxes is endemic helps to lend credence to the offender's claim to have been singled out and to be no more guilty than most people.

Tax offenders were more likely to have acted as individuals rather than as part of a group and, as a result, were more prone to account for their offenses by referring to them as either mistakes or the product of special circumstances. Violations were presented as simple errors which resulted from ignorance and poor recordkeeping. Deliberate intention to steal from the government for personal benefit was denied.

> I didn't take the money. I have no bank account to show for all this money, where all this money is at that I was supposed to have. They never found the money, ever. There is no Swiss bank account, believe

me. My records were strictly one big mess. That's all it was. If only I had an accountant, this wouldn't even of happened. No way in God's creation would this ever have happened.

Other offenders would justify their actions by admitting that they were wrong while painting their motives as altruistic rather than criminal. Criminality was denied because they did not set out to deliberately cheat the government for their own personal gain. Like the antitrust offenders discussed above, one tax violator distinguished between his own crime and the crimes of real criminals.

I'm not a criminal. That is, I'm not a criminal from the standpoint of taking a gun and doing this and that. I'm a criminal from the standpoint of making a mistake, a serious mistake. . . . The thing that really got me involved in it is my feeling for the employees here, certain employees that are my right hand. In order to save them a certain amount of taxes and things like that, I'd extend money to them in cash, and the money came from these sources that I took it from. You know, cash sales and things of that nature, but practically all of it was turned over to the employees, because of my feeling for them.

All of the tax violators pointed out that they had no intention of deliberately victimizing the government. None of them denied the legitimacy of the tax laws, nor did they claim that they cheated because the government is not representative of the people (Conklin, 1977:99). Rather, as a result of ignorance or for altruistic reasons, they made decisions which turned out to be criminal when viewed from the perspective of the law. While they acknowledged the technical criminality of their actions, they tried to show that what they did was not criminally motivated.

Violations of Financial Trust

Four offenders were involved in violations of financial trust. Three were bank officers who embezzled or misapplied funds, and the fourth was a union official who embezzled from a union pension fund. Perhaps because embezzlement is one crime in this sample that can be considered *mala in se* [Editor's

note: Latin for "evil in itself"], these offenders were much more forthright about their crimes. Like the other offenders, the embezzlers would not go so far as to say "I am a criminal," but they did say "What I did was wrong, was criminal, and I knew it was." Thus, the embezzlers were unusual in that they explicitly admitted responsibility for their crimes. Two of the offenders clearly fit Cressey's scheme as persons with financial problems who used their positions to convert other people's money to their own use.

Unlike tax evasion, which can be excused by reference to the complex nature of tax regulations or antitrust violations, which can be justified as for the good of the organization as a whole, embezzlement requires deliberate action on the part of the offender and is almost inevitably committed for personal reasons. The crime of embezzlement, therefore, cannot be accounted for by using the same techniques that tax violators or antitrust violators do. The act itself can only be explained by showing that one was under extraordinary circumstances which explain one's uncharacteristic behavior. Three of the offenders referred explicitly to extraordinary circumstances and presented the offense as an aberration in their life history. For example, one offender described his situation in this manner:

As a kid, I never even—you know kids will sometimes shoplift from the dime store—I never even did that. I had never stolen a thing in my life and that was what was so unbelievable about the whole thing, but there were some psychological and personal questions that I wasn't dealing with very well. I wasn't terribly happily married. I was married to a very strong-willed woman and it just wasn't working out.

The offender in this instance goes on to exlain how, in an effort to impress his wife, he lived beyond his means and fell into debt.

A structural characteristic of embezzlement also helps the offender demonstrate his essential lack of criminality. Embezzlement is integrated into ordinary occupational routines. The illegal action does not stand out clearly against the surrounding set of legal actions. Rather, there is a high degree of surface correspondence between legal and illegal behavior. To maintain this correspondence, the offender must exercise some restraint when committing his crime. The embezzler must be discrete in his stealing; he cannot take all of the money available to him without at the same time revealing the crime. Once exposed, the offender can point to this restraint on his part as evidence that he is not really a criminal. That is, he can compare what happened with what could have happened in order to show how much more serious the offense could have been if he was really a criminal at heart.

> What I could have done if I had truly had a devious criminal mind and perhaps if I had been a little smarter—and I am not saying that with any degree of pride or any degree of modesty whatever, [as] it's being smarter in a bad, an evil way—I could have pulled this off on a grander scale and I might still be doing it.

Even though the offender is forthright about admitting his guilt, he makes a distinction between himself and someone with a truly "devious criminal mind."

Contrary to Cressey's (1953:57-66) findings, none of the embezzlers claimed that their offenses were justified because they were underpaid or badly treated by their employers. Rather, attention was focused on the unusual circumstances surrounding the offense and its atypical character when compared to the rest of the offender's life. This strategy is for the most part determined by the mechanics and organizational format of the offense itself. Embezzlement occurs within the organization but not for the organization. It cannot be committed accidentally or out of ignorance. It can be accounted for only by showing that the actor "was not himself" at the time of the offense or was under such extraordinary circumstances that embezzlement was an understandable response to an unfortunate situation. This may explain the finding that embezzlers tend to produce accounts that are viewed as more sufficient by the justice system than those produced by other offenders (Rothman and Gandossy, 1982). The only plausible option open to a convicted embezzler trying to explain his offense is to admit responsibility while justify-ing the action, an approach that apparently strikes a responsive chord with judges.

Fraud and False Statements

Ten offenders were convicted of some form of fraud or false statements charge. Unlike embezzlers, tax violators, or antitrust violators, these offenders were much more likely to deny committing any crime at all. Seven of the ten claimed that they, personally, were innocent of any crime, although each admitted that fraud had occurred. Typically, they claimed to have been set up by associates and to have been wrongfully convicted by the U.S. Attorney handling the case. One might call this the scapegoat strategy. Rather than admitting technical wrong-doing and then justifying or excusing it, the offender attempts to paint himself as a victim by shifting the blame entirely to another party. Prosecutors were presented as being either ignorant or politically motivated.

The outright of any crime whatsoever is unusual compared to the other types of offenders studied here. It may result from the nature of the crime of fraud. By definition, fraud involves a conscious attempt on the part of one or more persons to mislead others. While it is theoretically possible to accidentally violate the antitrust and tax laws, or to violate them for altruistic reasons, it is difficult to imagine how one could accidentally mislead someone else for his or her own good. Furthermore, in many instances, fraud is an aggressively acquisitive crime. The offender develops a scheme to bilk other people out of money or property, and does this not because of some personal problem but because the scheme is an easy way to get rich. Stock swindles, fraudulent loan scams, and so on are often so large and complicated that they cannot possibly be excused as foolish and desperate solutions to personal problems. Thus, those involved in large-scale frauds do not have the option open to most embezzlers of presenting themselves as persons responding defensively to difficult personal circumstances.

Furthermore, because fraud involves a deliberate attempt to mislead another, the offender who fails to remove himself from the scheme runs the risk of being shown to have a guilty mind. That is, he is shown to possess the most essential element of modern conceptions of criminality: an intent to harm another. His inner self would in this case be exposed as something other than what it has been presented as, and all of his previous actions would be subject to reinterpretation in light of this new perspective. For this reason, defrauders are most prone to denying any crime at all. The cooperative and conspiratorial nature of many fraudulent schemes makes it possible to put the blame on someone else and to present oneself as a scapegoat. Typically, this is done by claiming to have been duped by others.

Two illustrations of this strategy are presented below.

> I figured I wasn't guilty, so it wouldn't be that hard to disprove it, until, as I say, I went to court and all of a sudden they start bringing in these guys out of the woodwork implicating me that I never saw. Lot of it could be proved that I never saw.

> Inwardly, I personally felt that the only crime that I committed was not telling on these guys. Not that I deliberately, intentionally committed a crime against the system. My only crime was that I should have had the guts to tell on these guys, what they were doing, rather than putting up with it and then trying to gradually get out of the system without hurting them or without them thinking I was going to snitch on them.

Of the three offenders who admitted committing crimes, two acted alone and the third acted with only one other person. Their accounts were similar to others presented earlier—and tended to focus on either the harmless nature of their violations or on the unusual circumstances that drove them to commit their crimes. One claimed that his violations were only technical and that no one besides himself had been harmed.

> First of all, no money was stolen or anything of that nature. The bank didn't lose any money. . . . What I did was a technical violation. I made a mistake. There's no question about that, but the bank lost no money.

Another offender who directly admitted his guilt was involved in a check-kiting scheme. In a manner similar to embezzlers, he argued that his actions were motivated by exceptional circumstances.

> I was faced with the choice of all of a sudden, and I mean now, closing the doors or doing something else to keep that business open. . . . I'm not going to tell you that this wouldn't have happened if I'd had time to think it over, because I think it probably would have. You're sitting there with a dying patient. You are going to try to keep him alive.

In the other fraud cases more individuals were involved, and it was possible and perhaps necessary for each offender to claim that he was not really the culprit.

Discussion: Offenses, Accounts, and Degradation Ceremonies

The investigation, prosecution, and conviction of a white-collar offender involves him in a very undesirable status passage (Glaser and Strauss, 1971). The entire process can be viewed as a long and drawn-out degradation ceremony with the prosecutor as the chief denouncer and the offender's family and friends as the chief witnesses. The offender is moved from the status of law-abiding citizen to that of convicted felon. Accounts are developed to defeat the process of identity transformation that is the object of a degradation ceremony. They represent the offender's attempt to diminish the effect of his legal transformation and to prevent its becoming a publicly validated label. It can be suggested that the accounts developed by white-collar offenders take the forms that they do for two reasons: (1) the forms are required to defeat the success of the degradation ceremony, and (2) the specific forms used are the ones available given the mechanics, history, and organizational context of the offenses.

Three general patterns in accounting strategies stand out in the data. Each can be characterized by the subject matter on which it focuses: the event (offense), the perpetrator (offender), or the denouncer (prosecutor). These are the natural subjects of accounts in that to be successful, a degradation ceremony requires each of these elements to be presented in a particular manner (Garfinkel, 1956). If an account giver can undermine the presentation of one or more of the elements, then the effect of the ceremony can be reduced. Although there are overlaps in the accounting strategies used by the various types of offenders, and while any given offender may use more than one strategy, it appears that accounting strategies and offenses correlate.

References

Casper, Jonathon D. 1978. *Criminal Courts: The Defendant's Perspective.* Washington, D.C.: U.S. Department of Justice.

Conklin, John E. 1977. *Illegal But Not Criminal: Business Crime in America.* Englewood Cliffs, NJ: Prentice-Hall.

Cressey, Donald. 1953. *Other People's Money.* New York: Free Press.

Denzin, Norman K. 1977. Notes on the criminogenic hypothesis: A case study of the American liquor industry. *American Sociological Review* 42: 905-920.

———. 1984. *On Understanding Emotion.* San Francisco: Jossey-Bass.

Edelhertz, Herbert. 1970. *The Nature, Impact, and Prosecution of White Collar Crime.* Washington, D.C.: U.S. Government Printing Office.

Garfinkel, Harold. 1956. Conditions of successful degradation ceremonies. *American Journal of Sociology* 61:420-424.

Glaser, Barney G. and Anselm L. Strauss. 1971. *Status Passage.* Chicago: Aldine.

Katz, Jack. 1979. Legality and equality: Plea bargaining in the prosecution of white collar crimes. *Law and Society Review* 13:431-460.

Rothman, Martin and Robert F. Gandossy. 1982. Sad tales: The accounts of white collar defendants and the decision to sanction. *Pacific Sociological Review* 4:449-473.

Searle, John R. 1969. *Speech Acts.* Cambridge: Cambridge University Press.

11

How Doctors Defraud Medicaid: Doctors Tell Their Stories

Paul Jesilow
Henry M. Pontell
Gilbert Geis

For *this selection, an excerpt from their book,* Prescription for Profit: How Doctors Defraud Medicaid, *Jesilow, Pontell, and Geis interviewed 42 physicians who had been sanctioned for Medicaid violations in California and New York. All of the sanctioned doctors had been suspended from practice and two-thirds of them had been convicted of crimes associated with Medicaid fraud. The researchers compared the responses of the sanctioned physicians with a control group of non-sanctioned physicians.*

The authors found that while the physicians admitted the basic facts of their cases, they explained away the criminality of the acts through the use of rationalization and justification, in much the same manner as did the subjects in Benson's research ("Denying the Guilty Mind," in this book) on white-collar offenders. Scully and Marolla ("Convicted Rapists' Vocabulary of Motive," in this book) reported similar uses of rationalization and excuse with a study population of convicted rapists.

In the course of our research we interviewed forty-two physicians apprehended for Medicaid scams. To hear them tell it, they were innocent sacrificial lambs led to the slaughter because of perfidy, stupid laws, bureaucratic nonsense, and incompetent bookkeepers. At worst, they had been a bit careless in their record keeping; but mostly they had been more interested in the welfare of their patients than in deciphering the arcane requirements of benefit programs. Certainly, the Medicaid laws are complex and, by many reasonable standards, unreasonable. But we were surprised by the number of rationalizations that these doctors offered, by the intensity of their defenses of their misconduct, and by their consummate skill in identifying the villains who, out of malevolence or ineptitude, had caused their downfall. In these doctors' system of moral accounting, their humanitarian deeds far outweighed their petty trespasses against Medicaid. . . .

Rationales and Rationalizations

The sanctioned doctors generally appeared open and candid, at ease and involved with the subject. Most were perfectly accurate in response to our opening question—which asked them to provide the factual details of their cases—though these recitals were interladen with a plethora of self-excusatory observations. Throughout the interview, we gave the respondents a great deal of leeway in responding, and we sought to avoid putting words in their mouths or guiding them in any particular direction. They could be rude or polite to us (most were very polite), satisfied or disgusted with the government, and optimistic or pessimistic about the futures of their careers. At times, some doctors told us more than they realized. It is difficult in a long, sometimes emotional interview to camouflage strongly held convictions.

All the doctors in the sanctioned group had been suspended from billing the Medicaid program, and about two-thirds had been convicted of a criminal offense. Nonetheless, a doctor often would ask us, "What did I do that was so bad?" Clearly, their interpretations of the ethical and legal character of their actions were quite unlike those made by the law enforcement authorities.

One way to explain this dissonance is by reference to the classic sociological work of

Gresham Sykes and David Matza on juvenile delinquents. According to Sykes and Matza, these young criminals "neutralize" the negative definitions that they know "respectable" people apply to their delinquent behaviors. By learning these neutralization techniques in delinquent subcultures, juveniles can render social controls inoperative and be free to engage in delinquency without serious harm to their self-images. Thus, the delinquent can remain committed to law-abiding norms but can also "qualify" them in order to make violations excusable, if not altogether "right." Sykes and Matza observe that "much delinquency is based on what is essentially an unrecognized extension of defenses to crimes, in the form of justifications for deviance that are seen as valid by the delinquent but not by the legal system or society at large." From a study of embezzlers incarcerated in federal prisons, Donald Cressey concluded that these wrongdoers used "vocabularies of adjustment" to justify their behaviors to themselves. They told themselves that they were merely "borrowing" the money, which they would replace just as soon as they resolved a momentary problem. This self-deception enabled the embezzlers to see themselves as basically decent although they were altering records and stealing money.

Because we carried out our interviews several years after the offenses had taken place, we could not determine whether the doctors had fashioned their explanations before or after they committed the abuses—an analytical issue that has bedeviled all researchers attempting to verify the importance of neutralization techniques in lawbreaking. Most likely, we heard explanations of both types. Our data do tend to support the hypothesis that neutralization often constitutes an important element of what has been called the "drift" into illegal behavior, a period during which the perpetrator's episodic lawbreaking often goes unattended and thus begins to lose whatever unsavory moral flavor it might have possessed.

Denial of Responsibility

Few physicians took full personal blame for their violations in the sense of describing them as volitional, deliberate acts of wrongdoing. They were apt to call their activities "mistakes," and some blamed themselves for not having been more careful. This neutralization practice corresponds to what Sykes and Matza call denial of responsibility: "Denial of responsibility . . . extends much further than the claim that deviant acts are an 'accident' or some similar negation of personal accountability. . . . By learning to view himself as more acted upon than acting, the delinquent prepares the way for deviance from the normative system without the necessity of a frontal assault on the norms themselves."

The wrongdoing physicians did engage in a frontal assault on Medicaid norms, but they typically laid the blame on a wide variety of persons other than themselves. Several blamed patients' demands, portraying their own behavior as altruistic. One insisted she was doing no more than trying to see to the essential health of needy people: "Some of the kids didn't have any Medicaid, and you get a mother saying, 'Look, my child is sick. I don't have any Medicaid. Could you put it on the other kid's Medicaid?' It probably wasn't their child to begin with. It was like a sister's child." The physician admitted that she complied with the mother's request, and her "goodheartedness" got her into trouble with the government. She says that during the investigation, "the mother who brought in her sister's child forgot that this kid was treated because it was like a year ago." The mother's lapse of memory or fabrication, the doctor suspected, occurred because the mother hoped to avoid implicating herself in the fraud.

The same physician also insisted she had been victimized by thieves who stole Medicaid cards from beneficiaries and then presented themselves for treatment. Her practice was in "a bad area," and such thefts were common, she pointed out. When the itemization of treatment services came to the legitimate cardholders, they would complain to the authorities. Even if this was true, however, her explanation sidestepped the issue of her responsibility to match the Medicaid card with the person presenting it. . . .

Another physician got into trouble for accepting kickbacks from a laboratory.

(Physicians can bill Medicaid for laboratory tests if they own the testing facility; otherwise the laboratory bills Medicaid.) This physician told us he had decided to do his own lab work in order to increase his income. A former employee, whom the physician held responsible for his misfortune, offered the doctor a deal:

> My lab technician quit to start his own laboratory. He said: "Why don't you give me all the lab work." I said: "Fine, you bill Medicaid, and I'll bill my private patients."
>
> They were doing the tests for so much, and I charged them the going rate, and he was giving me a good deal, and that was a private deal. The Medi-Cal, he was doing it all and billing it himself.
>
> Then I told him: "I'm going to get a technician so I can have the benefits of the laboratory, of Medi-Cal too." [But] eventually he says: "I'll give you some benefits on your private patients. For instance, your bill is $300. I'll cut it down to $200 or something so we'll make it up somehow." I said: "All right."

Another physician who took kickbacks portrayed himself as an unwary, passive participant, motivated only by amiability and generosity, in a plan hatched by a hospital. The initiative came from the hospital, and the direct beneficiaries were his employees, so, as far as he was concerned, he had done nothing wrong in allowing the hospital to underwrite his payroll:

> [The] [h]ospital, privately owned, was in the habit of giving kickbacks to physicians using the hospital. I had arranged for three of the girls that worked for me to receive part-time pay to the tune of about $250 each, per month.
>
> This lasted about two years before it was stopped, and the amount of work that they did for the money they received was negligible. So they were able to show in court that this was an indirect type of kickback. Even though the money was not paid to me, by the girls receiving this money, it obviously made them happier or better employees or whatever you want to call it.
>
> I felt that if I didn't accept it, that if I let the girls take it, and then made sure that

they got their full salaries and their Christmas bonuses, that I wasn't actually getting any benefit out of it. I thought that therefore I was immune.

> And I really wasn't getting any benefit out of it. I had three employees—two of them were getting divorces, and one of them had a third child. The hospital wanted to give kickbacks, let them have it, you know.

An obstetrician, perhaps truthfully, cast responsibility on the welfare department, which had told him how to circumvent an inconvenient regulation:

> Even the [welfare] department told me to change dates . . . to be within the letter of the law. For example, some girl delivers the baby, she decides to have her tubes tied. Now, according to the state, there has to be an application thirty days ahead of tubular ligation, and it has to be submitted, approved, and thirty days given for the patient to make up her mind, to decide.
>
> If she hadn't given us any indication to the ligation, and she has to have one, what do we do now? I can't say, "You have to go home and come back in thirty days." And so they [the welfare caseworkers] told me, as well as the other doctors for Medicaid, they'd just say: "Backdate the request thirty days."

Commonly, denials of responsibility were blended with other self-justifications. A psychiatrist who illegally submitted bills under his name (and took a cut) for work done by psychologists not qualified for payment under Medicaid blamed the therapists but also added that he did it for the benefit of his patients:

> There were times I wanted to quit, but the therapist would say that these people are in need of therapy, and it is going well. It seemed to make sense at the time. They were qualified people. I couldn't do it myself; I wasn't there all the time. It was partly a moral thing. I was persuaded to keep doing it, and a good percentage of patients were getting something out of it. I should have been more responsible, but it also had to do with my trust in people, and that trust was misplaced.

This physician, perhaps as a reflexive bow to a major postulate of his vocation, commented, "I don't want to think of myself as a victim, so I want to take responsibility for what I did." Yet he found irresistible the idea that it was his essential goodness—his trust in people and his sympathy for patients—that had led him astray.

Denial of Injury

Justifying lawbreaking by citing the superordinate benefits of the act—such as the psychiatrist's comment on the value of the therapy for his patients—is called denial of injury in the roster of Sykes and Matza's techniques of neutralization. As they point out, "wrongfulness may turn on the question of whether or not anyone has clearly been hurt by [the] deviance, and this matter is open to a variety of interpretations." Physicians often depicted Medicaid regulations, which assuredly can be both onerous and mercilessly nitpicking, as bureaucratic obstacles, erected by laypeople, that threatened patient care. By breaking or bending the Medicaid rules, the sanctioned physicians argued, they were responding to their higher calling and helping—not hurting—patients.

Taking this tack, a physician who treated obesity by performing surgery emphasized that he was motivated only by "medical reasons" and "didn't give a goddamn what Medi-Cal said":

> Consider patients on welfare. There's a huge group of people who are on welfare because they cannot work. Nobody will give them a job. Their obesity serves as an excuse for remaining in the welfare system. To themselves they just say: "Well, I'm fat; I cannot get a job; therefore, I have to be on welfare." And they're satisfied with it. To alter that situation is hazardous, both from the emotional standpoint, but particularly in terms of physical aspects of it because if they eat enough, no matter how you loused up their gut, they're going to manage to remain obese. Earlier on, fifteen years ago, I did a few welfare patients, and I soon recognized the problem that particular group has especially. The bottom line is that there is a subconscious need for obesity.

> Well, I came up with the idea many years ago of saying: "OK, if you want this done, I've got no handle on what your subcon-

> scious state is, how much you need your obesity; there's no test for it. But the pocketbook is pretty close to the subconscious mind. If you are willing to pay for something, chances are you want it." Doesn't work that great; but at least it's a way. So what I started doing was charging them in advance: You want surgery, you come up with the money. Your insurance company happens to pay it back, you know, pay the full fee; well, I'll give it right back to them.

> I must admit that I did some Medi-Cal patients before I came up with this gimmick. And one or two of them worked very well. They became employable and very successful. But on the other hand, for every successful one, I would find two or three that became a disaster and had to be taken down and reoperated, all kinds of problems.

> So, anyway, I started this business. So I go: "OK, you want this surgery; you pay half of it." Now, at that particular point in time, I didn't give a goddamn what Medi-Cal said. I mean, if the patient wants this done, whether it's legal or illegal. I said I'm doing this for my reasons—medical reasons. What they'd have to come up with was maybe $100 or $500, whatever. The fee that Medi-Cal was paying at that time, plus the $500, was still less than what it would be for a private patient. Medi-Cal was paying maybe $500 or $600.

> I didn't give a damn about the money. It wasn't as if I got a patient in the emergency room and Medi-Cal only paid me $150, but my fee was $600, and so I tried to collect the balance. That wasn't my intent at all. Welfare patients do not expect to pay you. But this was a volitional thing. They knew about it in advance. It was not an emergency. It was purely elective, cosmetic. I knew I couldn't bill. That's the only part of the regulations I knew and recognized.

> It wasn't as though there was fraud involved. I wasn't defrauding anybody. If you want this surgery, you pay me before surgery, not afterwards. If I were billing them afterwards, I recognize that was bad. But this isn't the same thing. I still don't think so.

> I really thought I had some really nice results on a few of them. I did have some disasters. That is why I started this. If I had

just had the disasters and said "the hell with it, there's no answer to this, get out," I would have avoided it, because I didn't need it. It didn't amount to that much money. I could have been doing a private patient and come out way ahead.

Of course, the physician could have employed tactics other than reaching into a beneficiary's wallet to determine the patient's motivation—for example, adherence to a diet and exercise regimen prior to the operation. That the preoperative payment was intended to preclude reneging on the fee, rather than to measure motivation, is implicit in the physician's subsequent statement:

Now, plastic surgeons, for example, have done this for years. If you want to have your nose fixed, you pay them right up front. And for the same reason. Because they know that if you have to try to collect afterwards, the patient's going to find five hundred reasons why their nose isn't the way they thought it was going to be. If you've already paid for it, they'll be happy and satisfied.

Such comparisons with other specialties were common among doctors seeking to explain away their violations of the law. The Medicaid rules were capricious, and their own interpretation of fairness was far more sensible than that of the bureaucrats. Consider this psychiatrist's self-righteous indignation:

My wife is an eminently qualified psychiatric nurse. She had a medical teaching appointment on a medical school staff, supervisor of their inpatients, very qualified individual. So, anyhow, the basic problem was, she worked for me. They accused me—I don't know what the hell they accused me of—charging [Medicaid] for her services.

She was my nurse employee, just like I've had nurse employees everywhere I've been. I have always billed, like when the nurse gave a shot, you didn't bill it through her name. I don't even understand this concept, you know. I still don't understand what basis they can say arbitrarily that she is any different than a nurse that works for an obstetrician.

The way people are supervised in psychiatry is different than for general medicine. They never understood the difference, and still don't, and don't want to know. You can't talk with other physicians about it because they don't know anything about psychiatry, and don't want to know. You are in an esoteric field, that you have to be in to understand.

In a similar vein, another psychiatrist found the regulations senseless and the work he was doing eminently valuable for his patients. Besides, he had been able to bill in another setting for therapy provided by non-physicians, so he could not comprehend why such an action was not permitted under Medi-Cal:

I worked as a convalescent lead psychiatrist at one time. Now that means working in one of these county clinics where you are seeing patients and the social worker is seeing patients. These people are being charged the full rate, and it is only the psychiatrist who has a Medi-Cal number. If it is all right in the agency, why isn't it all right in private practice?

I was aware of putting down my name and not any other therapist, you know, who wouldn't be honored. But nevertheless, they were still my patients, and everything that went on was under my signature and my supervision. Some social workers are better than some psychiatrists in the analysis of a problem. Some psychiatrists are not that good in understanding human behavior.

I will stand by unequivocally that the patients that were seen by me, in conjunction with others, were getting far more for their dollar, whether it is paid for by them, their company, or by Medi-Cal. They were getting far more from my clinic than they would get anywhere from one practitioner, and it was because there were certain areas in my training and intuition, my skills, where someone else could do better, and vice versa. As far as I am concerned, they are quality people—something I insisted upon.

My idea was with Medi-Cal, or with whatever I was doing, do what was right for the patients and for the patients' good. I consider four eyes better than two eyes, four arms better than two arms, and four ears better than two ears, and these patients were getting more in their hourly fee. . . .

Denial of a Victim

A third neutralization technique, denial of a victim, occurs when an offender grants that his or her behavior caused injury but insists "the injury is not wrong in light of the circumstances." In our interviews, the sanctioned physicians claimed that although the law had been broken, the excess reimbursement they had received represented only what they deserved for their work. They saw overcharging for services and ordering excessive tests as ways to "make back" what they *should* have been paid.

One physician, for example, granted that his excessive billings were wrong, especially because Medicaid participation was voluntary; but he maintained that the regulations and payment schedules encouraged—even necessitated—cheating, so that doctors in the program could earn fees equivalent to those paid by private insurance:

> If you voluntarily choose to accept Medicaid patients, you have to put up with their baloney, and if you're not willing to put up with their baloney, then maybe you shouldn't take Medicaid patients. So in that sense, it's difficult to say something is not fair and you shouldn't do it. . . .
>
> But the system has got many flaws in it and loopholes and irregularities which necessitate abuses to take place. Otherwise, you can't see patients because of the reimbursement attitude.
>
> Let's take an example. A patient comes in for the first time and is examined. For that it would be, let's say, $60. Now, if the patient goes to a general practitioner for the first time with a cold, he [the doctor] will get that amount. If the patient goes to an internist, who has to evaluate the patient for a complicated situation, such as diabetes, heart disease, god knows what, and spends a lot of time with that patient, he will get compensated the same amount. So it's all the same because it is a new patient visit.
>
> Now for that reason, it is virtually impossible to [receive treatment] at this time in this area. There are virtually no internists

> in this area that I know who accept Medicaid, because if a patient comes to an internist, they expect a thorough going-over, which they devote anywhere from half an hour to forty-five minutes, and yet the reimbursement rate is exactly the same as if the patient went to a general practitioner with a cold and spent five minutes with him.
>
> Now the system, of course, does ask, when you bill for this visit, whether you spent a lot of time with the patient or a little time. You are supposed to voluntarily say that it was a brief visit and, if you state that, they will pay you a less amount. However, very few people I know do that. They will always bill the maximum amount because that maximum amount is actually less than we charge our private patients. This is one door of abuse that virtually everyone I know who takes Medicaid is using. If they billed the patient with a cold for a very brief visit, then they get paid as little as $12. There's no one I know who can function in this area, with an office and a staff and insurance and all these things, and accept a patient for $12. I would say that form of abuse exists in 90 to 100 percent of doctors that I know who take Medicaid. They're all using the maximum [reimbursement] levels.

This physician's conviction that virtually all his colleagues engaged in billing scams provided fuel for self-justification. As Sykes and Matza note, such a belief allows the perpetrator to transform the violation from a "gesture of complete opposition" to one that represents no more than "an extension of common practice."

An anesthesiologist, caught billing the government for excess time, argued that he was reasonably charging for the patients' recovery time—a charge he knew was against Medicaid regulations:

> We saw no reason why we should do abortions on the garbage of the ghettos and barrios and be responsible for their recovery time and not be paid for it. I really think that it was gray, not black. I'm not defending it. In the context of the time, it wasn't really that bad. But it was stupid to try and do it considering how little money was involved and the horrible consequences. I should have known better. If

you are going to steal from the system, it was a very stupid act. I don't think it was really a basically crooked act. I guess you could say it was, but it depends on how you look at it.

When I did it, it was being done by at least 50 percent or 70 percent of the anesthesiologists in Southern California—at least 50 percent. People were fudging time, particularly on Medicaid.

Another physician also blamed the government for creating intolerable conditions that pressed practitioners toward fraud in order to meet patients' needs.

The doctor illustrated what he saw as his dilemma by telling of a fourteen-year-old girl who was having her third abortion in less than six months. He had given the girl birth control pills, but she obviously hadn't taken them. When she came back for the third abortion, he coaxed her into allowing him to insert an IUD: "It's very simple, very easy. We'll put it in right now, immediately after the abortion." The doctor then billed Medicaid for the IUD and its insertion, but the program would not pay because the insertion was done at the same time as the abortion for a fee the agency decreed reasonably covered both procedures. The doctor was irritated:

> So they don't give a damn. It has to be a separate visit. So, then there's the question of getting this patient back. She's already got a local anesthetic in for the abortion. She says, "OK, do it. I won't feel it." You try to convince that same girl a week later or two weeks later? "Oh, no, I don't want those shots again" or "No, it's going to hurt. I don't want an IUD. I'll take the pill." It's another way of driving up costs. It drives up costs because they're going to have the girl pregnant again, and they're going to be perfectly willing to pay for more abortions rather than violate their rule. I paid $7, $8, $9 for an IUD. If I've been foolish enough to insert it immediately after an abortion—I can just forget getting paid. That's too bad. That's my problem. I should have made her come back in two weeks.

Now that's a medical decision that they have no business getting involved in. One of the ways I can handle this problem with this fourteen-year-old, if I've decided that

the most important thing is her welfare, is I'm going to put in the goddamn IUD and put on the chart that I put it in tomorrow. Right? Because your health really should come before some bureaucrat, and there's no reason why I should be asked to throw away my money. . . .

Various complaints about the nature of Medicaid recipients were offered by physicians in support of their view that Medicaid practice was more demanding than "normal" medicine and, by implication, should pay more rather than less. One doctor flaunted his disgust to us: "The Medicaid patients are filthy. They keep the place in turmoil. They are the toughest type to treat. The Medicaid patient is more demanding as a rule, and is not as cooperative in their treatment programs. I found this to be very troublesome at times."

Even if one were to accept the doctors' premise that the regulations were too inflexible given the difficulties of working with Medicaid patients, one has to wonder about the structural conflict between the physicians' interest in their patients' well-being and their own financial self-interest. For example, the physician who inserted IUDs after performing abortions argued that he was offering important care to patients. Yet he was unwilling to assume the small cost of the IUD and the minimal extra time to insert it; instead, he chose to cheat Medicaid and reap illegitimate profits. Before the advent of Medicaid, of course, many physicians performed services for indigent patients without charge. They spread the cost of care for the indigent among their fee-paying and insured patients. Government benefit programs now offer—if one is willing to cheat—the opportunity both to proclaim a humanitarian interest in the welfare of poor patients and to get paid at or above the going rate for that interest.

One physician we spoke with harkened to the theme of pro bono service, but quickly added that he was always ready to circumvent the law in order to obtain his fee from Medicaid:

> I would say personally I am disappointed with my colleagues in medicine. All of them are interested in their business. They are not concerned about the health of their

patients. They want to make money. And, of course, they will make money. But the primary objective should be the care of patients. In medicine, the fee you get is a side effect.

I was satisfied with the Medicaid reimbursement because I always knew that if somebody didn't pay me, my conscience would make me treat them anyway. I figured it was better to get Medicaid than to treat them free. Some of the regulations are annoying, but you could always get around them. I would first treat the patient, then deal with Medicaid.

This blend of decency, self-righteousness, and a thoroughly high-handed attitude about "annoying" regulations that "you could always get around" nicely satisfied this doctor's conscience and cash flow.

Getting around the rules, playing the Medicaid game, working the system for maximum profit—many of the doctors we spoke with defined their illegal activities in such terms. . . .

Condemning the Condemners

Sykes and Matza describe condemning the condemners as a fourth neutralization technique: "The delinquent shifts the focus of attention from his own deviant acts to the motives and behavior of those who disapprove of his violations." This shift enables violators to minimize responsibility for their behavior by construing it as trivial compared to the misdeeds of the rule makers or as rational compared to the irrational expectations of the rule makers.

In a typical condemnation of the Medicaid program, one of our respondents insisted that Medicaid not only invited but demanded cheating:

It's not related to reality, you know. It's done by people who are not medical people, who know nothing about the services being provided. One of the peculiarities that they do is that they make arbitrary decisions about things totally unrelated to the services you provide. They're constantly irritating and aggravating the doctors and their staff.

They say, "What we used to do, we're not going to do anymore." And you're already

three months into your new billing system. I could keep you here the rest of the day giving you examples of their kind of idiocy, that they somehow manage to make sense out of in their little peculiar world that's unrelated to ours. They've built in systems that either ask for somebody to cheat, you know, or to cheat the patient on the type of care that's provided. You put somebody in the position where lying is the most reasonable course, and they will lie. The patients will lie; the doctor may even lie on what they say about what happened.

This physician illustrated his point by citing the often criticized Medicaid rule that three months must elapse between compensable abortions. Suppose, he argued, a young woman had undergone an abortion in his office one week short of three months ago. According to the rules, he should tell her to come back the following week. But suppose she insists that she has to visit her sick mother in another state. This puts "everybody in a position because somebody has made some rule that doesn't make sense." A "naive" doctor would do the young woman "a favor" and postdate the reimbursement form. But, he concluded, "I don't know whether there's any naive doctors around anymore; they've been so hassled and harassed by this system."

That the Medicaid regulations might represent an attempt, however flawed, to control abuse, rather than an effort to harass or second-guess doctors, did not enter into the thinking of doctors who condemned the system as arbitrary, capricious, and unreasonable. One doctor could only fall back on the word "ridiculous":

I think they are ridiculous. We ask permission; we send them proof, we send them everything. One of them even asked me for a picture of the patient. I told him: "Who do you think I am, a crook or what? I am telling you this big long hernia there is hanging out of the testicles." I said: "Well, what do I send a picture of? Oh man, you are crazy." And that's what I do; I sent a picture, but it was absolutely ridiculous.

They are spending so much money. So many secretaries they have. They check all the cases in the hospitals, the Medicaid cases that go in, all the welfare cases they check. . . .

Although the sanctioned physicians focused their scorn on particular aspects of the program that related to their own misconduct, they had fewer complaints about reimbursement levels and "unnecessary" regulation than our comparison group of nonsanctioned physicians. Slightly more than half (57 percent) of the sanctioned physicians felt reimbursement was too low, an opinion shared by 73 percent of the nonsanctioned doctors. And almost two-thirds of the sanctioned physicians (62 percent), compared to only 23 percent of the nonsanctioned, said they had no complaints about unnecessary Medicaid regulations. This pattern of self-serving selective disapproval resembles a phenomenon observed in prison culture, where "common criminals" are notably hostile to child molesters and traitors.

Appeal to Higher Loyalties

The fifth and final neutralization technique discussed by Sykes and Matza is the appeal to higher loyalties. Delinquents engage in law-breaking, they say, to benefit smaller and more intimate groups to which they belong, such as their gangs or their friendship networks. Laws are broken "because other norms, held to be more pressing or involving a higher loyalty, are accorded precedence." For the sanctioned physicians, such higher loyalties included service to patients and adherence to professional standards. In an unusual case, one physician insisted that being diagnosed with cancer prompted his cheating. He was worried about whether his infant son would have an adequate inheritance. In addition, he said he was despondent, angry, and bitter and wanted to get caught because of a wish to destroy himself or "to get back at the world" for his illness.

A Subculture of Delinquency?

Every sanctioned doctor we interviewed relied on one or more neutralization techniques to explain what had happened, and only rarely did we hear even the most elemental acknowledgment of self-serving motives. The structure of Medicaid, as we have noted, offers more than ample opportunities to harvest rationalizations that locate blame on factors other than the offender's lack of restraint. At times, doctors agreed that they might have been more careful and diligent about supervising others or challenging unusual goings-on, but such admissions were most often accompanied by claims to have been concerned with more important, socially valuable matters. On occasion, we heard physicians suggest that their own stupidity led to their apprehension—but it was the method of cheating, not the cheating itself, that they regretted.

The tenor of the interviews indicated that the cavalier attitudes these doctors had adopted toward the government benefit programs had been at least partially absorbed from others in the profession, and that professional values may effectively neutralize conflicts of conscience. Here we took our cue from Matza's discussion of a "subculture of juvenile delinquency—a setting in which the commission of delinquency is common knowledge among a group" and which provides norms and beliefs that "function as the extenuating conditions under which delinquency is permissible." A subculture of medical delinquency, we concluded, arises, thrives, and grows in large part because of the tension between bureaucratic regulation and professional norms of autonomy.

Physicians who cheated government programs were not committed to a life of crime and undoubtedly did not cheat on all their billings. Nor did they always steal from Medicaid or from private insurance programs; they probably were honest in much of their work. But when these doctors did defy Medicaid's legal requirements, they typically offered professional justifications in lieu of defining their activities as deviant, illegal, or criminal. . . .

Conclusion

The establishment of the Medicaid program provided new opportunities for doctors and other medical practitioners and organizations to commit criminal acts and to violate administrative regulations. Our research did not yield a composite portrait of physicians typically get into trouble with Medicaid, though there are some recurring traits in the roster of physicians dealt with by the authorities. The stereotypical image of the violator as an inner-city doctor associated with a Medicaid mill is misleading: Offenders include some of the most respectable members of the profession and physicians of all ages, specialties, and attitudes toward patients and government medical benefit programs.

References

Cressey, D. 1953. *Other People's Money*. Glencoe, IL: Free Press.

Sykes, G. and D. Matza. 1957. "Techniques of Neutralization: A Theory of Delinquency." *American Sociological Review* 22:667-70.

Section IV

Violent Crime

Violent crime refers to any criminal act committed through the threat of or actual physical harm to the victim. Violent crimes such as robbery, rape, and murder have profoundly affected the way we live and have clearly altered our lifestyles. This fear is not without a basis in reality. While the per capita crime rates for violent crime decreased slightly in the 1990s, due to increased population, the overall incidence of violent crime has increased significantly in the past two decades.

Violent crime is often considered less rationally conceived than property crime. Violent behavior is often expressed in the "heat of passion"—during periods of great emotional turmoil. The violent act is thought to be more expressive than instrumental, having no real functional purpose or acceptable rationale.

However, recent studies have shown that violence can be highly instrumental. Wright and Decker ("Creating the Illusion of Impending Death") reported that violence can play an important role in the commission of armed robberies by overcoming the resistance of the victims. Violence is thus rationally employed to accomplish the goal of the robbery.

Floyd Feeney's subjects ("Robbers as Decision Makers") reported the use of "irrational force" committed out of anger, fear,

rejection, and indifference. However, the study also provides examples of "strategic violence"—rationally conceived to further the efficient commission of a crime. Several of his respondents reported that they used physical force at the outset of the robbery to establish control over the situation. One reported that, while he felt violence was necessary to the commission of the crime, he hit the victim on the shoulder rather than on the head for fear that a head blow "might kill him."

Diana Scully and Joseph Marolla ("Convicted Rapists' Vocabulary of Motive") analyze the excuses and justifications used by convicted rapists to explain their behavior. The authors view rape as learned behavior. The learning also includes the excuses and justifications used to diminish responsibility. In this sense, the rapist responds more like the occupational criminal than other violent offenders. The occupational criminal has difficulty perceiving him- or herself as a criminal and thus attempts to negotiate a nondeviant identity. The rapist has committed one of the most socially repugnant crimes, repudiated by criminals and noncriminals alike. His excuses and justifications are designed to place the act in a more appropriate context. In much the same way, the occupational criminal attempts to recast his or her criminal behavior as "necessary" for the survival of the business or as merely sharp business practice.

In these selections we see violent crime as having both expressive and instrumental roots. The motives for their behavior, strategies employed by the offenders to accomplish their crimes, and rationalizations used to avoid responsibility for their acts are graphically illustrated in this anthology. ✦

12

Robbers as Decision Makers

Floyd Feeney

Robbery is one of the most feared of all street crimes. It is the quintessential predatory crime, involving face-to-face confrontation between a victim and an offender, where force or threat of force is used to obtain goods. In this piece Floyd Feeney presents findings from a study of robbery in California. The study population consisted of 113 male offenders convicted of robbery or an offense related to robbery. The data were reanalyzed for the purpose of examining the decision-making processes of the robbers, particularly the rational processes involved in the motivation and decision to commit a robbery and the planning involved in the commission of the act. Not unlike the findings in previous chapters (Shover and Honaker; Åkerström; Cromwell, Olson, and Avary), the decision to commit a robbery was largely unplanned and opportunistic. However, rational processes, in a broad sense of the term, were present in most of the reported robberies. While many of the offenses described by the offenders appeared to be unplanned and spur-of-the-moment, Feeney suggests that the sheer experience of the offenders, having committed hundreds or even thousands of previous robberies, substituted for planning of individual robberies. He writes, "There is clearly a thinking process involved. It is not Benthamite [completely rational], but it is not much different from what people do in their everyday lives."

Because of its suddenness and its potential for serious injury or death, robbery is one of the most feared of all crimes. It is the most frequent stranger-to-stranger crime involving violence, and its rapid increase over the past several decades has been a major corro-

sive force in contemporary urban life in the United States and to a lesser extent in Britain and Europe. The prevention and control of robbery is consequently an important item on the social agenda on both sides of the Atlantic.

As a legal term, robbery covers a fairly broad spectrum of criminal activity, from the Great Train Robbery worth millions of pounds to schoolyard bullies taking lunch money from their classmates—a kind of robbery that is often not reported. As a practical matter most robberies dealt with by the police and the courts fall into a narrower range largely consisting of two categories: muggings and other attacks on individuals on the street and holdups of commercial establishments. This chapter addresses the question whether it is useful in developing policies for the control of robbery to focus on how decisions about robbery are made by the robbers themselves. The conclusion is that this is a useful perspective for addressing the robbery problem, although obviously not the only approach that may be fruitful.

This chapter is based primarily on interviews with 113 northern California offenders charged with robbery and convicted of robbery or an offense related to robbery. Although this means that the offense of conviction is in some instances not a robbery, this sample was thought to be more representative of persons doing robberies than one based wholly on persons convicted of robbery itself. The sample was stratified to include both adults and juveniles, blacks and whites, offenders involved in commercial and in individual robberies, and offenders given both long prison sentences and shorter local sentences. As robbery is largely a male enterprise, only males were interviewed. The interviews were conducted in 1971 and 1972 (Weir, 1973) and were reanalyzed for the purpose of this chapter. The discussion is based on unweighted figures. Northern California had a very high robbery rate during the period of the interviews.

Like other human beings, individuals who commit robberies make many decisions. For all but the most prolific robbers, most of these decisions concern everyday life and have nothing to do with robbery. Of those that do involve robbery, some are strategic, career-type decisions such as the decision to get involved in crime, to commit a first robbery, to continue robbing, or to desist. Others are much more tactical, such as how to choose a victim, whether to use a gun, and how to escape. It is not possible to discuss all these different kinds of decisions here, but an attempt will be made to cover some of the more important decisions and to give the flavor of the decision-making process. Some of the argument that follows is based on solid empirical evidence. Where necessary, however, this has been supplemented with impressions and fragmentary evidence.

Logically the decision to rob is a very complex matter involving the whole past of the individual considering the crime as well as that person's present situation. As robbery is generally thought of as an economic crime, it might be expected that the typical individual considering a robbery goes through some kind of mental calculus to determine whether he has a need for money and what the legitimate opportunities for getting money are—whether through work or from family or friends. If these calculations indicate a need that cannot be satisfied through legitimate means, consideration might then be given to committing a crime to acquire the money, and if so, to which crime is the most suitable. Presumably in making this calculation the individual considers the relative financial gains that might be expected from the various kinds of crimes possible and the relative risks of getting caught or otherwise harmed. Presumably also the individual considers what actions he will be required to perform in committing the crime and how he feels about undertaking these actions.

Because robbery is a serious crime with severe penalties and significant possibilities for getting hurt, individuals considering robbery might be expected to pay particular attention to these matters, and those deciding to commit the crime might be expected to give careful thought to the choice of a target and the development of a plan for reducing the chances of apprehension. It is surprising therefore to find that the northern California robbers studied do not fit this description very well. Fewer than 60% stated money as the primary aim of their robbery, over half said they did no planning at all, and over 60% said that before the robbery they had not even thought about being caught.

The Decision to Rob

The decision to rob begins with some kind of desire. As previously indicated, fewer than 60% of the robbers said they wanted money. Twenty-four percent wanted something other than money, and 19% were involved in what might be called "accidental robberies" burglaries, fights, or other acts that were not originally intended to involve both theft and violence but which came to do so as events unfolded. . .

Nearly a third of those seeking money wanted it for drugs, and almost as many wanted specific things such as clothes or a car. The remainder seeking money needed food or shelter or just had a general desire for money. Most of those who wanted drugs were adult heroin addicts. Some said that their habits required only a few dollars a day, whereas others said they needed $100 a day or more. Many stressed the difficulty of their situations:

> But see, I would have been able to support my family if I wouldn't have had to pay for the heroin, so it didn't matter which way you split the money—whether it went for the heroin or whether it went to the family. I mean it was still for the heroin, because if it wasn't for the heroin I wouldn't have had debts to make money for. Well, I had a family to take care of and the heroin got to the point that I didn't keep food in the refrigerator and the rent paid and bills paid, phone bill, electric bill, and it was hard to handle both things, and that's when I got into robberies.

Many of those who wanted specific things had current problems or financial needs. Several wanted money to leave the state to avoid arrest. Another was trying to pay traffic tickets to avoid being put in jail. Several juveniles had run away from a juvenile camp and wanted to leave town. Another adult had given money to his roommate for several months to pay the rent. The roommate used the money for other things, however, and suggested a robbery when the manager demanded the back rent. The offender was not earning enough at his job to cover the loss and reluctantly agreed.

Those who wanted food and shelter were generally not destitute, but their circumstances were often poor. One was in a very low-paying job:

I had a little $1.65 job working 20 hours a week, which wasn't very much, but I was still trying to make it on the legit side, but there just wasn't nothing open to me. I don't mind working, but $1.65 is kind of ridiculous. . . [Robbing] was the only thing open to me at the time.

Others had no jobs but were looking for work. One adult with a good employment record was trying to find a new job. Finally he tried robbery—his first—when he ran out of other places to turn:

I needed the money for food. I tried welfare. I tried to borrow all the people that I could borrow from. Nobody else that I could borrow from. I didn't have any sources of money. I was just flat broke. I was getting it out of the savings and borrowing money from my mother, but I was getting kind of run out because she was starting to need more. I didn't even think about how much I wanted to get. I just felt that anything I got would help. It was better than nothing.

Another explained that he had a family:

There wasn't no food in the house, you know. Scrounging. And I'm forced into having to do something like this. I knew I was desperate. Besides, I was going out stealing anything I could get a hold of, get a little money to get some food.

Many in the group who said they just wanted money were not really able to explain why:

I have no idea why I did this. Well, I guess it was for money, but I didn't have no money problem, really, then. You know, everybody got a little money problem, but not big enough to go and rob somebody. I just can't get off into it. I don't really know why I did it.

The large number of juveniles who said they just wanted money were particularly

vague. One apparently wanted to avoid the inconvenience of going to the bank:

For the money. I think that being involved I could use, at that time I could use the money. Yeah. I was accumulating money. Many reasons. 'Cause I got low on my pocket and I needed some pocket money. 'Cause I didn't want to go to the bank.

Over 40% of the offenders indicated that money was not the real purpose of the robbery. A quarter of these were involved in arguments or fights. One became angry at a racial slur:

I was mad at Mom. This old broad had made me mad. I seen the lady coming out of the store. I said, "Help," you know. And she said something, she mumbled something but all I know was "black," I hear that. So I got mad.

Another took a wig from a young woman who had rejected his attempt to pick her up. He did it:

Because I felt she was disrespecting me, kind of. I did it 'cause I seen fear in her. So I knew if I took this, she might start acting right . . to punish her the way she was talking.

A drunk juvenile got mad when the victim bumped into him:

It was just a sudden thing. I didn't really mean to do it. I didn't plan or nothing; it just happened. Just like that. Because he offered it to me. There's no reason. I just took it. I beat him up, you know. I was happy I beat him up. I was going to walk away and leave him there but he gave me $4. He thought I was going to cut his throat. He gave it to me. I wouldn't cut his throat. I didn't want to get busted for murder.

Some were just generally angry—one because his apartment had just been "ripped off." Another was mad at everyone:

I was mad and I had to do something to get it out of my system. I was mad at my cousins and my girlfriend. I was mad at my mom at the time.

Both also had other reasons, however:

I get a kick out of it really. Watch people's faces when they see you. They scared. I robbed because he gave me a smart answer. [Did several robberies that same evening.]

I don't know. It sounded easy and I guess we needed the money. We didn't really need it but we wanted to do something. Something to do. I don't know.

A surprising number of offenders got involved primarily because of partners. One, who had done no previous robberies, tried to help a friend and wound up in prison:

Because he asked me to help him out. He done a favor for me before. I didn't really want the money. It was an emotional thing more than anything else. Like the guy did me a hell of a favor.

Juveniles often cited the influence of friends. Several were just trying to prove they could do robberies. One had $265 in his pocket but robbed to show that he was not "scared." Another said, "People got to prove things to people. My partner didn't think I could do it."

Six percent of the offenders said their partners started something and they just went along:

Oh, in a simple sentence, I was either going to take part in the robbery then or, you know, stay there and be a part of it already as far as my mind was going then. It might have been an irrational thing because I was with the gentleman, and if the guy would have turned to me, well, I would have been caught, and blamed and made to give it up anyway. Well, we was. I felt a part of it, you know, when he [partner] committed the act right then. I know it sounds silly, but that's the way my mind was going then.

Another sizable group of offenders simply wanted excitement or a change of some kind in their lives:

Just to cause some trouble. Well, we just wanted to try that, you know. Goof around, you know. have some fun—jack up somebody. . . We thought we were really big and stuff like that.

I don't really have any fear of prisons or things like that. I always sort of felt like I

was going back someday. [I was] disillusioned with myself . . and with some of the compromises I was forced to make in life. And "capering" appealed to me.

I did it because I didn't care. I felt I didn't have anything to live for anyway so what the heck's the difference.

Another group did not think of themselves as trying to rob at all. They were attempting to recover money they claimed was either theirs or owed to them. Their motivation was to get what they thought belonged to them. A number had money with them or at home.

There was little difference between blacks and whites in the motivations expressed for committing their current robberies. They were about evenly divided between those saying that money was the primary reason and those saying that reasons other than money prompted the robberies.

Surprisingly, one-fourth of the adult commercial robbers said that money was not their primary motivation. All of those who said they were disillusioned or depressed were commercial robbers, as were the adults who were primarily interested in excitement and a number of the adults who just went along with their partners.

Planning

Most of the robbers appear to have taken a highly casual approach to their crimes. . . Over half said they did no planning at all. Another third reported only minor planning such as finding a partner, thinking about where to leave a getaway car, or whether to use a weapon. This minor, low-level planning generally took place the same day as the robbery and frequently within a few hours of it. The longest lead time was generally that needed to get a weapon if one was not already available.

Fewer than 15% or so had any kind of planned approach. The largest number of these (9%) simply followed an existing pattern for their offenses. They did little new planning for their current offenses because they already had an approach that they liked. Fewer than 5% of the robbers planned in any detail. These robbers—all adults and all involved in commercial robberies—stole getaway cars, planned escape routes, detailed each partner's actions, evaluated contingencies, and observed the layout of prospective targets. As might be expected, commercial robberies were planned more often than those of individuals (60% versus 30%).

The robbers varied greatly in the number of robberies committed. Forty percent of those seeking to commit a robbery said they were committing their first robbery, 26% said they had committed 2 to 9 robberies, 24% reported 10 to 49 robberies, and 10% reported 50 or more robberies. The repeat offenders had many fewer arrests than the number of robberies mentioned, and virtually all said the police did not know about the offenses for which they had not been arrested.

Generally the amount of planning increased with the number of robberies committed. None of those not fully intending a robbery did any planning, and none of the first-time robbers did any planning other than minor planning. Twenty-one percent of those who said they had committed 2 to 9 robberies did some planning beyond the minor variety, as compared with 23% of those who reported 10 to 49 robberies and 33% of those who reported 50 or more.

The impulsive, spur-of-the-moment nature of many of these robberies is well illustrated by two adult robbers who said they had passengers in their cars who had no idea that they planned a robbery. One passenger, who thought his friend was buying root beer and cigarettes, found out the hard way what had happened. A clerk chased his robber-friend out the door and fired a shotgun blast through the windshield of the passenger's car. Other robbers, who had no transportation of their own, persuaded friends to drive them to robbery sites. In most of these incidents the friends dropped the robbers off and drove on, wholly unaware of what was about to happen.

The generally casual approach to the crime is also illustrated by the approach of many offenders to the possibility of apprehension. Over 60% of the robbers said they had not even thought about getting caught before the robbery. . . Another 17% said that they had thought about the possibility but did not believe it to be a problem. Only 21% considered the possibility a risk to be concerned about. Some, who had given no thought to getting caught before the robbery began, said that they did think about it during or immediately after, particularly when things started going wrong or they became involved in hot-pursuit chases. A few began to worry only after they had already escaped. The greatest concern was shown by the first-time robbers. A quarter of this group thought the risk of apprehension was a problem.

Decisions Concerning Means

Only 22% of the robbers indicated that they considered doing some crime other than robbery as a means of accomplishing their ends. Of those who did consider other crimes, burglary was the crime most frequently considered and shoplifting the second. A number of robbers were also selling drugs.

Most of those who considered burglary preferred robbery. Some did so because there was more money or no need to fence the loot, some because they thought robbery was safer or because they were fearful about going into houses. Others had been caught doing burglaries. One drug user had been shoplifting to support his habit but had moved to a town where the price of the drugs was twice what he had previously been paying. He decided to rob stores because the money was better and faster:

> That's the reason I went into robbing the stores. [When I came here] my habit immediately jumped to $100 a day, just the difference in dope. The dope down there and the dope up here was that different. So I said, "I can't be running around boosting and beating people on the head and doing whatever, $100 a day, man. That's crazy."

Another had been dealing drugs but quit because the police were getting suspicious. A few preferred burglaries but decided on impulse to try robbing. Three incidents began as burglaries but turned into robberies when the victim returned home unexpectedly. One shoplifting turned into a robbery in much the same way.

Fewer than 10% of those whose objective was something other than money considered any other crime. Half, however, of the highly active robbers responsible for 50 or more robberies considered some other crime. Many of those who said they did not consider any other crime had a prior arrest record for burglary or shoplifting. Although the offenders did not say so, it is possible that this prior history affected their decision to rob.

No systematic information is available as to how many offenders considered satisfying their needs through legitimate opportunities. Many of the robbers mentioned their inability to find work as a factor in their general situation, however. None of the juveniles and only 20% of the adults who robbed for money had jobs at the time of the robbery, and most of these were in low-paying or part-time jobs. White adults who robbed for money were more often working than black adults. About half of those who robbed for something other than money were working.

One of the most important tactical choices that a robber must make is whom to rob. In line with the general lack of planning, the robbers' comments as to how they chose victims were much more matter of fact than expected. Over 20% said that they chose their victims because of convenience, 15% said that the victim appeared to have money, and another 15% chose their victims because a fast getaway was possible or the risk otherwise appeared to be low. Others gave mixed reasons or did not know why they had chosen. Some typical comments as to convenience:

Just where we happened to be, I guess. Don't know.

Nothing else open at 2:00 a.m. Had been there before.

We thought it would be the quickest, you know, it's a small donut shop.

Another important tactical choice concerns the location of the robbery. A nearby site obviously is the most convenient and familiar but also carries the highest risk of recognition. Despite this risk over a third of the robbers attacked victims in their own neighborhoods and over 70% in their own towns. Moreover, only half of the 30% who robbed in another town had gone there for the purpose of committing a robbery. Fifteen percent just happened to be in the other town. Some were visiting friends or relatives; others were passing through when they decided to do a robbery.

Even when in another town for the purpose of committing a robbery, most apparently were there for reasons other than the idea that going out of town was the best approach. One was in a town 15 miles away simply because that was the only place where he could find a gas station open after midnight. Another was driving around looking for a motel to rob, and most of the motels in the area were outside the town where he lived. His partner had suggested one closer to home, but the robber rejected it as a target because he knew one of the employees. Of the adults who went to another town to rob, only one went to a town other than one contiguous to the town in which he lived. The one exception was a fairly well-planned robbery at a major resort which involved traveling several hundred miles.

One of the juveniles who was out of town for the purpose of doing a robbery wandered around for nearly 150 miles before selecting a robbery site; another drove 100 miles from home, and a third, 56. All had decided to do the robberies on the same day and apparently were attempting to ensure success by getting a long way from home.

Decisions Concerning Weapons and Force

Eighty percent of the offenders used some kind of weapon: 53% used guns, 19% knives, and 8% other weapons. Most said they were trying to intimidate their victims and gain control over the situation rather than to harm or dominate the victims. Most felt that showing the weapon was enough to accomplish their purpose but were prepared to use force if the victim resisted or the police came by.

A surprising percentage had qualms about the use of the weapons they carried, however, and made deliberate decisions to forego some of their advantage. Nearly 30% of those who used a "gun" used a weapon that was either not loaded or that was simulated. Sixteen percent carried guns that were not loaded, 7% simulated weapons, and another 5% toy weapons. Most wanted to be sure that no one was hurt and explained that if they had no bullets in the guns, there was no chance that they could accidentally shoot anyone:

> I didn't want a real gun because I might get jittery or something. Or if I would jam somebody that got out of line. I don't know. I wouldn't shoot nobody.

> It couldn't have been loaded. I made sure of that. I just didn't want it loaded. I didn't want to hurt nobody. Just wanted to more or less scare them to give me some money.

Others used a simulated weapon or kept their weapon hidden in the belief that the penalty would be less severe if they were caught:

> I felt that if I got caught it'd be a lot lighter on me if I didn't have a gun than if I did.

> [Gun not displayed.] Yeah, we told her we had a weapon, but we didn't show it to her. She didn't believe it because we didn't show it to her. We didn't want to hurt anyone. Man, we'd been in jail for life if we'd got caught.

For a few offenders the decision was hasty and pragmatic rather than deliberate. One explained his unloaded gun: "Probably because I didn't have any bullets handy for it." Another simulated a gun because he didn't have one but wanted the money.

Ninety percent of the commercial robbers used a weapon of some kind, and 80% used a gun. Of those who used a gun, nearly 80% used a loaded gun. Seventy percent of those who robbed individuals also carried weapons. Only a third carried guns, however, and only half of those used a loaded gun.

Eight percent of the offenders used weapons other than a gun or a knife: a, screwdriver, a lug wrench, a metal bar, a pool cue, a shovel and a board, some dog spray, or a broken beer bottle. In almost every instance the weapon used was something handy when the need arose rather than an instrument carried by careful design.

Sixty percent of those who did not use weapons failed to do so because the robbery itself was an impulsive act and no weapon was readily available. Whether they would have chosen to use a weapon if they had taken more time is not known.

A few offenders deliberately chose not to use a weapon for moral or legal reasons:

> I couldn't see using a weapon on a lady. I figured I could catch her off guard and grab her purse and run.

> I tried to make it nonviolent. I figured if I had to go [was caught] I would go on as less as I could.

One third of the robbers or their partners hurt someone during the robbery for which they were convicted. One additional adult reported that he had shot at a victim but missed. Robbers of individuals hurt their victims more than twice as often as the commercial robbers. Juvenile offenders harmed their victims more often than did adult offenders.

Most of the offenders who hurt victims said they did so because the victims resisted. Most chose to hit their victims with their fists or a weapon rather than to shoot or cut the victim. A sixth of those encountering resistance did, however, take drastic action: shooting, cutting, or spraying liquid into the eyes of their victims.

Around 15% of the robbers used physical force right at the outset, usually to establish initial control over the situation and usually striking without warning. One said he attacked in this way because the victim "was big." Another said it was his first robbery and that he wasn't sure what to do. He got a tire jack out of the truck, and:

> See, first I think, "Well, if I hit him in the head that might kill him," so I hit him on the shoulder.

A juvenile used force to flee a burglary when the house occupant unexpectedly returned.

Around 10% of the offenders hurt their victims unintentionally. In one the victim ran into another room slamming the door behind him. When the robber chased after him, the door hit the robber's gun hand, causing the gun to fire. The bullet accidentally struck the victim. Another robber deliberately pointed his gun away from the victim and sought not to fire. The gun fired accidentally, however, and the bullet struck the victim after ricocheting off a wall. In other cases, one victim suffered a heart attack, and another jumped out of a moving car. The robbers were concerned because they had neither intended nor foreseen the possibility of harm to the victims.

A quarter of those who hurt somebody did so in an attempt to recover money they had some claim to. A number of these arose out of drug-selling and gambling situations. Another victim had refused to "spot" a good location for a burglary after being paid to do so. Although these victims were certainly not asking to be robbed or hurt, they were certainly not totally innocent either. In every instance in which there was an attempt to recover money someone was hurt. Whether this was because the offenders were angry or because they met resistance is not clear.

Overall, the robbers did not generally appear to use gratuitous force. In some instances the force applied was greater than necessary, but generally the robbers did not appear to take any abstract pleasure in hurting people. Only one reported the use of force for its own sake. He said that after he had hit the victim with a lug wrench, his partner then hit the victim several more times. In commenting on why his partner had done this, he said, "Knowing him, he did it for meanness. He likes to hurt people."

Learning and Decisions to Continue

The process by which some of those committing one or two robberies become highly active offenders committing 50 or more robberies is obviously important. For some offenders this progression seems to involve an escalation from shoplifting to burglary to robbery. Several of the highly active robbers studied, however, went much more directly into robbery and at a very early age.

The information in this study is too limited to be more than suggestive. There are strong hints, however, that the key transitions take place very early. Most of the first-time robbers indicated that they felt fear and apprehension as they approached their robberies. Most also tended to be very tentative about the robberies. Many reported that they would have considered leaving the money if the victim said

he would lose his job or that he needed the money for rent. The more experienced robbers, however, were much more hardened. They were much less tentative and fearful, were unmoved by any difficulties that the crime might create for the victim, and tended to view victims as objects rather than persons. This harder kind of outlook was generally present after only a few robberies.

Seventy percent of the robbers said that they did not plan to commit another offense, 14% said that they might, and 4% said that they probably would. . . The remaining 12% said that they did not know whether they would or not. Thus a total of 30% of the offenders were willing to give some overt indication that they might commit further robberies. These indications show greater realism and honesty than might have been expected.

Rationality

Many of the decisions described are clearly rational in the sense used by Clarke and Cornish (1985). The individuals making these decisions had desires and needs that they chose to satisfy by committing robberies. Whether they were generalists who also committed other crimes or specialists who concentrated on robbery, they definitely had made robbery a deliberate part of their repertoire. Although these decisions would seem more rational if they involved more planning and more concern about the possibility of apprehension, the decisions nonetheless easily meet the standards of minimum rationality. There is clearly a thinking process involved. It is not Benthamite, but it is not much different from what people do in their everyday lives. This is particularly true for the decisions made by highly experienced robbers. Although these robbers frequently say that they undertake no planning, their experience is in a sense a substitute. Many of these robbers seem to feel that they can handle any situation that arises without specific planning.

Many of the decisions involved in robberies committed for reasons other than money also seem rational in this sense. Taking property from someone you are fighting with can be instrumental in accomplishing the aims of the fight. Going along with your friends or trying to recover property can also be instrumental acts. Some of the decisions described do not meet this kind of rationality test, however. Impulse decisions to commit serious crimes while loaded on drugs or alcohol cannot easily be called rational. Even these acts can be instrumental, however, in accomplishing goals that the actor—in his stupefied state—wants. Whether it is useful to treat these as rational for the purpose of developing theories of explanation, prevention, or control is not altogether clear. It is worth noting, however, that the criminal law often does so (LaFave and Scott, 1972).

Implications for Research

Whatever the scientific validity of the rational actor model for the purposes of developing criminological theory, the model is clearly useful for many purposes. It provides an excellent framework for analyzing and understanding the decision-making process used by offenders and puts a healthy emphasis on gaining information from offenders and on dealing with specific crime problems.

The emphasis on obtaining information directly from offenders is particularly important. Detailed discussions with offenders about their crimes and their methods of thinking and operation have already had considerable payoff in recent years, in the fine work on burglary and crime prevention that has been done in Britain (Bennett and Wright, 1984; Clarke, 1983; Maguire, 1982; Walsh, 1980) [and] in the contribution that self-report studies have made to the study of criminal careers. . . . This kind of work is in its infancy, however, and there is a great deal more to be learned.

The greatest payoffs are likely to come from increased attention to the strategic decisions made by offenders and the learning process involved—the decision to rob, to continue robbing, and to desist from robbing. Studies in the past decade (Chaiken and Chaiken, 1982; Farrington, 1979; Greenwood, 1982; Wolfgang et al., 1972) have taught us a great deal about the importance of criminal careers, but we need to understand more than just the number of offenses and the

sequences involved. We need to understand the thought processes and the decisions as well. In this context "decision" should not be defined too narrowly. Often there may be no single "decision" to begin robbing, to continue robbing, or even to desist from robbing. Rather, the offender has a whole thought process and belief system that ultimately lead to some kind of conclusion.

There are also likely to be substantial payoffs to further gathering of information about tactical decisions and the factual contexts as seen by the robbers. If headway is ever to be made in dealing with crime, we must access the information that offenders have and use this for purposes of prevention and control. Robbers know a lot about themselves and about robberies that no one else knows. A foreign journalist who tried to project the course of future events in Berlin in 1932 by studying only voting returns and demographics, to the exclusion of *Mein Kampf* and the Nazi platform, would today be considered very foolish.

The emphasis on particular crime problems is also timely and helpful. There are no doubt purposes for which it is useful to aggregate thinking about the Brighton hotel bombing, pilfering from the neighborhood market, and marijuana sales. For most practical purposes, however, it is much more useful to treat these as separate problems. If the solutions that emerge from separate analyses suggest some greater aggregation, that will be the appropriate time to have greater aggregation.

Implications for Policy

The studies to date tell us some useful and important things about the decision-making process employed by robbers and help point the way toward the more sophisticated research needed to obtain a fuller picture. The extent to which this information has implications for policy in its present fragmentary state is less clear.

The robbers themselves had some ideas. . . The most frequent suggestion they made as to ways of preventing robberies was to supply jobs or job-training programs to persons like themselves. This suggestion was made by

37% of the robbers. Fourteen percent of the robbers, however, said that it was not possible to stop people from robbing and that nothing could be done. Other suggestions made by a few offenders each included more counseling, more drug programs, target hardening, and letting offenders know the penalties in order to improve deterrence.

Some of the study findings tend to confirm the traditional police concern with apprehension. Whereas many offenders said that they did not think about being caught, some also said that they chose to rob rather than to burgle or shoplift because of prior apprehensions for those crimes. One chose to rob because he was on probation for burglary and was fearful of getting caught for that again.

There are some hints that the aversive effect of apprehension is strongest for first-time offenders who are still learning how to rob. This suggests that if apprehension could be made to take place early in the offender's career, it might be possible to interrupt the learning process and steer the offender away from robbery. This might be a gain even if the offender continued to commit some other crime such as shoplifting. The learning curve for robbery appears to be very rapid, however, and it is easier to describe the possible effects of early apprehension than to make early apprehensions. In any event, it would be useful to have more information from offenders about the effects of apprehensions and nonapprehensions at the various stages of their careers.

A more practical possibility is that of obtaining more convictions of offenders when valid arrests are made. This is particularly important in the United States where 30% to 60% of all robbery arrestees are not convicted, usually for reasons of evidence rather than innocence (Feeney et al., 1983; McDonald, 1982). This is one of the few areas in which rapid progress might be possible if the political will to address the issue existed. Its importance is indicated by the experience of one offender in the study. This offender began robbing and shooting heroin at age 13. By age 26 he had plausibly and conservatively committed over a thousand robberies without a conviction until his present sentence. He had been arrested on five occasions, but in each instance the charges were dropped. Is it any wonder that he did not worry too much about being caught?

The findings on decision making could also have implications for sentencing. If the reports that even the most active robbers do relatively little planning and rarely think about getting caught are accurate, this weakens the appeal of deterrence as a strategy for controlling robbery. Steep penalties are unlikely to deter those who do not believe they will be caught. Such penalties may, however, deter others, who then decide not to commit robberies. The fact that some offenders leave the bullets out of their guns because of the possible penalties suggests that some offenders worry about penalties more than they indicate. This may be particularly true for first offenders. The relative ineffectiveness of deterrence on those who actually rob strengthens the case for incapacitation, as incapacitation provides some measure of control over the impulsive as well as the calculating robber.

The findings suggest that, to be at all successful, prevention efforts must be very selective and highly targeted. There are some indications that robbers who plan little and act on impulse can be successfully thwarted by prevention schemes that make obtaining money more difficult and more time consuming, such as no-change bus fares and the holding of limited cash at gasoline stations (Misner and McDonald, 1970). There are also indications, however, that robbers are much less affected by prevention devices, such as bank cameras, which essentially operate on deterrence principles.

References

Bennett, T. and R. Wright (1984) *Burglars on Burglary.* Aldershot, Hants, England: Gower.

Chaiken, J. and M. Chaiken (1982) *Varieties of Criminal Behavior.* Santa Monica, CA: Rand.

Clarke, R. (1983) Situational crime prevention: its theoretical basis and practical scope. Pp. 225-56 in M. Tonry and N. Morris (eds.), *Crime and Justice: An Annual Review of Research*, Volume 4. Chicago: University of Chicago Press.

Clarke, R. and D. Cornish (1985) "Modelling offenders' decisions: A framework for research and policy." Pp. 147-85 in M. Tonry and N. Morris (eds.), *Crime and Justice: An Annual Review of Research*, Volume 6. Chicago: University of Chicago Press.

Farrington. D. (1979) "Longitudinal research on crime and delinquency." Pp. 289-348 in N. Morris and M. Tonry (eds.), *Crime and Justice: An Annual Review of Research*, Volume 1. Chicago: University of Chicago Press.

Feeney, F., F. Dill and A. Weir (1983) *Arrests Without Conviction*. Washington, DC: U.S. Government Printing Office.

Greenwood. P. (1982) *Selective Incapacitation*. Santa Monica. CA: Rand.

LaFave, W. and A. Scott (1972) *Criminal Law*. St. Paul, MN: West.

Maguire, M. (1982) *Burglary in a Dwelling*. London: Heinemann.

McDonald, W. (1982) *Police-Prosecutor Relations in the United States*. Washington, DC: U.S. Government Printing Office.

Misner, G. and W. McDonald (1970) *The Scope of the Crime Problem and Its Resolution*. Volume II of *Reduction of Robberies and Assaults of Bus Drivers*. Berkeley, CA: Stanford Research Institute and University of California.

Walsh, D. (1980) *Break-Ins: Burglary from Private Houses*. London: Constable.

Weir, A. (1973) "The robbery offender." Pp.100-211 in F. Feeney and A. Weir (eds.), *The Prevention and Control of Robbery*, Volume 1. Davis, CA: University of California.

Wolfgang, M., R. Figlio and T. Sellin (1972) *Delinquency in a Birth Cohort*. Chicago: University of Chicago Press.

Floyd Feeney, "Robbers as Decision Makers." In *The Reasoning Criminal: Rational Choice Perspectives on Offending*, edited by Derek B. Cornish and Ronald V. Clarke. Copyright © 1986 by Springer-Verlag. Tables deleted. Reprinted with permission. ✦

13

Creating the Illusion of Impending Death: Armed Robbers in Action

Richard T. Wright
Scott H. Decker

This selection is derived from a larger study by Wright and Decker in which they interviewed 86 active armed robbers in St. Louis. The interviews were semi-structured and conducted in a casual manner. The researchers focused on the robbers' thoughts and actions before, during, and after their crimes. In this selection they report on the strategies used by the robbers to compel their victims' compliance. The findings are consistent with those by Indermauer (in this volume) in that robbers are found to use violence or the threat of violence as a means of controlling the situation and to obtain victims' cooperation.

As such, violence is seen as instrumental to the commission of the crime. Wright and Decker's subjects reported that they created an illusion of impending death to scare victims into a state of compliance. The robbers attempted to maintain the illusion without having to actually make good on the threat. When, however, the victims did not comply as expected, the offenders usually responded with severe violence to bring victims back to compliance. The robbers reported that seldom did they want to kill their victims, although some were prepared to do so if necessary.

Unlike most sorts of street crime, successful armed robberies are never secret or ambiguous. By definition, they require offenders to confront intended victims directly. As David Luckenbill (1981:25) has observed, there is a strong interactional component to armed robbery; offenders and victims must develop "a common definition of the situation" and co-orient their actions to meet the demands of the offense. This does not happen automatically. After all, why should stick-up victims willingly participate in their own fleecing?

It is important to develop a clear understanding of the strategies used by armed robbers to compel the cooperation of would-be victims. Such information could offer citizens some guidance about how best to act and react should they be confronted by a robber. It also could provide policy makers and criminal justice officials with a better appreciation of offenders' aims and intentions during robberies, thereby enabling them to make more informed crime prevention and sentencing decisions.

In an attempt to learn more about the tactics employed by offenders to commit stick-ups, we located and interviewed 86 currently active armed robbers in St. Louis, Missouri. Armed robbery is a serious problem in St. Louis. In 1994, the year our research began, the city had 6,025 stick-ups reported to the police and ranked second in the nation in robberies per capita. The armed robbers for our study were recruited through the efforts of two field-based informants—an ex-offender, and a small-time heroin dealer and street criminal. Working through chains of street referrals, the field recruiters contacted active armed robbers, convinced them to take part in our project, and assisted us in conducting interviews that lasted up to two hours. In the pages that follow, we report just a small portion of what the offenders said during those interviews, focusing on how they actually commit their offenses.

Approaching the Victim

To be successful, armed robbers must take control of the offense from the start. They immediately have to impose on the interaction a definition favorable to their ends, allowing intended victims no room for negotiation. This typically is accomplished by creating an illusion of impending death.

> Robbery itself is an illusion. That's what it's about. . . . Here is a person that you stick a gun in his face, they've never died, they don't know how it feels, but the illusion of death causes them to do what you want them to do. (aka Robert Jones)

A large part of creating such an illusion involves catching potential victims off guard; the element of surprise denies them the opportunity to adopt an oppositional stance.

> Sometimes people be alert; they be watchin' so you got to be careful of what you do. You got to be alert. . . . Pretty soon [the intended victim] falls asleep, and then [h]e ain't even trippin'. He over there lookin' at some girl. . . . [H]e probably just take his eyes off what he's doin', watchin' out, [which is] what he's supposed to be doin', and just turn his head on some girls. And [the stick-up] be on. (aka Andrew)

The offenders in our sample employ two different methods to approach would-be victims without arousing their suspicion. The first method involves using stealth or speed to sneak up on unwitting prey.

> [Whoever I am going to rob. I] just come up on you. You could be going to your car. If you are facing this way, I want to be on your blind side. If you are going this way, I want to be on that side where I can get up on you [without you noticing me] and grab you: "This is a robbery, motherfucker, don't make it no murder!" I kind of like shake you. That's my approach. (aka Richard L. Brown)

The second method involves "managing a normal appearance" (Luckenbill, 1981:29). The offenders' aim is to fit into the social setting such that victims see their presence as normal and non-threatening, thereby allowing them to get close enough for a surprise attack.

> Well, if I'm walking, say you got something that I want, I might come up there [and say], "Do you have the time?" or "Can I get a light from you?" something like that.

"Yeah, it's three o'clock." By then I'm up on you, getting what I want. (aka Loco)

The method chosen to approach potential victims typically is dictated more by situational factors than by the idiosyncratic preferences of individual offenders. Depending on the situation, most of the armed robbers are prepared to use either speed and stealth or the presentation of a non-threatening self to move within striking range of their victims. The offender quoted below, for example, reported that he and his partners usually initiate their commercial stick-ups simply by charging through the front door of the establishment, ski masks pulled down and guns drawn.

> When I approach the door [of a would-be commercial target] generally we got ski masks that rolls up into a skull cap; it's a skull cap right now and as we get to the door, right prior to walking in the door, we pull our masks down. Once we come in, we got these masks down [so] we got to come in pulling our weapons, might even have them out prior to going in, just concealed. As soon as we pull those masks down, we are committed [because our intention is obvious]. (aka Robert Gibson)

He added, however, that circumstances occasionally require them to enter intended targets posing as customers. Doing so helps them to avoid tipping their hand too early, which is crucial in situations where the victim is likely to be armed.

> Say for instance [the target is] a tavern and the guy behind the bar . . . might be the kind of guy that got a pistol. Most bartenders and most people that's cashing checks, they got pistols on them. Believe me, they got pistols. . . . So in that particular situation, you got to . . . get in the door before you go into motion because you got to know where they are at. You've got to make sure that you've got a real chance to get up on them and make it not worth their risk to try to reach the pistol [before you betray your intentions]. (aka Robert Gibson)

Regardless of the manner in which the offenders make their approach, the aim almost invariably is the same: to "establish co-presence" with the victim without betraying their intentions (Luckenbill, 1981:29). This gives would-be victims little opportunity to recognize the danger and to take steps to repel the attack. Not only is this far safer for the offenders, it also puts them in a strong position when it comes to compelling the victim's immediate cooperation.

Announcing the Crime

By announcing a stick-up, armed robbers commit themselves irrevocably to the offense. Any semblance of normality has been shattered; from this point onward, the victim will act and react in the knowledge that a robbery is being committed. The offenders we interviewed saw this as the "make or break" moment. The challenge for them was "to dramatize with unarguable clarity that the situation ha[d] suddenly and irreversibly been transformed into a crime" (Katz, 1988:176). In effecting this transformation, they seek to establish dominance over their intended prey, thereby placing themselves in a position to dictate the terms of the unfolding interaction.

> When I first come up on [my victims], I might scare them, but then I calm them down. It's a control thing. If you can get a person to listen to you, you can get them to do just about anything. . . . That's the way the world is made. (aka Tony Wright)

Most of the offenders said that they typically open their armed robberies with a demand that the would-be victim stop and listen to them.

> I say [to the victim], "Look here, hey, just hold up right where you at! Don't move! Don't say nothing!" (aka James Minor)

They often couple this demand with an unambiguous declaration of their predatory intentions.

> [I tell my victims], "It's a robbery! Don't nobody move!" (aka John Lee)

That declaration, in turn, usually is backed by a warning about the dire consequences of failing to do as they instruct.

> [I say to the victim], "This is a robbery, don't make it a murder! It's a robbery, don't make it a murder!" (aka Wallie Cleaver)

All of the above pronouncements are intended to "soften up" victims; to inform them that they're about to be robbed and to convince them that they are not in a position to resist. Having seized initial control of the interaction, offenders then must let victims know what is expected of them. As one armed robber reminded us: "You have to talk to victims to get them to cooperate. . . . They don't know what to do, whether to lay down, jump over the counter, dance, or whatever." This information typically is communicated to victims in the form of short, sharp orders laced with profanity and, often, racial epithets.

> [I say to victims], "Hey motherfucker, give me your shit! Move slow and take everything out of your pockets!" (aka James Love)

> [I grab my victims and say], "Take it off girl! Nigger, come up off of it!" (aka Libbie Jones)

The "expressive economy" with which the offenders issue instructions can in part be accounted for by a desire to keep victims off balance by demonstrating an ominous insensitivity to their precarious emotional state (see Katz, 1988:177). Clearly, the swearing and racial putdowns help to reinforce this impression.

Almost all of the offenders typically used a gun to announce their stick-ups. They recognized that displaying a firearm usually obviated the need to do much talking. One put it this way: "A gun kinda speaks for itself." Most of them believed that "big, ugly guns" such as 9MMs or 45s were the best weapons for inducing cooperation.

> [The 9MM] got that look about it like it gonna kill you. It talk for itself. "I'm gonna kill you." Looking at a 9 pointed at you, that's what goes through your head: "He gonna kill me if I don't give him this money." (aka Prauch)

In practice, however, many of the armed robbers actually carried somewhat smaller firearms because they were more easily concealed and simpler to handle.

> I like the 32 because it's like a 38, small, easy and accessible. And it will knock [the

victim] down if you have to use it. (aka Bob Jones)

A few offenders maintained that very small caliber pistols (e.g., 22s, 25s) made poor robbery weapons because many potential victims were not afraid of them.

[With] 22s or 25s people gonna be like, "Man, he using this little gun. I ain't worried." A 22 is real little, they gonna be, "Man, that ain't gonna do nothing but hurt me. Give me a little sting." (aka Syco)

That said, the majority of respondents felt that even the smallest handguns were big enough to intimidate most people. As one observed: "A person's gonna fear any kind of gun you put in their face. So it don't matter [what you use]. If it's a gun, it's gonna put fear in you."

The dilemma faced by offenders in relying on a gun to induce fear is that the strategy might work too well. Jack Katz (1988) has noted that the display of a firearm can easily be misinterpreted by victims as the precursor to an offense far more serious than robbery (e.g., rape, kidnapping, murder). Offenders are keen to avoid such misinterpretations because they can stun victims into a state of incomprehension or convince them that determined resistance represents their only chance of survival. When armed offenders warn victims—"This is a robbery, don't make it a murder!"—they are doing more than issuing a credible death threat. Paradoxically, they also are seeking to reassure the victims that submission will not put their lives in jeopardy.

Transferring the Goods

No doubt the most difficult aspect of pulling off an armed robbery involves managing the transfer of goods. The difficulty inheres in the fact that offenders must keep victims under strict control while, at the same time, attempting to make sure that they have gotten everything worth taking. What is more, all of this must be accomplished as quickly as possible. The longer the stick-up lasts, the more risk offenders run of being discovered by police or passersby.

The armed robbers we talked to used two different strategies to manage the transfer of goods. The first involved simply ordering victims to hand over their possessions.

I tell [my victims], "Man, if you don't want to die, give me your money! If you want to survive, give me your money! I'm not bullshitting!" So he will either go in his back pocket and give me the wallet or the woman will give me her purse. (aka Tony Brown)

By making victims responsible for the transfer of goods, the offenders are able to devote their undivided attention to watching for signs of danger.

I rather for [victims] to give [their valuables] to me because I have to be alert. If they reach for something, I'll have to shoot them. (aka K-Money)

There is, however, one serious drawback to giving victims responsibility for the transfer; it is difficult to know whether they really have turned over all of their valuables. Recognizing this, many of the offenders employed tough talk and a fierce demeanor to discourage victims from attempting to shortchange them.

You say, "Is that everything?" You can kinda tell if they lyin' sometimes: "That's all I got, man, that's all!" You'll say, "You're lyin', man, you lyin'!" and just make them think that you're getting pissed because he's lying to you. So basically you got this gun [pointed] at they head, so sometimes it be like, "Okay, I got some more." (aka Damon Jones)

A few of them went so far as to rough up their victims, especially those who appeared confused or hesitant, to reinforce the message that holding something back would be a risky proposition.

Well, if [the victim] hesitates like that, undecided, you get a little aggressive and you push 'em. Let them know you mean business. I might take [the] pistol and crack their head with it. "Come on with that money and quit bullcrapping or else you gonna get into some real trouble!" Normally when they see you mean that kind of business they . . . come on out with it. (aka Burle)

But most of the offenders who allowed victims to hand over their own possessions simply accepted what was offered and made good their escape. As one explained: "You just got to be like, 'Well, it's cool right here what I got.' When you get too greedy, that's when [bad] stuff starts to happen."

The second strategy used by the armed robbers to accomplish the transfer of goods involved taking the victims' possessions from them without waiting for what was offered.

> I get [the victim's money] because everybody not gonna give you all they got. They gonna find some kind of way to keep from giving it all. (aka Richard L. Brown)

A number of the offenders who preferred this strategy were reluctant to let victims empty their own pockets for fear that they were carrying a concealed weapon.

> I don't let nobody give me nothing. Cause if you let somebody go in they pockets, they could pull out a gun, they could pull out anything. You make sure they are where you can see their hands at all times. (aka Cooper)

To outsiders, these offenders may appear to be greatly overestimating the risk of encountering an armed victim. Such a perspective, however, betrays a respectable, middle-class upbringing. In the desperate inner-city neighborhoods in which almost all of the armed robbers reside, and in which many of them ply their trade, weapons are a ubiquitous feature of everyday life.

As already noted, all of the crime commission strategies adopted by the offenders are intended, at least in part, to minimize the possibility of victim resistance. Generally speaking, these strategies work very well. Nevertheless, almost all of the armed robbers we talked to said that they occasionally encountered victims who steadfastly refused to comply with their demands.

> [O]n the parking lot, if you grab somebody and say, "This is a robbery, don't make it a murder!" I've had it happen that [the victim just says], "Well, you got to kill me then." (aka Richard L. Brown)

Faced with a recalcitrant victim, most of the offenders responded with severe, but non-lethal, violence in the hope of convincing the person to cooperate. Often this violence involved smacking or beating the victim about the head with a pistol.

> It's happened [that some of my victims initially refuse to hand over their money, but] you would be surprised how cooperative a person will be once he been smashed across the face with a 357 Magnum. (aka Tony Wright)

Occasionally, however, a robbery involved shooting the victim in the leg or some other spot unlikely to prove fatal.

> [If the person refuses to do what I say] most of the time I just grab my pistol, take the clip out and just slap 'em. If I see [the victim] trying to get tough, then sometimes I just straight out have to shoot somebody, just shoot 'em. I ain't never shot nobody in the head or nothing, nowhere that I know would kill 'em, just shoot them in they leg. Just to let them know that I'm for real [and that they should] just come up off the stuff. (aka Cooper)

While a majority of the armed robbers preferred to use non-lethal violence to subdue resistant victims, several of them admitted to having been involved in fatal encounters in the past. One of the female offenders, for instance, described how she had watched from the car while one of her male companions shot and killed an uncooperative robbery victim.

> We was in the car and, I didn't get out this time, one of the dudes got out. The [victim], he wasn't gonna let nobody rob him: "Nigger, you got to kill me! You got to kill me!" And that's what happened to him. Just shot him in the head. It was like, God!, I had never seen that. When [my accomplice] shot him, it wasn't like he was rushing to get away. He shot him, walked back to the car, put the gun back up under the seat and just, you know, we watched [the victim] when he fell, blood was coming out of his mouth, he was shaking or something. (aka Ne-Ne)

Such incidents are rare; few of the offenders entered into armed robberies intending to kill or seriously injure their prey. Indeed, some admitted that they probably would abandon an intended offense rather than use deadly force to subdue an uncooperative victim.

> I really ain't gonna shoot nobody. I think a lot of people are like that. I wouldn't shoot nobody myself, if they gave me too much of a problem, I might just take off. (aka Mike J.)

That said, it must be noted that armed robbers typically are acting under intense emotional pressure to generate some fast cash by any means necessary in an interactional environment shot through with uncertainty and danger. Is it any wonder that the slightest hint of victim resistance may provoke some of them to respond with potentially deadly force? As one observed: "When you're doing stuff like this, you just real edgy; you'll pull the trigger at anything, at the first thing that go wrong."

Making an Escape

Once offenders have accomplished the transfer of goods, it only remains for them to make their getaway. Doing that, however, is more difficult than it might appear. Up to this point, the offenders have managed to keep victims in check by creating a convincing illusion of impending death. But the maintenance of that illusion becomes increasingly more difficult as the time comes for offenders to make good their escape. How can they continue to control victims who are becoming physically more distant from them?

In broad terms, the offenders can effect a getaway in one of two ways; they can leave the scene themselves or they can stay put and force the victim to flee. Other things being equal, most of them preferred to be the ones to depart. Before doing so, however, they had to make sure that the victim would not attempt to follow them or to raise the alarm. A majority of the offenders responded to this need by using verbal threats designed to extend the illusion of impending death just long enough for them to escape unobserved.

> I done left people in gangways and alleys and I've told them, "If you come out of this alley, I'm gonna hurt you. Just give me 5

or 10 minutes to get away. If you come out of this alley in 3 or 4 minutes, I'm gonna shoot the shit out of you!" (aka Bennie Simmons)

A few offenders, however, attempted to prolong this illusion indefinitely by threatening to kill their victims if they *ever* mentioned the stick-up to anyone.

> I done actually took [the victim's] ID and told them, "If you call the police, I got your address and everything. I know where you stay at and, if you call the police, I'm gonna come back and kill you!" (aka Melvin Walker)

Some of the armed robbers were uncomfortable relying on verbal threats to dissuade their prey from pursuing them. Instead, they took steps to make it difficult or impossible for victims to leave the crime scene by tying them up or incapacitating them through injury.

> [I hit my victims before I escape so as to] give them less time to call for the police. Especially if it's somebody else's neighborhood [and] we don't know how to get out. You hit them with a bat just to slow his pace. If you hit him in the leg with a bat, he can't walk for a minute; he gonna be limping, gonna try to limp to a payphone. By then it be 15 or 20 minutes, we be hitting the highway and on our way back to the southside where our neighborhood is. (aka Antwon Wright)

While most of the offenders wanted to be the first to leave the crime scene, a number of them preferred to order the victim to flee instead. This allowed the offenders to depart in a calm, leisurely manner, thereby reducing the chances of drawing attention to themselves.

> I try not to have to run away. A very important thing that I have learned is that when you run away, too many things can happen running away. Police could just be cruising by and see you running down the street. I just prefer to be able to walk away, which is one of the reasons why I tend, rather than to make an exit, I tell the victim to walk and don't look back: "Walk away, and walk fast!" When they walk, I can make my exit walking. (aka Stick Going)

What is more, forcing the victim to leave first permitted the offenders to escape without worrying about being attacked from behind—a crucial consideration for those unwilling or unable to incapacitate their prey prior to departure.

> [Afterward,] I will tell [the victim] to run. You wouldn't just get the stuff and run because he may have a gun and shoot you while you are turning around running or something like that. (aka Damon Jones)

Beyond such instrumental concerns, several of the armed robbers indicated that they forced the victim to flee for expressive reasons as well; it demonstrated their continuing ability to dominate and control the situation. The clearest example of this involved an offender who routinely taunted his victims by ordering them to leave the scene in humiliating circumstances: "I like laughing at what I do, like, I told . . . one dude to take off his clothes. I just do a whole bunch of stuff. Sometimes I'll make a dude crawl away. I'll tell him to crawl all the way up the street. And I'll sit there in the alley watching him crawl and crack up laughing."

Conclusion

In short, the active armed robbers we interviewed typically compel the cooperation of intended victims through the creation of a convincing illusion of impending death. They create this illusion by catching would-be victims off guard, and then using tough talk, a fierce demeanor, and the display of a deadly weapon to scare them into a state of unquestioning compliance. The goal is to maintain the illusion for as long as possible without having to make good on the threat. This is easier said than done. Armed robbery is an interactive event and, for any number of reasons, victims may fail to behave in the expected fashion. When this happens, the offenders usually respond with severe, but nonlethal, violence, relying on brute force to bring victims' behavior back into line with their expectations. Very few of them want to kill their victims, although some clearly are prepared to resort to deadly force if need be.

References

Katz, Jack. 1988. *Seductions of Crime.* New York: Basic Books.

Luckenbill, David. 1981. "Generating Compliance: The Case of Robbery." *Urban Life* 10:25-46.

Richard T. Wright and Scott H. Decker, "Creating the Illusion of Impending Death: Armed Robbers in Action." In *The HFG Review,* 2(1) pp. 10–19. Fall 1997. Reprinted with permission. ✦

14

Convicted Rapists' Vocabulary of Motive: Excuses and Justifications

Diana Scully
Joseph Marolla

In *this chapter, Diana Scully and Joseph Marolla analyze the excuses and justifications which a group of convicted rapists used to explain themselves and their crimes. The researchers conducted extensive interviews with 114 male convicted rapists incarcerated in seven maximum- or medium-security prisons in Virginia. For the purpose of determining the validity of the information obtained, the offenders' accounts were cross-checked with information contained in pre-sentence investigation reports on file at the prison. These reports contained, among other things, police and victims' versions of the crimes for which the rapists had been convicted. Scully and Marolla classified the participants as* admitters *or* deniers. *Admitters told essentially the same account of their crimes as did police and victims. Interview accounts by deniers differed significantly from police and victims' versions.*

The rapists utilized excuses and justifications which allowed a majority of them to view themselves as nonrapists or "ex-rapists." Many of the rapists, through this form of self-delusion, saw their behavior as appropriate to the situation or as a reasonable adaptation or rational response to the situation they found themselves in.

The following selection, excerpted from the research, is divided into two sections. In the first the authors discuss the accounts which the rapists used to justify their behavior. In the second, they discuss the accounts which the rapists used to excuse the rape. The authors' analysis and conclusions follow.

Justifying Rape

. . . deniers attempted to justify their behavior by presenting the victim in a light that made her appear culpable, regardless of their own actions. Five themes run through attempts to justify their rapes: (1) women as seductresses; (2) women mean "yes" when they say "no"; (3) most women eventually relax and enjoy it; (4) nice girls don't get raped; and (5) guilty of a minor wrongdoing.

1) Women as Seductresses

Men who rape need not search far for cultural language which supports the premise that women provoke or are responsible for rape. In addition to common cultural stereotypes, the fields of psychiatry and criminology (particularly the subfield of victimology) have traditionally provided justifications for rape, often by portraying raped women as the victims of their own seduction (Albin, 1977; Marolla and Scully, 1979). For example, Hollander (1924:130) argues:

> Considering the amount of illicit intercourse, rape of women is very rare indeed. Flirtation and provocative conduct, i.e. tacit (if not actual) consent is generally the prelude to intercourse.

Since women are supposed to be coy about their sexual availability, refusal to comply with a man's sexual demands lacks meaning and rape appears normal. The fact that violence and, often, a weapon are used to accomplish the rape is not considered. As an example, Abrahamsen (1960:61) writes:

> The conscious or unconscious biological or psychological attraction between man and woman does not exist only on the part of the offender toward the woman but, also, on her part toward him, which in many instances may, to some extent, be the impetus for his sexual attack. Often a women [sic] unconsciously wishes to be

taken by force—consider the theft of the bride in Peer Gynt.

Like Peer Gynt, the deniers we interviewed tried to demonstrate that their victims were willing and, in some cases, enthusiastic participants. In these accounts, the rape became more dependent upon the victims' behavior than upon their own actions.

Thirty-one percent . . . of the deniers presented an extreme view of the victim. Not only willing, she was the aggressor, a seductress who lured them, unsuspecting, into sexual action. Typical was a denier convicted of his first rape and accompanying crimes of burglary, sodomy, and abduction. According to the pre-sentence reports, he had broken into the victim's house and raped her at knife point. While he admitted to the breaking and entry, which he claimed was for altruistic purposes ("to pay for the prenatal care of a friend's girlfriend"), he also argued that when the victim discovered him, he had tried to leave but she had asked him to stay. Telling him that she cheated on her husband, she had voluntarily removed her clothes and seduced him. She was, according to him, an exemplary sex partner who "enjoyed it very much and asked for oral sex. Can I have it now?" he reported her as saying. He claimed they had spent hours in bed, after which the victim had told him he was good looking and asked to see him again. "Who would believe I'd meet a fellow like this?" he reported her as saying.

In addition to this extreme group, 25 percent . . . of the deniers said the victim was willing and had made some sexual advances. An additional 9 percent . . . said the victim was willing to have sex for money or drugs. In two of these three cases, the victim had been either an acquaintance or picked up, which the rapists said led them to expect sex.

2) Women Mean 'Yes' When They Say 'No'

Thirty-four percent . . . of the deniers described their victim as unwilling, at least initially, indicating either that she had resisted or that she had said no. Despite this, and even though according to pre-sentence reports a weapon had been present in 64 percent . . . of these 11 cases, the rapists justified their behavior by arguing that either the victim had

not resisted enough or that her "no" had really meant "yes." For example, one denier who was serving time for a previous rape was subsequently convicted of attempting to rape a prison hospital nurse. He insisted he had actually completed the second rape, and said of his victim: "She semi-struggled but deep down inside I think she felt it was a fantasy come true." The nurse, according to him, had asked a question about his conviction for rape, which he interpreted as teasing. "It was like she was saying, 'rape me'." Further, he stated that she had helped him along with oral sex and "from her actions, she was enjoying it." In another case, a 34-year-old man convicted of abducting and raping a 15-year-old teenager at knife point as she walked on the beach, claimed it was a pickup. This rapist said women like to be overpowered before sex, but to dominate after it begins.

> A man's body is like a coke bottle, shake it up, put your thumb over the opening and feel the tension. When you take a woman out, woo her, then she says "no, I'm a nice girl," you have to use force. All men do this. She said "no" but it was a societal no, she wanted to be coaxed. All women say "no" when they mean "yes" but it's a societal no, so they won't have to feel responsible later.

Claims that the victim didn't resist or, if she did, didn't resist enough, were also used by 24 percent . . . of admitters to explain why, during the incident, they believed the victim was willing and that they were not raping. These rapists didn't redefine their acts until some time after the crime. For example, an admitter who used a bayonet to threaten his victim, an employee of the store he had been robbing, stated:

> At the time I didn't think it was rape. I just asked her nicely and she didn't resist. I never considered prison. I just felt like I had met a friend. It took about five years of reading and going to school to change my mind about whether it was rape. I became familiar with the subtlety of violence. But at the time, I believed that as long as I didn't hurt anyone it wasn't wrong. At the time, I didn't think I would go to prison, I thought I would beat it.

Another typical case involved a gang rape in which the victim was abducted at knife point as she walked home about midnight. According to two of the rapists, both of whom were interviewed, at the time they had thought the victim had willingly accepted a ride from the third rapist (who was not interviewed). They claimed the victim didn't resist and one reported her as saying she would do anything if they would take her home. In this rapist's view, "She acted like she enjoyed it, but maybe she was just acting. She wasn't crying, she was engaging in it." He reported that she had been friendly to the rapist who abducted her and, claiming not to have a home phone, she gave him her office number—a tactic eventually used to catch the three. In retrospect, this young man had decided, "She was scared and just relaxed and enjoyed it to avoid getting hurt." Note, however, that while he had redefined the act as rape, he continued to believe she enjoyed it.

Men who claimed to have been unaware that they were raping viewed sexual aggression as a man's prerogative at the time of the rape. Thus they regarded their act as little more than a minor wrongdoing even though most possessed or used a weapon. As long as the victim survived without major physical injury, from their perspective, a rape had not taken place. Indeed, even U.S. courts have often taken the position that physical injury is a necessary ingredient for a rape conviction.

3) Most Women Eventually Relax and Enjoy It

Many of the rapists expected us to accept the image, drawn from cultural stereotype, that once the rape began, the victim relaxed and enjoyed it. Indeed, 69 percent . . . of deniers justified their behavior by claiming not only that the victim was willing, but also that she enjoyed herself, in some cases to an immense degree. Several men suggested that they had fulfilled their victims' dreams. Additionally, while most admitters used adjectives such as "dirty," "humiliated," and "disgusted," to describe how they thought rape made women feel, 20 percent . . . believed that their victim enjoyed herself. For example, one denier had posed as a salesman to gain entry to his victim's house. But he claimed he had a previous sexual relationship with the victim, that she agreed to have sex for drugs, and that the opportunity to have sex with him produced "a glow, because she was really into oral stuff and fascinated by the idea of sex with a black man. She felt satisfied, fulfilled, wanted me to stay, but I didn't want her." In another case, a denier who had broken into his victim's house but who insisted the victim was his lover and let him in voluntarily, declared "She felt good, kept kissing me and wanted me to stay the night. She felt proud after sex with me." And another denier, who had hid in his victim's closet and later attacked her while she slept, argued that while she was scared at first, "once we got into it, she was ok." He continued to believe he hadn't committed rape because "she enjoyed it and it was like she consented."

4) Nice Girls Don't Get Raped

The belief that "nice girls don't get raped" affects perception of fault. The victim's reputation, as well as characteristics or behavior which violate normative sex role expectations, are perceived as contributing to the commission of the crime. For example, Nelson and Amir (1975) defined hitchhike rape as a victim-precipitated offense.

In our study, 69 percent . . . of deniers and 22 percent . . . of admitters referred to their victims' sexual reputation, thereby evoking the stereotype that "nice girls don't get raped." They claimed that the victim was known to have been a prostitute, or a "loose" woman, or to have had a lot of affairs, or to have given birth to a child out of wedlock. For example, a denier who claimed he had picked up his victim while she was hitchhiking stated, "To be honest, we [his family] knew she was a damn whore and whether she screwed one or 50 guys didn't matter." According to pre-sentence reports this victim didn't know her attacker and he abducted her at knife point from the street. In another case, a denier who claimed to have known his victim by reputation stated:

> If you wanted drugs or a quick piece of ass, she would do it. In court she said she was a virgin, but I could tell during sex [rape] that she was very experienced.

When other types of discrediting biographical information were added to these sexual slurs, a total of 78 percent . . . of the deniers used the victim's reputation to substantiate their accounts. Most frequently, they referred to the victim's emotional state or drug use. For example, one denier claimed his victim had been known to be loose and, additionally, had turned state's evidence against her husband to put him in prison and save herself from a burglary conviction. Further, he asserted that she had met her current boyfriend, who was himself in and out of prison, in a drug rehabilitation center where they were both clients.

Evoking the stereotype that women provoke rape by the way they dress, a description of the victim as seductively attired appeared in the accounts of 22 percent . . . of deniers and 17 percent . . . of admitters. Typically, these descriptions were used to substantiate their claims about the victim's reputation. Some men went to extremes to paint a tarnished picture of the victim, describing her as dressed in tight black clothes and without a bra; in one case, the victim was portrayed as sexually provocative in dress and carriage. Not only did she wear short skirts, but she was observed to "spread her legs while getting out of cars." Not all of the men attempted to assassinate their victim's reputation with equal vengeance. Numerous times they made subtle and offhand remarks like, "She was a waitress and you know how they are."

The intent of these discrediting statements is clear. Deniers argued that the woman was a "legitimate" victim who got what she deserved. For example, one denier stated that all of his victims had been prostitutes; pre-sentence reports indicated they were not. Several times during his interview, he referred to them as "dirty sluts," and argued "anything I did to them was justified." Deniers also claimed their victim had wrongly accused them and was the type of woman who would perjure herself in court.

5) Only a Minor Wrongdoing

The majority of deniers did not claim to be completely innocent and they also accepted some accountability for their actions. Only 16 percent . . . of deniers argued that they were totally free of blame. Instead, the majority of deniers pleaded guilty to a lesser charge. That is, they obfuscated the rape by pleading guilty to a less serious, more acceptable charge. They accepted being over-sexed, accused of poor judgement or trickery, even some violence, or guilty of adultery or contributing to the delinquency of a minor, charges that are hardly the equivalent of rape.

Typical of this reasoning is a denier who met his victim in a bar when the bartender asked him if he would try to repair her stalled car. After attempting unsuccessfully, he claimed the victim drank with him and later accepted a ride. Out riding, he pulled into a deserted area "to see how my luck would go." When the victim resisted his advances, he beat her and he stated:

> I did something stupid. I pulled a knife on her and I hit her as hard as I would hit a man. But I shouldn't be in prison for what I did. I shouldn't have all this time [sentence] for going to bed with a broad.

This rapist continued to believe that while the knife was wrong, his sexual behavior was justified.

In another case, the denier claimed he picked up his under-age victim at a party and that she voluntarily went with him to a motel. According to pre-sentence reports, the victim had been abducted at knife point from a party. He explained:

> After I paid for a motel, she would have to have sex but I wouldn't use a weapon. I would have explained. I spent money and, if she still said no, I would have forced her. If it had happened that way, it would have been rape to some people but not to my way of thinking. I've done that kind of thing before. I'm guilty of sex and contributing to the delinquency of a minor, but not rape.

In sum, deniers argued that, while their behavior may not have been completely proper, it should not have been considered rape. To accomplish this, they attempted to discredit and blame the victim while presenting their own actions as justified in the context. Not surprisingly, none of the deniers thought of himself as a rapist. A minority of the admitters attempted to lessen the impact of their crime by claiming the victim enjoyed being raped. But despite this similarity, the nature and tone of admitters' and deniers' accounts were essentially different.

Excusing Rape

In stark contrast to deniers, admitters regarded their behavior as morally wrong and beyond justification. They blamed themselves rather than the victim, although some continued to cling to the belief that the victim had contributed to the crime somewhat, for example, by not resisting enough.

Several of the admitters expressed the view that rape was an act of such moral outrage that it was unforgivable. Several admitters broke into tears at intervals during their interviews. A typical sentiment was,

> I equate rape with someone throwing you up against a wall and tearing your liver and guts out of you. . . . Rape is worse than murder . . . and I'm disgusting.

Another young admitter frequently referred to himself as repulsive and confided:

> I'm in here for rape and in my own mind, its the most disgusting crime, sickening. When people see me and know, I get sick.

Admitters tried to explain their crime in a way that allowed them to retain a semblance of moral integrity. Thus, in contrast to deniers' justifications, admitters used excuses to explain how they were compelled to rape. These excuses appealed to the existence of forces outside of the rapists' control. Through the use of excuses, they attempted to demonstrate that either intent was absent or responsibility was diminished. This allowed them to admit rape while reducing the threat to their identity as a moral person. Excuses also permitted them to view their behavior as idiosyncratic rather than typical and, thus, to believe they were not "really" rapists. Three themes run through these accounts: (1) the use of alcohol and drugs; (2) emotional problems; and (3) nice guy image.

1) The Use of Alcohol and Drugs

A number of studies have noted a high incidence of alcohol and drug consumption by convicted rapists prior to their crime (Groth,

1979; Queen's Bench Foundation, 1976). However, more recent research has tentatively concluded that the connection between substance use and crime is not as direct as previously thought (Ladouceur, 1983). Another facet of alcohol and drug use mentioned in the literature is its utility in disavowing deviance. McCaghy (1968) found that child molesters used alcohol as a technique for neutralizing their deviant identity. Marolla and Scully (1979), in a review of psychiatric literature, demonstrated how alcohol consumption is applied differently as a vocabulary of motive. Rapists can use alcohol both as an excuse for their behavior and to discredit the victim and make her more responsible. We found the former common among admitters and the latter common among deniers.

Alcohol and/or drugs were mentioned in the accounts of 77 percent . . . of admitters and 84 percent . . . of deniers and both groups were equally likely to have acknowledged consuming a substance—admitters, 77 percent . . . ; deniers, 72 percent. . . . However, admitters said they had been affected by the substance; if not the cause of their behavior, it was at least a contributing factor. For example, an admitter who estimated his consumption to have been eight beers and four "hits of acid" reported:

> Straight, I don't have the guts to rape. I could fight a man but not that. To say, "I'm going to do it to a woman," knowing it will scare and hurt her, takes guts or you have to be sick.

Another admitter believed that his alcohol and drug use,

> . . . brought out what was already there but in such intensity it was uncontrollable. Feelings of being dominant, powerful, using someone for my own gratification, all rose to the surface.

In contrast, deniers' justifications required that they not be substantially impaired. To say that they had been drunk or high would cast doubt on their ability to control themself or to remember events as they actually happened. Consistent with this, when we asked if the alcohol and/or drugs had an effect on their behavior, 69 percent . . . of admitters, but only 40 percent . . . of deniers said they had been affected.

Even more interesting were references to the victim's alcohol and/or drug use. Since admitters had already relieved themselves of responsibility through claims of being drunk or high, they had nothing to gain from the assertion that the victim had used or been affected by alcohol and/or drugs. On the other hand, it was very much in the interest of deniers to declare that their victim had been intoxicated or high: that fact lessened her credibility and made her more responsible for the act. Reflecting these observations, 72 percent . . . of deniers and 26 percent . . . of admitters maintained that alcohol or drugs had been consumed by the victim. Further, while 56 percent . . . of deniers declared she had been affected by this use, only 15 percent . . . of admitters made a similar claim. Typically, deniers argued that the alcohol and drugs had sexually aroused their victim or rendered her out of control. For example, one denier insisted that his victim had become hysterical from drugs, not from being raped, and it was because of the drugs that she had reported him to the police. In addition, 40 percent . . . of deniers argued that while the victim had been drunk or high, they themselves either hadn't ingested or weren't affected by alcohol and/or drugs. None of the admitters made this claim. In fact, in all of the 15 percent . . . of cases where an admitter said the victim was drunk or high, he also admitted to being similarly affected.

These data strongly suggest that whatever role alcohol and drugs play in sexual and other types of violent crime, rapists have learned the advantage to be gained from using alcohol and drugs as an account. Our sample were aware that their victim would be discredited and their own behavior excused or justified by referring to alcohol and/or drugs.

2) Emotional Problems

Admitters frequently attributed their acts to emotional problems. Forty percent . . . of admitters said they believed an emotional problem had been at the root of their rape behavior, and 33 percent . . . specifically related the problem to an unhappy, unstable childhood or a marital-domestic situation. Still others claimed to have been in a general state of unease. For example, one admitter said that at the time of the rape he had been depressed, feeling he couldn't do anything right, and that something had been missing from his life. But he also added, "being a rapist is not part of my personality." Even admitters who could locate no source for an emotional problem evoked the popular image of rapists as the product of disordered personalities to argue they also must have problems:

> The fact that I'm a rapist makes me different. Rapists aren't all there. They have problems. It was wrong so there must be a reason why I did it. I must have a problem.

Our data do indicate that a precipitating event, involving an upsetting problem of everyday living, appeared in the accounts of 80 percent . . . of admitters and 25 percent . . . of deniers. Of those experiencing a precipitating event, including deniers, 76 percent . . . involved a wife or girlfriend. Over and over, these men described themselves as having been in a rage because of an incident involving a woman with whom they believed they were in love.

Frequently, the upsetting event was related to a rigid and unrealistic double standard for sexual conduct and virtue which they applied to "their" woman but which they didn't expect from men, didn't apply to themselves, and, obviously, didn't honor in other women. To discover that the "pedestal" didn't apply to their wife or girlfriend sent them into a fury. One especially articulate and typical admitter described his feeling as follows. After serving a short prison term for auto theft, he married his "childhood sweetheart" and secured a well-paying job. Between his job and the volunteer work he was doing with an ex-offender group, he was spending long hours away from home, a situation that had bothered his wife. In response to her request, he gave up his volunteer work, though it was clearly meaningful to him. Then, one day, he discovered his wife with her former boyfriend "and my life fell apart." During the next several days, he said his anger had made him withdraw into himself and, after three days of drinking in a motel room, he abducted and raped a stranger. He stated:

> My parents have been married for many years and I had high expectations about marriage. I put my wife on a pedestal. When I walked in on her, I felt like my life had been destroyed, it was such a shock. I was bitter and angry about the fact that I hadn't done anything to my wife for cheating. I didn't want to hurt her [victim], only to scare and degrade her.

It is clear that many admitters, and a minority of deniers, were under stress at the time of their rapes. However, their problems were ordinary—the types of upsetting events that everyone experiences at some point in life. The overwhelming majority of the men were not clinically defined as mentally ill in court-ordered psychiatric examinations prior to their trials. Indeed, our sample is consistent with Abel *et al.* (1980) who found fewer than 5 percent of rapists were psychotic at the time of their offense.

As with alcohol and drug intoxication, a claim of emotional problems works differently depending upon whether the behavior in question is being justified or excused. It would have been counter-productive for deniers to have claimed to have had emotional problems at the time of the rape. Admitters used psychological explanations to portray themselves as having been temporarily "sick" at the time of the rape. Sick people are usually blamed for neither the cause of their illness nor for acts committed while in that state of diminished capacity. Thus, adopting the sick role removed responsibility by excusing the behavior as having been beyond the ability of the individual to control. Since the rapists were not "themselves," the rape was idiosyncratic rather than typical behavior. Admitters asserted a non-deviant identity despite their self-proclaimed disgust with what they had done. Although admitters were willing to assume the sick role, they did not view their problem as a chronic condition, nor did they believe themselves to be insane or permanently impaired. Said one admitter, who believed that he needed psychological counseling: "I have a mental disorder, but I'm not crazy." Instead, admitters viewed their "problem" as mild, transient, and curable. In-

deed, part of the appeal of this excuse was that not only did it relieve responsibility, but, as with alcohol and drug addiction, it allowed the rapist to "recover." Thus, at the time of their interviews, only 31 . . . percent of admitters indicated that "being a rapist" was part of their self-concept. Twenty-eight percent . . . of admitters stated they had never thought of themselves as a rapist, 8 percent . . . said they were unsure, and 33 percent . . . asserted they had been a rapist at one time but now were recovered. A multiple "ex-rapist," who believed his "problem" was due to "something buried in my subconscious" that was triggered when his girlfriend broke up with him, expressed a typical opinion:

> I was a rapist, but not now. I've grown up, had to live with it. I've hit the bottom of the well and it can't get worse. I feel born again to deal with my problems.

3) Nice Guy Image

Admitters attempted to further neutralize their crime and negotiate a non-rapist identity by painting an image of themselves as a "nice guy." Admitters projected the image of someone who had made a serious mistake but, in every other respect, was a decent person. Fifty-seven percent . . . expressed regret and sorrow for their victim indicating that they wished there were a way to apologize for or amend their behavior. For example, a participant in a rape-murder, who insisted his partner did the murder, confided, "I wish there was something I could do besides saying 'I'm sorry, I'm sorry.' I live with it 24 hours a day and, sometimes, I wake up crying in the middle of the night because of it."

Schlenker and Darby (1981) explain the significance of apologies beyond the obvious expression of regret. An apology allows a person to admit guilt while at the same time seeking a pardon by signalling that the event should not be considered a fair representation of what the person is really like. An apology separates the bad self from the good self, and promises more acceptable behavior in the future. When apologizing, an individual is attempting to say: "I have repented and should be forgiven," thus making it appear that no further rehabilitation is required.

The "nice guy" statements of the admitters reflected an attempt to communicate a message consistent with Schlenker's and Darby's analysis of apologies. It was an attempt to convey that rape was not a representation of their "true" self. For example,

It's different from anything else I've ever done. I feel more guilt about this. It's not consistent with me. When I talk about it, it's like being assaulted myself. I don't know why I did it, but once I started, I got into it. Armed robbery was a way of life for me, but not rape. I feel like I wasn't being myself.

Admitters also used "nice guy" statements to register their moral opposition to violence and harming women, even though, in some cases, they had seriously injured their victims. Such was the case of an admitter convicted of a gang rape:

I'm against hurting women. She should have resisted. None of us were the type of person that would use force on a woman. I never positioned myself on a woman unless she showed an interest in me. They would play to me, not me to them. My weakness is to follow. I never would have stopped, let alone pick her up without the others. I never would have let anyone beat her. I never bothered women who didn't want sex; never had a problem with sex or getting it. I loved her—like all women.

Finally, a number of admitters attempted to improve their self-image by demonstrating that, while they had raped, it could have been worse if they had not been a "nice guy." For example, one admitter professed to being especially gentle with his victim after she told him she had just had a baby. Others claimed to have given the victim money to get home or make a phone call, or to have made sure the victim's children were not in the room. A multiple rapist, whose pattern was to break in and attack sleeping victims in their homes, stated:

I never beat any of my victims and I told them I wouldn't hurt them if they cooperated. I'm a professional thief. But I never robbed the women I raped because I felt so bad about what I had already done to them.

Even a young man, who raped his five victims at gun point and then stabbed them to death, attempted to improve his image by stating:

Physically they enjoyed the sex [rape]. Once they got involved, it would be difficult to resist. I was always gentle and kind until I started to kill them. And the killing was always sudden, so they wouldn't know it was coming.

Summary and Conclusions

Convicted rapists' accounts of their crimes include both excuses and justifications. Those who deny what they did was rape justify their actions; those who admit it was rape attempt to excuse it or themselves. This study does not address why some men admit while others deny, but future research might address this question. This paper does provide insight on how men who are sexually aggressive or violent construct reality, describing the different strategies of admitters and deniers.

Admitters expressed the belief that rape was morally reprehensible. But they explained themselves and their acts by appealing to forces beyond their control, forces which reduced their capacity to act rationally and thus compelled to rape. Two types of excuses predominated: alcohol/drug intoxication and emotional problems. Admitters used these excuses to negotiate a moral identity for themselves by viewing rape as idiosyncratic rather than typical behavior. This allowed them to reconceptualize themselves as recovered or "ex-rapists," someone who had made a serious mistake which did not represent their "true" self.

In contrast, deniers' accounts indicate that these men raped because their value system provided no compelling reason not to do so. When sex is viewed as a male entitlement, rape is no longer seen as criminal. However, the deniers had been convicted of rape, and like the admitters, they attempted to negotiate an identity. Through justifications, they constructed a "controversial" rape and attempted to demonstrate how their behavior, even if not quite right, was appropriate in the situation. Their denials, drawn from common cultural rape stereotypes, took two forms, both of which ultimately denied the existence of a victim.

The first form of denial was buttressed by the cultural view of men as sexually masterful and women as coy but seductive. Injury was denied by portraying the victim as willing, even enthusiastic, or as politely resistant at first but eventually yielding to "relax and enjoy it." In these accounts, force appeared merely as a seductive technique. Rape was disclaimed: rather than harm the woman, the rapist had fulfilled her dreams. In the second form of denial, the victim was portrayed as the type of woman who "got what she deserved." Through attacks on the victim's sexual reputation and, to a lesser degree, her emotional state, deniers attempted to demonstrate that since the victim wasn't a "nice girl," they were not rapists. Consistent with both forms of denial was the self-interested use of alcohol and drugs as a justification. Thus, in contrast to admitters, who accentuated their own use as an excuse, deniers emphasized the victim's consumption in an effort to both discredit her and make her appear more responsible for the rape. It is important to remember that deniers did not invent these justifications. Rather, they reflect a belief system which has historically victimized women by promulgating the myth that women both enjoy and are responsible for their own rape.

While admitters and deniers present an essentially contrasting view of men who rape, there were some shared characteristics. Justifications particularly, but also excuses, are buttressed by the cultural view of women as sexual commodities, dehumanized and devoid of autonomy and dignity. In this sense, the sexual objectification of women must be understood as an important factor contributing to an environment that trivializes, neutralizes, and, perhaps, facilitates rape.

Finally, we must comment on the consequences of allowing one perspective to dominate thought on a social problem. Rape, like any complex continuum of behavior, has multiple causes and is influenced by a number of social factors. Yet, dominated by psychiatry and the medical model, the underlying assumption that rapists are "sick" has pervaded research. Although methodologically unsound, conclusions have been based almost exclusively on small clinical populations of rapists—that extreme group of rapists who seek counseling in prison and are the most likely to exhibit psychopathology. From this small, atypical group of men, psychiatric findings have been generalized to all men who rape. Our research, however, based on volunteers from the entire prison population, indicates that some rapists, like deniers, viewed and understood their behavior from a popular cultural perspective. This strongly suggests that cultural perspectives, and not an idiosyncratic illness, motivated their behavior. Indeed, we can argue that the psychiatric perspective has contributed to the vocabulary of motive that rapists use to excuse and justify their behavior (Scully and Marolla, 1984).

Efforts to arrive at a general explanation for rape have been retarded by the narrow focus of the medical model and the preoccupation with clinical populations. The continued reduction of such complex behavior to a singular cause hinders, rather than enhances, our understanding of rape.

References

Abel, Gene, Judith Becker, and Linda Skinner (1980) "Aggressive behavior and sex." *Psychiatric Clinics of North America* 3(2):133-151.

Abrahamsen, David (1960) *The Psychology of Crime*. New York: John Wiley.

Albin, Rochelle (1977) "Psychological studies of rape." *Signs* 3(2):423-435.

Athens, Lonnie (1977) "Violent crimes: A symbolic interactionist study." *Symbolic Interaction* 1(l):56-71.

Burgess, Ann Wolbert, and Lynda Lytle Holmstrom (1974) *Rape: Victims of Crisis*. Bowie: Robert J. Brady.

—— (1979) "Rape: Sexual disruption and recovery." *American Journal of Orthopsychiatry* 49(4):648-657.

Burt, Martha (1980) "Cultural myths and supports for rape." *Journal of Personality and Social Psychology* 38(2): 217- 230.

Burt, Martha, and Rochelle Albin (1981) "Rape myths, rape definitions, and probability of conviction." *Journal of Applied Psychology* 11(3):212-230.

Feldman-Summers, Shirley, Patricia E. Gordon, and Jeanette R. Meagher (1979) "The impact of rape on sexual satisfaction." *Journal of Abnormal Psychology* 88(l):101-105.

Glueck, Sheldon (1925) *Mental Disorders and the Criminal Law*. New York: Little Brown.

Groth, Nicholas A. (1979) *Men Who Rape*. New York: Plenum Press.

Hall, Peter M., and John P. Hewitt (1970) "The quasi-theory of communication and the management of dissent." *Social Problems* 18(1):17-27.

Hewitt, John P., and Peter M. Hall (1973) "Social problems, problematic situations, and quasi-theories." *American Journal of Sociology* 38(3):367-374.

Hewitt, John P., and Randall Stokes (1975) "Disclaimers." *American Sociological Review* 40(1):1-11.

Hollander, Bernard (1924) *The Psychology of Misconduct, Vice, and Crime*. New York: Macmillan.

Holmstrom, Lynda Lytle, and Ann Wolbert Burgess (1978) "Sexual behavior of assailant and victim during rape." Paper presented at the annual meetings of the American Sociological Association, San Francisco, September 2-8.

Kilpatrick, Dean G., Lois Veronen, and Patricia A. Resnick (1979) "The aftermath of rape: Recent empirical findings." *American Journal of Orthopsychiatry* 49(4):658-669.

Ladouceur, Patricia (1983) "The relative impact of drugs and alcohol on serious felons." Paper presented at the annual meetings of the American Society of Criminology, Denver, November 9-12.

Luckenbill, David (1977) "Criminal homicide as a situated transaction." *Social Problems* 25(2):176-187.

McCaghy, Charles (1968) "Drinking and deviance disavowal: The case of child molesters." *Social Problems* 16(l):43-49.

Marolla, Joseph, and Diana Scully (1979) "Rape and psychiatric vocabularies of motive." Pp. 301-318 in Edith S. Gomberg and Violet Franks (eds.), *Gender and Disordered Behavior: Sex Differences in Psychopathology*. New York: Brunner/Mazet.

Mills, C. Wright (1940) "Situated actions and vocabularies of motive." *American Sociological Review* 5(6):904-913.

Nelson, Steve, and Menachem Amir (1975) "The hitchhike victim of rape: A research report." Pp. 47-65 in Israel Drapkin and Emilio Viano (eds.), *Victimology: A New Focus*. Lexington, KY: Lexington Books.

Queen's Bench Foundation (1976) *Rape: Prevention and Resistance*. San Francisco: Queen's Bench Foundation.

Ruch, Libby O., Susan Meyers Chandler, and Richard A. Harter (1980) "Life change and rape impact." *Journal of Health and Social Behavior* 21(3):248-260.

Schlenker, Barry R., and Bruce W. Darby (1981) "The use of apologies in social predicaments." *Social Psychology Quarterly* 44(3):271-278.

Scott, Marvin, and Stanford Lyman (1968) "Accounts." *American Sociological Review* 33(1):46-62.

Scully, Diana, and Joseph Marolla (1984) "Rape and psychiatric vocabularies of motive: Alternative perspectives." In Ann Wolbert Burgess (ed.), *Handbook on Rape and Sexual Assault*. New York: Garland Publishing. Forthcoming.

Shore, Barbara K. (1979) *An Examination of Critical Process and Outcome Factors in Rape*. Rockville, MD: National Institute of Mental Health.

Stokes. Randall, and John P. Hewitt (1976) "Aligning actions." *American Sociological Review* 41(5):837-849.

Sykes, Gresham M., and David Matza (1957) "Techniques of neutralization." *American Sociological Review* 22(6):664-670.

Williams, Joyce (1979) "Sex role stereotypes, women's liberation, and rape: A cross-cultural analysis of attitude." *Sociological Symposium* 25 (Winter):61-97.

Section V

Gangs and Crime

The past 15 years have witnessed a renewed interest in gangs by the criminal justice system and academic researchers. Street youth gangs are increasing sharply in numbers and in violence. Unlike the turf-oriented gangs of the 1950s and 1960s, the youth gangs of today are heavily involved in a variety of criminal activities, including drug trafficking.

In this section Felix M. Padilla ("Becoming a Gang Member") examines the influences of the neighborhood, school, and interaction with police on the decision to affiliate with a gang.

As with many other decisions made by criminals, Padilla concludes that joining a gang has instrumental qualities, satisfies some basic needs, and/or serves as "a shield against conditions of injustice and suffering."

In the next selection, gang researcher John M. Hagedorn ("Homeboys, Dope Fiends, Legits, and New Jacks") identifies four categories of gang members based on commitment to gang life and drug dealing. He addresses a number of issues critical to understanding the phenomenon of gang life: What happens to gangs members as they age? How are drug sales and gang activity related? How might these findings be translated into effective social policy?

Most gang studies focus on street gangs. However, in recent years the emergence of prison gangs has caused a reappraisal of our concept of prison culture. Geoffrey Hunt and his associates examine these changes in "Changes in Prison Culture." They conclude that the relatively orderly prison culture of the past no longer exists.

The inmate social system—once organized about convict versus guard and black versus white divisions—has been deposed by the introduction of prison gangs, creating "an increasingly unpredictable world in which prior loyalties, allegiances, and friendships [are] disrupted."

In each selection, the offenders—both members of street gangs and prison gangs—provide an unfiltered glimpse into their lives and activities. ✦

15

Becoming a Gang Member

Felix M. Padilla

I*n this selection Felix M. Padilla examines the processes by which young Latinos become members of a street gang. He views the process as one of adaptation to the exigencies of life in the barrio. Padilla argues that influences in the neighborhood, school, and police attitudes are intertwined in a complex way to influence barrio youth to affiliate with gangs. He maintains that gangs provide youths protection, self-esteem, money, and other valued services which would not be so readily available outside the gang structure. In this sense, joining a gang is seen as a rational response to their situation.*

Padilla's subjects are members of a mostly Puerto Rican Chicago street gang—the Diamonds (a fictitious name given to the group by Padilla)—located in a neighborhood known as Suburbia five miles northwest of downtown Chicago. The research methodology conducted extensive open-ended interviews with participant-as-observer methods. Padilla spent over 16 months studying the gang, completing his research in 1990.

Neighborhood Influences

The youth gang made up a good part of the social and physical landscape of Suburbia during the preteen and adolescent years of the members of the Diamonds. Although it is a fact that Suburbia possesses and displays many middle-class characteristics, for nearly two decades this neighborhood has served as the home base for a large number of youth gangs. It is believed by most youngsters that the number of gangs and/or gang sections is still growing as attempts to create new drug-dealing turfs continue in earnest. My conversations with members of the Diamonds, how-ever, revealed ambiguous accounts of the history of their gang. Oral history accounts—those stories passed down from one generation to the next for the purpose of preserving and reinforcing, in this case, the history of the gang and maintaining its authenticity and identity—are hardly uniform. Similarly, they know just as little about other gangs. In most cases, however, some of the youngsters might recall the names of members who were really "down for the gang" (the most committed members) and some of the "courageous" sacrifices they carried out to save the gang from oblivion, though they are not capable of providing a thorough description of the particular actions taken. Many different and, at times, contrasting renditions of intergang fights represent the episodes most commonly described, and in these stories, of course, the Diamonds always emerge victorious.

One thing the youngsters are all certain about is that a large number of youth gangs were present in their neighborhood when they were growing up. Youngsters were unable to recall a day when the gang was not part of the neighborhood, as evidenced in the following exchange in which Coco speaks about living alongside several youngsters who were gang members.

Felix: Which gang members do you remember when you were a kid?

Coco: Oh, by my house—there was Jimmy and Francisco. They were cousins who lived in the same building. Not in my building, but they lived in the same building. That was next door to me.

Felix: Were there other gang members in your neighborhood?

Coco: At this time, of course. On my block there were several others. But, you see, gang members don't hang out on their block because they don't want their parents to know that they are bangers [members of a gang].

Felix: So, where did you see the other gang members?

Coco: Different corners, but mainly on the schoolyard. That was always their favorite place for hanging out. It still is.

For Flaco the gang represented a natural fixture of his neighborhood—an everpresent element of the physical and social environment. In an almost poetic way he stated:

Like the apartment buildings, the sidewalks, and trees of the neighborhood, we [the gangs] were all part of the same thing. You can't get the gangs out, they were there when I was a kid, and now we are here for the new kids. As a matter of fact, I don't think anyone can remember a day when there were no gangs in the city. A lot of people blame us for gangbanging, but there were gangbangers a hundred years ago. What do you think the Mafia was? That was a gang just like some of the ones in the neighborhood. They were really organized and had a lot of money, but, I tell you, some gangs today are developing that way. Maybe we will be one.

Indeed, the short-lived histories of members of the Diamonds have unfolded within a social environment wherein the youth gang has persistently played a central role. Thus, young people from the neighborhood have grown up witnessing and learning specific elements of gang culture. These youngsters have been altogether familiar with the workings of the gang for a very long time; at least, they have known about the more visible ingredients of the organization's cultural milieu.

Lobo's experience with the local neighborhood gang is a case in point. He grew up on a street block where several youngsters affiliated with a gang were his friends, from whom he witnessed what he defined as "the nuts and bolts of the gang." He recalls, in particular, the tightly knit relationships present among gang members and how those affiliations served as the major force for establishing and maintaining cohesiveness within the organization. When asked to elaborate on this idea Lobo responded:

The fact that those guys got along so well, that's what told me about how things worked with the gang. They cared for each other. They were brothers; the blood was the same. To me that's really what made the organization. People are always putting down gangs because they say we're punks and up to no good, but they don't understand what gangs are all about. I remember seeing these guys; hey, they cared

about each other more than a lot of other people who are not in gangs do. That's what I remember the most about the guys from the hood; they were always looking out for each other. And that's exactly what we did when we became gang members. I had several friends that I was really close with. They were like my brothers. We did everything together.

In the case of Tito, growing up among the local youth gang meant witnessing various fights and hearing the different explanations offered by gang members to justify their behavior. Tito recalled being in seventh grade when he first learned about gang-banging:

I didn't really know the meaning of gang-banging until one day on the schoolyard when I saw this fight. After the fight them were two guys who were cursing each other and talking bad about each other's gang. . . . After the fight in the schoolyard I learned that these guys didn't like each other, and the way to settle their differences was through throwing down. Then they began saying things like, "This is my hood. If I see you here again, I'm going to kick the shit out of you." So, to me the fights were started because some guy was in some neighborhood where he did not belong. I kind of thought that it made a lot of sense because I wouldn't want people from other places coming to my neighborhood and claiming it for themselves. My mother had told me stories about how Puerto Rican people used to live in different neighborhoods, like over there where you teach now at DePaul, and how other people came and took over their neighborhood. I thought, and still do, that we have to make claim to what is ours. We want our neighborhood for us, so we have to protect it. So, when I was in grade school, I saw these guys doing things that I thought were necessary to do, like protecting their section of the neighborhood from other gangs. And, you know what, ask any of these guys around here what they think about their neighborhood, they all going to tell you that is the most important thing for them. So, learn to care for the neighborhood—that's really important. I learned this lesson a long time. Not that I was making plans to join a gang in those days, but it's crazy that it would happen to me.

Youngsters learned to accept the neighborhood as something that was very personal, for its identity and character were believed to originate directly from all of its residents. Just as important, as Tito indicated, was having learned that maintaining neighborhood social harmony was an essential responsibility of gang members; any disturbance might make public a youngster's gang affiliation and identity as well as the drug-dealing business. Youngsters could hardly afford to reveal their covers since it might jeopardize their business routine and invite local parental involvement, which could, at the very least, lead to public embarrassment and humiliation. This point is well described by Coco:

The guys in the neighborhood never fought there, on the street. I learned something that I found was true when I turned [joined the gang], and that is that you take your business to the alley or to the schoolyard or even to someone's hood, but you don't do it in your own neighborhood. That's a sign of disrespect. Besides, you don't want people in your neighborhood to know you belong to a gang. They begin harassing you and stuff. Even to this day my mother doesn't believe that I'm a gangbanger. I have gotten locked up a couple of times, but, since this happened in other turfs, I always told her that I was jumped by punks from opposition gangs. . . . The first time I was locked up it happened in the hood of the opposition, so I had to call her to get me out. I told her that the cops fingered me because I looked like someone they were looking for. The police told her that I was a banger, but she believed me instead. And I kept telling her that they were lying and stuff like that. But, you see, if I was around the hood doing stupid shit and people saw me and told her, then she be like, "La Sra. [Mrs.] Maria told me this about you," and I couldn't deny it because Puerto Ricans believe a lot in what their neighbors tell them.

Association with neighborhood peers (nongang members) also served to fill out members of the Diamonds's mental images of gang culture. In most cases, friendship groups, sports teams, clubs, party groups, and other cliques were already long established, and, like other youngsters, members of the Diamonds joined these groups for companionship, social enjoyment, and recreation. And when a group member was acquainted with someone affiliated with the gang he would facilitate interaction and communication between the rest of the group and the gang. The role of this young man was to legitimize each group, for each was suspicious of the other. He would vouch for his neighborhood friends, endorsing them as trustworthy to his friends in the gang. On the other hand, his depiction of the gang was aimed at cultivating a clear and convincing picture with which his friends could evaluate the gang as an authentic and positive youth organization. Rafael describes the way he first made contact with members from his neighborhood gang:

I don't think I was really afraid of the gang. But, as you know, when you're a kid a lot of things scare you. You have your parents telling you all the time not to hang out with this group or that other group. Your older brothers and sisters tell you the same thing. But my friend knew some of the guys, and because of him I started hanging out with the guys. And because of him I was treated just like him. I was OK to them.

Elf experienced a similar process of gaining familiarity with the gang, as he indicates in the following dialogue:

Felix: When was the first time you came in contact with the gang?

Elf: I was young. Maybe eleven.

Felix: How did this happen?

Elf: Through my friends. Several homeys of mine who were connected brought us in. It was really no big deal.

Felix: Why not?

Elf: Well, I used to think that what those guys always wanted to do was to beat the shit out of you just for the fuck of it—something like wilding [doing crazy things]—you know, that they would beat up people because they didn't have anything else to do. And that they picked on guys like me because we were small and weak, and, you know, we were what you call helpless. You know, we couldn't defend ourselves. That's how I used to picture it.

Felix: So, what did you find out?

Elf: They were not like that. They talked to you. I was too young, so they were not interested in me as a member. They didn't mess with me. They treated me alright. At first I was surprised because they were cool with me, and I did not think that was the way I was supposed to be treated. But they did, and I'm glad.

Felix: What did you do with them?

Elf: Well, not much. Whenever I saw them or they saw me I would say, "What's up?" if I was in the hood and they were hanging out, sometimes they called me over. We would say, "What's up?" But it was something loose, but I became uptight with them and they with me.

A contrasting experience affecting the peer group also served to heighten youngsters' mental image of gang culture. There were many times when the peer group became the target of harassment from different neighborhood gangs because of the former group's determination to maintain a "neutron" status—that is, having no affiliation to any one gang. Though they lived in the same neighborhood, some youngsters chose to remain unaffiliated with the geographically immediate local gang and those from other neighborhoods (that is, they were "hanging in the middle"); as a result, their status of neutrality was constantly being tested by various competing gangs. Punishment inflicted on these youngsters, then, was not aimed at coercing them to "turn"; rather, it was meant to ensure that they would remember the importance of remaining neutrons. There is a constant fear on the part of gang members that neutrons might decide to become informants for another gang or, worse yet, be coerced into providing law enforcement agents with news and information of activities being carried out by some gangs. Even as neutrons, these youngsters learned the importance of loyalty within the gang's scheme of things. They witnessed the gang's activities and perceived the gang as an association committed to maintaining confidentiality among its members as well as by people in the neighborhood. As one young man expressed it:

Back when I was a neutron, I learned that with the gang it's the secret that counts. You got to be tight-lipped about what's going on. So, now I understand that it's important that you don't tell people anything you know about the gang. Even talking to someone like you is dangerous, except that they know you, so that's OK. In a way that's how things should be. I really like that. We don't want neutrons to be rats, to be telling people about our affairs. Another thing that we don't want is people in the neighborhood to be calling the cops on us. That's not cool. We don't let people get away with that shit, boy. If they give us this respect, then we give them the same thing. But, if they don't, then we are going to be on two different sides. We like the neutrons and other people to be on the same side with us.

It is important to add that trying to maintain a neutral status is no small task for youngsters growing up in Latino neighborhoods today. To grow up in an area controlled by one gang or, worse yet, by several gangs means having to identify oneself with at least the spatially nearest group. So Latino youngsters learn very quickly to adopt a series of protective or defensive schemes; in particular, they learn the cultural symbols of the nearby local gang as well as those of the various competing others in order to masterfully use this knowledge in appropriate situations. In this way they will not be accused of choosing sides or displaying more loyalty to a given group than to another. Tito recalls being in this plight:

Felix: What's the meaning of "represent"?

Tito: To know what gang they're from and what gang they dislike and know who's hood you're in.

Felix: So, what happens when you represent?

Tito: You throw up their signals. That tells them that you're straight. That you respect them.

Felix: When did you start learning about these things?

Tito: I was going to the seventh grade. That's when I started learning a lot about gangs and what they were really about.

Felix: What did you learn?

Tito: Their symbols and the signs and what hey mean and what's for the gangs. They write their symbols up, to tell people which are their symbols, and where they are at, and things like that. If the symbols are upside down that means another gang defaced the gang's wall. I learned that when that happens that's a sign of disrespect.

Felix: And which gangs were around your neighborhood?

Tito: They were opposites. There were Folks and People where I lived. They were all around, so I got to know all of them—where to hang out and where not to hang out.

Felix: So, you had to learn to be a neutron?

Tito: Right, and, if I did choose to be with the opposition, which one would be best for me? Like, if I lived in one territory, I should be more or less on their territory than on the other side. Because, if I had to spend most of my time there, I would have to be on their side. It depended on where I was at and where I would go.

Through these various neighborhood experiences, all of which occurred before their teen years, members of the Diamonds were able to accumulate a fairly extensive body of conceptual information as well as practical knowledge with which to form opinions about the functioning of gangs. Overall, their emerging views toward the gang were being shaped in a positive light. For them there was nothing necessarily immoral or inappropriate about being a gang member; in fact, they defined gang members as "straight," "cool," and "together"—people to be admired and not resented. Contrary to public opinion, which tends to prescribe a criminal label to gangs and their members, ever since their adolescent years youngsters belonging to the Diamonds, like Elf, have pictured the gang favorably.

Felix: You told me you knew things about the gang when you were in eighth grade. What exactly were your thoughts of the gang at that time?

Elf: It was cool—a bunch of guys who cared for each other and who were having a good time.

Felix: And that's what *cool* meant to you then?

Elf: Yeah, it said that you were part of a bunch of guys who trusted each other. The gang was cool in that way. There are some guys who don't know how to act cool. They are always showing off. They be trying to impress you. They think that's cool. But it's not. They be lying and telling stories about their homeys. In the gang you can't do that. In the gang you don't carry on that way because the rest of the guys are going to think that you are a big jerk. You ain't a nobody because nobody cares for you.

Felix: Are you saying that other youngsters were not cool because they did not belong to the gang?

Elf: I guess they could be cool, but, you see, the gang forces you to always be cool, together. You know, this is your homey, and brother, so take care of him, don't rat on him. That's what makes the whole thing cool, like a family. Everybody is a friend and brother. You treat people like a brother, like family.

In the same way Tito developed an affirmative and supportive impression of the gang. He still recalls early times when those who were known to belong to a gang were granted a great deal of fame:

I went to a school where there were all kinds of nice girls—you know, a bunch of really attractive Puerto Ricans and Latinas—and they were always checking us out. And, since I have always liked girls, I used to check them out, too. And the girls in school used to think that these guys [gang members] . . . everyone in school used to think that these guys were cool, and they were because they had all the girls and stuff. I thought that they were bad [meaning "good"]. They talked kind of bad, you know; they had their own kind of way of expressing themselves. They used to walk bad. They had this hip walk, and everybody knew that they were in gangs. And the clothes. Well, you know, everything about those guys was really together. Hey, I began wondering how it would be to be in a gang. These guys seemed to be having a good time all the time. Not that I went and joined the gang right there and then. I was still too young, I guess. I guess I was still scared. But I used to think in a good way about bangers at that time.

Benjy offers a similar characterization of the gang, perceiving it as the most rational organization for youth participation:

The gang seemed to control the things I wanted. I was kind of a dork when I was in elementary school. I was really into my studies, and I didn't get involved in any stuff that the gang was doing. But then I began to see that they had the girls, that people listened to them, and stuff like that. I never expected to become one of them, but at that time they were something to be admired. They were popular. You know, this is where it's at; that was my initial attitude of them. And, even though my parents and older brothers were always telling me to stay away from those guys, I kind of admired what they stood for and the way people used to like them.

School Environment

In addition to these neighborhood influences and motivations, a wide range of school-related experiences contributed immensely to the youngsters' positive outlook toward the gang, which in turn, led to their subsequent affiliation with it. Their affirmative judgment of the gang and decision to join were developed over time as contact and interaction with teachers and some schoolmates already familiar with or actually belonging to gangs resulted in their being labeled "deviants" and troublemakers and treated accordingly. Members of the Diamonds responded to these conditions by joining with others so labeled and engaging in corresponding behavior. In response to teachers' labelling them negatively, which in most cases occurred during their elementary school years, youngsters adopted different forms of "oppositional behavior" (for example, misbehaving in the classroom, refusing to do work in the classroom and at home, fighting with classmates, and cutting school). Additionally, some of the labeled adolescents began associating as an informal group, developing a distinctive subculture within

which they could examine and interpret what was going on in their lives and in school as well as determining the most appropriate set of activities for dealing with these conditions. Thus, beginning at the elementary school level, the oppositional, or resistance, behavior carried out by these youngsters in response to their being labeled was akin to gang activity. What was happening to these young people was that, unknowingly, they were undergoing early preparation for a later stage in their teenage years (during high school) when they would finally join the gang. Against the actions of high school classmates who were involved in gangs and who tended to consider them members of an opposition gang, Flaco, Coco, Elf, Lobo, and the others sought protection by turning. Since primary grade and high school years produced different experiences of nonconformist behavior, I will consider the two periods separately—the former first.

The Elementary School Experience

Some members of the Diamonds recall that as early as the fourth, fifth, and sixth grades some of their teachers were already ascribing the label of deviant to their activities. In turn, many of these youngsters sought out others similarly labeled for comfort and affiliation. Whether for misconduct or alleged academic deficiency, or both, some of the youngsters remember being publicly branded as deviant by their teachers. They responded by adopting the popular stereotype assigned to anyone bearing the label, and their classmates and other school peers treated them accordingly.

Even at the time that I met these youngsters it was difficult for many of them to talk about their days in elementary school. This experience was associated with much pain as teachers and staff refused to understand and respect their cultural and socioeconomic class background. In the case of Flaco, on several occasions he started mentioning how unfairly he had been treated, only to break sharply and stop talking altogether or discuss something totally unrelated. One day it finally happened: He carried the description of that "awful experience" to the end. It was a day I was spending with him and Benjy. Benjy began to tell me about his wife and child, his future plans, how confused he was, and how much assistance he could use to figure out how to accomplish some of the things he wants to do. He then asked me about how I managed to survive life in *el barrio*. How did I make it? I told him about my high school experiences. Afterward Benjy asked me to drop him off at a friend's house on the north side.

I then stopped at a Burger King with Flaco for some food for our way back. Flaco asked me again to talk about my high school experiences. I had already shared this part of my life with Flaco. Perhaps the first time it had not carried the significance that apparently developed during this second round. In any event, I repeated my difficulties with U.S. schools, especially having had to accept a grade demotion because I was not fluent in the English language when I transferred from a school in Puerto Rico to one in Chicago. I told him that I had been an excellent student in Puerto Rico, but in the Chicago school system teachers did not involve me in the goings-on of the classroom because they assumed that my language difference was obviously a sign of some sort of academic deficiency. I sounded angry when I told Flaco how I felt attending a school system that had defined me as defective because I spoke a language different from the one used formally there. My tone took on a sour quality when I told him how upset I had felt to be physically present in the classroom but with my teachers refusing to see me. I also told him how I was able to survive. Being a baseball player and participating on the school's baseball team was a means through which I gained self-respect.

It was at this point in our relationship, about five months since our initial contact, that Flaco opened up and began talking freely about his life as an elementary school student. I had shared information with Flaco about my personal life which he probably did not expect was even there. Apparently, he felt compelled to reciprocate and spoke openly to me.

Felix: On several occasions you have mentioned having failed the fourth grade. For what reasons?

Flaco: That's when I started grouping around with the boys.

Felix: How old were you?

Flaco: I was about ten, maybe nine. It was like my second fourth grade, though.

Felix: And what do you mean by hanging out with the boys?

Flaco: Well, the boys, we started groups, right? And there be groups where the guys you think you want to hang out with, you be classifying them, like, these guys, they cool, or these guys are nerds or act like dorks, or these guys are too smart for us and teacher's pets, and then other guys were alright. And, then, we'll judge each other, we'll be coming to school at a certain time and meeting each other there, and then we try to get seats next to each other and to talk to each other and stuff like that.

Felix: And which one of the groups did you belong to?

Flaco: I was with the bad ones—the ruthless.

Felix: Where does that classification come from?

Flaco: Well, 'cause that's how the teachers would put it in our heads, you know, and "You guys are the troublemakers," and "You guys are too loud" and "You're too this, and you just don't want to listen, and you just want to sit in your chairs and lay there."

Felix: Why were you placed in the group you called the bad ones?

Flaco: I don't really know. I guess I used to be hyper. I was always moving. It was no problem . . . it was no problem with other people. But in school the stuff was boring, and I would tell the teacher about it, so she kept saying no and to be quiet and shit like that. So, because I talked back and didn't want to sit still she started treating me like if I was retarded or like shit.

Felix: What happened after you were grouped into the bad ones?

Flaco: We started hating the other kids. The classification did not stop there because from there my fourth grade teacher would know the teacher you were going to next, so she already says, "Keep an eye out for these kids because these are the troublemakers," and stuff like that. And we would think, "Well, why bother because we're in the bad group already?" And then we'd say, "You see all the other kids in our class, too, but they're the smarter ones, or they're the dorks, this and that." And they just call us the troublemakers.

Coco's school experiences in his fifth grade are almost identical to Flaco's. In his opinion his teachers and other school personnel did not recognize and accept his excessively active behavior as part of his normal personality. Instead, it was misinterpreted as a sign of mental instability. As a result, he was summoned to take a series of diagnostic tests and later placed in a program for the learning disabled, to which he responded by displaying the kind of behavior prescribed in the label or anticipated by school personnel. He says:

I was put into a class for slow learners, you know, students that the school thought were disturbed and had problems with reading and math. They also thought that I had mental problems. You know, they said that, because our mental problems, we didn't know how to work with numbers or that we couldn't read. What they were saying was that I was stupid and retarded—you know, that these kids can't do the work because there is something wrong with them, in their head. And shit like that.

Anyway, that became my permanent class. . . . I was in a classroom where most of the students were Mexican and black and I was the only Puerto Rican, so they would pick on me and try busting me up. But one day one of my friends transferred to my classroom. They thought that he was retarded too, and the two of us began fighting with these other guys. We would fight, throw ourselves on the floor, and do crazy things like. And throughout all of this sometimes we would get caught, and sometimes we wouldn't. One day I really got caught, and the people there decided to give me tests to see if I was crazy. I told them that I wasn't crazy, that I behaved like that because that was what I wanted to do. But they gave me these tests, and

they placed me in this classroom, and I was there until seventh grade. From there I transferred to [another school], and they put me in a classroom with the so-called bad-ass kids. I told them to put me out because the problem was going to continue since I acted that way because I wanted to and not because I was retarded or crazy.

But, you see, people in school, like your teachers and principal, these people don't listen to you because they are supposed to be right all the time. They lied to my mother about the way I was acting. they convinced her that it was true that I was crazy. They told her that the best thing for me was to go into this classroom because there were going to be just a few of us and the teacher could work better with us. What we did was to fight all the time. But my mother, she knew how to speak English, but, you know, not that good. She is a Puerto Rican, and you know how that is. She didn't want to be disrespectful; she is always talking that talk. And then my father, he was working, so they didn't call him. She was tricked to sign that paper. She says it herself now. She knows that I'm hyper, but that's how I am.

In Lobo's earliest school memories one of his teachers' name-calling routines led to his subsequent stigmatization and treatment as a troublemaker. He described how, after being labeled a troublemaker for arriving late to class on several occasions, every mischievous act that happened in school was blamed on him.

One time . . . we were in the hallway, walking to the bathroom, and someone threw a rock through a window, and all the kids said, "Lobo did it." But since I was with everybody else in line they changed the story to "one of Lobo's friends did it." You know, I became the explanation for everything that went wrong in that school. So, I retaliated by fighting. And there were lots of fights.

My first fight was with a guy for stupid little reasons. This was about the fourth grade. I threw him into the filing cabinet. It was a stupid reason because the teacher wanted us to go around . . . we were doing something with science and using test tubes and then we had to collect them from each student. I collected them from one side, and he collected them from the other. We ended up running into each other in the middle, and I told him to leave them there and I'll bring them up to the front. He said, "No, I'll do it." So, I said fine, and I walked over to one of the small tables and put it on top there. I guess he was picking them up so fast that he hit the chair, and they all fell over. And then he blamed me for it. He told me that he thought I was going to take them all up to the front first and then let him come back and get the other stack. And I said no—I had figured he wanted to take them and left them right there for me to take up. Then he started yelling that it was my fault. I told him to fuck off. The teacher came and started yelling at the both of us, but primarily at me. And the minute she turned her back I slammed his ass into a filing cabinet where he had about five of his front teeth knocked out. Then I got suspended—like, big deal. Ever since then I had this attitude that, if you were going to mess with me, I was going to mess with you physically.

The stories of these and other youngsters serve as evidence of the difficulties of attending school while knowing that they were being viewed as the cause for every disruptive situation there. Always being blamed constituted part of the emotional attack these young people suffered so early in their school experiences. As the bearers of the troublemaker label, they remember being cut off from participation in activities involving other "normal" students, though they believe they possessed the academic skills and knowledge required for performing classroom work at the same level of proficiency as their peers. Lobo recalls never being called on by the teacher:

I was real good in science and math, but the teacher never bothered to let me work with the rest of the class. I was a troublemaker, and I was supposed to stay by myself. What was I supposed to do?

Not surprisingly, this treatment gave rise to a self-fulfilling prophecy whereby several mechanisms conspired to make Lobo, Coco, Flaco, and the others fit the image teachers and others had developed for them. As indicated earlier, all of these young men began

drifting into oppositional behavior by joining other students and friends who had been treated as they had been. These youngsters began to recognize the common fate they shared with others like themselves. In Coco's own words:

If the teachers and everyone else thought that we were bad, we started to show that we were. So, we started doing a lot of bad things, like hitting some kids and even talking back to the teacher and laughing at her. In a way, it was kind of fun because here are these teachers thinking we were nuts and we would act nuts. That made them feel good. Like I told you before, I'm sure they felt like they were right. But for me that was an opportunity to act stupid, to act silly and like a clown. It was fun because some of the other students liked to see us act stupid. So we had like a crowd, a crowd that we wanted to give a good time.

For several other youngsters this oppositional behavior was undertaken to serve as a rationale for neutralizing the treatment they believed their teachers and peers were unfairly bestowing upon them. Rafael describes it in the following dialogue:

Felix: What was your "acting up" like?

Rafael: We were bad. We didn't listen. We used to fight all the time.

Felix: What were you hoping to get from acting up?

Rafael: Well, it was no big deal. It was my way of getting even. You know, teachers were saying and doing all this nasty shit, and I wasn't going to put up with that anymore.

Felix: So, what were you doing these things for?

Rafael: I guess I was trying to protect my dignity. There was nothing wrong with me, but they didn't believe me. To them I was like shit. Just because you're Puerto Rican or Latino, they treat you like dirt. I guess I was trying to protect myself.

Felix: And about your fights with your classmates, what were you trying to show?

Rafael: Well, we used to think that they were always kissing the teacher's ass because they were put down, too. They thought that by being ass kissers they were going to be treated OK.

Felix: And why did you pick fights with them?

Rafael: We didn't like them. They were punks. And this was our way of saying "Hey, we're not afraid of the teachers or you." It made us feel good. We felt like we were in control. This was our way to feel powerful. You know, we didn't want to make people feel afraid, but we didn't have nothing to use to get at these people. So, like a lot of people do, like you see in the movies, the best weapon to use is force.

Clearly, resistance patterns of thinking and acting furnished these young people with reasons that appeared rational and sound for continuing to challenge the generalized view that they possessed undesirable traits allegedly associated with their culture and behavior. In other words, since the treatment given to these youngsters denied them the conventional means of carrying out the routines of everyday life in the classroom (including moral support), the youngsters, of necessity, developed an oppositional system of strategic activities.

For members of the Diamonds the disparaging treatment by teachers and peers dampened their interest in school and led them to conclude that it was far better to stay out of school than to be victimized by their teachers' constant verbal assault and sometimes physical punishment. These young people lost interest in school and stopped attending—or "cutting school," as this behavior is popularly referred to—as early as elementary school. They began experimenting with staying out of school, continued to do so on an occasional basis, and finally became regular "cutters." Tito explains his experience of despair and frustration with one of his teachers and how it influenced him to not bother taking school seriously:

Well, there was one lady, and I don't remember her name, I just remember that I was in fourth grade, and she was one of those ladies that liked to yell at the kids and call us names. She was always calling me names, like slow and someone who couldn't do work and stuff like that. And I

didn't like that. I guess that's what lost my interest. And this teacher had a triangle ruler, and if she caught us talking she would hit us on the hand for it, and I'm just one of those people that hates to be hit like that—I don't know why. So, that's why I never like to get into the school too much. I never went to school. When I went I never did any work or homework. I was never really interested in school when I went there. So, even at that age I found ways not to come to school. There were times when I left for school but never got there because I would go someplace else and hang out with my friends.

What was really upsetting for these young men was the constant explicit and implicit disapproval, or put-down, of those things that were at the core of their lives. It was extremely difficult for them to know that their culture was being assigned a negative value or, at best, not given appropriate respect. Carmelo reflects on how one of his teachers was always ridiculing and belittling Puerto Rican children in her class, at times suggesting that they voluntarily accept becoming welfare recipients. He recalls losing his respect for this particular teacher. He also believes that this experience took away much of his interest in school.

Felix: How did you like [your school]?

Carmelo: I did not care for it. The teacher was a crap. I remember a few times she would say things like "We are supporting your parents who are on welfare and are living off of us." She said this several times.

Felix: What grade was this? What was your teacher like?

Carmelo: Fifth grade. I was a child. She was a white teacher who lived in Northbrook—you know, one of the wealthy suburbs along the lakeshore and far away from people like you and me. I remember she'd be talking about how her daughter had a closet full of clothes.

Felix: And what?

Carmelo: And she would talk about her daughter. One time she [the daughter] complained that she needed another blouse, and she [the teacher] went into the closet and counted something like sixty blouses, or something like that—some outrageous number. Imagine, this bitch had sixty blouses and was complaining. Why did she [the teacher] have to tell us that shit? We were poor. Imagine sitting there hearing this shit when you know how tough things are at your house. But that's how this lady was. And several times, again, she would say how her and people that worked with her or people that were like her were supporting people who were on welfare. And I was on welfare—I was on welfare for many years.

Felix: How did you feel after hearing your teacher say these things?

Carmelo: I used to bring good grades home. I was taught to stay shut. I used to talk a lot but never to adults. I did not want the word to get out to my parents and grandmothers that I was being disrespectful. My grandmother was the last person I wanted to find out. She taught us manners the Puerto Rican way. You know, she lived with us for a very long time. When my mother and father were working she was the one that raised us. And she raised us the old Puerto Rican way. After my mother got sick, she [the grandmother] stayed living with us. I did not want her to get angry at me for doing bad in school. So I did not say or do anything when my teacher said those things.

Felix: How much did this bother you?

Carmelo: Obviously, it bothered me a whole lot because it still clicks in my mind. I still hear her saying that. When I left that class to go to another class I did not miss her at all.

Felix: What did you do to counter what your teacher was saying?

Carmelo: Well, as I told you earlier, I liked school a lot—even to this day. But I was little; I was a child at that time. So, I decided to forget about all this shit, so I would cut school as much as I could get way with. At that time we took most of our classes with the same teacher, so we couldn't simply cut one class. We had to cut the whole day. And I did. It was better not to attend school than to go to school. People tell you all the time to go to school—that without school you are nothing. Maybe that's true, but they never tell you about the kind of shit that you have to put up with in school. At that time I was not willing to put up with insults. I have changed very little over the years.

What was once a degrading and demeaning "in-school" experience became a pleasant, desired, and sought after "out-of-school" activity. Youngsters found pleasure in staying out of school, an experience that at first was very frightening.

Lobo: In the fifth grade I left for a semester. Almost half the year I missed out because I didn't want to go.

Felix: What happened?

Lobo: Just picking up trades from the streets. It just stole my attention away from school. So, as far as wanting to come to school, I'd leave early in the morning, making everybody think I was going to school, but I just hated school. After that I just stayed out.

Felix: So you were leaving home but not going to school?

Lobo: Right, that was all in the fifth grade. I just got really fed up. I figured leading a life of hanging out in the streets with my homeys on the corner or in a game room would sometimes be smoother than being in the classroom. These guys were better than classmates. These guys show you they care. They were better than anything that was inside those doors.

For these young people entering into associations with other labeled and/or mistreated peers signified their first unofficial connection with gang behavior. These youngsters were carrying out activities that closely resembled those of the gang, though they were not gang members. In addition, in several cases there were older youngsters already involved with the gang who made it possible for Lobo and Tito and the others to come into direct contact with the gang. Although these young people were not official members at this time, nonetheless they were provided with opportunities to witness for themselves several key activities being performed by the gang organization. And to these they responded affirmatively, developing an image of gang members as role models to be admired.

It is clear that these youngsters did not accept their elementary school experience as an anomaly or a transient social phenomenon. During their adolescent years the institution of education and its agents, the administrators and teachers, were already being experienced as antagonistic elements in their socialization rather than as facilitators of their goals.

The High School Experience

The above presentation indicates that during their elementary school years several members of the Diamonds had already participated in some of the activities of the gang, mainly hanging out, or "grouping," on the street, block or schoolyard. Their involvement during this time, however, remained marginal and unofficial. For the most part turning occurred when youngsters began attending high school.

Tito was sixteen years old and in his second year of high school when he became an official member of the Diamonds. His decision to join the gang was heavily influenced by a friend of whom he thought very highly and with whom he had developed a tight bond.

I was about in my sophomore year or, like, the end of my freshman year. . . . I had a friend who was in a gang and who was telling me about gangs and how things were, and, I don't know, just one day I went, and my friend was kind of bubbly because he had been drinking, and we went to his neighborhood, and I was talking to his chief and stuff, and, then, I just turned. When I joined, like, four or five other guys that were like my neighbors, right there by the crib, they turned too, and we all joined at one time. Since we were friends we all decided to join—because we used to hang with the gang, but we were neutrons, and we just decided that we might as well become something since we hung out on the corner and gang-bang anyway, and so we just decided to go for it. We just did it just like that. We didn't think about it or think, "Wow, what is this?" We just slid into it. We knew what we had to go through to become official gang members, but we were willing to. We

wanted to be part of the gang and be recognized like that.

That his friends played a major role in Tito's life can be witnessed from the way he talks and describes them. Tito always sounded exhilarated and proud, demonstrating a special enthusiasm for the relationship he and his friends have been able to maintain over the years. One such moment can be captured from his response to my prompt, "Tell me how you turned together":

Like, there was a main seven of us in my neighborhood. We stuck together all the time. When we joined this gang we became real good friends, and we always shared with one another. Like, my friend would need a boom box, and I would have it at my crib; I would say, "Here, take the box; you can use it." Or, like, if the summer was real hot and I would have an extra fan, I would give it to my friend and say, "Hey, here's a fan." Then we would talk about it. I would say that I needed a T-shirt, and sometimes they would go get me a T-shirt, or stuff like that. It became more like brothers instead of friends. We became like real true brothers, and we treated each other so good that it made sometimes being out there all right. It made it, like, you're out there with people you know. It's not like somebody you never saw or you never met in your life. You know you finally joined, and you'll be with people that you really know and trust. It's alright; it's not what a lot of people think.

And in my school there were other gangs that always thought of us as belonging to this other gang. And we always denied it because really we weren't. I mean, we would hang out, but we were not with them. One day one of our boys got smashed, and he was crippled really bad. So, we decided, if this is going to happen again, if the opposition is going to wait to catch us alone when there is no one around us, we might as well join. This way they know that messing with us is like messing with the whole organization. So, that was another reason that we finally hooked together.

Coco attributes his turning primarily to the influence one of his high school friends had on him. This friend was exceptionally regarded for he had served as one of Coco's sources of emotional support during elementary school. This particular friend had earned Coco's trust and confidence by sticking up for him at a time of need. So, when the friend recommended to Coco that he become a Diamond he replied affirmatively and with little hesitation. He recalls:

> Well, my friend from [this other school] had caused so much spill there that he was given a transfer and was accepted at [my school]. He turned Diamonds, and it looked to me that he was having so much fun in the organization—like, "Let's go and do this, or let's go and stump that punk or that other punk"—and that's how I always wanted to be. I had taken so much shit from my teachers and principals—I always wanted to get on top of someone and slam him to the street top. So, I decided that I wanted to be a Diamond. From there on I attended the meetings. We started chasing hoodlums from the opposition. I was dope [having fun].

Flaco also joined the Diamonds on the advice of some friends who had provided him with protection over time against other gangs. Flaco had grown up in a section of Suburbia which served as turf for several gangs, making it quite difficult for maintaining a neutron status. His friends helped him remain unaffiliated and sheltered; other gangs understood that to mess with Flaco could be considered an act of disrespect against the organization he was closest to. And, like in Tito's case, since he had spent so much time hanging out with a particular gang and had developed a close affinity with its members, deciding to become an official member seemed like the most natural and rational decision to make.

Felix: When did you join the Diamonds?

Flaco: Four and half years ago. I was a freshman in high school.

Felix: And what were the reasons for joining?

Flaco: Well, let me see. More or less the reason was because I was already hanging with them since I was small, so I was in the neighborhood. And I had a couple of real good buddies. And I had protection by them.

Felix: What exactly did your friends say to you?

Flaco: Not much. It wasn't like they were forcing me. They just told me to turn. It was no big deal.

Felix: And what did you do after this?

Flaco: I turned. I believed them. You know, I had to get my V-in [initiation ritual]; they told me about that. It wasn't like if I didn't know. It was tough, but we all had to go through that.

Felix: You mentioned earlier that your friends gave you protection. What's protection?

Flaco: Protection? I had backup. You have to have Folks on your side, 'cause, if you're not in one gang, you're not in another gang, and they always be asking if you got a sign, and if you're on this side, and you get rolled on anyway. And you have nobody on your side, so you're still 'gonna pick a favorite of your Folks or People. I don't know, kids could stay neutron, but it's very hard, and it's very rarely you see kids that are neutrons. And the ones that are neutrons—they still got a favorite; they like Folks better, or People. And the Folks or the People can't let you see them too much on the other side. Like, if you're a neutron, and you're in favor of Folks, if the Folks see you in People's neighborhoods, they're gonna think something about it. And then that's when you got problems.

Felix: So one of the reasons why you joined was for protection, for backup?

Flaco: Yeah. I liked chilling out with them, too.

Felix: What did you like about hanging out with them?

Flaco: Everything's fun. Sometimes we would ditch school or take a day off. We just go, we get a couple of cases of beer, we drink those, and then we'll go up to the top of the roofs and look over. Police come, and they chase us down. We just had a lot of fun, do a lot of kinds of things.

Rival gang labeling, as already suggested above, was another major reason for turning Diamond. It is a common practice for gang members in a high school to consider new, incoming students as belonging to the opposition. In doing so, when initial contact is made the new students are treated according to the views held about them.

Most confrontations tend to occur in schools where members from various rival groups are enrolled. Suburbia's school district is served by two high schools. According to members of the Diamonds, one is faced with rival gangs from different neighborhoods primarily because the community has a major busing program that enables students from areas other than Suburbia to be accepted for enrollment. Some believe that the school is represented by twenty different gangs from several neighborhoods. Additionally, members of the Diamonds were attending this particular school during the period of ethnic population change; there were, thus, racial clashes with several white gangs as well. In effect, the school atmosphere was filled with gang tensions.

The other high school is the home of a single gang. Therefore, gang rivalry and gangbanging is less frequent than in the other school. Most of the Diamonds attended the former; they indicated having experienced an enormous amount of gang-related problems there. In describing the reasons for joining the Diamonds, Elf recalls having been the target of one gang because some of its members believed he was with the opposition. He says,

> I was a smart student. I would never let things get in my way, school-wise. But once I got into high school that's where it all dropped out of sight. 'Cause I used to live in one neighborhood, and I would go to another neighborhood, and they would never see me there, and they would say, "What you be?" "What gang are you in?" "Where you live?" And I'd tell them were I lived, and they already assumed that I was one of them, when I wasn't. Or they assumed that I was with another gang when I wasn't that either. Then I decided, "Man, if they're going to keep on rolling on [jumping] me, and I ain't got nobody to back me up, I better turn. And I did.

Elf's response led me to probe further since I found it extremely difficult to identify or single out someone like him as a gang member with the same ease he had described. To me Latino youngsters from *el barrio* seem to look the same; they seem to dress, walk, and talk the same. So, I said to him, "Let me try to put this in some perspective. You're saying that, whether you are in a gang or not, once a gang identifies and labels you as a gang member, they start treating you like a gang member. Now explain to me, how is it that someone like you gets identified as a gangbanger?" Reaching back to touch the ponytail he was styling and then bringing his hand up to his left ear to touch his earring, Elf explained:

> At one time it used to be colors, but that's out. People don't wear colors anymore; that's too obvious of an identification. Colors are no good for the business. But it's usually the way a Latino looks or the way he expresses himself, the way he brings himself to people. Let's say, when you first saw me, what'd I look like to you? A little hoodlum, right? But you can't say that, but the way I look, usually the hair, the way I have my hair, the way I style my hair. It's things like that make me look like a gangbanger. I don't know, but there's a certain thing to a person, what he does, the way he walks. It's the way you bring yourself to people.

Rival gang labeling was the major reason Gustavo decided to turn. Gustavo was constantly picked on by gang members who believed that he was affiliated with an opposition gang. Turning for him came after having served as a punching bag for members of one gang.

Felix: How did it happen that you joined the Diamonds?

Gustavo: Well, my friends from grammar school were in a gang at my high school, and, since I used to hang out with them, the other gangs began considering me as a member of the gang. The gang itself did not consider me a member, but the other gangs did because they always saw me with these guys. These guys were my friends from grammar school. These were the guys that I grew up with, so I was going to hang out with them.

Felix: Are you saying that at this time you were not an official member of the gang?

Gustavo: No, I wasn't. I became an official member of the gang about three years later, during my junior year in high school.

Felix: What were the reasons for your decision to join the gang then—after all, you were so near graduation?

Gustavo: There were times when I would get into trouble, and the gang would try helping me, but the president of the gang would say that they couldn't do that because I was not an official member. Sometimes I would be chased by another gang because they thought that I was a member of this other gang, and this was happening, and I did not have the protection that other members did. So, finally, I turned. So that, if anything happened to me, I would be protected.

Benjy was having problems at home when he met an older Diamond who inspired him to turn.

Well, I started realizing that me and my parents didn't have this—I can't say we didn't love each other—we didn't have this closeness. I don't know if it was because of my dad's drinking. I can't really put the blame on him or my mom. I can't tell them that it is because of them. But my problems at home confused me a lot. Then, one day I met this guy—I still know him to this day—and he was an older guy. He was maybe twenty-five or twenty-six, and he had been in the gang all his life, since maybe he was eleven years old. He was married with kids; his wife left him; he didn't choose to leave the streets; he chose to stick with it. He recruited me because I was young and the gang needed to expand. So, I joined the gang and started recruiting friends, doing the same thing my friend did to me.

I met him on a Halloween night, and I was throwing eggs and stuff like that with the guys, doing things that normal teenagers would, but after he came things changed. He started mentioning "Let's go do this, and let's go shoot up." He sort of shook [scared] me at first because I never did things that were so criminal. My way of getting back at somebody was like stealing a radio or doing something minor. I was never much of a thief, either. After a while he started teaching me the tricks, how to burn people, how to deal, how to do this, and I made him money. He started turning me on to the gangs, the colors, the hand signals, and everything—how it was done,

how you shook someone's hand when you were on the street, and who to eye for. And we became pretty good buddies after about a year and a half.

Once a Diamond, Benjy's affiliation was firmly sealed by rival gang labeling and treatment.

I met my friend during eighth grade. I was still not an official member. Then I started attending high school. Usually, when you're a freshman in high school you feel intimidated by everybody. When you first get to high school you feel like you're taking the first step toward becoming an adult, and I was pretty intimidated by a lot of the students there, and I started fighting back against some of the kids, doing things to people, selling drugs at the school. I remember the first or second day there, a couple of people pointed me out—they knew me from the street—and I remember getting an apple splattered in my face, whipped across from, like, another room. Everyone thought it was funny, so after that I brought golf clubs to school, spray paint, and I started taking charge. I started taking things out physically and violently with other people.

When you hang around with people and you're seen often by members of another gang, at first they'll say, yeah, maybe he's a friend, but after they see you on the street corner a lot they'll say he is with them. I was just marked, I guess, for the rest of the year, and I guess they were just waiting for me to screw up and do something against one of the enemies of another gang.

Police Treatment

For other youngsters the way they were handled by the police served as another stimulus for their decision to turn. In the same way that rival gangs take action against neighborhood youngsters they label as belonging to the opposition, the police employ a similar approach. Some members of the Diamonds speak about how the police do not make distinctions when dealing with Latino youngsters from their neighborhood. They are steadily tormented by the police because they appear like gang members or because they are friends with known gang members. In the views of members of the Diamonds all

Latino young people, whether they're gang affiliates or not, are targets of a belittling process of police action.

Freddie makes this point very clear as he describes the reasons why he became a member of the Diamonds:

I wasn't a gangbanger. I used to hang out with them; they are my friends. The police started messing with me. They would pull me into their car and harass me. I kept telling them that I was not a banger. But they don't believe anything we tell them. They asked me questions about this and other friends, guys from the hood who are gangbangers, and, since I wouldn't tell them what they wanted to hear, they would say things like, "Yes, you are one of those hoodlums from this street. We've been watching you for a long time, and now we got you, and you're going to pay."

One day I was with my girlfriend and my friend and his girl—it was the four of us. So we were walking by the neighborhood—this was during Christmas. The police saw us and pulled us over to a corner. They went through their shit—you know, "Who you be?" "Where are the other boys?" So, we didn't say nothing. They got really pissed and, in front of our girls, told us to kneel down and sing "Jingle Bells." So, there we are singing "jingle bells, jingle bells, jingle bells" for these pricks. Can you imagine that shit? I wanted to kill them fuckers. How are you supposed to feel when they do that to you for no reason and then in front of your girl? And there's a lot of shit like that goes on all the time.

So, one day I told my friends, so we said, "Well, fuck it. Let's do it." It seems that we need a fuckin' license to be with our friends. If you're friends with people in a gang, forget it—the law will always be on your case. And to me there is nothing wrong with being friends with these guys; these are the guys I grew up with. We played ball together; we went on picnics together. We did everything together, and now the law comes and says I can't be with them. Well, fuck them. Now that I'm a gangbanger, they have other reasons for messing with me.

Turning for Tony was motivated by several factors; his relations with the police served as a leading one.

Tony: I wouldn't say that I turned because of one thing or the other. I don't believe there is one reason why guys join the gang. We join because of this and that. I joined because I was having problems in school, and then my parents were getting on my case for that, and then the law. . . .

Felix: What was happening at home?

Tony: My parents.

Felix: What about them?

Tony: It's a long story. But my parents were getting a divorce. And my mother wanted me with her, and I guess my father didn't like that, so he would come over and put all these ideas in my mind. He be telling things like I was something special and I deserved more than my mother. To tell him what I needed and stuff like that. My mother took me away from the neighborhood because she thought I could do better in some suburb. And I didn't. We moved, and we spent about six months in this suburb, and all that did was to make me more confused. Because I didn't fit in, and I didn't want to fit in. I wanted back to the hood with the guys. We were not bangers. We were just friends. Sometimes you have parents that try to be too protective and that's what happened with mine. They tried to control me all the time. And that doesn't work anymore. Maybe it did for them when they were growing up, but this is different today.

Felix: In terms of the police, what did they do to you?

Tony: There are cops, like Rocky, all right? Rocky is a straight up prick. When my girlfriend was younger Rocky tried to tell her to get in the car. Rocky beat this one homey who had a broken leg right in front of McDonald's one day, with his own crutch. The other day Rocky came up to gangbangers, and he tells them, "I'm going to bust you," and then he plants drugs on you. A friend of mine, Tiny, Tiny had a joint on him. One joint. They put it on the record that he had five dimes on him.

Felix: But what did they do to you that has anything to do with you joining the gang?

Tony: They do everything. They take your money when they bust you. They'll go through your wallets saying they're looking for an ID, and the next thing you see is some cops with cash, sticking it in his pocket. Over the years I don't know how much money I've lost to police officers. You know, the people who are supposed to uphold justice—you know, the American way and all this crap—these people rip you off just as much as we do.

Felix: So, they were really messing with you?

Tony: They blame all of this on us, and half the time it's ridiculous. Cops, they lie, and the only difference between them and us is that they have a uniform and a little piece of metal on their chest that says they can get away with this. Some narcs beat the shit out of me and I wasn't a banger. They get away with this. So, I decided if these pricks are going to mishandle me because they think I'm a Diamond I might as well be one. So I did. That's what went down.

Rafael also blames the police for his decision to turn.

The law has always messed with our people. The way they treat us today is not new. This is not something I'm making up. You can ask the older people in the hood. Ask them to tell you about the Puerto Rican riots. I was real little then, but I hear that several cops shot some Puerto Rican kids in the park. Nothing was done to those cops, and they know that they can get away with anything they decide to do to us.

I was picked up on several occasions by the law because I was Puerto Rican and was walking down the street. I wasn't into gangbanging, but the cops kept asking me about my gang and shit. One time, and this is what really did it for me—after this I decided to turn—I just said fuck it. But, anyway, two white blue boys picked me up and dropped me off in a white neighborhood on the north side. They took my money so I couldn't catch the bus back to the hood. The white dudes from that neighborhood had a field day with me. Well, I tried protecting myself and ran a lot, but I did get the shit smashed out of me. So, what do you do after something like that happens to you? A year ago there were some investigations of blue boys who were picking up black kids and dropping them off in white neighborhoods in the

south side or something. Listen, that shit has been happening to us for a long time, and nobody ever gave a shit about it. I didn't want no investigation. Can you imagine the law investigating itself?—in a case involving someone they believe to be a Puerto Rican hoodlum? Well, I resolved it. I turned. I became an official member of the Diamonds, and now they have the right when they stop and ask me questions.

There is also the case of Tomas, who was picked up by two white police officers because he was riding in a car with a couple of his neighborhood friends.

I was in my second year of high school when I got my driver's license. That summer I drove my father's car, and one of my friends, Junior, was also given permission to cruise in his father's ride. One night, about seven or eight, we were cruising through the neighborhood. It was just Junior and me, and we were driving, and these two law dogs pulled us to the side. We were not doing nothing wrong. They told us to get out of the car, and they started searching the car. I asked them what they were doing, and they told us to shut the fuck up. One of them looked at Junior and said, "Shut up, you little bastard, you spic, we are going to confiscate this car because we know you bought this with dope money." Junior got charged like hell and told them that the car belonged to my father, that we were not dope dealers. The same cop said to us, "It doesn't matter. You're gangbangers, we know the gang you belong to, and we plan to destroy it. We are going to harass you until you stop hanging out with your gang friends." We told them again that we were not bangers, but once again they didn't believe us. This went on for a long time, and finally they took us in. The charge was that we stole the car. After two or three hours at the police station they let us call our parents. Well, by then it was about twelve midnight, and my dad was really pissed. He came to the station to pick us up. The police told him and Junior's dad a bunch of bullshit about us. I didn't drive my father's car again—he didn't let me use it—and, instead, he started accusing me of being a gangbanger. So, I started to identify more and more with the Diamonds. They knew very well about the different ways the law is always trying to set us up—how the police don't care if they break up a family.

Let me give a better vision of this so you can understand it better. A few days ago on a Saturday, about two in the afternoon, one of my boys, we call him Red because he has red freckles and red hair. . . . Anyway, he was coming from the store with his mother and little brother when the law stopped them. These two big white cops walked over to Red, took a bag he was carrying, and started smacking him. They were hitting him in front of his mother. This cop that nobody likes . . . he kicked Red in the ribs with his flashlight. And, hey, that shit hurts. Anyway, Red's mom became hysterical, and all the law said was that this did not concern her. They also told Red that they had been looking for him for a long time and that he had it coming. After this they got in their mobile and left like if no shit had happened.

So, you can understand my attitude. This is the way we are treated everyday. Cops don't give a shit who they pick on; after all, we all look the same. We are all bangers to them. There is a war out there; the law has declared war on us. We are targets of abuse for the Chicago police department because they have a license to do what they want. So, if this is how it is going to be, then we have to protect ourselves. I don't have respect for blue boys.

You know, I didn't have to turn and become a Diamond—these guys knew me for a long time. I grew up together with some of these guys. But I don't regret it now. This is our defense against police brutality.

Clearly, a good part of the lives of members of the Diamonds revolved around the police. Police action made these youngsters feel defenseless and vulnerable in their own neighborhood. They are repeatedly subject to questioning; they are suspected of nearly every crime and made to prove their innocence. Youngsters have come to believe that, as long the police are protected by their status as officials, a system of harassment and dehumanization will persist. And, of course, the deep frustrations youngsters experience in their encounters with the police involve much more than physical fear, time lost, and inconvenience; they are damaging to their human integrity.

These varying accounts point out the very long and complex process youngsters undergo to become official gang members. As Tony indicated, many factors combine to shape the individual's decision to turn. There is no single reason to explain gang participation; however, it is noteworthy that these youngsters' determination to turn was rooted in early childhood experiences.

Flaco, Benjy, Coco, Lobo, and the others were earmarked for failure from day one. They were rejected in "normal" society and labeled as social problems first by the schools and later by the police. This early experience of rejection was devastating; it incapacitated them and broke them, and it denied them their individuality and integrity. To circumvent these consequences these young men sought oppositional forms of resistance. Clearly, for these youngsters the survival behavior that many conventional people consider destructive—participation in a gang—is the one great protection they have against a system in which failure is almost assured.

Intensifying their emerging feelings of antagonism, developed toward their teachers and other school personnel, was the fact that the school was trying to engage them in an almost impossible process of cultural adaptation at the same time they were undergoing the intense identity search of adolescence. During this phase in the socialization process the function of peer culture, shared by those of their kind, superseded all school efforts to mold them according to the latter's predetermined set of standards. The pressure to identify with a culture of resistance, not to reject it, was never greater. In other words, to develop personal identity and maintain integrity these youngsters had to become part of a culture with resistance as its centerpiece. Our mental images and perceptions of gang members do not usually take account of the painful and humiliating road they've traveled to get to where they are.

Adapted from Felix M. Padilla, *The Gang as an American Enterprise*, pp. 60–90. Copyright © 1992 by Felix M. Padilla. Reprinted with permission of Rutgers University Press. ✦

16

Homeboys, Dope Fiends, Legits, and New Jacks

John M. Hagedorn

Based on field research with Milwaukee gangs, gang researcher John Hagedorn delineates four categories of gang members based upon their orientation to conventional values and social institutions. Focusing on core members of drug-dealing gangs, Hagedorn argues that gang members may be classified along a "continuum of conventionality," ranging from former gang members now living a legitimate life to those who regard drug-dealing to be a career. The study addresses several issues important to both social science and public policy. First, what happens to gang members as they age? Do most gang members graduate from gangbanging to drug sales, as popular stereotypes might suggest? Is drug dealing so lucrative that adult gang members eschew work and become committed to the drug economy? Have changes in economic conditions produced underclass gangs so detached from the labor market that the only effective policies are more police and more prisons? Second, and related to these questions, are adult gang members basically similar kinds of people, or are gangs made up of different types? Might some gang members be more conventional and others less so? What are the implications of this "continuum of conventionality" within drug-dealing gangs for public policy?

The following selection includes interviews with present and former gang members Hagedorn classified as homeboys, dope fiends, legits, *and* new jacks. *They discuss their attitudes toward drug-dealing and conventional lifestyles, attitudes toward themselves, values, future plans, and their life chances. Gang*

members were largely classified according to their level of commitment to crime as a lifestyle and particularly to drug dealing.

In the conclusion, Hagedorn discusses criminal justice policy relating to gangs, drugs, and the "underclass" in society.

A Typology of Male Adult Gang Members

We developed four ideal types on a continuum of conventional behaviors and values: (1) those few who had gone *legit*, or had matured out of the gang; (2) *homeboys*, a majority of both African American and Latino adult gang members, who alternately worked conventional jobs and took various roles in drug sales; (3) *dope fiends*, who were addicted to cocaine and participated in the dope business as a way to maintain access to the drug; and (4) *new jacks*, who regarded the dope game as a career.

Some gang members, we found, moved over time between categories, some had characteristics of more than one category, and others straddled the boundaries (see Hannerz, 1969:57). Thus a few homeboys were in the process of becoming legit, many moved into and out of cocaine addiction, and others gave up and adopted a new jack orientation. Some new jacks returned to conventional life; others received long prison terms or became addicted to dope. Our categories are not discrete, but our typology seemed to fit the population of gang members we were researching. Our "member checks" (Lincoln and Guba, 1985:314-316) of the constructs with gang members validated these categories for male gang members.

Legits

Legits were those young men who had walked away from the gang. They were working or may have gone on to school. Legits had not been involved in the dope game at all, or not for at least five years. They did not use cocaine heavily, though some may have done so in the past. Some had moved out of the old neighborhood; others, like our project staff, stayed to help out or "give back" to the community. These are prime examples of Whyte's "college boys" or Cloward and Ohlin's Type I, oriented to economic gain and class mobility. The following quote is an example of a young African American man who "went legit" and is now working and going to college.

> Q: Looking back over the past five years, what major changes took place in your life—things that happened that really made things different for you?

> R#105: I had got into a relationship with my girl, that's one thing. I just knew I couldn't be out on the streets trying to hustle all the time. That's what changed me, I just got a sense of responsibility.

Today's underclass gangs appear to be fundamentally different from those in Thrasher's or Cloward and Ohlin's time, when most gang members "matured out" of the gang. Of the 236 Milwaukee male founders, only 12 (5.1%) could be categorized as having matured out: that is, they were working full time *and* had not sold cocaine in the past five years. When these data are disaggregated by race, the reality of the situation becomes even clearer. We could verify only two of 117 African-American and one of 87 Latino male gang founders who were currently working and had not sold dope in the past five years. One-third of the white members fell into this category.

Few African-American and Latino gang founders, however, were resigned to a life of crime, jail, and violence. After a period of rebellion and living the fast life, the majority of gang founders, or "homeboys," wanted to settle down and go legit, but the path proved to be very difficult.

Homeboys

"Homeboys" were the majority of all adult gang members. They were not firmly committed to the drug economy, especially after the early thrill of fast money and "easy women" wore off. They had reached an age, the mid-twenties, when criminal offenses normally decline (Gottfredson and Hirschi, 1990). Most of these men were unskilled, lacked education, and had largely negative experiences in the secondary labor market. Some homeboys were committed more strongly to the streets, others to a more conventional life. Most had used cocaine, some heavily at

times, but their use was largely in conjunction with selling from a house or corner with their gang "homies." Most homeboys either were married or had a "steady" lady. They also had strong feelings of loyalty to their fellow gang members.

Here, two different homeboys explain how they had changed, and how hard that change was:

> Q: Looking back over the past five years, what major changes took place in your life—things that happened that really made things different for you?

> R#211: The things that we went through wasn't worth it, and I had a family, you know, and kids, and I had to think about them first, and the thing with the drug game was, that money was quick, easy, and fast, and it went like that, the more money you make the more popular you was. You know, as I see it now it wasn't worth it because the time that I done in penitentiaries I lost my sanity. To me it feels like I lost a part of my kids, because, you know, I know they still care, and they know I'm daddy, but I just lost out. Somebody else won and I lost.

> Q: Is she with somebody else now?

> R#211: Yeah. She hung in there about four or five months after I went to jail.

> Q: It must have been tough for her to be alone with all those kids.

> R#211: Yeah.

> Q: What kind of person are you?

> R#217: Mad. I'm a mad young man. I'm a poor young man. I'm a good person to my kids and stuff, and given the opportunity to have something nice and stop working for this petty-ass money I would try to change a lot of things. . . . I feel I'm the type of person that given the opportunity to try to have something legit, I will take it, but I'm not going to go by the slow way, taking no four, five years working at no chicken job and trying to get up to a manager just to start making six, seven dollars. And then get fired when I come in high or drunk or something. Or miss a day or something because I got high smoking weed, drinking beer, and the next day come in and get fired; then I'm back in

where I started from. So I'm just a cool person, and if I'm given the opportunity and if I can get a job making nine, ten dollars an hour, I'd let everything go; I'd just sit back and work my job and go home. That kind of money I can live with. But I'm not going to settle for no three, four dollars an hour, know what I'm saying?

Homeboys present a more confused theoretical picture than legits. Cloward and Ohlin's Type III delinquents were rebels, who had a "sense of injustice" or felt "unjust deprivation" at a failed system (1960:117). Their gang delinquency is a collective solution to the failure of institutional arrangements. They reject traditional societal norms; other, success-oriented illegitimate norms replace conventionality.

Others have questioned whether gang members' basic outlook actually rejects conventionality. Matza (1964) viewed delinquents' rationalizations of their conduct as evidence of techniques meant to "neutralize" deeply held conventional beliefs. Cohen (1955:129-137) regarded delinquency as a nonutilitarian "reaction formation" to middle-class standards, though middle-class morality lingers, repressed and unacknowledged. What appears to be gang "pathological" behavior, Cohen points out, is the result of the delinquent's striving to attain core values of "the American way of life." Short and Strodtbeck (1965), testing various gang theories, found that white and African American gang members, and lower- and middle-class youths, had similar conventional values.

Our homeboys are older versions of Cohen's and Matza's delinquents, and are even more similar to Short and Strodtbeck's study subjects. Milwaukee homeboys shared three basic characteristics: (1) They worked regularly at legitimate jobs, although they ventured into the drug economy when they believed it was necessary for survival. (2) They had very conventional aspirations; their core values centered on finding a secure place in the American way of life. (3) They had some surprisingly conventional ethical beliefs about the immorality of drug dealing. To a man, they justified their own involvement in drug sales by very Matza-like techniques of "neutralization."

Homeboys are defined by their in-and-out involvement in the legal and illegal economies. Recall that about half of our male respondents had sold drugs no more than 12 of the past 36 months. More than one-third never served any time in jail. Nearly 60% had worked legitimate jobs at least 12 months of the last 36, with a mean of 14.5 months. Homeboys' work patterns thus differed both from those of legits, who worked solely legal jobs, and new jacks, who considered dope dealing a career.

To which goal did homeboys aspire, being big-time dope dealers or holding a legitimate job? Rather than having any expectations of staying in the dope game, homeboys aspired to settling down, getting married, and living at least a watered-down version of the American dream. Like Padilla's (1992:157) Diamonds, they strongly desired to "go legit." Although they may have enjoyed the fast life for a while, it soon went stale. Listen to this homeboy, the one who lost his lady when he went to jail:

Q: Five years from now, what would you want to be doing?

R#211: Five years from now? I want to have a steady job, I want to have been working that job for about five years, and just with a family somewhere.

Q: Do you think that's gonna come true?

R#211: Yeah, that's basically what I'm working on. I mean, this bullshit is over now, I'm twenty-five, I've played games long enough, it don't benefit nobody. If you fuck yourself away, all you gonna be is fucked, I see it now.

Others had more hopeful or wilder dreams, but a more sobering outlook on the future. The other homeboy, who said he wouldn't settle for three or four dollars an hour, speaks as follows:

Q: Five years from now, what would you want to be doing?

R#217: Owning my own business. And rich. A billionaire.

Q: What do you realistically expect you'll be doing in five years?

R#217: Probably working at McDonald's. That's the truth.

Homeboys' aspirations were divided between finding a steady full-time job and setting up their own business. Their strivings pertained less to being for or against "middle-class status" than to finding a practical, legitimate occupation that could support them (see Short and Strodtbeck, 1965). Many homeboys believed that using skills learned in selling drugs to set up a small business would give them a better chance at a decent life than trying to succeed as an employee.

Most important, homeboys "grew up" and were taking a realistic look at their life chances. This homeboy spoke for most:

Q: Looking back over the past five years, what major changes have taken place in your life—things that made a difference about where you are now?

R#220: I don't know, maybe maturity. . . . Just seeing life in a different perspective . . . realizing that from sixteen to twenty-three, man, just shot past. And just realizing that it did, shucks, you just realizing how quick it zoomed past me. And it really just passed me up without really having any enjoyment of a teenager. And hell, before I know it I'm going to hit thirty or forty, and I ain't going to have nothing to stand on. I don't want that shit. Because I see a lot of brothers out here now, that's forty-three, forty-four and ain't got shit. They's still standing out on the corner trying to make a hustle. Doing this, no family, no stable home and nothing. I don't want that shit. . . I don't give a fuck about getting rich or nothing, but I want a comfortable life, a decent woman, a family to come home to. I mean, everybody needs somebody to care for. This ain't where it's at.

Finally, homeboys were characterized by their ethical views about selling dope. As a group, they believed dope selling was "unmoral"—wrong, but necessary for survival. Homeboys' values were conventional, but in keeping with Matza's findings, they justified their conduct by neutralizing their violation of norms. Homeboys believed that economic necessity was the overriding reason why they could not live up to their values (see Liebow,

1967:214). They were the epitome of ambivalence, ardently believing that dope selling was both wrong and absolutely necessary. One longtime dealer expressed this contradiction:

Q: Do you consider it wrong or immoral to sell dope?

R#129: Um-hum, very wrong.

Q: Why?

R#129: Why, because it's killing people.

Q: Well how come you do it?

R#129: It's also a money maker.

Q: Well how do you balance those things out? I mean, here you're doing something that you think is wrong, making money. How does that make you feel when you're doing it, or don't you think about it when you're doing it?

R#129: Once you get a [dollar] bill, once you look at, I say this a lot, once you look at those dead white men [presidents' pictures on currency], you care about nothing else, you don't care about nothing else. Once you see those famous dead white men. That's it.

Q: Do you ever feel bad about selling drugs, doing something that was wrong?

R#129: How do I feel? Well a lady will come in and sell all the food stamps, all of them. When they're sold, what are the kids gonna eat? They can't eat the dope cause she's gonna go smoke that up, or do whatever with it. And then you feel like "wrong." But then, in the back of your mind, man, you just got a hundred dollars worth of food stamps for thirty dollars worth of dope, and you can sell them at the store for seven dollars on ten, so you got seventy coming. So you get seventy dollars for thirty dollars. It is not wrong to do this. It is not wrong to do this!

Homeboys also refused to sell to pregnant women or to juveniles. Contrary to Jankowski's (1991:102) assertion that in gangs "there is no ethical code that regulates business ventures," Milwaukee homeboys had some strong moral feelings about how they carried out their business:

R#109: I won't sell to no little kids. And, ah, if he gonna get it, he gonna get it from someone else besides me. I won't sell to no pregnant woman. If she gonna kill her baby, I want to sleep not knowing that I had anything to do with it. Ah, for anybody else, hey, it's their life, you choose your life how you want.

Q: But how come—I want to challenge you. You know if kids are coming or a pregnant woman's coming, you know they're going to get it somewhere else, right? Someone else will make their money on it; why not you?

R#109: 'Cause the difference is I'll be able to sleep without a guilty conscience.

Homeboys were young adults living on the edge. On the one hand, like most Americans, they had relatively conservative views on social issues and wanted to settle down with a job, a wife, and children. On the other hand, they were afraid they would never succeed, and that long stays in prison would close doors and lock them out of a conventional life. They did not want to continue to live on the streets, but they feared that hustling might be the only way to survive.

Dope Fiends

Dope fiends are gang members who are addicted to cocaine. Thirty-eight percent of all African-American founders were using cocaine at the time of our interview, as were 55% of Latinos and 53% of whites. African-Americans used cocaine at lower rates than white gang members but went to jail twice as often. The main focus in a dope fiend's life is getting the drug. Asked what they regretted most about their life, dope fiends invariably said "drug use," whereas most homeboys said "dropping out of school."

Most Milwaukee gang dope fiends, or daily users of cocaine, smoked it as "rocks." More casual users, or reformed dope fiends, if they used cocaine at all, snorted it or sprinkled it on marijuana (called a "primo") to enhance the high. Injection was rare among African-Americans but more common among Latinos. About one-quarter of those we interviewed, however, abstained totally from use of cocaine. A majority of the gang members

on our rosters had used cocaine since its use escalated in Milwaukee in the late 1980s.

Of 110 gang founders who were reported to be currently using cocaine, 37% were reported to be using "heavily" (every day, in our data), 44% "moderately" (several times per week), and 19% "lightly" (sporadically). More than 70% of all founders on our rosters who were not locked up were currently using cocaine to some extent. More than one-third of our male respondents considered themselves, at some time in their lives, to be "heavy" cocaine users.

More than one-quarter of our respondents had used cocaine for seven years or more, roughly the total amount of time cocaine has dominated the illegal drug market in Milwaukee. Latinos had used cocaine slightly longer than African Americans, for a mean of 75 months compared with 65. Cocaine use followed a steady pattern in our respondents' lives; most homeboys had used cocaine as part of their day-to-day life, especially while in the dope business.

Dope fiends were quite unlike Cloward and Ohlin's "double failures," gang members who used drugs as part of a "retreatist subculture." Milwaukee dope fiends participated regularly in conventional labor markets. Of the 110 founders who were reported as currently using cocaine, slightly more were working legitimate jobs than were not working. Most dope fiends worked at some time in their homies' dope houses or were fronted an ounce or an "eightball" (3.5 grams) of cocaine to sell. Unlike Anderson's "wineheads," gang dope fiends were not predominantly "has-beens" and did not "lack the ability and motivation to hustle" (Anderson, 1978:96-97). Milwaukee cocaine users, like heroin users (Johnson et al., 1985; Moore, 1978; Preble and Casey, 1969), played an active role in the drug-selling business.

Rather than spending their income from drug dealing on family, clothes, or women, dope fiends smoked up their profits. Eventually many stole dope belonging to the boss or "dopeman" and got into trouble. At times their dope use made them so erratic that they were no longer trusted and were forced to leave the neighborhood. Often, however, the gang members who were selling took them back and fronted them cocaine to sell to put them back on their feet. Many had experienced problems in violating the cardinal rule, "Don't get high on your own supply," as in this typical story:

R#131: . . . if you ain't the type that's a user, yeah, you'll make fabulous money but if you was the type that sells it and uses it and do it at the same time, you know, you get restless. Sometimes you get used to taking your own drugs. . . . I'll just use the profits and just do it . . . and then the next day if I get something again, I'd just take the money to pay up and keep the profits. . . . You sell a couple of hundred and you do a hundred. That's how I was doing it.

Cocaine use was a regular part of the lives of most Milwaukee gang members engaged in the drug economy. More than half of our respondents had never attended a treatment program; more than half of those who had been in treatment went through court-ordered programs. Few of our respondents stopped use by going to a treatment program. Even heavy cocaine use was an "on-again, off-again" situation in which most gang members alternately quit by themselves and started use again (Waldorf et al., 1991).

Alcohol use among dope fiends and homeboys (particularly 40-ounce bottles of Olde English 800 ale) appears to be even more of a problem than cocaine use. Like homeboys, however, most dope fiends aspired to have a family, to hold a steady job, and to find some peace. The wild life of the dope game had played itself out; the main problem was how to quit using.

New Jacks

Whereas homeboys had a tentative relationship with conventional labor markets and held some strong moral beliefs, new jacks had chosen the dope game as a career. They were often loners, strong individualists like Jankowski's (1991) gang members, who cared little about group norms. Frequently they posed as the embodiment of media stereotypes. About one-quarter of our interview respondents could be described as new jacks: they had done nothing in the last 36 months except hustle or spend time in jail.

In some ways, new jacks mirror the criminal subculture described by Cloward and Ohlin. If a criminal subculture is to develop, Cloward and Ohlin argued, opportunities to learn a criminal career must be present, and close ties to conventional markets or customers must exist. This situation distinguishes the criminal from the violent and the retreatist subcultures. The emergence of the cocaine economy and a large market for illegal drugs provided precisely such an opportunity structure for this generation of gang members. New jacks are those who took advantage of the opportunities, and who, at least for the present, have committed themselves to a career in the dope game.

Q: Do you consider it wrong or immoral to sell dope?

R#203: I think it's right because can't no motherfucker live your life but you.

Q: Why?

R#203: Why? I'll put it this way . . . I love selling dope. I know there's other niggers out here love the money just like I do. And ain't no motherfucker gonna stop a nigger from selling dope . . . I'd sell to my own mother if she had the money.

New jacks, like other gang cocaine dealers, lived up to media stereotypes of the "drug dealer" role and often were emulated by impressionable youths. Some new jacks were homeboys from Milwaukee's original neighborhood gangs, who had given up their conventional dreams; others were members of gangs that were formed solely for drug dealing (see Klein and Maxson, 1993). A founder of one new jack gang described the scene as his gang set up shop in Milwaukee. Note the strong mimicking of media stereotypes:

R#126: . . . it was crime and drug problems before we even came into the scene. It was just controlled by somebody else. We just came on with a whole new attitude, outlook, at the whole situation. It's like, have you ever seen the movie *New Jack City*, about the kid in New York? You see, they was already there. We just came out with a better idea, you know what I'm saying?

New jacks rejected the homeboys' moral outlook. Many were raised by families with long traditions of hustling or a generation of gang affiliations, and had few hopes of a conventional future. They are the voice of the desperate ghetto dweller, those who live in Carl Taylor's (1990:36) "third culture" made up of "underclass and urban gang members who exhibit signs of moral erosion and anarchy" or propagators of Bourgois's (1990:631) "culture of terror." New jacks fit the media stereotype of all gang members, even though they represent fewer than 25% of Milwaukee's adult gang members.

Discussion: Gangs, the Underclass, and Public Policy

Our study was conducted in one aging postindustrial city, with a population of 600,000. How much can be generalized from our findings can be determined only by researchers in other cities, looking at our categories and determining whether they are useful. Cloward and Ohlin's opportunity theory is a workable general theoretical framework, but more case studies are needed in order to recast their theory to reflect three decades of economic and social changes. We present our typology to encourage others to observe variation within and between gangs, and to assist in the creation of new taxonomies and new theory.

Our paper raises several empirical questions for researchers: Are the behavior patterns of the founding gang members in our sample representative of adult gang members in other cities? In larger cities, are most gang members now new jacks who have long given up the hope of a conventional life, or are most still homeboys? Are there "homeboy" gangs and "new jack" gangs, following the "street gang/drug gang" notion of Klein and Maxson (1993)? If so, what distinguishes one from the other? Does gang members' orientation to conventionality vary by ethnicity or by region? How does it change over time? Can this typology help account for variation in rates of violence between gang members? Can female gang members be typed in the same way as males?

Our data also support the life course perspective of Sampson and Laub (1993:255), who ask whether present criminal justice policies "are producing unintended criminogenic effects." Milwaukee gang members are like the persistent, serious offenders in the Gluecks' data (Glueck and Glueck, 1950). The key to their future lies in building social capital that comes from steady employment and a supportive relationship, without the constant threat of incarceration (Sampson and Laub, 1993:162-168). Homeboys largely had a wife or a steady lady, were unhappily enduring "the silent, subtle humiliations" of the secondary labor market (Bourgois, 1990:629), and lived in dread of prison. Incarceration for drug charges undercut their efforts to find steady work and led them almost inevitably back to the drug economy.

Long and mandatory prison terms for use and intent to sell cocaine lump those who are committed to the drug economy with those who are using or are selling in order to survive. Our prisons are filled disproportionately with minority drug offenders (Blumstein, 1993) like our homeboys, who in essence are being punished for the "crime" of not accepting poverty or of being addicted to cocaine. Our data suggest that jobs, more accessible drug treatment, alternative sentences, or even decriminalization of nonviolent drug offenses would be better approaches than the iron fist of the war on drugs (see Hagedorn, 1991; Reinarman and Levine, 1990; Spergel and Curry, 1990).

Finally, our typology raises ethical questions for researchers. Wilson (1987:8) called the underclass "collectively different" from the poor of the past, and many studies focus on underclass deviance. Our study found that some underclass gang members had embraced the drug economy and had forsaken conventionality, but we also found that the majority of adult gang members are still struggling to hold onto a conventional orientation to life.

Hannerz (1969:36) commented more than two decades ago that dichotomizing community residents into "respectables" and "disrespectables" "seems often to emerge from social science writing about poor black people or the lower classes in general." Social science that emphasizes differences within poor communities, without noting commonalities, is one-sided and often distorts and demonizes underclass life.

Our data emphasize that there is no Great Wall separating the underclass from the rest of the central-city poor and working class. Social research should not build one either. Researchers who describe violent and criminal gang actions without also addressing gang members' orientation to conventionality do a disservice to the public, to policy makers, and to social science.

References

Anderson, Elijah (1978) *A Place on the Corner.* Chicago: University of Chicago Press.

—— (1990) *Streetwise: Race, Class, and Change in an Urban Community.* Chicago: University of Chicago Press.

Blumstein, Alfred (1993) Making rationality relevant. *Criminology* 31:1-16.

Bourgois, Phillippe (1990) In search of Horatio Alger: culture and ideology in the crack economy. *Contemporary Drug Problems* 16:619-649.

Cloward, Richard and Lloyd Ohlin (1960) *Delinquency and Opportunity.* Glencoe, Ill: Free Press.

Cohen, Albert (1955) *Delinquent Boys.* Glencoe, Ill.: Free Press.

Coleman, James S. (1988) Social capital in the creation of human capital. *American Journal of Sociology* 94:95-120.

Cummings, Scott and Daniel J. Monte (1993) *Gangs.* Albany: State University of New York Press.

Fagan, Jeffrey (1990) Social processes of delinquency and drug use among urban gangs. In C. Ronald Huff (ed.), *Gangs in America.* Newbury Park: Sage.

—— (1991) Drug selling and licit income in distressed neighborhoods: The economic lives of street-level drug users and dealers. In Adele V. Harrell and George E. Peterson (eds.), *Drugs, Crime, and Social Isolation.* Washington: Urban Institute Press.

Glueck, Sheldon and Eleanor Glueck (1950) *Unraveling Juvenile Delinquency.* New York: Commonwealth Fund.

Gottfredson, Michael and Travis Hirschi (1990) *A General Theory of Crime.* Stanford: Stanford University Press.

Hagedorn, John M. (1988) *People and Folks: Gangs, Crime, and the Underclass in a Rustbelt City.* Chicago: Lakeview.

—— (1991) Gangs, neighborhoods, and public policy. *Social Problems* 38:529-542.

Hamid, Ansley (1992) The developmental cycle of a drug epidemic: the cocaine smoking epidemic of 1981-1991. *Journal of Psychoactive Drugs* 24:337-348.

Hannerz, Ulf (1969) *Soulside: Inquiries into Ghetto Culture and Community.* New York: Columbia University Press.

Huff, C. Ronald (1990) *Gangs in America.* Newbury Park: Sage.

Jankowski, Martin Sanchez (1991) *Islands in the Street: Gangs and American Urban Society.* Berkeley: University of California Press.

Johnson, Bruce D., Paul J. Goldstein, Edward Preble, James Schmeidler, Douglas S. Lipton, Barry Spunt, and Thomas Miller (1985) *Taking Care of Business: The Economics of Crime by Heroin Abusers.* Lexington, Mass.: Heath.

Klein, Malcolm W. (1971) *Street Gangs and Street Workers.* Englewood Cliffs, NJ.: Prentice-Hall.

—— (1992) The new street gang . . . or is it? *Contemporary Sociology* 21:80-82.

Klein, Malcolm W. and Cheryl L. Maxson (1993) Gangs and cocaine trafficking. In Craig Uchida and Doris Mackenzie (eds.), *Drugs and the Criminal Justice System.* Newbury Park: Sage.

Klein, Malcolm W., Cheryl L. Maxson, and Lea C. Cunningham (1991) Crack, street gangs, and violence. *Criminology* 29:623-650.

Liebow, Elliot (1967) *Tally's Corner.* Boston: Little, Brown.

Lincoln, Yvonna S. and Egon G. Guba (1985) *Naturalistic Inquiry.* Beverly Hills: Sage.

MacCoun, Robert and Peter Reuter (1992) Are the wages of sin $30 an hour? Economic aspects of street-level drug dealing. *Crime and Delinquency* 38:477-491.

MacLeod, Jay (1987) *Ain't No Makin' It: Leveled Aspirations in a Low-Income Neighborhood.* Boulder: Westview.

Matza, David (1964) *Delinquency and Drift.* New York: Wiley.

Merton, Robert K. (1957) *Social Theory and Social Structure.* New York: Free Press.

Miller, Walter B. (1969) Lower class culture as a generating milieu of gang delinquency. *Journal of Social Issues* 14:5-19.

Moore, Joan W. (1978) *Homeboys: Gangs, Drugs, and Prison in the Barrios of Los Angeles.* Philadelphia: Temple University Press.

—— (1991) *Going Down to the Barrio: Homeboys and Homegirls in Change.* Philadelphia: Temple University Press.

Padilla, Felix (1992) *The Gang as an American Enterprise.* New Brunswick: Rutgers University Press.

Preble, Edward and John H. Casey (1969) Taking care of business: The heroin user's life on the street. *International Journal of the Addictions* 4:1-24.

Reinarman, Craig and Harry G. Levine (1990) Crack in context: politics and media in the making of a drug scare. *Contemporary Drug Problems* 16:535-577.

Rose, Harold M., Ronald S. Edari, Lois M. Quinn, and John Pawasrat (1992) *The Labor Market Experience of Young African American Men from Low-Income Families in Wisconsin.* Milwaukee: University of Wisconsin. Milwaukee Employment and Training Institute.

Sampson, Robert J. and John H. Laub (1993) *Crime in the Making: Pathways and Turning Points through Life.* Cambridge: Harvard University Press.

Short, James F. and Fred L. Strodtbeck (1965) *Group Process and Gang Delinquency.* Chicago: University of Chicago Press.

Skolnick, Jerome H. (1990) The social structure of street drug dealing. *American Journal of Police* 9:1-41.

Spergel, Irving A. and G. David Curry (1990) Strategies and perceived agency effectiveness in dealing with the youth gang problem. In C. Ronald Huff (ed.), *Gangs in America.* Beverly Hills: Sage.

Strauss, Anselm L. (1987) *Qualitative Analysis for Social Scientists.* Cambridge: Cambridge University Press.

Sullivan, Mercer L. (1989) *Getting Paid: Youth Crime and Work in the Inner City.* Ithaca: Cornell University Press.

Taylor, Carl (1990) *Dangerous Society.* East Lansing: Michigan State University Press.

Thrasher, Frederick (1927) *The Gang.* 1963. Chicago: University of Chicago Press.

Waldorf, Dan (1993) *Final Report of the Crack Sales, Gangs, and Violence Study*: Alameda: Institute for Scientific Analysis.

Waldorf, Dan, Craig Reinarman, and Sheigla Murphy (1991) *Cocaine Changes: The Experience of Using and Quitting.* Philadelphia: Temple University Press.

Whyte, William Foote (1943) *Street Corner Society.* Chicago: University of Chicago Press.

Williams, Terry (1989) *The Cocaine Kids.* Reading, Mass.: Addison-Wesley.

Wilson, William Julius (1987) *The Truly Disadvantaged.* Chicago: University of Chicago.

17

Changes in Prison Culture: Prison Gangs and the Case of the 'Pepsi Generation'

Geoffrey Hunt
Stephanie Riegel
Tomas Morales
Dan Waldorf

This selection measures recent changes in

This selection measures recent changes in prison life as a function of the growth of prison gangs. Information was obtained from a series of in-depth interviews with a sample of California ex-prisoners. The respondents had all been released from prison in the Oakland and San Francisco area and were located and interviewed in 1991 and 1992. Thirty-nine men were eventually located through a snowball sampling procedure initiated through contacts with ex-offender groups, education programs, and through respondents in a study of street gangs. The ethnic backgrounds of the men were as follows: 16 Chicanos, 14 African Americans, five whites, two Native Americans, one French Creole, and one Chilean. Sixty-two percent (24) identified themselves as gang members or former gang members. Semi-structured, open-ended interviews elicited information about their knowledge of prison gangs and their perceptions of changes in prison life.

Since Clemmer (1958) published *The Prison Community* in 1940, sociologists and criminologists have sought to explain the culture of prisons. A key debate in this literature cen-

ters on the extent to which inmate culture is either a product of the prison environment or an extension of external subcultures. Those in the former camp, such as Sykes and Messinger (1977), Cloward (1977), and Goffman (1961), have argued that the inmate social system is formed "as a reaction to various 'pains of imprisonment' and deprivation inmates suffer in captivity" (Leger and Stratton 1977:93). These writers saw the prison as a total institution in which the individual, through a series of "status degradation ceremonies," gradually became socialized into prison life. Analysts such as Irwin and Cressey (1977) challenged this view of prison life, arguing that it tended to underestimate the importance of the culture that convicts brought with them from the outside. They identified two dominant subcultures within the prison—that of the thief and the convict—both of which had their origins in the outside world.

Our interview material did not clearly support one or the other of these opposing views and instead suggested that other dynamics of prison life were key to understanding inmates' experiences. Salient in inmate interviews was a greater degree of turmoil than was common to prison life in the past. The reasons for this turmoil were complex and included newly formed gangs, changes in prison population demographics, and new developments in prison policy, especially in relation to gangs. All these elements coalesced to create an increasingly unpredictable world in which prior loyalties, allegiances, and friendships were disrupted. Even some of the experienced prisoners from the "old school" were at a loss as to how to negotiate this new situation. Existing theories were not helpful in explaining our findings, for the current dynamics could not be attributed solely to forces emanating from inside the prison or outside it. . . .

The Established California Prison Gangs

According to various accounts (Camp and Camp 1985; Davidson 1974; Irwin 1980; Moore 1978; Porter 1982), the first California prison gang was the Mexican Mafia—a

Chicano gang, believed to have originated in 1957 in the Dueul Vocational Institution prison. This Chicano group began to intimidate other Chicanos from the northern part of the state. The non-aligned, predominantly rural Chicanos organized themselves together for protection. They initially called themselves "Blooming Flower," but soon changed their name to La Nuestra Familia. Like the Mexican Mafia, La Nuestra Familia adopted a military style structure, with a general, captains, lieutenants, and soldiers. However, unlike the Mexican Mafia, La Nuestra Familia had a written constitution consisting of rules of discipline and conduct.

The Texas Syndicate, a third Chicano gang, followed the model of the Mexican Mafia and La Nuestra Familia and utilized a paramilitary system with a president at its head. Its members are mainly Mexican-American inmates, originally from Texas, who see themselves in opposition to the other Chicano groups, especially those from Los Angeles, who they perceive as being soft and too "Americanized."

Both black and white prisoners are also organized. The general view on the origins of the Black Guerilla Family (B.G.F.)—the leading black gang—is that it developed as a splinter group of the Black Family, an organization reportedly created by George Jackson. The authorities were particularly wary of this group, both because of its revolutionary language and reports that its members, unlike those of other gangs, regularly assaulted prison guards.

The Aryan Brotherhood—the only white gang identified in California prisons—originated in the late 1960s. It is said to be governed by a 3-man commission and a 9-man council who recruit from white supremacist and outlawed motorcycle groups. According to prison authorities, it is a "Nazi-oriented gang, anti-black, [which] adheres to violence to gain prestige and compliance to their creed" (Camp and Camp 1985:105).

The available sociological literature on older prison gangs is divided on the issue of their relationship to street gangs. On the one hand, Moore, in discussing Chicano gangs argues that they were started by "state-raised youths and 'psychos'" (1978:114) inside the prisons, while Jacobson sees them as an extension of street gangs. Although Moore sees the gangs as initially prison inspired, she describes a strong symbiotic relationship between the street and the prison. In fact, she notes that once the gangs were established inside the prisons, they attempted to influence the street scene. "The Mafia attempted to use its prison-based organization to move into the narcotics market in East Los Angeles, and also, reputedly, into some legitimate pinto-serving community agencies" (1978:115).

Institutional Attempts to Control the Gangs

Prison authorities see gangs as highly undesirable and have argued that an increase in extortion, intimidation, violence, and drug trafficking can be directly attributed to their rise. In responding to prison gangs, the California Department of Corrections (CDC) introduced a number of strategies and policies, for example, using "confidential informants," segregating gang members in different buildings and prisons, intercepting gang communications, setting up task forces to monitor and track gang members, locking up gang leaders in high security prisons, and "locking down" entire institutions. These changes were perceived by our respondents who saw the CDC as increasingly tightening its control over the prison system and the gangs.

Prison Guards

In spite of the "official" view that gangs should be eradicated, many prison authorities hold a more pragmatic view and feel that the gangs have "had little negative impact on the regular running of prison operations" (Camp and Camp 1985:xii). Moreover, as Cummins (1991) has noted, there is often a considerable discrepancy between the official stance and what takes place within particular prisons. This point was emphasized by our respondents who portrayed guards' attitudes toward the gangs as complex and devious, and saw the guards as often accepting prison gangs and in some cases even encouraging them. In supporting this view, they gave three reasons why guards would allow gangs to develop or continue.

First, some noted guards' financial incentive to encourage gang behavior. They suggested that guards are keen to create "threats to security" which necessitate increased surveillance and, consequently, lead to overtime work.

> They have a financial interest in getting overtime.... Anything that was "security" meant that there were no restrictions in the budget. So if there are gangs, and there are associations, if there is some threat in that focus of security, they make more money. (Case 17)

Others went even further and told us that some guards benefited from gangs' illegal activities.

> Well, you know the guards, aren't . . . you'd be surprised who the guards affiliated with. Guards have friends that's in there. They have their friends outside, you know. Guards'll bring drugs in. Sell 'em. Guards will bring knives in, weapons, food. The guards play a major role. (Case 7)

Not only were guards involved in illegal activities, but the practice was often overlooked by other guards. For example, as one respondent philosophically replied in answer to our question: "Were individual guards involved in illegal gang activities?"

> Well, I think you have guards that are human beings that . . . don't really want to do more than they have to. So if they see a guard doing something a little shady, it's easy to turn a blind eye because of the hassle it would take to pursue it. (Case 16)

Finally, in addition to these financial incentives, some believed that guards encouraged gang activities and conflict in order to control the prison inmates more effectively and "keep the peace out of prisons" (Case 32).

> They perpetuated the friction because, for instance, what they would do is . . . give false information to different groups. . . . Something to put the fear so that then the Latino would prepare himself for a conflict. . . . And so everybody's on point and the next thing you know a fight would break out and the shit would come down. So it was to their interest to perpetuate division amongst the inmates so that they would be able to better control the institu-

tion. Because if you are spending your time fighting each other you have no time . . . to fight the establishment. (Case 34)

This divide and rule policy was emphasized by many of our respondents and was seen as a major contributory factor in prisoner conflicts.

Jacketing and the Use of Confidential Informants

According to our respondents, another prison administration tactic was "jacketing"—officially noting in a prisoner's file that he was a suspected gang member. Once identified as a gang member, a prisoner could be transferred to a high security prison or placed in a special housing unit. "Jacketing," which is similar to the "dirty jacket" procedure outlined by Davidson (1974), was seen by our respondents as a particularly arbitrary process and one in which the prisoner had little or no recourse.

> Like I said, if you're a sympathizer you could be easily jacketed as a gang member. You hang around with 'em. You might not do nothing. But hang out with 'em. Drive iron with 'em. Go to lunch with 'em. (Case 1)

Many respondents felt the process was particularly unfair because it meant that a prisoner could be identified as gang member and "jacketed" purely on the basis of information from a confidential informant. Confidential informants or "snitches" supplied intelligence information to prison authorities about inmate activities, especially gang-related activities.

> Now let's say you and I are both inmates at San Quentin. And your cellie gets in a fight and gets stabbed. So all of a sudden, the Chicano who is a friend of your cellie says that he'll get the boys and deal with this. They talk about it but nothing happens. All of a sudden one of the snitches or rats, says I think something is cooking, and people are going to make a move to the administration. What will happen is that they [the administration] will gaffel up you and me and whoever else you associate with and put us all on a bus straight to Pelican Bay. They will say we have confidential reliable information that you guys are planning an assault on

Billy Bob or his gang. . . . And you're wondering, you've never received a disciplinary infraction. But by God now, information is in your central file that you are gang affiliated, that you're involved in gang violence. (Case 16)

Our respondents distinguished between two types of snitching: dry and hard.

Dry snitching is a guy who will have a conversation with a guard and the guard is just smart enough. He'll say you talk to Joe, don't ya? You say, oh, yeah, Joe's a pretty good ol' boy, I heard he's doing drugs but don't believe it. He might smoke a few joints on the yard, but nothing hard. He just dry snitched. He indirectly dropped a lug on Joe. And then you got the guy who gets himself in a jam and goes out and points out other inmates. (Case 16)

Dry snitching could also refer to a prisoner supplying general information to guards without implicating anyone by name. This allowed the prisoner to develop a "juice card" or a form of credit with the guard.

A "juice card" is that you have juice [credit] with a particular guard, a lieutenant, a sergeant or somebody that is part of staff. . . . Let's say that somebody is dry snitching. By dry snitching I mean that they might come up to their juice man that has a "juice card," let's just say it is a sergeant of the yard, and they might go up there and say, "Hey I hear that there is a rumble coming down. I can't tell you more than that but some shit is going to come down tonight." So they alert the sergeant right. The sergeant tells him, "I owe you one." Now the guy might come up to the sergeant and say, "Hey remember you owe me one, hey I got this 115 [infraction] squash it." "Okay I will squash it." That is the "juice card." (Case 34)

Many of our respondents felt there was a growing number of snitches (also see Stojkovic 1986). A key factor promoting this growth was the pressure exerted by the guards—a point denied by the prison authorities in Stojkovic's research.

Pressure could be applied in a number of ways. First, if for example a prisoner was in a high security unit, he often found himself unable to get out unless he "debriefed"; i.e.,

provided information on other gang members. Many respondents felt that this was an impossible situation because if they didn't snitch their chances of getting out were minimal. As one respondent remarked:

They [the guards] wanted some information on other people. . . . So I was put between a rock and a hard place. So I decided I would rather do extra time, than ending up saying something I would later regret. (Case 10)

Second, if the guards knew that a prisoner was an ex-gang member, they might threaten to send him to a particular prison, where he would be attacked by his own ex-gang.

See there is a lot of guys in there that are drop outs from whatever gang they were in, and they are afraid to be sent to a joint where some other tip might be. They even get threatened by staff that if they don't cooperate with them they will be sent to either Tracy, or Soledad and they are liable to get hit by their own ex-gang, so they cooperate. (Case 40)

However, it would be inaccurate to suggest respondents accused only the prison authorities, since many also pointed out other developments within the prison system, and especially within the prison population, to explain what they described as a deteriorating situation.

Prison Crowding, the New Gangs, and the 'Pepsi Generation'

Since 1980, the California prison population has increased dramatically from 24,569 to 97,309 (California Department of Corrections 1991). The net effect of this expansion has been severe overcrowding in the prisons. In 1970, prison institutions and camps were slightly underutilized and the occupancy rate stood at 98 percent. By 1980, they were full, and in 1990, the rate had risen dramatically to 180 percent of capacity. Currently, the inmate population stands at 91,892, while bed capacity is only 51,013. In order to cope with this overcrowding, institutions have been obliged to use all available space, including gymnasiums and dayrooms.

Many respondents graphically described the problems created by this situation and complained about the deterioration in prison services. However, in talking about prison overcrowding they tended to concentrate more on the changes in the characteristics of the inmates currently arriving. Specifically, they focused on the growth of new gangs, the immaturity of new inmates, and the problems they caused within the prison. Respondents felt this change in prison population characteristics had a major effect on day-to-day activities, and contributed to the fragmentary nature of prison life.

The New Gangs

According to our respondents, although all five of the older gangs still exist, their importance has diminished. The reasons for this appear to be twofold. First, many of the older gang members have either dropped out, gone undercover, or have been segregated from the rest of the prison population. Second, a new crop of gangs has taken center stage. In other words, prison authorities' efforts to contain the spread of gangs led, unintentionally, to a vacuum within the prison population within which new prison groupings developed.

Information on these new gangs is relatively limited in comparison with information on the older gangs. Thus it is difficult to be precise about their structure and composition. Moreover, a further complication is whether or not these groups fit current definitions of what constitutes a gang. For instance, if we adapt Klein and Maxson's (1989) definition of a street gang—community recognition as a group or collectivity, recognition by the group itself as a distinct group, and activities which consistently result in negative responses from law enforcement— then these new groupings constitute gangs if the prison is considered the community. However, if we compare them with the Mexican Mafia, La Nuestra Familia, or the Black Guerilla Family, which have developed hierarchies or clearly articulated constitutions, they constitute instead territorial alliances which demand loyalties and provide security and protection. Regardless of whether these groups fit traditional definitions, respondents made it clear they had a significant impact on the traditional prison loyalties and allegiances and contributed to conflicts amongst the prisoners.

Chicano and Latino Gangs. Among Chicanos, the Nortenos and the Surenos are the most important groupings or gangs. These two groups are divided regionally between the North and South of California, with Fresno as the dividing line. Although regional loyalties were also important for the Mexican Mafia and La Nuestra Familia, the regional separation between North and South was not as rigid as it is today for Surenos and Nortenos.

In addition to the Nortenos and the Surenos, two other groups were mentioned— the New Structure and the Border Brothers. Our respondents provided differing interpretations of the New Structure. For instance, some noted it was a new Chicano group made up of Nortenos which started in San Francisco, while others implied it was an offshoot of La Nuestra Familia. Opinions differed as to its precise relationship to La Nuestra Familia.

The Border Brothers are surrounded by less controversy. Their members are from Mexico, they speak only Spanish and, consequently, keep to themselves. Most of our respondents agreed this was a large group constantly increasing in size, and that most members had been arrested for trafficking heroin or cocaine.

Although, there was little disagreement as to the Border Brothers' increasing importance, which was partly attributed to their not "claiming territory," there was, nevertheless, some dispute as to their impact on the North/South issue. Some respondents saw the Border Brothers as keeping strictly to themselves.

> The Border Brothers don't want to have anything to do with the Surenos-Nortenos —they keep out of that 'cause it's not our fighting and all of that is stupid. . . . Either you are a Chicano or you're not. There is no sense of being separated. (Case 3)

Others predicted that in the future, the Border Brothers will become involved in the conflict and will align themselves with the Surenos against the Nortenos.

It used to be Border Brothers over there and Sureno and Norteno, stay apart from each other. . . . But now what I see that's coming out is that the Border Brothers are starting to claim Trece now. What I think is going to happen, to the best of my knowledge, is that the Surenos instead of them knockin' ass with the Nortenos, they're going to have the Border Brothers lock ass with the Nortenos due to the fact that they're South and all that. Maybe in a few years we will see if my prediction is true or not. (Case 36)

Black Gangs. The Crips, originally a street gang from South Central Los Angeles, is the largest of the new black gangs. It is basically a neighborhood group.

Interviewer: So the Crips is more a neighborhood thing than a racial thing?

Respondent: Oh yeah! That's what it stems from. It stems from a neighborhood thing. There's one thing about the Crips collectively, their neighborhoods are important factors in their gang structures. (Case 5)

The Bloods are the traditional rivals of the Crips. Although, like the Crips, they are a neighborhood group, they do not attribute the same importance to the neighborhood.

They're structured geographically in the neighborhood, but it's not as important as it is for the Crips. Only in LA is it that important. Bloods from LA, it's important for them but they don't have as many neighborhoods as the Crips. But anywhere else in Southern California the neighborhoods are not that important. Only in LA. (Case 5)

The 415s is a third black prison gang emerging recently. The group is made up of individuals living within the 415 San Francisco Bay area telephone code. Although the group's visibility is high, especially in the Bay area, the organization appears to be loosely structured, so much so that one of our respondents suggested that the 415s were more an affiliation rather than a gang.

All of these gangs are said to be producing a significant impact on prison life. Whereas previously there were four or five major gangs, today there are nine or ten new groupings, each with its own network of alliances

and loyalties. These crosscutting and often conflicting allegiances have a significant impact on prison life. They produce a confusing, disruptive situation for many prisoners and can even produce problems for existing friendships. As one Puerto Rican respondent noted, "When I first started going to the joints . . . it wasn't as bad to associate with a guy from the North and the South. It wasn't that big of a deal" (Case 39). But as the fragmentation increased and dividing lines became more rigid, this type of friendship was much less acceptable. According to many of our respondents, another consequence of fragmentation was an increase in intraethnic conflict, especially amongst the black population.

Back then there was no Crips, there was no Bloods, or 415s. It is a lot different now. The blacks hit the blacks. When the blacks at one time were like the B.G.F. where the blacks would stick together, now they are hitting each other, from the Crips, to the Bloods, to the 415, are pretty much all enemies. (Case 39)

The picture provided by our respondents is one of an increasing splintering of prison groupings. Allegiances to particular groups, which had previously seemed relatively entrenched, are now questioned. Friendships developed over long prison terms are now disrupted, and where previously prisoners made choices about joining a gang, membership has now become more automatic, especially for Chicanos. Today, what counts is the region of the state where the prisoner comes from; if he comes from South of Fresno, he is automatically a Sureno, if he is from North of Fresno, he becomes a Norteno.

'Pepsi Generation'

Respondents not only described the conflict arising from the new divisions within the prison population, but also attributed this conflict to new prison inmates. They emphasized that the new generation of prisoners differed from their generation—in their dress, attitudes, and behavior toward other prisoners and the prison authorities. Respondents described themselves as convicts who represented the "old school."

In my point of view there is what is called the old school. . . . And the old school goes back to where there is traditions and customs, there is this whole thing of holding your mud, and there is something you don't violate. For instance you don't snitch, you are a convict in the sense that you go in and you know that you are there to do time. And there is two sides. There is the Department of Corrections and there is you as the convict. (Case 34)

A convict, in this sense, was very different from the present day "inmate" who they described as not having

a juvenile record or anything like that, and so that when they come in they have no sense of what it is to do time. . . . The inmate goes in there and he goes in not realizing that, so that they are doing everybody else's number or expect somebody else to do their number. Which means for instance, that if they can get out of something they will go ahead and give somebody up or they will go against the code. Say for instance, the food is real bad and the convict would say, look we have to do something about this so let's make up a protest about the food and present it to the warden. And the convict will go along with it because it is for the betterment of the convicts. The inmate will go and go against it because he wants to be a good inmate and, therefore, he is thinking about himself and not the whole population. (Case 32)

The prisons were full of younger prisoners who were described disparagingly by our respondents as "boys trying to become men," and the "Pepsi Generation," defined as

the young shuck and jive energized generation. The CYA [California Youth Authority] mentality guys in a man's body and muscles can really go out and bang if they want. They are the youngsters that want to prove something—how tough and macho and strong they are. This is their whole attitude. Very extreme power trip and machismo. The youngsters want to prove something. How tough they are. And there is really very little remorse. (Case 16)

According to our respondents, the "Pepsi Generation" went around wearing "their

pants down below their ass" (Case 40) and showing little or no respect for the older inmates, many of whom had long histories of prison life which normally would have provided them with a high degree of status. Disrespect was exhibited even in such seemingly small things as the way that the younger prisoners approached the older inmates.

They'll come up and ask you where you are from. I had problems with that. They come with total disrespect. It seems like they send the smallest, youngest punk around and he comes and tries to jam you. You know, you've been around for a long time, you know, you've got your respect already established and you have no business with this bullshit. . . . And here you have some youngster coming in your face, talking about "Hey man, where you from?" (Case 2)

This view was graphically corroborated by a 38-year-old Familia member who described the young inmates in the following way:

They're actors. Put it this way, they're gangsters until their fuckin' wheels fall off. . . . I'm a gangster too. But there is a limitation to everything. See I can be a gangster with class and style and finesse and respect. Get respect and get it back. That's my motto, my principle in life. Do unto another as you would like to have done to you. These kids don't have respect for the old timers. They disrespect the old men now. (Case 36)

The "younger generation" was not only criticized for its disrespect, but for its general behavior as well. They were seen as needlessly violent and erratic and not "TBYAS"—thinking before you act and speak.

I think they're more violent. They are more spontaneous. I think they are very spontaneous. They certainly don't use TBYAS. I think their motivation is shallower than it was years ago. (Case 16)

Their behavior had the effect of making prison life, in general, more unpredictable, a feature many of our respondents disliked.

They have nothing but younger guys in prison now. And ah, it has just changed. I don't even consider it prison now anymore. I think it is just a punishment. It is just a place to go to do time. Which now since there are so many children and kids in prison it is hard to do time now. It is not like it used to be where you can wake up one morning and know what to expect. But now you wake up and you don't know what to expect, anything might happen. (Case 12)

Inmate Culture Reassessed

Inmates' picture of prison life is of increasing uncertainty and unpredictability; more traditional groupings and loyalties are called into question as new groups come to the fore. Whereas previously, prisoners believed a clear dividing line existed between convicts and authorities, today they see this simple division disintegrating. This occurs because, in their attempt to control the spread of prison gangs, authorities introduced a series of measures which contained the gangs, but also unexpectedly created a vacuum within the organizational structure of the prison populations—a vacuum soon filled by new groups. Group membership was taken from newer inmates, who, according to our respondents, had not been socialized into the convict culture. The dominance of these groups soon led to an environment where the rules and codes of behavior were no longer adhered to and even the more experienced prisoners felt like newcomers. Moreover, the ability of prisoners to remain nonaligned was hampered both by developments amongst the prisoners and by the actions of the authorities. For example, a Norteno arrested in the South and sentenced to a southern prison would find himself in a very difficult and potentially dangerous situation.

You'll see some poor northern dude land in a southern pen, they ride on [harass] him. Five, six, seven, ten deep. You know, vice versa—some poor southern kid comes to a northern spot and these northern kids will do the same thing. They ride deep on them. (Case 2)

Study respondents portrayed prison culture as changing, but the change elements they identified were both inside and outside the institution. The available theoretical approaches, which have tended to dichotomize the source of change, fail to capture the complexity and the interconnectedness of the current situation. Furthermore, the information we received produced no conclusive evidence to prove whether or not the street scene determined the structure of gangs inside the prison or vice versa. For example, in the case of the Crips and the Bloods, at first glance we have a development which supports the approaches of Jacobs (1974) and Irwin and Cressey (1977). The Crips and the Bloods originated in the neighborhoods of Los Angeles and transferred their conflicts into the prison environment. In fact, according to one respondent, once in prison, they bury their intragang conflicts in order to strengthen their identities as Crips and Bloods.

Even when they are "out there" they may fight amongst themselves, just over their territory. . . . But when they get to prison they are wise enough to know, we gotta join collectively to fend off everyone else. (Case 5)

However, although the Crips and Bloods fit neatly into Jacobs' perspective, when we consider the case of the 415s and the Nortenos and the Surenos, we find their origins fit more easily into Cloward's (1977) alternative perspective. According to two accounts, the 415s began in prison as a defense group against the threatening behavior of the Bloods and the Crips.

It [the 415s] got started back in prison. In prison there is a lot of prison gangs . . . and they were put together a lot. They got LA gangs like the Bloods and the Crips, and they are putting a lot of pressure on the people from the Bay area. And we all got together, we got together and organized our own group. (Case G189)

Originally, the Nortenos and Surenos existed neither on the streets nor in the adult prisons but within the California Youth Authority institutions. Gradually this division spread to the adult prisons and soon became powerful enough to disrupt the traditional loyalties of more established gangs. Furthermore, in-prison conflicts soon spread to the outside and, according to information from our San Francisco study, Norteno/Sureno conflicts are beginning to have a significant impact on the streets.

Conclusion

As Irwin (1980) noted over ten years ago, prisons today are in a turmoil. From both the Department of Corrections perspective and the interview material, it is clear that the prison system is under immense pressures. As the prison population expands and the Department of Corrections attempts to find more bed space, the problems within the prisons multiply. The impact of this situation on the inmates is clear from the interviews— they complain about the increased fragmentation and disorganization that they now experience. Life in prison is no longer organized but instead is viewed as both capricious and dangerous.

For many, returning to prison after spending time outside means being confronted by a world which they do not understand even though they have been in prison many times before. Where once they experienced an orderly culture, today they find a world which operates around arbitrary and ad hoc events, and decisions seem to arise not merely from the behavior of their fellow prisoners but also from prison authorities' official and unofficial decisions. Where before they understood the dominant prison divisions—prisoners versus guards and black versus white inmates—today they find new clefts and competing allegiances. The Chicanos are split not only between the Mexican Mafia and La Nuestra Familia but also North versus South. A relatively unified black population is divided into different warring camps of Crips, Bloods, and 415s.

The world portrayed by our respondents is an important corrective both to the criminal justice literature, which portrays prison life in very simplistic terms, and to those theoretical approaches which attempt to explain prison culture solely in terms of internal or external influences. Our interviews have shown that the linkages between street activities and prison activities are complex and are the result of developments in both arenas. Therefore, instead of attributing primacy to one set of factors as opposed to the other, it

may be more useful and more accurate to see the culture and organization of prison and street life as inextricably intertwined, with lines of influence flowing in both directions.

References

Beaird, Lester H. (1986) "Prison gangs: Texas." *Corrections Today* 48 July: 12, 18-22.

Biernacki, Patrick, and Dan Waldorf (1981) "Snowball sampling: Problems and techniques of chain referral sampling." *Sociological Methods and Research* 10:141-163.

Buentello, Salvator (1984) "The Texas Syndicate." Texas Department of Corrections. Unpublished report.

California Department of Corrections (1991) *Historical Trends: Institution and Parole Population, 1970–1990.* Offender Information Services Branch. Data Analysis Unit. Sacramento.

Camp, George, M., and Camille, G. Camp (1985) *Prison Gangs: Their Extent, Nature and Impact on Prisons.* U.S. Department of Justice, Office of Legal Policy, Federal Justice Research Program. Washington, D.C.

Castenedo, Esteban P. (compiler) (1981) *Prison Gang Influences on Street Gangs.* Sacramento, Calif.: California Department of Youth Authority.

Clemmer, Donald (1958) *The Prison Community.* New York: Rinehart and Co.

Cloward, Richard (1977) "Social control in the prison." In *The Sociology of Corrections,* ed. Robert G. Leger and John R. Stratton, 110-132. New York: John Wiley and Sons.

Conrad, John (1978) "Who's in charge? Control of gang violence in California Prisons." In *Report on Colloquium on Correctional Facilities,* 1977, ed. Nora Harlow. Sacramento, Calif: Department of Corrections.

Crist, Roger W. (1986) "Prison gangs: Arizona." *Corrections Today* 48 July: 13, 25-27.

Cummins, Eric (1991) "History of gang development in California prisons." Unpublished paper.

Davidson, R. Theodore (1974) *Chicano Prisoners: The Key to San Quentin.* Prospect Heights, Ill.: Waveland Press, Inc.

EMT Associates, Inc. (1985) *Comparative Assessment of Strategies to Manage Prison Gang Populations and Gang-related Violence.* Vol. 1-8. Sacramento, Calif: California Department of Corrections. Unpublished report.

Fong, Robert S. (1990) "The organizational structure of prison gangs: A Texas case study." *Federal Probation* 54:1.

Fong, Robert, and Salvator Buentello (1991) "The detection of prison gang development: An empirical assessment." *Federal Probation* 55:1.

Goffman, Erving (1961) *Asylums*. Garden City, N.J.: Anchor.

Irwin, John (1980) *Prisons in Turmoil*. Boston: Little, Brown and Company.

Irwin, John, and Donald Cressey (1977) "Thieves, convicts, and the inmate culture." In *The Sociology of Corrections*, ed. Robert G. Leger and John R. Stratton, 133-147. New York: John Wiley and Sons.

Jacobs, James (1974) "Street gangs behind bars." *Social Problems* 21:395-409.

—— (1977) *Stateville: The Penitentiary in Mass Society*. Chicago: University of Chicago Press.

Klein, Malcolm W., and Cheryl L. Maxson (1989) "Street gang violence." In *Violent Crime, Violent Criminals*, ed. Neil Allen Weiner and Marvin E. Wolfgang. Newbury Park, Calif.: Sage.

Lane, Michael. P. (1989) "Inmate gangs." *Corrections Today* July: 98-128.

Leger, Robert G., and John R. Stratton (1977) *The Sociology of Corrections: A Book of Readings*. New York: John Wiley and Sons.

Moore, Joan W. (1978) *Homeboys: Gangs, Drugs, and Prison in the Barrios of Los Angeles*. Philadelphia: Temple University Press.

Porter, Bruce (1982) "California prison gangs: The price of control." *Corrections Magazine* 8:6-19.

Stojkovic, Stan (1986) "Social bases of power and control mechanisms among correctional administrators in a prison organization." *Journal of Criminal Justice* 14:157-166.

Sykes, Gresham M., and Sheldon L Messinger (1977) "The inmate social system." In *The Sociology of Corrections*, ed. Robert G. Leger and John R. Stratton, 97-109. New York: John Wiley and Sons.

Section VI

Drugs and Crime

One of the enduring arguments in criminology is that surrounding the relationship between drugs and crime. While no one disputes the correlation—that drugs and crime seem to be interrelated in some manner—the issue of causation is controversial. Do drugs *cause* crime, or are they related in some other manner?

Recent Drug Use Forecasting (DUF) data clearly show that male arrestees tend to test positive for drugs. During one period, 78 percent of arrestees in Philadelphia tested positive for at least one illegal drug. Drug use for female arrestees ranged from less than 50 percent in San Antonio to over 85 percent in Manhattan.

In the first selection Patricia A. Adler ("Dealing Careers") provides a unique opportunity to view the world of upper-level drug dealing *from the inside.* In this chapter she describes how one becomes a drug dealer, then moves up in the business, and finally how experience and age combine to terminate or at least redirect the drug dealer's career.

In the next selection, Charles E. Faupel ("The Drugs-Crime Connection Among Stable Addicts") considers the role that criminal activity plays in facilitating drug use. Using ethnographic interviews with a population of stable addicts (seasoned, mature heroin users), Faupel argues that the drugs-crime connection is much more complex than the "drugs

cause crime" hypothesis of popular currency. Instead, he reports that increased heroin consumption is *preceded* by increased criminal activity. He further debunks the myth of "crazed drug fiends" by examining the rational processes involved in maintaining a drug habit through criminal activity.

In the next selection, Tom Mieczkowski ("Life With Crack") examines what might be considered the polar opposite of the drug dealers in Adler's study and also much different from the "stable addicts" studied by Faupel. The world of the crack addict represents the bottom of the drug dealing and using world. In this selection, Mieczkowski compares the problems and strategies of female crack dealers with those of their male counterparts. He found that while men and women faced many of the same problems, women encountered dilemmas not faced by men.

In the final selection, Bruce Jacobs ("The Social Organization of Crack Sales") takes the reader to the mean streets of the St. Louis drug markets. Here he describes the decline of the crack market and the strategies used by crack dealers to maintain their "market share."

From the top of the drug dealing world to the bottom, drug users and dealers tell their stories, discuss their problems, and reveal their strategies. ✦

18

Dealing Careers

Patricia A. Adler

In the early 1970s Patricia Adler and her husband Peter moved to Southwest County (pseudonym) to begin their graduate studies in sociology. There they made friends with "Dave," a neighbor whom they later learned was involved in high-level drug smuggling and dealing. As their friendship with Dave developed, they were introduced to a group of Dave's friends and associates, all involved in illegal drug dealing. As friendship and trust continued to develop between the Adlers and Dave and his associates, the two were slowly granted access to the world of smuggling, dealing, and drug use. For the next six years, with the knowledge and active assistance of Dave and his friends, the Adlers studied this drug-dealing and smuggling community, conducting interviews and observing their activities.

In this selection taken from her book, Wheeling and Dealing: An Ethnography of an Upper-Level Drug Dealing and Smuggling Community, *Patricia Adler explains how thrill seeking, spontaneity, emotionality, and other expressive concerns characterize the lifestyle of these upper-level drug dealers. She follows their careers, first by examining the process of becoming a drug trafficker, then considering the various routes to upward mobility, and finally the experience of aging in the career. Clearly noted are themes of the "glamour and excitement," the hedonism and fast life that attract some to the criminal lifestyle. Like Shover's persistent property offenders and Åkerström's thieves, Adler's drug dealers experienced "burn out" in the later stages of their careers. They reported disillusionment with the glamour and increased concern with the risks associated with a criminal life.*

Becoming a Drug Trafficker

Becoming a drug trafficker was a gradual process, where individuals progressively shifted perspective as they became increasingly involved in the social networks of dealers and smugglers (Lieb and Olson 1976). As Ray (1961) has noted for the careers of heroin addicts, joining these social networks required a commitment to the drug world's norms, values, and lifestyle, and limited the degree of involvement individuals subsequently had with nondeviant groups.

Recruitment

I observed three entry routes to this deviant career. These routes were different for dealing and smuggling, and varied according to the level of trafficking where individuals entered the field.

Dealing. Individuals began dealing drugs through their own initiative, entering the occupation via *self-propulsion*. They fell into two groups, marked by different levels of entry and characterized by significantly varied experiences.

People who began dealing with a low-level entry followed the classic path portrayed in the literature (see Anonymous 1969; Blum et al. 1972; Carey 1968; Goode 1970; Johnson 1973). These initiates came from among the ranks of regular drug users, since, in practice, using drugs heavily and dealing for "stash" (one's personal supply) were nearly inseparable. Out of this multitude of low-level dealers, however, most abandoned the practice after they encountered their first legal or financial bust, lasting in the business for a fairly short period (see Anonymous 1969; Carey 1968; Lieb and Olson 1976). Those who sought bigger profits gradually drifted into a full-time career in drug trafficking. Their careers as dealers were therefore entwined with their careers as drug users, which usually began by late adolescence (between the ages of 15 and 22). Because of this early recruitment into dealing, low-level entrants generally developed few, if any, occupational skills other than dealing. Although it was difficult to attain the upper level of the drug trade from these humble beginnings, a small but significant percentage of the dealers I observed in Southwest County got their start in this fashion.

A larger percentage of Southwest County dealers made a middle-level entry. Future big dealers usually jumped into transacting in substantial quantities from the outset, buying 50 kilos of commercial marijuana or one to two ounces of cocaine. One dealer explained this phenomenon:

> Someone who thinks of himself as an executive or an entrepreneur is not going to get into the dope business on a small level. The average executive just jumps right into the middle. Or else he's not going to jump.

This was the route taken by Southwest County residents who had little or no previous involvement in drug trafficking. For them, entry into dealing was precipitated by their social relations with local dealers and smugglers (naturally, this implies a self-selecting sample of outsiders who became accepted and trusted by these upper-level traffickers, based on mutual interests, orientation, and values). Through their friendships with dealers, these individuals were introduced to other members of the dealing scene and to their fast life. Individuals who found this lifestyle attractive became increasingly drawn to the subculture, building networks of social associations within it. Eventually, some of these people decided to participate more actively. This step was usually motivated by their attraction to the money and the lifestyle. Dave recounted how he fell in with the drug world set:

> I used to be in real estate making good money. Through my property management and investment services I started meeting some rich people. I was the only person at my firm renting to longhairs and dealing with their money. They all paid me in cash from a giant wad of bills. They never asked for a receipt and always had cash, 24 hours a day. I slowly started getting friendly with them, although I didn't realize how heavy they were. I knew ways of buying real estate and putting it under fictitious names, laundering money so that it went in as hot cash and came out as spendable income. I invested their money in gems, metals, cars. But the whole time

I never asked any questions. I just took my commission and was happy. Then one guy asked me to clear some checks for him through my bank account—said he was hiding the money from his ex-wife and the Treasury people. This was the beginning. I slowly got more and more involved with him until I was neglecting my real estate business and just partying with him all the time. My spending went up, but my income went down, and suddenly I had to look around for another way to make money fast. I took the money I was cashing for him, bought some bricks from another dealer friend of his and sold them out of state before I gave him back the cash. Eventually I started to deal with him too, on a front basis. Within six months I was turning 100 bricks at a time.

Once individuals decided to try dealing, they rarely abandoned it after one transaction. Earning money was intoxicatingly alluring, stimulating their greed for more, while losing money usually necessitated becoming involved in another deal to recoup what they lost.

People who entered drug dealing at these middle levels were usually between the ages of 25 and 35, and had worked in some other occupation before dealing seriously. Many drifted into the lifestyle from jobs already concentrated in the night hours, such as bartending, waiting tables, and nightclub door bouncing. Still others came from fields where the working hours were irregular and adaptable to their special schedules, such as acting, real estate, inventing, graduate school, construction, and creative "entrepreneurship" (more aptly called hand-to-mouth survival, for many). The smallest group was tempted into the drug world from structured occupations and the professions.

Smuggling. Smuggling, in contrast, was rarely entered in this self-directed manner. Only a small minority of upper-level dealers were able to make the leap into importation on their own. The rest became involved in smuggling through a form of *solicitation*. The complex task of importing illegal drugs required more knowledge, experience, equipment, and connections than most people possessed. Those who got into drug smuggling usually did so at the invitation of an established smuggler. About half of the people smugglers recruited had not dealt before, but came directly into importation from the drug world's social scene. This implies, like middle-level entry into dealing, that recruits were attracted to the drug crowd and its lifestyle, and that they had prior acquaintance with dealers and smugglers. The other half of the recruits were solicited from among the ranks of middle-level Southwest County dealers.

Recruits who were solicited were likely to have some skill or asset which the experienced smuggler needed to put his operation together. This included piloting or navigating ability, equipment, money, or simply the willingness to handle drugs while they were being transported. One smuggler described the criteria he used to screen potential recruits for his smuggling crew:

> Pilots are really at a premium. They burn out so fast that I have to replace them every six months to a year. But I'm also looking for people who are cool: people who will carry out their jobs according to the plan, who won't panic if the load arrives late or something goes wrong, 'cause this happens a lot . . . and I try not to get people who've been to prison before, because if they haven't they'll be more likely to take foolish risks, the kind that I don't want to have to.

Learning the Trade

Once people experienced some initial success in dealing, their attitude shifted from hesitancy to enthusiasm. Despite the amount of time and effort they invested, most people felt as if they had earned a lot of money for very little work. This was because dealing time and work differed structurally from legitimate work: the latter usually took place within a well-defined physical and temporal framework (the 9-to-5 hours at the office), while dealing was accomplished during discretionary, or recreational, hours and settings.

As business began to go well, the danger translated into excitement, making it seem like fun. Novice drug traffickers felt as if they were earning "gravy" money while simultaneously enjoying themselves. This definition of the situation helped them overcome any remaining reluctance and plunge themselves more deeply into the occupation. They then became eager to learn more about concrete strategies of conducting business safely and successfully.

Learning the trade involved acquiring specific knowledge of potential business connections, ways of organizing transactions profitably, ways of avoiding legal detection and arrest, ways of transporting illegal goods, ways of coordinating participants, types of equipment, and myriad other details. This knowledge was acquired through either *on-the-job* training (Miller and Ritzer 1977:89) or *sponsorship*.

Dealers underwent on-the-job training, refining their knowledge and skills by getting experience and learning from their mistakes. Their early experiences often included getting burned with inferior merchandise, getting "short counted" with low volume, and getting ripped off through carelessness in selecting their dealing associates. While some people abandoned dealing because of these early errors, many returned, better educated, to try again.

Socialization into the technical aspects of smuggling was not as isolated as it was for dealing. Most future smugglers were recruited and trained by a sponsor with whom they had an apprentice/mentor relationship. Those who had been dealers previously knew the rudiments of drug transactions. What they learned from the smuggler was how to fill a particular role in his crew. From there they became familiar with many other roles, learned the scope of the whole operation, and began to meet suppliers and customers. This mentor relationship often led apprentices to form an enduring loyalty to their sponsor. . . .

Identity Shift

Developing a dealing or smuggling self-conception involved more than simply committing illegal acts. A transition in the locus of self was required. Some people assumed the dealing identity immediately and eagerly, having made a conscious decision to pursue dealing as an occupation. Others displayed a more subtle identity shift, as they gradually drifted into membership in the drug world (Matza, 1964). Many individuals, then, became drug dealers by their actions well before they consciously admitted this to themselves. One dealer described his transformation:

> I had a job, school, and I was doing volunteer work, but I was also deviant and the deviant part was the part I secretly got off on. I was like a Dr. Jekyll with a Mr. Hyde side. When I got into my dealing bag people would pay homage to me; I'd get respect and recognition. . . . Eventually the two worlds intermingled and the facade [dealing side] became the reality.

Becker and Carper (1956) have asserted that individuals' identities are based on their degree of commitment to an occupation. Thus, those people who maintained their ties to other occupations took longer to form a dealing identity. They did not become fully committed to dealing until some external event (i.e., an arrest, or the conflicting demands of their legitimate and illegitimate businesses) forced them to make a conscious choice. One dealer related how he faced this decision:

> I had been putting off thinking about it for all those months but the time squeeze finally became such a thing that I couldn't ignore it any more. I was working at the office all day and staying up dealing and doing drugs all night. My wife was complaining because I'd fall asleep at odd hours and I never had any time for the kids. I knew I had to choose between my two lives—the straight and the dealing. I hated to give up my job because it had always been my security, and besides, it was a good business cover, but I finally decided I was more attracted to dealing. I was making better money there in fewer hours and this way, I'd have more time to be with my kids during the day.

Upward Mobility

Once they had gotten in and learned the trade, most dealers and smugglers strove for upward mobility. This advancement took different forms, varying between dealing and smuggling.

Dealers experienced two types of upward mobility: *rising through the ranks* and *stage-jumping*. The gradual rise exemplifies the way upward mobility has historically been portrayed in the sociological literature on dealing (Anonymous 1969; Carey 1968; Redlinger 1975). Individuals from the lowest levels expanded their range of contacts, realized that they could earn greater profits by buying in greater quantities, and began to move up the hierarchy of dealing levels. Rick described his early stage of involvement with dealing:

> I had dealt a limited amount of lids and psychedelics in my early college says without hardly taking it seriously. But after a while something changed in me and I decided to try to work my way up. I probably was a classic case—started out buying a kilo for $150 and selling two pounds for $100 each. I did that twice, then I took the money and bought two bricks, then three, then five, then seven.

This type of upward mobility, though characteristic of low-level dealers, was fairly atypical of the upper-level drug crowd. Two factors combined to make it less likely for low-level entrants to rise through the ranks to the top. The first was psychological. People who started small thought small; most had neither the motivation nor the vision to deal large quantities of drugs. The second and more critical factor was social. People who started at the bottom and tried to work their way up the ladder often had a hard time finding connections at the upper levels. The few people who did rise through the ranks generally began dealing in another part of the country, moving to Southwest County only after they had already progressed to the middle levels. These people were lured to the region by its reputation within drug circles as an importation and wholesale trafficking market.

More commonly, dealers and smugglers stage-jumped to the higher levels of drug trafficking. Beginning at a middle level, and progressing so rapidly that they could hardly acclimate to their increasing involvement and volume, these people moved quickly to the top. Jean described her mode of escalation:

> When I started to deal I was mostly looking for a quick buck here or there, something to pay some pressing bill. I was middling 50 or 100 bricks at a time. But then I met a guy who said he would front me half a pound of coke, and if I turned it fast,

I could have more, and on a regular basis. Pretty soon I was turning 6, 7, 8, 9, 10 pounds a week—they were passing through real fast. I was clearing at least 10 grand a month. It was too much money too fast. I didn't know what to do with it. It got ridiculous, I wasn't relating to anyone anymore. I was never home, always gone. . . . The biggest ego trip came when all of a sudden I turned around and I was selling to the people I had been buying from. I skipped their level of doing business entirely and stage-jumped straight past them.

Southwest County's social milieu, with its concentration of upper-level dealers and smugglers, thus facilitated forming connections and doing business at the upper levels of the drug world.

Within smuggling, upward mobility took the form of individuals *branching out on their own* (Redlinger 1975). By working for a smuggler, some crew members developed the expertise and connections to run their own operation. There were several requirements for such a move. They could fairly easily acquire the technical knowledge of equipment, air routes, stopovers, and how to coordinate personnel after working in a smuggling area for six months to a year. It was difficult to put together their own crew, though, because skilled employees, especially pilots, were hard to find. Most new smugglers borrowed people from other crews until they were established enough to recruit and train their own personnel. Finally, they needed connections for buying and selling drugs. Customers were plentiful, but it often required special breaks or networks to serve a foreign supplier.

Another way for employees to head their own smuggling operations was to take over when their boss retired. This had the advantage of keeping the crew and style of operation intact. Various financial arrangements were worked out for such a transfer of authority, from straight cash purchases to deals involving residual payments. One marijuana smuggler described how he acquired his operation:

I had been Jake's main pilot for about a year and next after him I knew the most about how his operation was run. We were really tight, and he had taken me all up and down the coast with him, meeting his customers. Naturally I knew the Mexican end of the operation and his supplier, Cesar, since I used to make the runs, flying down the money and picking up the dope. So when he told me he wanted to get out of the business, we made a deal. I took over the set-up and gave him a residual for every run I made. I kept all the drivers, all the dealers, all the connections—everything the guy had—but I found myself a new pilot.

In sum, most dealers and smugglers reached the upper levels of doing business not so much as a result of their individual entrepreneurial initiative but through the social networks they formed in the drug subculture. Their ability to remain in these strata was largely tied to the way they treated these drug world relationships.

Aging in the Career

Up to this point I have discussed dealers and smugglers separately because they displayed distinctive career patterns. However, once individuals rose to the highest levels, they faced a common set of problems and experiences. I will therefore discuss them together below.

Once they entered the drug world and established themselves at its upper levels, dealers and smugglers were capable of wheeling and dealing on a major scale. Yet this period brought with it a growth of malaise. As they aged in the career, the dark side of their occupation began to surface.

The first part of their disillusionment lay in the fading of glamour and excitement. While participation in the drug world brought thrills and status to novices, the occupation's allure faded over time. Their initial feelings of exhilaration began to dull as they became increasingly jaded by their exorbitant drug consumption. Already inclined toward regular use, upper-level dealers and smugglers set no limits on their drug intake once they began trafficking and could afford all the cocaine they desired. One smuggler described how he eventually came to feel:

It was fun, those three or four years. I never worried about money or anything. But after a while it got real boring, there was no feeling or emotion or anything about it. I wasn't even hardly relating to my old lady anymore. Everything was just one big rush.

After a year or more of serious drug trafficking, dealers and smugglers became increasingly sensitized to the extreme risks they faced. Cases of friends and associates who were arrested, imprisoned, or killed (because of natural hazards) began to mount. The probability that they were known to the police increased. They gradually realized that the potential legal consequences they faced were less remote than they had earlier imagined. Many individuals became convinced that continued drug trafficking would inevitably lead to arrest ("It's only a matter of time before you get caught").

Dealers and smugglers generally repressed their awareness of danger, treating it as a taken-for-granted part of their daily existence. Periodic crises shattered their casual attitudes, however, evoking strong underlying feelings of fears. One dealer talked about his feelings of paranoia:

You're always on the line. You don't lead a normal life. You're always looking over your shoulder, wondering who's at the door, having to hide everything. You learn to look behind you so well you could probably bend over and look up your ass. That's paranoia. It's a really scary, hard feeling. That's what makes you get out.

These feelings caused dealers and smugglers to assume greater security precautions. After especially close brushes with danger, they intensified their precautions temporarily, retreating into near isolation until they felt that the heat was off. They also gradually incorporated more precautions into their everyday routines, abandoning their earlier casualness for greater inflexibility and adherence to their rational rules of operating (see Lieb and Olson 1976). This went against their natural preference, and they found it unspontaneous and cumbersome.

Drug world members also grew progressively weary of their exclusion from the legitimate world and the series of deceptions they had to manage to sustain that separation. Initially, the separation had been surrounded by an alluring mystique. As they aged in the career, however, the mystique was replaced by the hassle of everyday boundary maintenance and their feelings of being expatriated from conventional society. One smuggler described the effects of this separation:

I'm so sick of looking over my shoulder, having to sit in my house and worry about one of my nondrug world friends stopping in when I'm doing business. Do you know how awful that is? It's like leading a double life. That's what makes it not worth it.

Thus, while the drug world was somewhat restricted, it was not an encapsulated community. As Reuter (1983:174) has noted, criminals maintain an involvement with the legitimate world:

Criminals do not inhabit a social and physical world that is different from the rest of society. They walk the same streets, dine in the same restaurants, and send their children to the same schools.

This constant contact with the straight world reminded them of the comforts and social ease they had left behind, and tempted them to go straight.

For upper-level dealers and smugglers, then, the process of aging in the career was one of progressive *burnout*. With the novelty worn off, most dealers and smugglers felt that the occupation no longer resembled their earlier impressions of it. Once they had reached the upper levels, their experience began to change and they changed with it. No longer were they the carefree people who lived from day to day without a thought for the future. No longer were they so intoxicated with their glamour that their only care in the world was the search for new heights of pleasure. Elements of this lifestyle remained, but they were tempered with the harsher side of the reality. In between episodes of intensive partying, veteran dealers and smugglers were struck by anxiety. They began to structure their work to encompass greater planning, caution, secrecy, and insulation. They isolated themselves from the straight world for days or weeks at a time, imprisoned and haunted by their own suspicions. They never renounced their hedonism or materialism, but the price they paid increased. Eventually, the rewards of trafficking no longer seemed to justify the strain. It was at this point that the straight world's formerly dull ambience became transformed (at least in theory) into a potential haven.

Shifts and Oscillations

Despite the gratifications dealers and smugglers derived from the easy money, material comfort, freedom, prestige, and power associated with their careers, most of them decided, at some point, to quit the business. This stemmed, in part, from their initial perceptions of the career as temporary ("Hell, nobody wants to be a drug dealer all their life"). Supplementing these early intentions was the process of rapid aging in the career, where dealers and smugglers became increasingly aware of the sacrifices their occupations required and got tired of living the fugitive life. As the dealing life began to look more troubling than rewarding, drug traffickers focused their energies on returning to the straight life. They thought about, talked about, and in many cases, took steps toward getting out of the drug business. But like entering the field, disengaging from drug trafficking was rarely an abrupt act (Lieb and Olson 1976:364). Instead, it more often resembled a series of transitions, or oscillations out of and back into the business. For once out of the drug world, dealers and smugglers were rarely successful at making it in the legitimate world because they failed to cut down on their extravagant lifestyle or drug consumption. Many thus abandoned their efforts to reform and returned to deviance, sometimes picking up where they left off and other times shifting to a new mode of operating. For example, some shifted from trafficking in cocaine to trafficking in marijuana, some dropped to a lower level of dealing, and others shifted their role within the same group of traffickers. This series of phase-outs and reentries, combined with career shifts, endured for years, dominating the pattern of their remaining involvement with the business. It also represented the method by which many eventually broke away from drug traf-

ficking, for each phase-out had the potential to be an individual's final departure.

Phasing Out

Making the decision to quit a deviant occupation is difficult. Several factors served to hold dealers and smugglers to the drug world. First, the hedonistic and materialistic satisfactions were primary. Once individuals became accustomed to earning large amounts of easy money, they found it exceedingly difficult to go back to the income scale of the straight world. They were also reluctant to abandon the pleasures of the fast life and its accompanying drugs, sex, and power. Second, dealers and smugglers formed an identification with and commitment to the occupation of drug trafficking. Their self-images were tied to that role and could not be easily disengaged. Their years invested learning the trade, forming connections, building reputations served as "side-bets" (Becker 1960), strengthening their involvement with both the deviant occupation and the drug community. And since their relationships were social as well as business-oriented, members' friendship ties bound them to dealing. As one dealer, in the midst of struggling to phase out, explained:

> The biggest threat to me is to get caught up sitting around the house with friends that are into dealing. I'm trying to stay away from them, change my habits.

Third, dealers and smugglers hesitated to voluntarily quit the field because they knew it would be difficult to find another way of earning a living. They feared that they would be unable to account to prospective employers for their years spent in illicit activities. This narrowed their occupational choices considerably, leaving self-employment as one of the few remaining avenues open.

Once dealers and smugglers made the decision to phase out, they generally pursued one of several routes out of dealing. The most frequent pattern involved resolving to quit after they executed one last big deal. While the intention was sincerely uttered, individuals who chose this route rarely succeeded; the big deal too often remained elusive. One marijuana smuggler offered a variation on this theme:

> My plan is to make a quarter of a million dollars in four months during the prime smuggling season and get the hell out of the business.

A second pattern involved individuals who planned to get out immediately, but never did. They announced that they were quitting, yet their outward actions never varied. Bruce, with his problems of overconsumption and debt escalation, described his involvement with this syndrome:

> When I wake up I'll say, "Hey, I'm going to quit this cycle and just run my other business." But when you're dealing you constantly have people dropping by ounces and asking, "Can you move this?" What's your first response? Always, "Sure, for a toot."

In the third pattern of phasing-out, individuals actually suspended their dealing or smuggling activities, but did not replace them with an alternative source of income. Such withdrawals were usually spontaneous and prompted by exhaustion, the influence of a person from outside the drug world, or problems with the police or other associates. As one dealer's case illustrated, these phase-outs usually lasted only until their money ran out:

> I got into heavy legal trouble with the FBI a while back and I was forced to quit dealing. Everybody just cut me off completely, and I saw the danger in continuing myself. But my high class tastes never dwindled. I borrowed money here and there. Before I knew it I was in hock over $30,000. Even though I was hot, I was forced to get back into dealing to relieve some of my debts.

In the fourth pattern of phasing-out, traffickers attempted a move into another line of work. Alternative occupations they tried included: occupations they had pursued before dealing or smuggling; front businesses maintained on the side while they were trafficking in drugs; and new occupations altogether. While some people successfully accomplished this transition, there were problems in all three alternatives.

Most people who tried to resume their former occupations found that these had changed too much while they were away from the field. In addition, they themselves had changed: they enjoyed the self-directed freedom and spontaneity associated with dealing and smuggling, and were unwilling to relinquish it.

Those who turned to their legitimate front business often found that these businesses were unable to support them. Designed to launder rather than earn money, most of these ventures had become accustomed to operating under a continuous subsidy from illegal funds. Once their drug funding was cut off, they could not survive for long.

Many dealers and smugglers utilized the business skills and connections they had developed in drug trafficking to create a new occupation. For some, the decision to prepare a legitimate career for retirement followed an unsuccessful attempt to phase out into a front business. One husband-and-wife dealing team explained how these legitimate side businesses differed from front businesses:

> We always had a little legitimate scam going, like mail-order shirts, wallets, jewelry, and the kids were always involved in that. We made a little bit of money on them. Their main purpose was for a cover and a legitimate business both. But [this business] was different; right from the start this was going to be a legal thing to push us out of the drug business.

Dealers and smugglers often formed these legitimate side occupations by exchanging their illegal commodity for a legal one, going into import/export, manufacturing, wholesaling, or retailing other merchandise. One former dealer described his current business and how he got into it:

> A friend of mine knew one of the major wholesalers in Tijuana for buying Mexican blankets, ponchos, and sweatshirts. After I helped him out with a favor when he was down, he turned me on to his connections. Now, I've cornered the market on wholesaling them to surf shops and swap meet sellers by undercutting everybody else.

The most future-oriented dealers and smugglers thus began gradually tapering off their drug world involvement, transferring their time and money into a selected legitimate endeavor. They did not try to quit drug trafficking altogether until they felt confident that their legitimate business could support them. But like spontaneous phase-outs, many of these planned withdrawals into legitimate businesses failed to generate enough money to keep individuals from being lured back into the drug world.

In addition to the voluntary phase-outs dealers and smugglers attempted after they became sufficiently burned out, many of them experienced an involuntary "bustout" at some point in their careers. Forced withdrawals from dealing or smuggling were usually sudden and necessitated by external factors, either financial, legal, or reputational. Financial bustouts generally occurred when dealers or smugglers were either burned or ripped off by others, leaving them in too much debt to rebuild their operation. Legal bustouts occurred when individuals got so hot from arrest or incarceration that few of their former associates would deal with them. Reputational bustouts occurred when individuals burned or ripped off others (regardless of whether they intended to do so) and were banned from business by their former associates. One smuggler gave his opinion on the pervasive nature of forced phase-outs:

> Some people are smart enough to get out of it because they realize, physically, they have to. Others realize, monetarily, that they want to get out of this world before this world gets them. Those are the lucky ones. Then there are the ones who have to get out because they're hot or someone else so close to them is hot that they'd better get out. But in the end when you get out of it, nobody gets out of it out of free choice; you do it because you have to.

Death, of course, was the ultimate bustout. Some pilots met this fate because of the dangerous routes they navigated (hugging mountains, treetops, other aircraft) and because of the sometimes ill-maintained and overloaded planes they flew. However, despite much talk of violence, few Southwest County drug traffickers died at the hands of fellow dealers.

Reentry

Phasing out of the drug world was usually only temporary. For many, it represented merely another stage in their dealing careers (although this may not have been their original intention), to be followed by a period of reinvolvement. Depending on the situation, reentry into the drug world represented either a *comeback* (from a forced withdrawal) or a *relapse* (from a voluntary withdrawal).

Most people forced out of drug trafficking were anxious to return. They had never decided to withdraw, and their desire to get back was based on many of the same reasons which drew them into the field originally. While it was possible to come back from financial, legal, and reputational bustouts, it was difficult and not always successfully accomplished. Dealers and smugglers had to reestablish their contacts, rebuild their organization and fronting arrangements, and raise any necessary operating capital. More important, they had to overcome the circumstances surrounding their departure; once they resumed operating they often found their former colleagues suspicious of them. They were therefore informally subjected to a trial period in which they had to re-prove their reliability before they could once again move easily through the drug world.

Dealers and smugglers usually found that reentering the drug world after they had voluntarily withdrawn from it involved a more difficult decision-making process, but was easier to implement. As I noted earlier, experienced dealers and smugglers often grappled with conflicting reasons for wanting to quit and wanting to stay with the occupation. When the forces propelling them out of the drug world were strongest, they left. But once out, these forces weakened. Their images of and hopes for the straight world often failed to materialize. Many could not make the shift to the norms, values, and lifestyle of the straight society and could not earn a living within it. Yet the factors enticing individuals to resume drug trafficking were not the same as those which motivated their original entry. They were no longer awestruck by the glamorous lifestyle or the thrill of danger. Instead, they got back in to make money both to pay off the debts they had accumulated while "retired" and to build up and save so that their next phase-out would be more successful. Dealers and smugglers made the decision to reenter the drug world, then, for some very basic reasons: the material perquisites; the drugs; the social ties; and the fact that they had nowhere else to go.

Once this decision was made, the actual process of reentry was relatively simple. One dealer described how the door back into dealing remained open for those "who left voluntarily":

> I still see my dealer friends, I can still buy grams from them when I want to. It's the respect they have for me because I stepped out of it without being busted or burning someone. I'm coming out with a good reputation, and even though the scene is a whirlwind—people moving up, moving down, in, out—if I didn't see anybody for a year I could call them up and get right back in that day.

People who relapsed thus had few problems obtaining fronts, reestablishing their reputations, or readjusting to the scene. Yet once back in, they generally were again unsuccessful in accumulating enough of a nest egg to ensure the success of their subsequent phase-outs. Each time they relapsed into drug trafficking they became caught up once again in the drug world's lifestyle of hedonism and consumption. They thus spent the money they were earning almost as fast as they earned it (or in some cases, faster). The fast life, with its irrationality and present orientation, held a grip on them partly because of the drugs they were consuming, but most especially because of the pervasive dominance of the drug subculture. They thus started the treadmill spinning again so that they never got enough ahead; they never amassed the stockpile that they had reentered the drug world to achieve.

Career Shifts

Dealers and smugglers who reentered the drug world, whether from a voluntary or forced phase-out, did not always return to the same activity, level, or commodity which characterized their previous style of opera-tion. Upon returning after a hiatus, many individuals underwent a "career shift" (Luckenbill and Best 1981) and became involved in some new segment of the drug world. The shifts were sometimes lateral, as when a member of a smuggling crew took on a new specialization, switching from piloting to operating a stash house, for example. One dealer described how he used friendship networks upon his reentry to shift from cocaine to marijuana trafficking:

> Before, when I was dealing cocaine, I was too caught up in using the drug, and people around me were starting to go under from getting into base. That's why I got out. But now I think I've got myself together and even though I'm dealing again I'm staying away from coke. I've switched over to dealing grass. It's a whole different circle of people. I got into it through a close friend I used to know before, but I never did business with him because he did grass and I did coke.

Vertical shifts moved operators to different levels. For example, one former smuggler returned and took up dealing; another wholesale marijuana dealer came back to find that the smugglers he knew had disappeared and he was forced to buy from other dealers.

A third type of shift relocated drug traffickers in different styles of operation. One dealer described how, after being arrested, he tightened his security measures:

> I just had to cut back after I went through those changes. Hell, I'm not getting any younger and the idea of going to prison bothers me a lot more than it did ten years ago. The risks are no longer worth it when I can have a comfortable income with less risk. So I only sell to four people now. I don't care if they buy a pound or a gram.

A former smuggler who sold his operation and lost all his money during his phase-out returned as a consultant to the industry, selling his expertise to individuals with new money and fresh manpower:

> What I've been doing lately is setting up deals for people. I've got foolproof plans for smuggling cocaine up here from Colombia. I tell them how to modify their airplanes to add on extra fuel tanks and to fit in more weed, coke, or whatever they

bring up. Then I set them up with refueling points all up and down Central America, telling them how to bring it up here, what points to come in at, and what kind of receiving unit to use. Then they do it all, and I get 10 percent of what they make.

Reentry did not always imply a shift to a new niche, however. Some returned to the same circle of associates, trafficking activity, and commodity they worked with before their departure. Thus, drug traffickers' careers often peaked early and then displayed a variety of shifts from lateral mobility, to decline, to holding fairly steady.

A final alternative involved neither completely leaving nor remaining in this deviant occupation. Many individuals straddled the deviant and respectable worlds forever by continuing to dabble in drug trafficking. As a result of their experiences in the drug world they had developed a deviant self-identity and a deviant *modus operandi*. They did not want to bear the social and legal burden of full-time deviant work, but neither were they willing to assume the drudgery of the straight world. They therefore moved into the entrepreneurial realm, where their daily activities involved some sort of hustling in an assortment of legitimate, quasi-legitimate, and deviant ventures, and where they were their own boss. In this way they were able to retain certain elements of the deviant lifestyle and to socialize on the fringes of the drug community. For these individuals, drug dealing shifted from a primary occupation to a sideline, but they never abandoned it altogether.

Leaving Drug Trafficking

This pattern of oscillation into and out of active drug trafficking makes it somewhat problematic to speak of leaving deviance in the sense of a final retirement. Clearly, some people succeeded in voluntarily retiring. Of these, a few managed to prepare a post-deviant career for themselves by transferring their drug money into a legitimate enterprise. A larger group was forced out of dealing and either did not or could not return; their bustouts were sufficiently damaging that either they never attempted reentry or they abandoned their efforts after a series of unsuccess-

ful comeback attempts. But there was no way of determining in advance whether an exit from the business would be temporary or permanent. Here, dealers' and smugglers' vacillating intentions were compounded by the complexity of operating successfully in the drug world. For many, then, no phase-out could ever be definitively assessed as permanent. As long as individuals had the skills, knowledge, and connections to deal, they could potentially reenter the occupation at any time. Leaving drug trafficking was thus a relative phenomenon, characterized by a trailing-off process where spurts of involvement occurred with decreasing frequency and intensity. This disengagement was characterized by a progressive reorientation to the legitimate world, where former drug traffickers once again shifted their social networks and changed their self-conceptions (Lieb and Olson 1976).

Summary

Dealing and smuggling careers were temporary, fraught with multiple attempts at retirement. Veteran drug traffickers quit their occupation because of the ambivalent feelings they developed toward their deviant life. As they aged in the career their experience changed, shifting from a work life that was exhilarating and free to one that became increasingly dangerous and confining. Just as their deviant careers were temporary, so too were their retirements. Potential recruits, therefore, were lured into the business by materialism, hedonism, glamour, and excitement. Established dealers were lured away from the deviant life and back into the mainstream by the attractions of security and social ease. But once out, retired dealers and smugglers were lured back in by their expertise, by their ability to make money quickly and easily. People who were exposed to the upper levels of drug trafficking found it extremely difficult to quit permanently. This stemmed, in part, from their difficulty in moving from the illegitimate to the legitimate business sector. Even more significant was the affinity they formed for their deviant values and lifestyle. Thus few of the people I observed were successful in leaving deviance entirely. What dealers and smugglers intended, at the time, to be a permanent withdrawal from drug trafficking can be seen in retrospect as a pervasive occupational pattern of shifts and oscillations.

References

Anonymous. 1969. "On selling marijuana." In Erich Goode, ed., *Marijuana*, pp. 92-102. New York: Atherton.

Becker, Howard, and James Carper. 1956. "The development of identification with an occupation." *American Journal of Sociology* 66:32-42.

Blum, Richard, et al. 1968. *The Dream Sellers*. San Francisco: Jossey-Bass.

Carey, James T. 1972. *The College Drug Scene*. Englewood Cliffs, NJ: Prentice-Hall.

Goode, Erich. 1970. *The Marijuana Smokers*. New York: Basic.

Johnson, Bruce D. 1973. *Marijuana Users and Drug Subcultures*. New York: Wiley.

Lieb, John, and Sheldon Olson. 1976. "Prestige, paranoia and profit; on becoming a dealer of illicit drugs on a university community." *Journal of Drug Issues*. 6:356-69.

Luckenbill, David F., and Joel Best. 1981. "Careers in deviance and respectability: the analogy's limitations." *Social Problems* 29:197-206.

Matza, David. 1964. *Delinquency and Drift*. New York: Wiley.

Miller, Gale, and George Ritzer, 1977. "Informal socialization: deviant occupations." In George Ritzer, *Working*, 2nd ed., 83-94. Englewood Cliffs, NJ: Prentice-Hall.

Ray, Marsh. 1961. "The cycle of abstinence and relapse among heroin addicts." *Social Problems* 9:132-140.

Redlinger, Lawrence J. 1969. "Dealing in dope: market mechanisms and distribution patterns in illicit narcotics." Ph.D. diss., Northwestern University.

——. 1975. "Marketing and distributing heroin." *Journal of Psychedelic Drugs* 7:331-53.

19

The Drugs-Crime Connection Among Stable Addicts

Charles E. Faupel

In *this piece Charles E. Faupel examines in detail the lifestyles and career patterns of hardcore heroin addicts and the controversial issue of the relationship between drugs and crime. He also considers the question of whether addict criminals are skilled, rational "professional" criminals or opportunists. Faupel arrives at many of the same conclusions regarding opportunism versus rationality as have other researchers represented in this book (see Cromwell et al.; Shover and Honaker; Decker and Wright; and Feeney). The lifestyle depicted by Faupel as representative of the addict criminal is also similar to that noted by Shover and Honaker in their study of persistent property criminals. Regarding the drugs-crime nexus, Faupel concludes that drug use does not cause crime, but may be caused by crime or at least facilitated by it. His treatment of these issues supports an understanding of the heroin addict as a much more rational being than previously believed.*

Faupel notes four phases in the heroin-using career: the occasional user, the stable addict, the free-wheeling junkie, and the street junkie. In this selection, he focuses on the stable addict—the mature, seasoned heroin user. He characterizes this stage in the heroin addict's life as analogous to the productive, established period in conventional careers.

In terms of research methodology this article is drawn from a long-term study of the relationship of drugs to crime. It is based on life history interviews with hard-core heroin addicts in the Wilmington, Delaware, area. Thirty heroin addicts were extensively interviewed—10 to 25 hours each in sessions lasting from two to four hours. The subjects were paid a small stipend for their time.

The subjects all had extensive criminal histories and at the time of the interviews, 24 were under correctional supervision (incarcerated, probation, parole, or work release). Women were slightly overrepresented, constituting 12 of the 30 respondents.

The sample consisted of 22 blacks and eight whites. Latinos were not represented because there is not a sizeable Latino drug-using population in the area where the study was conducted.

The complexity of the drugs-crime connection is perhaps most fully apparent during the stable-addict phase. One clear feature is the role that criminal activities plays in facilitating drug use. The participants in this study strongly concurred that their level of heroin consumption was a function of their ability to afford it, which was usually enhanced by criminal activity. "The better I got at crime," remarked Stephanie, "the more money I made; the more money I made, the more drugs I used." She went on to explain, "I think that most people that get high, the reason it goes to the extent that it goes—that it becomes such a high degree of money—is because they make the money like that. I'm saying if the money wasn't available to them like that, they wouldn't be into drugs as deep as they were."

Contrary to the "drugs cause crime" hypothesis, which suggests that increases in the level of heroin consumption are necessarily followed by stepped-up criminal activity, the dynamics reported by the addicts in this study are quite the opposite: increased heroin consumption is preceded by increased criminal activity as measured by estimated criminal income. This does not necessarily imply a greater frequency of crime, for, as I shall highlight below, stable-addict status usually brings with it greater sophistication in skill and technique, often resulting in higher proceeds per criminal event.

These life history data also reveal, however, that the relationship between drug use and crime is much broader and more complex than simple causality. As I suggested earlier, increased criminal income not only enhances drug availability, but also provides the basis for an expanded life structure, an alternative daily routine. Because these criminal routines usually provide greater flexibility than do most forms of legitimate employment, they free the addict from prohibitive roles and social contacts that may be imposed by more rigid schedules. Drug-using activities are certainly facilitated under these more flexible routines. Nevertheless, criminal routines do impose certain constraints on the addict life-style. Moreover, they provide an important structure to one's drug-using activities. It is in this respect that Old Ray likened the routine of dealing drugs to legitimate employment: "When you're working, the world has its rhythm, its time clock. You have your eight-to-five time clock. Well, it's the same way with dealing drugs." The result is a curious paradox. Criminal activity not only enhances availability thereby providing for heavier drug consumption, but also places broad limits on the amount of heroin consumed by providing some semblance of structure and routine. There is yet another paradox in the drugs-crime relationship for the stable addict. While it is true that crime facilitates heroin use, many of the addicts I interviewed indicated that heroin and other drugs played a utilitarian role in their commission of crime as well. While it is commonly assumed that addicts are most likely to commit crimes when they are sick and desperate for a fix, the addicts in this study reported quite the opposite. The following comments from Joe and Belle highlight the importance of being straight (not experiencing withdrawal) when committing crimes:

[Joe] It would be awful hard for me if I was sick to be able to hustle. A lot of times if you're sick you go in and grab stuff. And run without caution. But if I was high it was a different story. I could take my time and get what I wanted.

[Belle] Most people say about drug addicts [that] when they're sick is when they do their most damage. But that's the lying-est thing in the world. When a dope addict is sick, he's sick. He can't raise his hand if

he's a drug addict. . . . They say when a dope fiend's sick he'll do anything to get money, but how the hell is he going to do it if he can't even go on the street and do it?

The prostitutes I interviewed found heroin especially functional in their criminal activities. Never knowing if their next *trick* (client) might be a freak (one who enjoys violence or sadomasochistic acts), carry a disease, or simply have unpleasant body odor, prostitutes understandably approach many of their dates with a good deal of apprehension. They reported that heroin allows them to work under otherwise difficult conditions:

[Belle] I think that a woman that tricks has to do something. If they wasn't an alcoholic, they had to be a dope fiend. 'Cause a woman in her right sense, you just can't sit up and do some of the things you do with a trick.

[Penny] If I didn't have no heroin in me, I couldn't trick, because it turns my stomach. . . . I didn't feel nothin' then, I just went on and do it. . . . I always was noddin' before I even get to the date. And then when I get to the date, I go to the bathroom and get off again.

[Helen] I could forget about what I was doing; I didn't give a damn about anything. I just felt good.

Heroin is not the only drug that addicts use for functional reasons in their commission of crimes. Amphetamines are also sometimes used to maintain necessary energy levels on particularly busy days. Boss, who was an armed robber among other things, reported that he would frequently use barbiturates before going out on a robbery. He found that they put him in the necessary belligerent mood to play the "tough guy" in order to pull off the robbery successfully. He also reported that he would frequently celebrate a successful robbery with heroin or cocaine or perhaps even a speedball (a heroin and cocaine combination): "They'd be like a toast. Maybe nine-thirty or ten o'clock we'd done pulled a good score off and we're sitting there and say, 'Hey man, let's go get us some good motherfucking dope.' And it would carry you until two o'clock. Nodding in the apartment, everybody feeling all right because they got away with the crime, planning what you're gonna do with your half of the money. So it'd be like the cap for you. It'd be like a toast for a job well done."

Finally, the data from these life histories suggest that both drug use and criminal behavior are interrelated elements of a broader subcultural experience that cannot be fully understood in terms of a simple causal relationship. Particularly as stable addicts, these respondents regarded both drug use and crime as important parts of a challenging lifestyle. On the one hand, it is true that drugs provide an important perceptual framework from which addicts interpret their behavior. Boss commented on the importance of drugs in defining the meaning that he attached to his activities: "The money is good, but I wouldn't want the money if I couldn't have what goes along with selling the money [for heroin]. . . . Like with the whores, I wouldn't want the whores if I couldn't spend the money on dope. . . . It's like a working man. A working man, he wants a home and nice family. Just like in the life of crime you got to have all those essential things that go with it or it's nothing. It would be nothing if I couldn't spend that money the way [I want to]."

But while heroin is an important component of the subjective experience of addicts, it is only part of a more general lifestyle, the maintenance of which motivates the addict. Also part of that lifestyle for most addicts is a nice wardrobe, fancy cars (for men), a nice *crib* (home), and a reputation for generosity with friends. As Boss reflected: "See, my concern wasn't catching the habit. . . . My thing was being able to make enough money to supply that habit and make enough money to keep my thing up to par—you know, my clothes, and my living standards . . . to stay up to par enough so if my mother or sister or brother needed some money I could loan them some money, plus keep my habit, plus buy some shoes or something, you know, rent a car for the weekend and just hang out like the guy that didn't have the habit. And in the course of that, that called for more crime."

As important as drugs and the fast lifestyle are in motivating addict behavior, one important fact remains: crime is a way of life with stable addicts. These people take pride in their ability to hustle successfully. Criminal success is a mark of stature in the subculture, and the more lucrative or difficult the hustle, the greater the recognition one receives. "The type of criminal activity he engages in, and his success at it determine, to a large extent, the addict's status among fellow addicts and in the community at large. The appellation of *real hustling dope fiend* (a successful burglar, robber, con man, etc.) is a mark of respect and status" (Preble and Casey, 1969:20; italics in original). Crime is a challenge that most stable addicts find tremendously appealing. It provides a source of excitement and a sense of accomplishment, similar to the challenge of climbing formidable mountain peaks or rafting turbulent white water. Mario compared the excitement of burglarizing a house with the anticipation experienced by a young child at Christmastime. Each package (house) has its own surprises, its own challenges. Some are located in wealthy sections of the city and have fabulous exteriors (pretty wrappings). Some of these promising houses resulted in a valuable *take* (loot), while others did not. What kept Mario going was the anticipation he experienced with each crime.

Mario's feelings reflect those of many of the addicts who took part in this study. Their perceptions defy any attempt to characterize criminal behavior as somehow being "driven" by an overwhelming need for drugs, even though heroin and other drugs constitute an important feature of a stable addict's motivational structure. For these addicts, drugs and crime are mutually reinforcing elements of a broader lifestyle, both of which play an important role in defining one's position in the criminal-addict subculture. Harry expressed it this way: "It was never really the drug. It was the lifestyle I was trying to keep going. And the drug was a lot of that lifestyle. . . . Back then [before becoming a street junkie] . . . it was just that it was there and I had all this energy and no vent for it. And I had begun to vent it into getting drugs, knocking people in the head, taking their money, going into somebody's house, taking that stuff out, running into the fence, going to get the drugs—a full-time job. It was more than your basic forty hours a week. And that's what it was about, sustaining that lifestyle."

By way of summary, in contrast to the occasional-user period of addict careers where drug use and crime are independent, parallel activities, the stable-addict phase is marked by a close interdependence between these two sets of activities. This relationship is more complex than can be captured in the empiricist language of cause and effect, however. The transition to the status of stable addict is a function of increased drug availability and expanded life structure, which, in most instances, result from increased systematic criminal activities. In this respect, we might characterize the stable-addict period as one in which "crime causes drugs" or, at least, crime facilitates drug use. Having attained the status of stable addict, the user has succeeded in jockeying for position in the criminal-addict subculture. The stable addict is, at least by minimal definition, a successful participant in the subculture. Success in the subculture is defined by drug-using and criminal activity, both of which are motivating factors in the behavior of stable addicts. In this respect, the drugs-crime relationship is not so much causal as it is reciprocal, itself contributing to one's stature in the subculture.

Criminal Specialization Among Stable Addicts

The career transition to stable addict usually entails an increasing reliance on a small number of criminal hustles or, in some cases, on a single type of crime. I pointed out [earlier] that early occasional use is a time of experimentation, not only with various types of drugs, but also with a variety of criminal roles. As in other careers, this trial period usually gives way to more focused activity as developing addicts discover what criminal skills and penchants they may have by experimenting with different criminal routines. In short, assumption of the stable-addict role usually implies the development of one or more main hustles.

Developing a main hustle implies not only the achievement of increased specialization but also of increased skill and sophistication as a criminal. Stable addicts go beyond learning the nuts and bolts of their chosen trade(s)

to master the subtleties of these criminal enterprises with a finesse more characteristic of a craftsman than of a stereotyped common criminal. Old Ray may have stated it most succinctly when he remarked, "You got to have a Ph.D. in streetology." There are three broad types of skills that the successful criminal addict acquires: technical, social, and intuitive skills (Faupel, 1986).

Technical Skills

This category of criminal skills entails both the knowledge of how to perform the task as well as the physical adeptness for carrying it out successfully. Shoplifters stress the importance of being able to *roll* clothing items tightly with one hand with the clothes still on the hanger. Rolling loosely will not allow as many clothes to be packed in the bag, and keeping clothes on the hanger is important because empty hangers arouse suspicion. This must all be done with one hand because the other hand is used to finger through items on the rack, thereby creating the impression that the shoplifter is a legitimate customer. A slip in any one of the maneuvers involved in the complex process may mean failure to reach a quota for the day or, even more seriously, possible detection and arrest. Moreover, shoplifters must continually keep abreast of technological innovations designed to detect theft, including cameras, one-way mirrors, and alarm devices attached inside expensive clothing items.

Prostitutes also report the importance of developing technical skills, particularly streetwalkers who regularly *beat their johns* (rob their clients) out of credit cards and cash. Belle described her strategy, for successfully stealing from her clients: "The car was sweeter than anything else as far as getting money. Because once you get a dude's pants down, you got him where you want him. He just automatically forgets about he's got money in his pocket. . . . All she's thinking about is getting him in a position to get his mind off his pocket long enough for her to get in there. . . . She might take his pants with her and leave him stripped for nothing— 'cause I've done it." A prostitute must also be able to determine where her trick keeps his wallet, take the wallet from his pocket, and then return it—all in a matter of minutes and without the client's being aware that this activity is taking place. These are skills not readily acquired; developing them takes time and practice, as Penny described: "When I started off I was scared. It took a little longer. . . . It might take four or five hours [on an all-night date] to get his wallet. . . . [Later] it didn't take me but a minute to get it and put it back in."

The acquisition of technical skills is critical to the success of other hustles as well. The technical skills required by burglars have been extensively discussed in the literature on professional crime (Letkeman, 1973; Sutherland, 1937). These same skills were also reported by the burglar-addicts who participated in this study. An intimate knowledge of alarm systems is part of the seasoned burglar's stock-in-trade. Moreover, because most burglars prefer to enter unoccupied homes, they commonly case a residential area for days or even weeks, meticulously noting the mobility patterns of the residents. Burglars working business districts also case their working areas to determine patterns of police surveillance. Paige recalled "staying up all night watching the pattern of the police officers and seeing how regularly he made his rounds of the establishment—and charting all that stuff down and trying to get a fix on when's the best time for me to rip that store off."

Stable addicts are also involved in many other types of criminal offenses. The addicts in this study reported engaging in main hustles such as armed robbery, pickpocketing, forgery, fencing stolen goods, pimping, and drug dealing at one time or another during their careers. Each of these criminal enterprises involves its own modus operandi and requires the acquisition of specialized technical skills if one is to be a reasonably successful hustler.

Social Skills

Most criminal hustles require the addict to be verbally and socially skilled as well as technically adept. These social skills involve verbally and non-verbally manipulating the setting to the criminal's advantage such that the offense can be carried out smoothly and without risk of apprehension or arrest.

Social skills, like technical skills, are quite specialized. Shoplifters who work in pairs, for example, frequently find it necessary to engage in small talk with salespersons, thereby diverting attention from the actions of their partners. Moreover, when they are detected, good boosters are often successful in talking their way out of an arrest. Gloria found that she could intimidate lower-level sales personnel from referring her to management by taking on the persona of an indignant, falsely accused customer. Some shoplifters, such as Slick, used a modus operandi that relied primarily on verbal agility. In contrast to the surreptitious strategies employed by many shoplifters, such as hiding stolen goods in garbage bags and false-bottom boxes or underneath one's own clothing, Slick opted for the bold strategy of walking out of the store with his stolen merchandise in full view of store personnel, as if he had paid for it: "I would take McCullough chain saws. . . . I would just pick up the big box, set it up on my shoulders, and even get the store security guard at the door to open the door for me. I just got bold." Then, rather than sell the chain saw to a fence for about one-third the retail value, Slick would rely on his verbal skills once again by returning the item the next day to the very store he had stolen it from (or bring it to another store in the chain) for a full refund.

Needless to say, this sort of strategy requires a unique ability to play the role of a legitimate customer. A shoplifter with highly developed social skills tends to assume this role so completely that he or she takes on the attitudes, feelings, and perspective of the customer. To use Mead's (1934) term, the shoplifter quite literally "takes the role of the other." Socially skilled shoplifters do not take the role of just any customer, however; they assume the role of an assertive customer who takes complete command of the situation. Indeed, they must do so. A legitimate customer can perhaps afford not to be assertive, but a timorous shoplifter may well forfeit his or her career by failing to command credibility as a legitimate customer.

Check forgers make use of some of the same social skills employed by shoplifters. Indeed, social agility can probably be said to constitute the principal stock-in-trade of the check forger. The entire act revolves around successfully convincing a bank employee that the signature on the check is in fact that of the individual whose name it bears, and that the forger is that individual and therefore the rightful recipient of the amount of the check. All of this involves the ability to assume the role of an assertive individual with a legitimate claim, an ability Old Ray cultivated to his advantage: "I found the hardest teller I could find and she sent me to the manager's office. . . . I went in there telling about this godsent check—a tragedy in my life. It was all acting. . . . You got to story-tell. But it was my check. It became my check the minute I walked into the bank. . . . Once I packed up that type attitude, I became the role. And it's easier to go to the top than the bottom. It's easier at the top to get to anybody. . . . The guy at the bottom, he's gonna give you hell . . . but the man at the top, he can afford to be benevolent."

Other criminal hustles require social skills of a slightly different nature. Prostitutes point out the importance of maintaining a position of dominance in the interaction between them and their tricks. Rose advised: "Always try to keep control of the conversation. Never let them see that you're soft. . . . They see one time that you stutter or aren't in control, they're gonna try to take advantage of you." By maintaining such control, the prostitute is also able to direct and focus her client's attention, which allows her to engage in acts of theft. Penny was so successful at this strategy that she was frequently able to rob her clients without even having to *turn the trick* (engage in sexual acts).

Drug dealing entails social skills with still another focus. Here the primary task is to maintain a relatively stable clientele. This involves advertising one's drugs and establishing a reputation as having "righteous" dope. Harry, who was heavily involved in burglary as well as selling drugs, understood successful dealing to be little more than hype and good salesmanship: "Conning was part of everything. The whole thing is an image. Believe it or not, it's the American way! . . . So you learn how to hype. . . . One of my favorite lines was 'You better do only half of one of these.' And that just made them get all that much more motivation to do three or four of them. And they'd do three or four and they'd come back and say, 'Hey, that shit was good!' Of course, if they did three or four of them, they did get fucked up."

Inevitably, however, drug dealers are confronted with dissatisfied customers who have reason to believe that they have been ripped off with poor-quality dope. There was no consensus among the dealers I interviewed regarding how they respond to discontented clients. Some would play it tough, on the theory that to give in to a client's demands sets a bad precedent and may serve as a signal to others that here is a dealer who can easily be taken. Others saw themselves as conscientious businesspeople and would quite readily supply a dissatisfied customer with more dope, urging them to spread the word that they were treated fairly. In either event, to borrow a phrase from the subculture of pickpockets, dealers must "cool the mark out," employing all of the social skills they have at their disposal to maintain a stable clientele.

Intuitive Skills

This last category of hustling skills entails an acute sensitivity to one's environment. Sutherland (1937) describes this characteristic as *larceny sense*, a term that Dressler also employs to describe the professional criminal: "Larceny sense, it seems, is the ability to smell out good hauls, to sense the exact moment for the kill, and to know when it is wiser to desist" (1951:255). Maurer (1955) applies the term *grift sense* to describe intuitive skills in his classic analysis of the professional pick-pocket. But these skills are by no means limited to professional criminals. Gould et al. observe this ability among active heroin users: "Most successful dope fiends show an ability to size up people they meet in terms of trustworthiness and motivation, and have a good memory for people" (1974:45-46).

The addicts I interviewed also emphasized the importance of intuitive skills. Like technical and social skills, intuitive skills are manifested differently in various criminal contexts, but their general purpose is to help facilitate the commission of a crime or to help the criminal avoid detection and arrest.

Intuitive skills can facilitate the commission of crime by providing the addict with the ability to sense a profitable and reasonably safe opportunity. "I could see money. I could smell money," claimed Old Ray. "I could walk by a store and see if it was vulnerable. . . . I could sense the whole setup." These are the skills that contribute to larceny (or grift) sense, and many of the participants in this study explicitly acknowledged their importance. Representative observations of a prostitute, a pickpocket, and a shoplifter illustrate how these skills are applied in various hustles:

> [Rose—a prostitute] Look for the nice dates. When you spot a man with the raggediest car and the oldest clothes, he's probably got the money. Because he's cheap, he don't wanna spend all of that money. It's usually the man that's got all this and that [who] ain't got a dime because he's paying out so many bills. [Rose went on to point out that she would probably have to steal his money because he is unlikely to be generous with her either.]

> [Boss—a pickpocket] As I got better, I could spot people with decent money, and you play them. Whereas in the beginning, on the amateur thing, I might play anywhere from ten to fifteen wallets. But when I got professional, I might just play one or two wallets.

> [Booter—a shoplifter] All days aren't the same for boosting. . . . If there's no situation where you can make some money you just don't go in and make a situation. You understand what I'm saying? The situation has to be laid out for you. And to be really good at it, you got to be the type of person that can recognize a laid-out situation. If you get in there and try to make a situation, then you're rearranging the whole thing and it could be detrimental.

Intuitive skills are also instrumental in avoiding detection and arrest. The addict criminals in this study repeatedly stressed the importance of being able to detect and avoid undercover police officers, floorwalkers, and potential informants. This ability was re-

garded as absolutely crucial to their success in criminal roles:

> [Harry—regarding drug dealing] I learned the ropes . . . how you spot cops. He [a friend] pointed out . . . those undercover detectives with the bee stingers on their cars, little teeny antennae on top; and how you could pick those cars out; and how two detectives in a car, how there were certain characteristics about them that were always the same. You could smell them a mile away. He really schooled me criminally, you know.

> [Stephanie—a check forger] When she [the bank teller] sees the check, if she has to look up [or] if she has to call another teller or something like that, it ain't no good. . . . If the teller has to pick up the phone, then you tell her, "That's all right, there's something I have to do."

> [Penny—on shoplifting] I can tell [who the floorwalkers are]. They constantly keep walking the floor looking at me. . . . They're still in that same department and ain't bought nothing.

> [Fred—a drug dealer] Never take a deal that sounds too good to be true. . . . This guy came by and wanted to buy fifteen bags for $10 apiece—no shorts. Now any kind of a hustler junkie coming off the street and he's got $150, he's not gonna come to you wanting fifteen bags. He's gonna come to you wanting twenty-five or thirty. You know what I'm saying? The deal was too good to be true.

These observations illustrate the diffuse qualities characteristic of intuitive skills—it was difficult even for the study respondents to articulate their precise nature. Pagie recalled: "I always had a knack for sensing the police. I don't know why. I don't know if it's an ESP thing or what, but I always could sense when the police was there." It is because of their rather imperceptible quality that I have used the term *intuitive skills* to refer to this important set of abilities. It is important to understand, however, that they are not hereditary talents. These are skills that are acquired through the same process of socialization as are technical and social skills. Together, these three sets of skills distinguish successful stable addicts from beginning occasional users.

I have attempted in this discussion to demonstrate that contrary to stereotyped depictions of addict criminality, stable addicts are skilled criminal entrepreneurs. The level of criminal sophistication required to sustain a livelihood of the magnitude reported by these hard-core addicts is acquired only after spending considerable time in the sub-culture. Such skills are simply not part of the beginning occasional user's stock-in-trade. In the process of becoming stable addicts, however, most users narrow the range of their criminal activities considerably. I certainly do not wish to represent the stable addict as a professional in the tradition of a Chic Conwell (Sutherland, 1937) or Vincent Swaggi (Klockars, 1974) nor necessarily as specialized as Preble and Casey (1969) imply in their watershed study of addict criminals. The addicts I interviewed, however, do favor a small number of crimes among the vast variety they could be committing. I am suggesting that as stable addicts, these hard-core users are sufficiently successful at their main hustles such that they seldom find it necessary to deviate from their preferred crimes. They attain a level of specialization not characteristic of amateurs nor even of their own criminal patterns during other periods of their careers. Indeed, I contend that it is only by such specialization that these addicts are able to develop the requisite skills for a successful career. There is thus a mutually reinforcing relationship between the development of a main hustle and the acquisition of technical, social, and intuitive skills that correspond to this specialization. The acquisition of these skills is, in the first place, dependent upon some level of specialization; at the same time, these skills provide the very foundation for stable addicts to maintain their main hustles.

These main hustles, which constitute more or less full-time criminal roles, also have other important consequences. As I suggested earlier, they provide an alternative basis for life structure that is capable of accommodating higher levels of drug use and consumer activity generally. At the same time, however, the routine nature of the main hus-

tle prevents one's habit from getting out of hand. The stable addict's heroin use still takes place within a rather well defined, though modified, life structure. Moreover, full-time hustler roles provide addicts with increased dependable income. Unlike the marginal criminality of occasional users, the main hustle is both a primary means of income and a source of identity and prestige in the subculture. The study respondents were quick to distinguish between a main hustle typical of stable addicts and the more amateur or impulsive *flat-footed hustling* style characteristic of less criminally routine lifestyles. Gloria emphasized her distinctive status as a booster: "I'm not a thief—I'm a booster. There's a difference between a thief and a booster. A thief . . . takes anything and everything from anywhere." Booter understood his role as a pimp in entrepreneurial terms, viewing his *who's* (prostitutes) as an investment: "You try not to spend too much money unless it's important. You're playing economics here. Like I got some stock. . . . In order for her to collect the capital, she has to be a product. You have to have something that you can sell. You don't try to give up too much, but say you are into a new girl. . . . You have to put some clothes on her, put some capital into that to make her look presentable. . . . You're expecting her to get that money back."

Thus, the stable-addict phase is characterized by a comparatively high degree of criminal specialization, complete with the technical, social, and intuitive skills that contribute to success in the criminal role. As shown by this research and in previous studies, stable addicts are successful and sophisticated criminal entrepreneurs.

References

Faupel, Charles E. (1986). "Heroin use, street crime and the main hustle: implications for the validity of official crime data." *Deviant Behavior* 7: 31-45.

Gould, Leroy, Andrew L. Walker, Lansing E. Crane, and Charles W. Lidz (1974). *Connections: Notes From the Heroin World.* New Haven, CT: Yale University Press.

Klockars, Carl (1974). *The Professional Fence.* New York: The Free Press.

Letkeman, Peter (1973). *Crime as Work*. Englewood Cliffs, NJ: Prentice-Hall.

Maurer, David W. (1955). *Whiz Mob: A Correlation of the Technical Argot of Pickpockets with Their Behavior Patterns*. Gainesville, FL: American Dialect Society.

Mead, George Herbert (1934). *Mind, Self, and Society*. Edited by C.W. Morris. Chicago: University of Chicago Press.

Preble, Edward and John H. Casey (1969). "Taking care of business: the heroin user's life on the streets." *International Journal of the Addictions*, 4, 1 (March): 1-24.

Sutherland, Edwin H. (1937). *The Professional Thief*. Chicago: University of Chicago Press.

20

Life With Crack: Women's Experiences and Voices

Tom Mieczkowski

I*n this selection the author examines the role of women in selling crack cocaine. This excerpt from a larger study examines various coping strategies employed by the subjects in dealing with the challenges and dangers that are an aspect of drug selling. These strategies are compared to those of male crack sellers. Tom Mieczkowski reports that women face many of the same problems common to all drug dealers and some that are unique to their gender. As a consequence, they cope with these problems in unique ways.*

The interviews were gathered by the author as part of the Detroit Crack Ethnography Project conducted in 1988 and 1989. The interview component of the study (from which this selection is drawn) consists of transcripts of taped interviews with 100 self-reported dealers and user/dealers of crack cocaine. Of these, 23 subjects were female. All the female crack dealers were black. All were clients of a drug treatment facility.

All 23 females were crack users who considered themselves addicted to the drug. Their mean age was 30.4 years of age. They ranged from 21 to 50 years of age. Volunteers were paid a $25 stipend for participation. Interviews varied from one to three hours.

Introduction: Women, Drugs, and Drug Dealing

In the large literature on drugs, drug addiction and drug-focused criminality data on women is relatively small. Drug selling in particular evokes images of largely "a male problem" (Datesman 1981; Henderson 1991). This situation is both a particular aspect of the construction and presentation of the drug subculture. It is also an analog to the larger and longer-term issue of the neglect of women in the general study of criminology and deviance (Warren 1981; Pohl and Boyd 1992). The Detroit Crack Ethnography Project (DCEP), sensitive to these critiques, gathered data on women crack cocaine sellers.

In general, the DCEP found that women in the study sample were actively involved in distributing crack cocaine and other drugs. They carried out these activities in a variety of organizational formats and also worked at many different levels within drug distribution organizations. As sellers of illegal drugs they experienced problems common to all persons involved in drug dealing. But, as women, they also faced unique aspects of those problems that were linked to their gender. Consequently, female dealers often coped in unique ways with their problems.

The objective of this article is to present findings on the female dealers by providing relevant sociodemographic data on these women, and examining and reflecting on descriptions of their experiences as crack dealers. The objective is to add to the slender amount of information available about female crack sellers, and to address several issues raised in the traditional literature regarding the roles women play in drug distribution systems. . . .

Opportunity and Entrepreneurial Drug Models

Recent work on street-level crack sales have emphasized the entrepreneurial aspects of the trade (see Reuter et al. 1990; Mieczkowski 1989; Johnson et al. 1992). Entrepreneurial markets can be highly resistant to control and restriction of entry. If the market is highly fluid, penetrable, and entrepreneurial, then it is feasible for women entrepreneurs to succeed in various ways within the market system. In essence, these models are consistent with opportunity theories. Economic opportunity offers a mechanism by which roles may change or evolve beyond the constraints that tradition applies. Female participation in crack sales represents one aspect of opportunity realization.

If the entrepreneurial aspects of street drug sales promote greater social fluidity, have women been able to take advantage of this by acting in roles historically associated with males? Has this movement included a lessening of the traditional sex-linked vision of females as adjuncts to males in the selling situation?

For most of the women in the DCEP study, becoming a drug dealer was an opportunistic extension of their life experiences. Thus, their experiences reflect Datesman's contention that female drug dealing is not as exceptional as one might believe. Drug dealing, for these subjects, was a mode of surviving that represented a variation on a class of "hustling" activities they had pursued. Driven by choice, necessity, or a combination of both, to be independent, to make one's own way in life, led to the decision that, like many other hustles, drug dealing was simply a good way to "get over." In this regard the women reflected a choice pattern that was indistinguishable from the males in the study.

Quite often the women in this study operated within a range of sex-linked roles that included elements of dependence upon, interdependence with, and sometimes dominance over males. Furthermore, because of their gender, these women faced some unique problems and had to develop specific coping strategies. The degree of systematic and organizational independence from males varied from almost none (a woman who simply stood by or handed out drugs for a boyfriend or employer) to complete autonomy and the operation of multiple drug selling sites. The excerpts presented in the following section will illustrate some of this variety.

Describing Role Types

We begin by describing the relative degrees of independence from or dependence on male partners or associates, as well as the particular type of dealing activity that the subjects report. The objective of this section is to document the variety which the data reveal, and to show the complexity of these typologies, and the degree to which they are "mixed" in the experience of the subjects of the study. There has been a tendency to emphasize single role descriptions in the literature of women drug dealers. They are characterized as "male dependent," "hustlers," "loners," and the like. While these characterizations are not in and of themselves inaccurate, they tend to mask the developmental history and complicated role transformations experienced by female participants in the drug-selling subculture. We shall examine aspects of role transformation in this next section by looking at the relative dependence and independence of female dealers. We shall also examine the need to manage violence and violent encounters as part of the dealer role.

Relative Independence

We start with subject #10, a thirty-three-year-old black female. She represents a relatively independent seller who marketed, at different times, both heroin and crack.

Subject #10 manifests a relatively high degree of entrepreneurial action and an absence of dependence on an opposite-sexed relationship in her business activities. This is demonstrated in three different ways. First, she organized and operated her own business on her initiative once she received an opportunity to sell. Second, she employed males—teenage "runners" to carry out retail street transactions. Third, she entered into an arrangement with another woman to secure a selling locale—using her residence in exchange for supplying the occupant with drugs. She was dependent on male suppliers. She did not conceptualize her selling activity as exceptional. She viewed it purely as a sensible, efficient, and even necessary means for funding her heroin habit, and later her crack habit.

Interview: Subject #10

(Tell me how you started selling drugs)

How I got into selling heroin? Well, I used to hang around a lot of people that uh sold drugs. It was easier to sell it and that way you would always have some although it never really worked out like that. I was thirty-one when I started selling it (crack). Sold it in the rock form for $20 hits and $10 hits basically. I did that on my own. At someone's house they said I could sell it outta there and all I'd do was give em like $20 or a $20 rock. I bought my own drugs, but they gave me a place to stay. . . . This lady let me sell drugs outta her house. She had teenage kids that did the running, you know. They would go down and get the money. I never really came in contact with the people.

Subject #19, like subject #10, viewed her drug selling as "a job," an instrumental means to obtain income either in the absence of other sources of income, or at higher rates than any legitimate employment could provide her. Subject #19 was a small-time crack seller, twenty-four years old, never arrested or charged with a crime. She was a small-scale user/dealer, primarily interested in funding her own crack use. She did not experience any extraordinary violence or problems during her selling activities. She did not realize she was dependent on crack until "the money ran out," and primarily focused on the interference the drug caused with her ability to maintain her regular employment as a secretary. She relied upon males as her source for cocaine, but she paid for her drugs in advance ("up front") and was primarily interested in selling enough to support her own crack use. She did rely mainly on male friends to "rock up" for her. She also sold primarily to men, but reported no serious problems in dealing with male customers.

Interview: Subject #19

(So you bought powder and rocked it up yourself?)

Well, I didn't know how to rock it, but I would have somebody do it for me.

(You didn't know?)

I always called somebody.

(Never got ripped off?)

No, uh, but like they wanna credit or borrow some money and I don't get it back . . . but then I let that pass 'cause I feel like they'll need me again, or access to get some. 'Cause I use to have good credit.

(Deal with men customers?)

Mostly men.

(Ever threaten you?)

Oh, no.

Moving Away From Independence: Female Rollers

"Rollers," as the term is typically used, are people who sell drugs as salespersons for others. Such persons are not independent entrepreneurs, but rather act as selling agents for a larger organization. The roller does not typically pay in advance ("up front") for their drug consignment. They sell it and then pay back the consignee with the cash proceeds. In the literature developed around heroin, rollers have always been reported as males (Mieczkowski 1986; Johnson et al. 1985). "Rollers" mostly work in groups, involving at least one "boss," and sometimes full-time security personnel. Several female subjects in this sample worked as rollers. These rollers worked as crew in crack houses, retailing crack from occupied dwellings or abandoned buildings. Subject #94 is a good illustration of female rolling.

Interviewee #94 was twenty-one years old and a black female who rolled for a male crew boss. She was a user/dealer, one who just worked to "get high." She first began by selling powder cocaine provided on consignment to her by a male friend (with whom she got high). She typically received cocaine powder for which she would have to pay $100, and was able to sell it for about $300 at retail. She "never had any problems doing this" because she sold to people she knew— "most of the people who came over I grew up with."

However, she began smoking crack cocaine and became in her words "quickly dependent, the first time I did it." She became a heavy user and experienced a number of difficulties because, although she was supposed to be selling crack for her male friend, she typically would smoke up large portions of the consignment, resulting in her being "fired." She also lost conventional jobs as a cashier for pilfering cash, or else would pilfer cash and quit before she was discovered and move on to another job. She eventually entered a nonresidential treatment program, but upon release began using again. She re-entered a one-month residential treatment program, but relapsed quickly and began to fund her drug use via prostitution. She then went through a series of further negative experiences. This woman's history illustrates not only some specific aspects of rolling as an activity, but the complex manner in which an individual can go through role transformations. This subject's experiences illustrate the transitory element that is often a part of life arrangements. Individuals will occupy many different roles over a period of time.

Interview: Subject #94

I sold crack for a guy and sold it in a dope house. There would be a person at the front door, a person at the window with a gun and you come to the side door or window. And I would be there and sell the crack. The customer stayed outside. You pass through the window. The money comes in first and then the crack goes out. I was paid $10 off of every $50. I would make about $80—$100 a day. I took it in cash and spent it on rock, so eventually we took it in rock. We really didn't make no money. I was just working to get high. Some crack houses I worked in paid $75 a day and some gave you a $1 off of every $10.

The statement here of "not really making any money" should be understood as describing a result not an intent. At least superficially, all "rolling operations" are supposed to be profitable. Generally, crew bosses do not care if the crew wants its pay in drugs. However, they are not generally permitted to use those drugs while "on duty." Note, for example, how violence ensues as a result of smoking in the "house."

Interview: Subject #94

Once in the crack house I got beat up. This one guy that I was staying with, I had his dope and he gave me so much for myself and the workers in the crack house. This

one girl was really begging me for one. I told her that I would give her some, but it would have to come out of her pay. He was sleeping and I had the dope, so I gave her one. While she was smoking, he woke up and he automatically jump on me because they weren't suppose to be smoking. He stomped me in my back and threw me down a flight of stairs, sprang my arm and I was in the hospital for about two days.

Further Complex Role Transitions

In addition to rolling out of a crack house, some female subjects transited through several types of different selling circumstances. In the following case, subject #33 acted early in her selling involvement in very much a dependent role. The "roller/runner" role has traditionally been dominated by males, with females involved only as peripheral personnel (Adler 1985; Mieczkowski 1986). Women are described as companions or minor helpers to boyfriends who deal. Starting from this position, subject #33 evolved into a relatively independent seller. Ultimately, however, she was overcome by her own addiction to crack and turned to prostitution to fund her drug use. While her prostitution was independent and entrepreneurial, its business productivity was erratic, and one would be hard pressed to call it even moderately successful. This subject did not ever work for a pimp or turn her earnings over to a male during her time in the role of prostitute.

Subject #33, an attractive and articulate young women, was thirty years old. After completing her high school education, she worked as a seamstress and tailor for a custom clothier. She had some post-high school education and was trained in both fashion design and upholstery design.

Interview: Subject 33

(Interviewee #33 stated that she started dating a man who was a "big time dealer" and he had given her the first powder cocaine she ever had for a birthday present.) I'm very much attracted to material things. He had a lot of money, nice car, nice house and we weren't living together at the time. He had a lot of money and that sucked me right in. Right after that I was selling it pretty good to my co-workers.

Notice here, that when she refers to being "sucked in" she means that her boyfriend had succeeded in recruiting her to work for him by vending cocaine to her coworkers. She became increasingly involved in helping market cocaine for her boyfriend, spending long periods of time with him at his house (from where he sold), assisting him with various aspects of the business. Eventually she became a trusted stand-in for him, doing some of his business.

Interview: Subject 33

A lot of his associates would come to his home and if he wasn't around, then I would take care of the business. Still no one is coming to *my* house.

(What quantities were you selling it in?)

We would break it down into grams, $125 to $150. This went on on a consistent basis. I wouldn't work that many hours there because he knew that I had to be at work at 9:00 a.m., so after I got off in the evenings, I would go and stay sometimes to 12:00 midnight and he would make sure that I got home.

It is interesting that she comments so directly on his provision of protection and security, for example, "making sure" she got home. Also in the next passage, it is interesting that although she apparently was trusted to manage some aspects of his business, she did not consider herself a "lieutenant" in the sales organization.

Interview: Subject 33

(Was he there with you frequently?)

Sometimes he would be and sometimes he would leave all his lieutenants to watch over me. He'd hold a gun. I had a pistol too.

(Didn't this scare you?)

No, not at all. I felt real powerful because I wasn't using it. I'm pointing the finger, right. I didn't consider myself an addict because I only smoked weed. I didn't drink. If it was tropical weed, I smoke a half a joint and be nice and mellow for about four or five hours. So I didn't consider myself an addict. Okay, so we are selling now and he would make sure I got

home. I got a car and a lot of material things. He gave me money and it was just what he felt like giving me. If I asked for me, he would give it to me.

(This was satisfactory to you?)

Yes, it was very satisfactory, because my money that I worked for was all mine (money she made as a seamstress and tailor). He would pay my bills so I could take my money and do what I want. At the time I was buying a lot of clothes, fabric, shoes, jewelry anything I felt like buying. I didn't have to be responsible because my bills were taken care of.

This person's account is quite a contrast to the first two examples. This woman is involved in this situation not simply as some instrumental mechanism to acquire drugs. She initially is in an emotional relationship that takes on increasing functional aspects. She also evidences various components of dependency. She readily admits her attraction to the male's financial resources, her requests for and acceptance of his money, and her dependence on him for physical security.

Eventually, after struggling with increasingly problematic crack addiction, she broke up with this boyfriend and went to Narcotics Anonymous at the encouragement of her mother. She was "clean" for about one year and resumed working in tailoring and clothes making. Then her sister was murdered in a drug-related incident and her life began again to experience major difficulties. These resulted in a return to crack and alcohol involvement, but now in a very different fashion from her first experiences. Also, her life became increasingly involved in violence.

Interview: Subject 33 (continued)

I quit my job and left home. I got my own place after we buried my sister. I met this guy and asked him to move in with me and he was a crack user too. We didn't get along very well. He jumped on me and I left the house with him. I moved out some of my things, the main thing was that I left there and started roaming the streets, living here and there, sleeping in crack houses, sleeping on the streets. The last couple of weeks I was sleeping in a truck on 8 Mile Road. I didn't care where I slept.

(Did you try and sell any drugs?)

Yea, it was crazy. Depending on how many "dates" ("tricks" or prostitution customers) I would turn. Sometimes I would make $200–$300 a night, depending on how I wanted to work. I would get a motel room and stay where I knew they didn't have any crack. I would go and sit and try to sell some. Like if they were out, I would go there and try and sell mine.

(The people operating the crack house didn't mind?)

No, because they knew me and they would say when we get back on, you got to go. That was okay as long as I could keep a supply for me. Even though I was still smokin, I managed to keep some to sell and money to buy me some more crack later on that night.

Subject #33 was operating in an independent, entrepreneurial mode here, and was not acting subordinate to a male, that is, a pimp, procurer, or boyfriend. However, "independence" in this regard has a rather circumscribed meaning, since it could not be characterized as a happy or fulfilling situation for her. The transformation from her early experiences was profound.

Interview: Subject 33

(You were turning over $200–$300 a night selling crack?)

No, not that much maybe $100. In selling my body, I would make $200 to $300.

(So, total income is $300–$400?)

Yes.

(How did you find the time to turn the tricks?)

$50 a trick, but then it got down to $20–$15 a trick.

(Were you working the street?)

Yea, and I had regulars, pay $50 and pay for the room so I didn't have to worry about a place to sleep for that night.

(Where did you sleep literally?)

Sometimes I wouldn't go to sleep for four or five days and just stayed high on crack all day long and all night until my body couldn't take it anymore. I'd go to an associate's or girlfriend and lay down for a couple hours, wash up. My clothes were scattered by the way. I would change clothes and go right back out.

(Did anybody ever pay you in drugs for tricks?)

No. I had to have the money, I made that clear.

(You didn't have a pimp?)

No.

(Because you didn't, did you ever have any problems?)

Yea.

(How did you deal with customers who wouldn't pay?)

I threatened them, lied, and told them that my boyfriend was watching when I really didn't have anybody. I tell them that he was behind us in a car and had their license plates. I wouldn't date black guys because they were really street smart.

Subject #33 invokes a fictive boyfriend as a means of protection. This action demonstrates a unique strategy opportunity for females. Males create security by grouping, by arming themselves, and by trying to cultivate a "scandalous" reputation, a reputation defined primarily by irrationality in the use of violence and volatility of temper. These are designed to control problem behaviors by overwhelming physical force. Females rarely use these devices, instead employing guile, sometimes arranging male protection, and only rarely carrying weapons. It is also interesting that she preferred white customers simply because she found them to be more gullible regarding the various defenses she could use to help enhance security, given her situation.

Danger and Violence

The experiences of subject #33 indicate that confronting violence and strategies for coping with violence impinge on the "independence" of entrepreneurial female drug dealers. Females in the DCEP have identifiably different coping mechanisms than males. The male drug domain is controlled ultimately by a reliance on threats of violence and actual violence, often unrestrained and sometimes lethal. Comparing male and female dealers within this sample reveals a distinct contrast.

Female dealers in this study rarely used physical force unilaterally, or rarely threatened it, though it is not unreported completely. For example, subject #33 reported carrying a weapon along with her boyfriend. But her statement about her feelings toward the weapon are purely symbolic and non-functional from a damage-infliction point of view—"I felt real powerful because I wasn't using it."

Females in this project (in contrast to many male subjects) generally do not report pulling out guns, shooting people, or ostentatiously carrying weapons. Yet they do not infrequently report having to cope with violence or the threat of violence, or are the objects of violence on the part of others. Recall that subject #94 reported her supplier "jumped on her" and then "stomped" her and threw her down some stairs for permitting smoking of the inventory. And recall that subject #33 reported the need to refer to an imaginary "boyfriend" or "pimp" to deal with prostitution customers who could only be controlled by insinuation of violence.

A few women report repeated violent confrontations, which they occasionally resisted with force themselves. Interview subject #26 was a twenty-nine-year-old black female who began using crack with a boyfriend and whose crack use "eventually got totally out of control." The result was that she turned to street prostitution in order to raise money for crack. She, like subject #33, worked without a pimp or protector. She experienced violent encounters with customers. The circumstances for these violent encounters included a variety of factors. One was simply a desire by the customer to receive the sex for free and the belief that he could so exploit her and "get away with it." Another was the customer's attempts to coerce the prostitute into performing sex acts that she did not wish to perform. Consider the following excerpt:

Interview: Subject #96

I had borrowed all the money I could and couldn't pay back anything, so I started hustling. I stood on Woodward Avenue prostituting. On the weekends I could make $50 or $60 and on a slow day $30. Sometimes I would run into trouble where a trick may want to take his money back or (want me to) do it for free. They say "yes" (to the prostitute's proposition), take you to a place, and pull out knives and use different things or use physical force to make you do things. So some nights I might run into one of them.

However, she was also victimized because of the resentment of "tricks" who themselves were previously victimized by another prostitute who "burned" them for their money. It was not unusual that a prostitute wanted to get her money "up front" in order to purchase and consume her crack prior to providing sexual services to her "trick." This meant that the trick/prostitute relationship can become extended over time. Thus, the conceptualization of street sex as a brief and fleeting interlude ("wham, bam, thank you, mam") is not necessarily accurate. The relationship can become extended in time while the female goes to a crack source and makes a purchase. Since the "trick" has fronted money to the prostitute, he is going to accompany her in order to protect his money. They then would consume the crack, and if the "deal" went well, they would then have sex while smoking crack or right after the crack was consumed. This extended involvement of prostitute and customer meant opportunities for other scenarios to play out, and in many ways increased risk for the prostitute. Subject #96 speaks to this possibility in the next excerpt. She begins by gesturing to a prominent scar on her forehead.

Interview: Subject #96

[How did I get] this scar on my forehead? This guy had picked up a lady before picking me up and she ran off with his $20. And he didn't get what he paid for. So when he picked me up, he was already mad, but I didn't know this. So, I wanted a rock bad, I am desperate by now and trying to talk him into it. I finally do get him to go along with me and when he is about there he pulls out a knife cause I was asking for the money up front. He said "no." [I said] that is okay. I said I will meet you half way and do this and that, and if you don't like it you don't have to give me the money or you can just take your money back. Just when I am getting ready to say forget it, I don't want to do it, he pulls out a knife. I kept trying to explain to him that I am not the one that ran off with your money and that I am not trying to hurt you. Why are you trying to hurt me? I said to myself that if I don't go on and fight this motherfucker back, he is going to hurt you anyway, so go and fight. I fought my way up out of the car.

In a later encounter subject #96 told of having to jump out of a moving car to escape a "trick" in similar circumstances. She was once again attempting to secure money prior to providing sex in order to smoke crack before "servicing" her customer. She injured herself quite severely and walked with a limp as a result of the injury she sustained.

Interviewee #28 illustrates another type of violent confrontation with yet another alternative coping strategy. This subject was a twenty-seven-year-old black female who was introduced by a relative to selling crack. She also used the common technique of working out of another's dwelling in exchange for providing the tenant with drugs. She was savvy and experienced, a relatively independent dealer who showed considerable initiative in establishing her business. She had been a live-in girlfriend for a prominent heroin dealer. He was eventually imprisoned. Using contacts established through her relationship with him, she was able to establish a cocaine distribution business.

Interview: Subject #28

(How did you get involved in dealing?)

I started selling it on my own, but never out of my house. I would sell it out of these people's house around the corner. I would give them so much cane for exchange of selling out of their apartment.

(How about security?)

We only sold it to people we know, you have to know me in order to cop from me.

However, even with these precautions a "customer" confronted her on the street in order to rob her.

Interview: Subject #28

These guys said I know you got this money, give it to me. I was high at the time and it is strange to see the courage you get when you high. I'm lookin at this dude and he has this (gestures as a gun) in his hand and I said I ain't got no money. My little girl was with me and I said you do anything you want to me, but you let that woman with that baby in her arms keep right on walking because that is my daughter and if anything happens to her, hey I can deal with you messing with me, but that woman with that baby you better let them keep right on walking. He asked me if I was crazy, I said no but that is how high I was and he finally backed off and I was surprised. I could have got killed. He searched her, but didn't search me and I had $200 in my pocket.

Subject #28's approach can best be described as a "bravado" strategy. This sort of response more closely resembles a male description of challenge. However, it is also true that the dynamics of this challenge, from a female to male, is fundamentally different than if a male-to-male encounter occurred. The woman, in her response established "face," a setting of limits, but also conceding power; you can do "x" but you can't do "y." In this case it is established around the child. Interestingly, in segments from subject #29 we will find a similar strategy revealed during her explanation of a robbery she experienced.

Another reported strategy for female dealers is to surround oneself with hired male security. This is most feasible in relatively highly organized selling circumstances (e.g., a crack house operation). In these conditions one can, if successful, generate enough income to employ armed "security guards." These conditions may also allow additional "fortifying" of the selling location, which can also enhance physical protection against any violence. However, this will not work if there are lapses in the security services performed, the security personnel are not trustworthy, or one leaves the secure circumstances, or allows breaches of the security system. Case #29 demonstrates these points. This subject was the most successful of the female dealers, in terms of income, operations size, and longevity. She operated and maintained a profitable multi-site marijuana selling and crack selling organization.

Interview: Subject #29

(So you had a successful business. What did you do with the money?)

Partying. Spending it on myself and my son and made sure he had everything and . . . eventually I got me a house and then I was selling like big time out of my house.

(So, what was your weekly income?)

I would make something like $1,500 a day and that was on a slow day. I had so much money I couldn't keep track of it. I started hiring people to work my door. Sell the weed for me and I stayed there with my son at the time and so much money that it all went to my head. I was bringing it out of another house and had people running out of there.

(So you were working two places?)

Yeah. The fascination was, that I was a woman. It was my own and I wasn't selling it for nobody and I had the big head cause it is like everybody respected me. It's the action and the game, you know.

The next segment documents a violent robbery she experienced within her home at the hands of a male predator. A robber gained access to her house because she broke her own security rules by staying "open" past operational hours, and permitting a customer entrance when there was no security on the premises. Also, quite interestingly, the robber, reacting to her position and her gender, chastised her for being in a "man's" business. He made no attempt to sexually assault her.

Interview: Subject #29

(I'm sure that it must have occurred to you that other men out there dealing must of said hey this is a woman, we can go take this woman out. Weren't you worried about that?)

Yeah, at first it didn't dawn on me like that until I got stuck up in the house.

(Tell me about that.)

It must have been at about 12:00 midnight, and I went to the door . . . . usually close at 11:00 p.m. And I let these people in and I usually never let nobody in, but this particular time I let somebody in.

(A man?)

Yeah, and he said let me get a dime and I said I ain't got no dime. He said let me see what your ounces look like. I grabbed an ounce out the bag and when I was grabbing the ounce, he pulled a gun out and he said get on the floor. So I got on the floor and he held the gun to my head and said I don't want no sex, I want all your money. Where is your money, where is the weed at? I said I ain't got no money, I ain't got no more weed. This is it in the bag. He said I want you to know that you are a woman and we have been watching it. We set you up, we been watching you for about two weeks. We know your program, when you come and when you go. . . . My nephew was asleep in the house. I said don't hurt my kids. Are you going to hurt my kids 'cause I wanted to know 'cause if you was I would have tried something. He said no. I ain't going to hurt you, I just want all your money and want you to know that you are a woman and you can't be playing this game. Who is you to be rolling, you ought to have a man like me to roll for you. I said how am I going to let you roll for me and you sticken me up? He said put your head to the floor. He started searching the house and asking where the gun at, where the gun at. So he never found the gun, he kept finding money in my drawers.

(Did you have a gun in the house?)

Yes, he kept finding [money], like $10 or $20 here. But all the money was on me, in my pocket.

(How much did you have on you?)

About $3,000. I had about five pounds of weed upstairs under the chair. I stapled it back. He said if I find some more money, I am going to kill you. What kept running through my mind is whether I should go in my pocket and say here. Cause he never searched me. I had on a nightgown. I had just got through playing baseball and my jersey was real low and I had on baseball sweats, but you couldn't tell that.

(So, he didn't think about you having a pocket?)

Right, that's why he kept say I don't want no sex.

(So, he wasn't worried about you having a gun?)

Yeah, he was saying where the gun, where the gun, he was looking all around for the gun. I said ain't no gun. He never found the gun. The gun was up under the seat. He searched everywhere, he pulled my rugs up, my drawers in the kitchen, the refrigerator, everywhere and he never found the weed or nothing. He took my son's jar of money and said I'm going to fuck you up if I find some more money. So after he searched all these places and kept moving me from room to room while he searched. So finally one time he turned his back and I reached in my pocket and threw all the money up under this chair he had already searched just in case he searched me, but he never did and he told me to turn my face and put it in the corner and to count to ten and he ran out of the door.

As traumatic as it was for her, the robbery experience did not drive this woman from the drug trade. Ultimately, she lost her business due to her very high levels of personal crack use. This incident illustrates, however, how a male predator was conscious of and upset by the reality of a woman "rolling" in what he considered a "man's business."

Summary

The information gathered as a part of the DCEP project shows that women are involved actively in distributing crack cocaine, as well as other drugs, and appear to work at many levels within distribution systems. While they face problems common to all illicit drug dealers, they also face unique aspects of those problems tied to their gender. As a consequence, they cope in unique ways with those problems.

Considering these women as a group, they are young, relatively well educated, quite likely to be employed, and typically have been involved in using various drugs, especially alcohol and marijuana. These women are likely to report dependencies on marijuana much more frequently than alcohol. The usual route by which they become involved in drug selling is via associations with males, although these associations may range rather widely, from casual and instrumental to intense and emotional. Women can become deeply, and even dominantly, involved in drug distribution processes, and may work in roles ranging from "gofers" for males to the "chief executive" of operating distribution syndicates. Most importantly, many of these women transited through multiple roles, each role quite distinct in characterization and content. Based on this data one thing seems quite clear: monotonic statements about women's involvement in drug trafficking are likely to be oversimplifications.

While women dealers experience distinctive aspects of the world of drug distribution, they also encounter in many ways the same general problems with which male drug dealers must grapple. These "generic" problems center around violence and its consequences, the problems of order maintenance while conducting business, and the need to exert self-control around the drug inventory.

Women crack dealers obviously encounter unique circumstances and problems related to their gender. A central and overwhelming problem is the potential for exploitation by mates, either through manipulation of a "trusted" male, or the possible predation by males who view women as weak and inappropriate in a "man's business" of selling cocaine (Adler 1985). Women in this regard have ambiguous and sometimes hostile feelings for men, reciprocating the ambivalence and hostility of males toward them. Females often invoke the protection of males (either real or fictive). But the use of that "protection" can be itself risky. These male protectors may be lovers, relatives, friends, or business associates but their "protection" can be exploitive. Subject #29's situation demonstrated this, and other women in the study made direct and even poignant comments about this relationship. Subject #99, for example, commented with irony. . . :

The mistake I made was putting my life in some man's hands. I placed my well-being or whatever you call it in the hands of a man or a brother. There was always a man somewhere. If I screwed up, I would only call and they would make everything alright . . . why can't I get myself together?

These data show that women face a host of problems as dealers. In spite of this, some women became considerably self-reliant, and were successful in curtailing violence. But the vulnerability that women feel in these circumstances and the concomitant stress is also quite telling. Women do feel a special sense of vulnerability in the crack world, and that vulnerability, while tied into the general risks all crack users face, is amplified by their gender. Subject #100, in reflecting back on her sales to male customers, noted that

They said "Look at this young lady. She is getting over, why can't I do it? So why not take it from her and go start off like she has done?" As a result it is nothing but total madness. The scene is total madness and that is why I am here.

The data of this project support further and more detailed examination of the roles women play in drug dealing, and support further analysis of the explicit or implicit conceptualization of a purely patriarchal drug distribution system. Women do succeed in operating on many levels in crack selling, from minor to major. They face a host of problems endemic to drug dealing, but they mostly face them in a different manner than male dealers.

References

Adler, P. (1985) *Wheeling and Dealing.* New York: Columbia University Press.

Datesman, S. K. (1981) "Women, drugs, and crime." In *The Drugs-Crime Connection*, ed. J. Inciardi. Beverly Hills, Calif.: Sage.

Henderson, D. (1991) *Sexuality, Relationships, and Self-Correlates to Women's Crack Cocaine Use.* Unpublished Master's Thesis. University of Michigan.

Johnson, B. D., A. Hamid, and H. Sanabria (1992) "Emerging models of crack distribution." In *Drugs, Crime, and Social Policy*, ed. T. Mieczkowski. Boston: Allyn and Bacon.

Mieczkowski, T. (1986) "Geeking up and throwing down: Heroin street life in Detroit." *Criminology* 24(4):645-66.

Mieczkowski, T. (1989) *The Economic Concepts of Crack Dealers in Detroit: An Examination of Market Dynamics.* Paper presented at the American Society of Criminology Annual Meetings, Reno, Nevada.

Pohl I, and C. Boyd (1992) "Female addiction: a concept analysis." In *Drugs, Crime, and Social Policy*, ed. T. Mieczkowski. Boston: Allyn and Bacon.

Reuter, P., R. Macoun, and P. Murphy (1990) *Money from Crime: A Study of the Economics of Drug Dealing in Washington, D.C.* Santa Monica: The RAND Corporation.

Warren, M., (ed.) (1981) *Comparing Female and Male Offenders.* Beverly Hills, Calif.:Sage.

Tom Mieczkowski, "The Experiences of Women Who Sell Crack: Some Descriptive Data from the Detroit Crack Ethnography Project." In *Journal of Drug Issues*, 24(2), pp. 227, 233–248. Notes deleted. Copyright © 1994 by *The Journal of Drug Issues*. Reprinted with permission. ✦

21

The Social Organization of Crack Sales

Bruce Jacobs

In *this selection, adapted from his book,* The Twilight of Cocaine Corners: Crack in Decline *(Northeastern University Press, forthcoming), Bruce Jacobs analyzes the social organization of street-corner crack sales. Jacobs argues that the crack epidemic is in a state of decline as anticrack conduct norms have arisen in response to the personal and social devastation the drug has brought about. To be labeled a "crackhead" is the "lowest of the low" in the hierarchy of the streets. The active crack market, according to Jacobs, is saturated and becoming increasingly unprofitable. This state of affairs has had a major negative impact on those who make their living as crack dealers. In this selection he focuses on the changes in the crack market and how these changes affect street-corner dealing strategies and organization.*

Ethnographic research in criminal environments is difficult and dangerous, doubly so in the highly fluid, socially unstable, and paranoid environment of the drug subculture. The subjects are criminals and are hard to locate as they lead clandestine lives. Once located, they are reluctant to share information about themselves or their activities.

For this study Jacobs spent several weeks "hanging out" on the streets of the city where large-scale drugs sales were occurring. He became a familiar figure to the underworld inhabitants of the area, but the dealers and drug culture hangers-on remained suspicious of him. He was thought to be an undercover police officer. Ultimately, he made contact with several crack dealers who agreed to interviews with him. They continued, however, to be suspicious of his activities. During the course of the first few weeks of his study, Jacobs was stopped, questioned, and searched by police while in the presence of his drug dealer subjects. They believed him to be a college student in the neighborhood to score drugs. His credibility with the research subjects increased each time he was harassed by the police. Eventually, they began to treat him for what he said he was, a college professor doing research. He initially recruited five subjects directly through the dealers he initially approached. These five led to a chain of referrals which resulted in 40 subjects. An additional 10 subjects were located later in the year. Open-ended, semi-structured interviews were conducted with the subjects over a period of about 18 months in 1995 and 1996.

Though crack is legally proscribed, [a] "tarnished good" (Shover 1975), it is bought and sold in a marketplace like any other. The distinguishing characteristics of the crack market are a bit unique. There is constant exposure to violence or its threat (see also Mieczkowski 1992a:157). Transactions are exceedingly vulnerable to exploitation and duplicity on the part of both customers and sellers is so common as to be institutionalized (see also Shover 1975). Overall, instability reigns and predatory arrangements thrive between actors at all levels (see also Johnson et al. 1992).

A freelance system of distribution dominates the St. Louis street crack scene, as it does most urban drug markets (Johnson et al. 1992). Scholars had predicted that this system—with its individualistic, every-man-for-himself orientation—would weaken, or perhaps even disappear, over time. As demand became more established and competition increasingly virulent, crack markets were thought likely to become hierarchically organized as a precondition to survival (Johnson et al. 1992:65). Freelancers would form loose confederations and ultimately "vertical business" operations characterized by pooled interdependence, vertical differentiation, and well-defined employer-employee relationships (Johnson et al. 1992). Recognizing that vertical business models are ideal-types, nothing approaching an evolution has occurred in St. Louis. Although open air, curbside crack sellers no longer predominate, those who remain face both a mature demand and predatory competition, yet arguably are the least organized dealing strata of any drug market.

Copping One's Supply

In any retail enterprise, no merchandising is possible without first procuring a product to sell. Though street gangs neither direct nor control street crack distribution (Klein et al. 1991), gang membership provides affiliated sellers access to supply, and the connections necessary to do business (see Decker and Van Winkle 1996). For the majority of offenders in my sample, suppliers were ubiquitous and easily accessible—typically older gang-affiliated brothers, cousins, other sellers within the set, or persons affiliated with a friendly gang constellation nearby. Customary purchases were 50s ($50 worth of crack wholesale, about a gram) boppers ($100 of crack wholesale, about two grams or ten $20 rocks), quarter-ounces ($250 wholesale), and, less frequently, half-ounces ($500 wholesale). Fifties and boppers comprise the modal purchases and generally could be bought within the neighborhood.

Price and quality, though fairly uniform, varied enough so that sellers had an incentive to shop around. Convenience was overriding, but if individual sellers thought they could readily get a better "play," they would look for it. As Prus (1984:250) notes, buyers want a good product at a fair price, but "buying is far from a static or simple dollars and cents exchange." It requires a degree of "reflective planning" and is "strikingly qualified" by the activities of those whose services buyers seek. Sellers who are able to keep abreast of prices, quantities, and locations of suppliers stood to get the best deals. Social organization is about information (Scott 1968), about who knows what and how one uses it to their advantage.

Though commonplace in the heroin and cocaine powder eras of the 1960's, 70's, and early 80's, buying on consignment is not customary among street-level crack distributors (Johnson et al. 1992). By and large, the dealers in my sample were reticent to be fronted,

and reportedly would do so only when necessary. Dependence means owing somebody something, since "assistance of any type is limited and has reciprocal costs" (Sanchez-Jankowski 1991:24-5). Self-reliance, by contrast, "earns for offenders a measure of respect from peers for their demonstrated ability to 'get over' "(Shover and Honaker 1992:285). As Bo Joe put it,

> I don't let somebody front me 'cause if it don't come out the way it supposed to be, you don't get yo' money, he don't get his money. . . . It's all just a big commotion between you and yo' friends.

Sellers typically purchased their supply already rocked up. To rock it up oneself required time and effort, access to a kitchen, and the know-how to manufacture the product correctly—a skill not all sellers possess. As Fade explained,

> It's best to get the shit hard. They [suppliers] already know how much to put in of what. How to cut it up. How much water and all that.

Crack can be rocked up in any number of ways, but each requires boiling water and baking soda to bind with the cocaine and free it from its hydrochloride salt (Chitwood et al. 1996:11). A variety of comeback agents—baby laxative, inositol, or milk sugar, for example—can be mixed in during the cooking process to increase the volume of the product while retaining the drug's psychoactive effect, thereby making individual sales more profitable. In powder form, the quality of cocaine also can be quite difficult to gauge. Any number of nonpsychoactive cutting agents (e.g., lidocaine, procaine) can be added after the cooking process is complete to mimic the texture, taste, color, and numbing sensation produced by cocaine hydrochloride.

Though buying is always a gamble—taking place in a setting of "shifting uncertainties" and reflecting dependencies on others outside the exchange process (Prus 1984:256)—procuring a prefabricated product eased sellers' fears of being swindled. Nonetheless, it behooved more inexperienced sellers to bring smokers with them to verify a purchase's authenticity. More seasoned vendors did not bother with "tasters," as they were able to discern product quality by smell, touch, and sight. Good crack will have a yellowish or off-white tinge, be hard but brittle, and have a characteristic odor—even before heat is applied.

After purchasing their "bundle," the offenders package individual quantities for retail. Typically, they cut out the corners of sandwich baggies, place rocks of particular sizes inside, and knot each end—sometimes burning the ends for extra closure. In these tightly knotted balls, rocks can easily be swallowed or spat out in the event of a police chase. Meanwhile, excess inventory can be buried in secret places and protected from the elements. The packaging process is more often than not imprecise, with quantities typically eyed rather than scaled (though some offenders did weigh individual retail units). The denomination packaged and sold generally depended on how much a given dealer purchased at any one time. A bopper purchased wholesale, for example, might be broken down into 10 20-dollar rocks—yielding $200 in sales, or double the initial investment. Quarter-ounces purchased wholesale for $250 might be broken down into some combination of $50s, $20s and $10s that equaled, when retailed, $500. Half-ounces purchased wholesale for $500 might be broken down into boppers, $50s, and $20s equal to $1000 at retail.

The goal is to double one's money. More often than not, this is a goal and nothing more. As K-Rock explained, "The only way to double your money like that for real is to sell twenties. You need all twenty sales to make a straight profit." On the street, dealers confront desperate and financially strapped users wanting to "get over"—soliciting $20s for $12, $50s for $40, or $10s for $3–4. Buyers would sometimes reportedly bring the full amount to a transaction and attempt to either hide this fact, or more brazenly, ask for change from the dealers they were trying to short (e.g., to purchase alcohol or cigarettes to temper the inevitable crash). To maintain profit margins, dealers might bite open a baggie, break off the quantity requested, and sell the remainder later for its marginal value— or even better, at full price to some dupe. Breaking off pieces, however, is inconven-

ient, imprecise, messy (crumbs might be dropped), and time-consuming. In the meantime, the sale might be lost to competition or, worse yet, observed by police.

To avoid this, a small number of $5 and $10 rocks might be prepackaged. Such nickel and dime sales, however—referred to on the streets as "kibbles and bits"—were disliked (Inciardi et al. 1993a). Like most merchants, crack sellers want to make the fewest sales for the most money. This is particularly true for streetcorner dealers, whose lifestyle and risk of arrest make less work better: Fewer transactions for larger amounts reduce the chances of arrest and allow the sellers to dedicate more time to purely hedonistic pursuits.

The frequency with which sellers purchased supplies varied by the individual. As a general rule, most reported trying to time their purchases to coincide with periods of high demand—typically on, or shortly before, the first of the month (with the influx of public transfer payments). Social Security, AFDC, and Disability checks are in the several-hundred dollar range and sellers reportedly could expect to pocket a significant portion of these amounts from customers. Pee Wee Dancer remarked, "It be poppin' on the first, people be buyin' 50s [not just fives, tens, and twenties]. On the first, airybody wanta make some money." "The set be deep," continued Deuce Low. "Airybody be outside. Airybody tryin to get their issue off. Airybody tryin to get their ends on." "You make a killin' [around the first]" concluded Skates. To not have crack when public transfer money hit the streets would be to forego potentially substantial profits. As Bourgois et al. (1997:162-3) observe, the illicit drug economy is facilitated and energized by the very institutions of government that seek to suppress and inhibit illicit drug use. Recent welfare reform legislation is intended to address this problem by reducing the amount of transfer money and altering its form so as to make it less liquid.

After the arrival of government checks, ending with food stamp allotments on the fifteenth of the month, demand reportedly drops off. A number of offenders claim to branch off into marijuana sales to maintain cash flow and to generate additional funds to plow back into crack purchases before the next cycle of public transfer payments. Though product diversification may complicate matters, it can generate interest in a seller's other goods (Prus 1984:259)—crack in this case—which is beneficial when these sales became more frequent and lucrative (e.g., near the first of the month). More important, product diversification hedges the overall market risk and increases the likelihood that one will sell "something" (Prus 1984), no matter how slow things get. . . .

[T]he popularity of marijuana has skyrocketed in recent years. Weed sales reportedly are quite profitable. For $100, a seller could purchase an ounce or "zo" and package it into an assortment of $5 and $10 blunts— sometimes dunking them in "water" (PCP) to sell them as "dips" or rolling them with sprinkled crack to sell them as chewy blunts, primos, or woolas. Blunt sales typically resulted in a 50% to 80% return on the investment. Moreover, weed is perceived to sell regardless of the time of month. Tony Mack explained,

> Crack is more money [a lot of sales at one time], but weed sell faster [you make sales all the time, so] you make more money with weed.

Criminal sanctions were perceived correctly to be much less severe for marijuana than for crack, allowing income supplementation and risk reduction at the same time. In St. Louis, as in many other metropolitan jurisdictions around the country, criminal statutes for minor marijuana possession are weak. Any quantity under 35 grams carries a misdemeanor charge, anything over a felony. Considerably more than 35 grams is generally necessary to get circuit attorneys to proceed with a case. Police often are reluctant to enforce marijuana possession statutes to begin with, diluting further the threat of sanctions. As Skates remarked,

> Weed ain't that illegal like dope [crack] is. They [police] catch you wi a gang o' dope, they send you up to penitentiary. They catch you wi blunts, they say 'Don't lemme catch you wi no more of this,' then they let you go.

Whether or not one sells marijuana in down times, always having crack to sell, regardless of the time of the month, seemed to be the most profitable strategy. As Prus (1984) notes, profits, more than anything else, hinge on having merchandise available when customers want it. Customers will seek out the most reliable and wellstocked suppliers first—especially when the commodity involved is criminally sanctioned, high-risk, and hard-to-obtain. Those wise enough to maintain a baseline supply stood to capture the sales that did come through—no matter how meager or intermittent they were. By and large, however, most offenders were neither wellstocked nor reliable. They lived for the moment, were lazy, and were largely incapable of engaging in the kind of cost accounting that permitted maintenance of baseline inventories. This undermines attempts to cultivate a stable cadre of brand loyal customers, as we shall see shortly.

Street Selling

Consistent with previous research on gang-affiliated drug sellers (see e.g., Decker and Van Winkle 1996; Waldorf 1993), those in my sample typically sold by themselves, in pairs or trios, or in slightly larger groups (e.g., four to six individuals) within the study neighborhood. Individuals or cliques of sellers pock-marked the area, setting up shop on corners and vacant lot fronts. There were no formal rules dictating where or when a particular person or clique could establish itself—though certain sellers were more likely to be found on certain streets, corners, or housefronts. There also did not appear to be any hierarchical role interdependence, role specificity, or functional division of labor— three important operational measures of organization. As A-Train and Deuce Low observed respectively:

> We sell by ourself, but we all out together, but airybody sellin' for they self. My partners, they all be outside, but I'm not really slingin' with them. Anywhere I stand, somebody gonna be 'round, [but I sell by myself]. Each individual in they own area but we all as one. It's like a family. . . . [But] Airybody tryin' to get their issue off,

airybody tryin' to get their ends on [trying to make money]. Nobody answer to no-body. Everyone equal.

Though instances of rudimentary employer-employee relations were reported (where one dealer might "kick down" money or drugs to one or more others in return for serving as informal lookouts or protectors), such practices were infrequent and episodic. Sellers simply were not cohesive or organized enough to establish formal or lasting role structures (see also Klein 1995). Youthful street sellers—particularly gang-affiliated ones—are not bound by feelings of loyalty, duty, or solidarity (see Empey and Stafford 1991:243). They tend to hold each other in low esteem, and their relationships hinge on aggression, mutual insult, and the pervasive need to assert and protect their status (Miller 1958; Short and Strodtbeck 1965). Such qualities are not conducive to the formation of internally cohesive or interdependent functioning drug selling groups.

More often than not, group forms of selling were disordered, chaotic, and predatory—'with lots of individuals involved and little coherence to the tasks involved" (Decker and Van Winkle 1996:162). Indeed, "group behavior" seemed to be more a function of competing individuals joined at one place and time than anything else. This is illustrated best by the two modal forms of group orientation that did emerge, "get em got em" and the "bum rush."

Get em got em was the more innocuous of the two. In this "gable," dealers would compete to see who could spot the user first and thus "get" the sale first. Whoever did "got" it—hence "get em got em." As one respondent explained:

You be sittin' on the set and airybody be lookin' up the street for the dope fiend. Cause when he come, the first one who see him yells 'got 'em!' and they get the sale.

Sales were tied directly to acuity in spotting customers. There appeared to be no limit to the number of sales any seller could procure consecutively. Of course, the more consecutive sales a dealer got, the more quickly he would sell out and be removed from the competition, opening up opportunities for those

less attentive, creating a natural check of sorts.

Bum rushes, the second and more common form, were an animated and physically aggressive version of get em got em. In this competition, at least two sellers—but usually more—would make an entrepreneurial windsprint to a newly spotted customer. Whoever arrived first would get the sale or, at least, would be in the best position to get it. The more desperate for money one or more sellers were, and the more of them convened in space and time, the more prone to bum rushing the set appeared to become. As A-Train put it, "It be like ants tryin' to get a piece of crumb." Desperation was not the only prerequisite. Certain sellers are prone to hog customers; the presence of one greedy seller acting might be all it takes to start a stampede. Bum rushes represent collective retail behavior at its worst, a kind of mindless action that is the epitome of free expression yet one which also is inherently threatening to individuality (see Simmel 1908).

Like get em got em, bum rushing appeared to have a point that naturally checked the number of sellers who viably could participate: After a certain number of sellers had spotted a dope fiend and began rushing him, it soon became futile for more to do so. As Ice-D explained:

We see a customer, five'll start runnin' to get 'em. By time those five do, five mo' will just stand back and look. It's like, 'forget it, I get the next one [sale]' 'cause too much trouble [to run after everybody else already was] and you probably not get the sale anyway—damn too many [sellers there] already.

Being surrounded by a throng of hucksters, all proclaiming the superiority of *their* product, spitting rocks into their hands and clutching them with a death grip, shoving each other out of the way, and jostling the buyer in the process is no doubt disconcerting. The buyer does not know who to deal with, who is selling the real thing and who is not, whose rocks are the biggest and whose just look bigger by virtue of clever packaging, and if or when police will appear. All of this may occur in a context in which the buyer is crashing from a recent binge or is paranoid from ongoing use—adding to the aura of chaos. Transacting with the first seller on the scene—though expeditious—is not necessarily wise. Gankers—dealers who sell hardened wax, peanuts, velamints, and almonds—can be, and often are, the first ones to reach a prospective customer. Taking the first stone offered may allow users to leave the area quickly and reduce their risk of arrest, but they might not come away with the real thing. A better deal might be forthcoming with a little patience. Then again, patience is a scarce commodity on the streets—particularly given a customer's precarious psychological state coupled with the ever-present threat of being caught. Bum rushes create an indisputable dilemma, requiring the most scrutiny of the merchandise yet affording the least opportunity to do so.

Mobbed by a frenzied swarm of street youths with ambiguous and perhaps ominous intentions, it also is easy to see how a buyer already paranoid from ongoing use might misinterpret the bum rush as "an attack." As Tony-Mack mused,

> Dope fiend see a gang o' people runnin' at 'em, they think you fi'in [fixing] to rob 'em. Sometimes, they get scared like that and run off [before sellers are even copresent with them]. [As a result,] Not a lot of dope fiends comin' through [any more] and the ones that do, they be gettin' rushed by like five or six dudes.

Bum rushes were not all that well-liked by sellers either. Rushing is indiscreet, obtrusive, and risky. "Negotiation" with users on the open street (brief as it may be), comparing stones with those of other dealers, and "cajoling" users to purchase *their* stones takes time and generates a commotion. These issues notwithstanding, the desperation to beat everyone else to the buyers made those first to arrive most vulnerable to victimization, since they could not always be sure of who or what they were running up to.

Bo Joe and K-Rock understood that the lifeblood of bum rushes—greed—was potentially counterproductive. "You ain't gonna get nowhere tryin' to be greedy," said the former. "You try to be greedy," K-Rock added, "you try to get all the money, you get caught up. Can't be greedy in this business [and do it for

long]." Greed is lust and lust can destroy caution (Manning 1980) as one's "intellectual sentries" are overwhelmed (St. Augustine quoted in Lyman 1989:55).

At the same time, even greedy freelancers are capable of working out marketing arrangements "amicably, with little competition or violence" (Waldorf 1993:6). As Johnson et al. (1992:62) observe, "free-lance sellers may obtain their supplies independently of each other, [but they may also] make 'gentleman's agreements' not to compete for customers, territory, or prices in a specific locale." The rotation system was as close as the sellers got to establishing amicable marketing relations. Rotations involved the unsophisticated notion of taking turns:

> You take turns. I get a sale, then another one'll [customer] pull up and it they [others'] turn. If they be six people on the block, you just go 1-2-3-4-5-6 and start all over after that. Person out the longest get the next sale. (TreyTone)

Rotations, however, were reported infrequently, seldom observed, and generally more the exception than the rule. They appeared most likely to be used when a number of sellers had enough dope to sell, enough customers to sell to, and a particular selling clique was egalitarian enough to allow sharing—an uncommon state of affairs in this context. In the final analysis, group selling was neither feasible, popular, nor profitable.

Escaping from the stifling confines of the study neighborhood became the overriding objective. There were a number of tactics sellers used to achieve "separation from the crowd." The simplest way was to be out early and stay out late, monopolizing sales during inconvenient time slots. Though MacCoun and Reuter (1992:489) contend that dealers who use such strategies "will frequently find themselves in conspicuous isolation (i.e., at high risk and with few income generating opportunities)," Skates and Fade felt otherwise.

> Best time to sell in the mornin'. Six, 7 a.m. Ain't got to worry about nothin for real. No cats [rivals], no poh-lice trippin on you. They [police] think you on yo way to school. Ain't gonna trip on you.

I like sellin' late at night—3 am—ain't no-body out. The few car that do come through, they fixin to spend some money. When you see a car hit the corner, you already know who it is. Only a buyer . . . come through that late.

Of course, off-peak selling was avoided by many sellers precisely because it was incon-venient and unlikely to result in significant rewards per unit of time expended. "Going the extra mile" contradicted the sellers' indo-lent orientation to life and an underlying motivation for being on the streetcorner, sell-ing crack in the first place.

Late night, off-time sales also tend to at-tract the truly desperate crack fiend—one who is not wont (or able) to spend a good deal of money and/or one who may try to get credit or pull a scam. Yet given the fierce competi-tion and stagnating demand, stray sales be-come more important than ever. . . .

Being mobile was a more acceptable alter-native. Mobility allowed offenders the lati-tude to move about when and where *they* wanted to, at times when a selling environ-ment was more likely to be target-rich (see also MacCoun and Reuter 1992 on temporal peaks of drug distribution activity). Mobility helped to attenuate the negative effects of de-clining demand and intense competition—providing flexibility to sellers who could troll for sales rather than remaining to a fixed spot. As Deuce Low illustrated,

I get my rounds on round the hood. Half hour on Denny, half hour on Phillips, half hour on Joyner. I'm gettin my rounds on. Catchin a little somethin [a sale] here and there.

To be mobile was also to be elusive, essential in a context where being tied to a particular spot might draw the attention of patrolling police.

The more mobile the seller, however, the more likely he was to come upon already es-tablished sellers. Though Pee Wee Dancer claimed, "If he on it, he on it. Airybody makin' money. It's all good," in reality, selling spots might or might not be honored. Spots once respected might devolve quickly into a cha-otic, every-man-for-himself bum rush. The limited selling prospects contiguous to the study neighborhood only increased the like-lihood of this. The study site was bounded on three sides by rival drug sets; venturing to these areas was risky. "It be all staticky [threatening] and shit around here," noted K-Rock.

Much of north St. Louis city is quilted by a patchwork of gang-affiliated drug sets, en-meshing gang and nongang curbside sellers and circumscribing their options. In general, sellers seldom cross into "foreign" areas—particularly those designated by gang boundaries. Such boundaries represent geo-graphic as well as perceptual and psychologi-cal barriers to entry (Brantingham and Brantingham 1995)—deflecting potential in-truders by virtue of the socially-constructed ownership particular groups have over a given parcel of land. Extra-neighborhood mobility appeared to be limited to friendly constellations in other north side areas. Affili-ated sets claimed several sectors around the city, providing sellers (at least those with the means to get there) a semblance of a social network to allow occasional expansion of their bleak selling prospects. As K-Rock remarked,

Maybe I just be drivin' 'round for a blow [driving while smoking marijuana] and need to make me a little money. I just go down to Teller and Denny-there's some metro's down there—"who is you, blase, blase" they say. "I'm OG four deuce, I know so and so and so, and so and so. Need to make a little grip for a little while. That cool?" Make a few sales and go on about my business. There be metro's all 'round. Down on Garfield and Cleveland, Coolidge and Jackson, Lincoln and Ezra. Wherever [they are, I can sell]. I can sell all around 'cause there be nine-deuce, metro crips. I flash a sign, they flash me back, then I know what set they be claimin' [and if that set is friendly].

It was my sense, however, that such excur-sions were infrequent, ad hoc, spontaneous, and not available to the vast majority of sell-ers. It also was my sense that going to these sets might very well place dealers in the very selling conditions they sought to escape—high competition, limited demand, and indi-gent customers. The ability to move around the city itself, irrespective of gang affiliation, to sell for a few hours or days at a time in some specified location in which one had kin or friends, was preferable. As Blockett remarked,

> The key is to not stay in one place very long. I be movin' all the time. . . . I'll go to North City, Central West, and North County. I'll stack my grip [make money] each place and then just do the cycle all over again.

Jimmy Hat claimed that every Saturday his brother would take him to the south side. He spoke highly of these sojourns, claiming that transactions there were for 50s and boppers, that "there a lot of white people over there [with considerably more money to spend], and that police ain't too hot." Jimmy Hat described his strong desire to focus his selling efforts on the south side only:

> South side, ohhh man, I wish I could there about seven days [a week]! They ain't comin' with no $5, $10 over there. They comin' with $20, $25, $30, $50.

> Money be comin' like this. I makes 'bout $850 [over a week] on the south side.

South St. Louis is a mix of white and black residents and exhibits much less of the acute social disorganization of the underclass north side study setting. With a few exceptions, south city may fairly be characterized as working class. Compared to the north, per capita income is generally higher, unemployment less chronic, social organization less severe, and crack users more "affluent." Any opportunity to go south and sell to consumers who were not dependent on public transfer payments was welcome. Only well-connected dealers, however—those with associates, friends, or kin in these locales—could truly be mobile. By and large, the offenders in my sample lacked the necessary resources to move about, reinforcing the isolated nature of their selling position and compelling them to resort to more proximal strategies to obtain sales. Cultivation was just such a strategy.

Cultivation

Sellers somehow had to differentiate an undifferentiated product, setting it apart from that of a multitude of other sellers within and without the neighborhood who offer basically the same thing. Developing an inelastic demand with one or more customers can shield a given seller from withering competition. This requires a series of specific cultivation techniques. Cultivation techniques refer to the "courting and wooing activities engaged in by servicers in relations with those whom they service." They "are employed with the intent of either directly or indirectly gaining a reward (usually monetary)" (Bigus 1972:131). Through such techniques, sellers can increase the amount of control they exercise in relationships with particular buyers over time. Control over buyers, in turn, gives them control over other sellers within and without the neighborhood with whom they are in competition: Customers will seek out sellers that have "done them right," and them only.

The crucial importance of "loyalty invoking behavior" (Prus 1987) has been noted in a wide variety of contexts—licit and illicit, economic and noneconomic (see e.g., Adler 1985; Bigus, 1972; Prus 1987). In retail enterprise, repeat customers represent the backbone of most successful businesses. Regular customers are valued not only for their repeat purchasing, their predictability, and their familiarity, but also as a possible source of new referrals (Prus 1984:261). Insofar as sellers are concerned with the maintenance of working relations with a given set of customers, buyers may also be more likely to define the drugs they buy and the experience of buying within the context of these relations. To the extent that buyers perceive sellers to be effective "partners-in-trade," sellers' may enjoy both greater immediate rewards and longer-term stability (Prus 1984).

In the world of illicit street drugs, the mythic importance of a good connection cannot be overstated. Like others involved in the generic process of purchasing, crack buyers want the most and best product for the least amount of money. It is on this basis that evaluations of dealers are made; whoever is perceived to offer the best deal will be the most sought after (Agar 1973:89-90). This is especially true of the street fiends these sellers modally served, who tend to treat every transaction as an extensive and irretrievable investment (Bigus 1972). Unlike "normal" consumers, who tend to act in closer accordance with rational principles of supply, demand, value, and comparative shopping, hard-core crack users typically want to score as much as they can as fast as they can. Quite often, they have neither the time nor inclination to "shop around." Information about who has what, where and for how much, is therefore a "high-ranking need" that is not easily met, since street-level crack markets are in a constant state of flux (Lex 1990). Users' rationality is severely bounded and tracking down alternative suppliers—though possible—is disliked. Buyers will typically hedge their bets and seek the services of somebody with a proven track record (see also Prus 1984:259).

A number of sellers attempted to target their market strategies accordingly. Selling the fattest stones, offering more product for the money than was customary, and giving credit were all geared to entice customers to seek them and them only:

> The bigger ones [rocks] you serve, the more customers you get. You don't gotta worry about no on else gettin' the sale because they [users] want you. (Bo Joe)

> You give em more that what you should, because they look at their's [competitors'] and know that ain't what so and so gave me [last time]. (Ice-D)

> Airybody try to keep they own clientele. Homie spoiled a customer so much last night, he don't wanta deal wi' me. Only him. (Deuce Low)

Providing fat stones may hook customers into them but smaller quantities—provided sometimes at reduced cost or free of charge—keeps the addiction going. Cultivation is arguably the most effective—and most appreciated—when users are at their height of desperation. In the twilight of a binge, for example, even the most meager form of generosity can look colossal and reflect positively on the dealer "compassionate" enough to offer a free or cut-rate nugget.

> When a customer's geekin' . . . I'll break off some pieces, like give 'em a 15 for 10, or a 10 for 5, or just break off like two and three dollar pieces to someone who ain't got nothin' right now. . . . I kinda feel guilty—know they got kids. So I don't be taxin' like that. You're gonna lose money but you're gonna keep yo' clientele. You know they get paid at the first of the month and they gonna keep spendin' with me [because I did that for them]. I'm true to the smokers. . . . That why my clientele be so high [numerous]. (K-Rock)

Offering credit was a second important aspect of customer cultivation. In the world of street crack, credit is traditionally arranged only among sellers. As Skolnick (1997:174) notes, "Similar trust is rarely extended to street customers. . . .This is sometimes attributable to the lack of personal knowledge of the buyer, which precludes the building of the necessary trust, and sometimes to the simple fact that the buyer is a cocaine user and as such is perceived to be unreliable." Where the supply of dealers and demand for the substance they purvey is asymmetrical, however, an aggregate power imbalance will result and benefit those who are fewest in number. Clearly, buyers have the upper hand in a declining market, so sellers have to deploy whatever "leveling mechanisms" they can to try to balance things out (Bigus 1972).

Extending the right amount of credit at the right time can forge brand loyalty *and* be profitable at the same time. Several sellers reportedly timed their offerings to coincide with the last week of the month, so that memories would be fresh when money became abundant the following week. "Yeah, I give credit like around the first—if you know em and know they'll come back. When they get they [public transfer] money, they gonna come back and spend it wi me," explained Benzo. This could mean a real windfall, particularly if customers made their repayment along with an additional (and perhaps quite large) purchase. Other sellers extended credit to customers who had previously demonstrated enough financial wherewithal to be considered good risks—typically customers with regular jobs, steady access to cash (e.g, from petty hustles), or both. As Bo Joe remarked:

> Give somethin' on credit, ten or twenty dollars, and when they get they check they pay you back. When more money comin' in [when customers come into more cash], they keep comin' to me.

Interest rates varied by the offender and were usurious to say the least—from the more forgiving sum of $5 a day on a $20 rock to a mafia-esque 100% rate—regardless of the amount involved—to be paid the following day or week. To an outsider, such arrangements seem foolish but to thirsty crack users they make perfect sense. No matter how exorbitant the interest, those caught in the throes of an all-consuming addiction, without sufficient funds to continue using, often view getting crack on credit tantamount to getting crack free. Immediate gratification is essential and can occur at the expense of rational economic thinking.

To be sure, such arrangements may not be as sweet for dealers as they appear either. Although Fade emphasized the importance of extending credit only to "specific people that won't play wi' yo money," the objective conditions he and others faced mitigated against prompt repayment. Delinquent customers often were difficult to find or if found, unable to pay. Those most able to pay—by virtue of greater income, social capital, or control over their use—also were most likely to have alternative sources of supply and an effective means of evading repayment. Of course, the less credit dealers offered, the less they had to worry about coming up short or tracking down debtors. Yet the less credit dealers extended, the more restricted their sales and the more limited their customer base would be. As desperation mounts, sellers increase their risk of entering into shaky arrangements, in the misguided belief they will be paid back. The more interest they charge to make up for shortfalls, the less likely customers will be able to pay, and the more incentive there will be for debtors not to return. Arrangements intended to create inelastic demand in declining markets may have the opposite effect, resulting in the further erosion of one's client-base.

In the final analysis, cultivation tactics—whether in the form of credit offerings, fat stones, or donation nuggets—clearly were not used because buyers were a "valued, long-term resource, whose favor and custom should be curried" (Decker and Van Winkle 1996:168). The very tactics designed to make crack demand more inelastic helped perpetuate their customers' pharmacological enslavement. A kind of pseudofriendship guided such behavior, illustrated by the rather common expressions of "showing love" and "blessing" customers dealers made to describe their beneficent acts. Such is the world of illicit street drug sales, where friendship is sometimes measured by how generous one is in wreaking destruction on another only too willing to accept it. That the majority of sellers voiced some guilt about their behavior is ironic, but not remarkable. Their guilt was not necessarily heartfelt, and even if it was, market conditions and the hard reality of needing fast cash quickly overrode it. Double-D Loc, for example, claimed that he was often tempted to take his stash and throw it away out of guilt, but never did so because, in his words, "if I don't sell to them, they'll just go right over to someone else and they will make the money. It might as well be me." Skates agreed:

> I be sellin' that, it like killin' my brothers and sisters. It hurt my fillins when, I gets to thinkin' about it, it make me wanna go flush all my shit down the toilet. But if I do, I don't feel right 'cause they just go out and get more from somewhere else.

Walters (1990:132) refers to such sentiments as mollification, a process by which offenders attempt to "assuage, exonerate, or extenuate responsibility for [their] . . . activities by pointing out external considerations, which may or may not be true, but which have nothing to do with [their] own behavior." The point is that even if one seller decided to forego a particular cultivation episode, a host of others against whom they measured their status would step in to fill the void. Occupational ambivalence is common among most who deal in tarnished goods among "dirty" people (see Shover 1975).

Conclusion

Some commentators have speculated that drug dealing is a good substitute for formal business training. It instills entrepreneurial skills and socializes young participants into the art of customer, inventory, and cash flow management. Neophyte capitalists learn to get by in an unstable, competitive, and resource-scarce environment (see Fagan 1991; Padilla 1992). To be successful, however, one must infuse a certain degree of rationality into one's operations. This often means forming hierarchical organizations and becoming functionally interdependent. For those accustomed to the rhythm and freedom of street life, organization and hierarchy are untenable propositions (Shover 1996).

As freelancers, the offenders in my sample are individual functionaries operating without any meaningful organizational template, cohesive exchange structure, or interdependent flow of tasks. Cooperative forms of selling are shortlived, infrequently observed, and generally limited to respecting one another's selling spot. Groups that emerged reflected a decentralized distribution system rather than a "coherent, formal, or lasting organization" (Fagan 1991:117). Plans to expand market share characteristically were parasitic and limited to individual sellers becoming more attentive about getting sales that came through or being better about stealing customers from others.

Ironically, it was these sellers' collective orientation and its provision of a definable, exclusive, "protected" turf on which to sell that played the pivotal role in shaping their group selling forms. Traditionally, protected markets are thought to be advantageous—particularly for gang-affiliated freelancers—by limiting competition that might otherwise undermine profits. Members can sell drugs in their own neighborhood without encroaching on the turf of others, and can bar others from selling there since this "territorial monopoly" is backed by force (Skolnick et al. 1997:174). Gang affiliation also is said to "thwart the possibility of rip offs from would-be customers and robberies by rival gangs," to provide "lookouts to warn of police presence," and to offer a "measure of anonymity when police try to identify individual [sellers]" (Curcione 1997:249). The street gang is claimed to be an effective facilitator of drug sales because the collectivism it engenders complements the business side of dope selling (Decker and Van Winkle 1996:17).

A second look reveals such benefits to be superficial at best. Although collective identification provides a modicum of protection, the territoriality that goes with it ensures that a significant number of sellers will be vying for a finite number of sales in a limited geographic frame. Protected markets keep outsiders out, but they keep affiliated participants in. The chaotic, predatory, and parasitic group selling arrangements that I found are not surprising and become particularly troublesome in a declining streetcorner market. Since the amount of money any given seller could make is finite (and reportedly smaller compared to years gone by), maximizing one's own sales at the expense of others becomes even more important.

Whether, when, and how intense competition is likely to develop hinges on a number of factors. Surging prices serve as a signal for dealer entry (Riley 1998). Rising demand at certain times of the day, days of the week, or weeks of the month (e.g., Thursday evenings, weekends, near the first) make it easier or more profitable to sell in than others, and will attract a greater number of dealers than other times. As dealer-to-customer ratios rise, market organization will tend to destabilize and sellers will be more likely to rush to cars and passers-through in an attempt to steal sales from one another. With multiple persons vying for a finite but significant amount of cash, sellers also may be more likely to take risks about whom they sell to and generally, may be more indiscreet in how they go about their business. Low-volume sales periods need not necessarily change things all that much. The more diffused a restricted number of sales are, the more desperate sellers are likely to become and the more predatory their selling arrangements may be, at least in the short-term. The alternative argument could be made, that the promise of lower profits may actually check competition—assuming that the attractiveness of crack selling decreases in direct proportion to the allure of more convenient, available, or profitable substitutes. Sellers, for example, may choose to "lie low" and live off their savings until the volume of sales restabilizes, sell other substances (e.g., marijuana, heroin), or displace criminal activity to predatory, income-generating offenses.

The nature and degree of law enforcement also is likely to influence emergent selling forms. Very intense, visible police initiatives have a tendency to temper competition, and this can have a profoundly stabilizing effect on market organization (but see Riley 1998:195). Yet sellers do adapt. Windows of opportunity inevitably will be available, and pent-up transactional activity might be moved to these times. Indeed, it is conceivable for microbursts of selling activity to be sandwiched between even the most intense of crackdowns. Undercover surveillance and selectively-targeted, small-scale buy and bust tactics are unlikely to have the same kind of short-term effect. As learning curves come into play, however, increasing discretion on the part of sellers is more likely. The use of surveillance and other covert measures over time may actually have a more stabilizing effect on market organization than uniformed initiatives: Since offenders never know if or when they are being watched, a kind of global discretion may be triggered through a panopticon effect: "I might be watched right now so I better be careful about how I offend, lest I be caught and punished." . . .

Cultivating a brand-loyal cadre of personal customers becomes the most logical and effective response in the face of current market conditions. No matter how predatory conditions get, the more a seller is able to distinguish his product from that of the crowd, the more likely he is to have a chance at selling discreetly. Of course, doing the things necessary to establish inelastic demand (e.g., giving bigger rocks for the money, offering lenient credit arrangement, or providing rocks for free in times of user desperation) undermine a seller's fiscal footing and his ability to continue selling—especially in a declining streetcorner market where there is little margin for cultivation. Other sellers also can adopt the same tactics, neutralizing those who initiate them first, leveling the playing field, and making everyone worse off (see Prus 1987). The inferior product streetcorner sellers generally have to purvey—a function of drugs becoming progressively diluted as they move downward through the dealing chain—may make their product "uncultivatable" to begin with. This is to say nothing of the increased investment of time required to cultivate and the potential risk it brings. Street crack users, in this regard, are often perceived to be the most vexing to deal with—owing largely to their chronic dependence and desperation to make the best deal possible. "They try to be choicy," A-Train complained. "Takin' all day, tryin' to be foolin' around, tryin' to get over, [and in the meanwhile] police gonna swoop." Yet sellers could not dismiss the importance of cultivating brand loyalty, nor ignore the fact that this might require extended copresence (that is, time spent together completing a transaction). As demand continues to stagnate and buyer-seller relations become increasingly asymmetrical, the short-term outlook for curbside vendors is likely only to worsen.

References

Adler, Patricia A. 1985. *Wheeling and Dealing.* New York: Columbia University Press.

Agar, Michael 1973. *Ripping and Running: A Formal Ethnography of Urban Heroin Addicts.* New York: Seminar Press.

Bigus, Odis E. 1972. "The Milkman and His Customer: A Cultivated Relationship." *Urban Life and Culture* 1:131-165.

Bourgois, Philippe, Mark Lettiere, and James Quesada 1997. "Social Misery and the Sanctions of Substance Abuse: Confronting HIV Risk among Homeless Heroin Addicts in San Francisco." *Social Problems* 44:155-173.

Brantingham, Patricia and Paul Brantingham 1995. "Criminality of Place: Crime Generators and Crime Attractors." *European Journal on Crime Policy and Research: Special Issue on Crime, Environment, and Situational Prevention* 3:1-19.

Chitwood, Dale D., James E. Rivers, and James A. Inciardi 1996. *The American Pipe Dream:*

Crack Cocaine and the Inner City. New York: Harcourt Brace.

Curcione, N. 1997. "Suburban Snowmen: Facilitating Factors in the Careers of Middle-Class Coke Dealers." *Deviant Behavior* 18:233-253.

Decker, Scott H. and Barrik Van Winkle 1996. *Life in the Gang*. Cambridge: Cambridge University Press.

Empey, LaMar T. and Mark C. Stafford 1991. *American Delinquency*. Belmont: Wadsworth.

Fagan, Jeffrey 1991. "Drug Selling and Licit Income in Distressed Neighborhoods: The Economic Lives of Street-Level Drug Users and Dealers." Pp. 99-146 in Adele V. Harrell and George E. Peterson (eds.), *Drugs, Crime, and Social Isolation*, Washington, D.C.: The Urban Institute Press.

Fleisher, Mark S. 1995 *Beggars and Thieves*. Madison: University of Wisconsin Press.

Inciardi, James A., Ruth Horowitz, and Anne E. Pottieger 1993a. *Street Kids, Street Drugs, Street Crime*. Belmont, CA.: Wadsworth.

Johnson, Bruce D., Ansley Hamid, and Harry Sanabria 1992. "Emerging Models of Crack Distribution." Pp. 56-78 in Thomas Mieczkowski (ed.), *Drugs and Crime: A Reader*. Boston: Allyn and Bacon.

Klein, Malcolm W. 1995. *The American Street Gang*. Oxford: Oxford University Press.

Klein, Malcolm W., Cheryl Maxson, and Lea Cunningham 1989. "Crack, Street Gangs, and Violence." *Criminology* 4:623-650.

Lex, Barbara W. 1990. "Narcotics Addicts' Hustling Strategies: Creation and Manipulation of Ambiguity." *Journal of Contemporary Ethnography* 18:388-415.

Lyman, Stanford 1989. *The Seven Deadly Sins*. Dix Hills, NY: General Hall.

MacCoun, Robert and Peter Reuter. 1992. "Are the Wages of Sin $30 an Hour? Economic Aspects of Street-Level Drug Dealing." *Crime and Delinquency* 38:477-91.

Manning, Peter K. 1980. *The Narcs' Game*. Cambridge: MIT Press.

Mieczkowski, Thomas 1992a. "Crack Dealing on the Street: The Crew System and the Crack House." *Justice Quarterly* 9:151-163.

Miller, Walter B. 1958. "Lower-Class Culture as a Generating Milieu of Gang Delinquency." *Journal of Social Issues* 14:5-19.

Padilla, Felix M. 1992. *The Gang as an American Enterprise*. New Brunswick, N.J.: Rutgers University Press.

Prus, Robert 1987. "Developing Loyalty: Fostering Purchasing Relationships in the Marketplace." *Urban Life* 15:331-366.

Prus, Robert 1984. "Purchasing Products for Resale: Assessing Suppliers as 'Partners-in-Trade.' " *Symbolic Interaction* 7:249-278.

Riley, K. Jack 1998. "Homicide and Drugs: A Tale of Six Cities." *Homicide Studies* 2:176-205.

Sanchez-Jankowski, Martin 1991. *Islands in the Street*. Berkeley: University of California Press.

Short, James F. Jr., and Fred L. Strodtbeck 1965. *Group Process and Gang Delinquency*. Chicago: University of Chicago Press.

Shover, Neal 1996. *Great Pretenders*. Boulder: Westview.

Shover, Neal 1975. "Tarnished Goods in the Marketplace." *Urban Life and Culture* 3:471- 488.

Shover, Neal and David Honaker 1992. "The Socially-Bounded Decision Making of Persistent Property Offenders." *Howard Journal of Criminal Justice* 31: 276-93.

Skolnick, Jerome H., Theodore Correl, Elizabeth Navarro, and Roger Rabb 1997. "The Social Structure of Street Drug Dealing." Pp 159-191 in Larry K. Gaines and Peter B. Kraska (eds.), *Drugs, Crime, and Justice*, Prospect Heights, Ill: Waveland Press.

Simmel, Georg 1908. "The Stranger." In Donald Levine (ed.) *Georg Simmel* Chicago: University of Chicago Press, 143-149.

Waldorf, Dan 1993. "Don't Be Your own Best Customer—Drug Use of San Francisco Gang Drug Sellers." *Crime, Law, and Social Change* 19:1-15.

Walters, Glenn B. 1990. *The Criminal Lifestyle*. Newbury Park: Sage.

Adapted from Bruce Jacobs, *The Twilight of Cocaine Corners: Crack in Decline*. Northeastern University Press, forthcoming. Reprinted with permission. ✦